New Developments in Autism

of related interest

Autism, Brain and Environment
Richard Lathe
ISBN-13: 978 1 84310 438 4   ISBN-10: 1 84310 438 5

Understanding the Nature of Autism and Asperger's Disorder
Forty Years of Clinical Practice and Pioneering Research
Edward R. Ritvo MD, Professor Emeritus, UCLA School of Medicine
Foreword by Tony Attwood
ISBN-13: 978 1 84310 814 6   ISBN-10: 1 84310 814 3

The Development of Autism
A Self-Regulatory Perspective
Thomas L. Whitman
ISBN-13: 978 1 84310 735 4   ISBN-10: 1 84310 735 X

Autism – From Research to Individualized Practice
Edited by Robin L. Gabriels and Dina E. Hill
Foreword by Dr Gary B. Mesibov
ISBN-13: 978 1 84310 701 9   ISBN-10: 1 84310 701 5

The Complete Guide to Asperger's Syndrome
Tony Attwood
ISBN-13: 978 1 84310 495 7   ISBN-10: 1 84310 495 4

Asperger's Syndrome
A Guide for Parents and Professionals
Tony Attwood
Foreword by Lorna Wing
ISBN-13: 978 1 85302 577 8   ISBN-10: 1 85302 577 1

Autism – The Search for Coherence
Edited by John Richer and Sheila Coates
ISBN-13: 978 1 85302 888 5   ISBN-10: 1 85302 888 6

Children, Youth and Adults with Asperger Syndrome
Integrating Multiple Perspectives
Edited by Kevin P. Stoddart
Hardback ISBN-13: 978 1 84310 268 7   ISBN-10: 1 84310 268 4
Paperback ISBN-13: 978 1 84310 319 6   ISBN-10: 1 84310 319 2

Finding You Finding Me
Using Intensive Interaction to get in touch with people whose severe
learning disabilities are combined with autistic spectrum disorder
Phoebe Caldwell
ISBN-13: 978 1 84310 399 8   ISBN-10: 1 84310 399 0

New Developments in Autism

The Future is Today

Edited by Juan Martos Pérez,
Pedro M. González,
María Llorente Comí
and Carmen Nieto

Jessica Kingsley Publishers
London and Philadelphia

First published in 2007
by Jessica Kingsley Publishers
116 Pentonville Road
London N1 9JB, UK
and
400 Market Street, Suite 400
Philadelphia, PA 19106, USA

www.jkp.com

Library of Congress Cataloging in Publication Data

New developments in autism : the future is today / edited by Juan Martos Pérez ... [et al.]. -- 1st American ed.
  p. cm.
Includes bibliographical references and index.
ISBN-13: 978-1-84310-449-0 (pbk. : alk. paper)
ISBN-10: 1-84310-449-0 (pbk. : alk. paper) 1. Autism. 2. Autism--Research. I. Pérez, Juan Martos.
RC553.A88N55 2007
616.85'8820072--dc22

                    2006005792

British Library Cataloguing in Publication Data
A CIP catalogue record for this book is available from the British Library

ISBN-13: 978 1 84310 449 0
ISBN-10: 1 84310 449 0

Printed and bound in Great Britain by
Athenaeum Press, Gateshead, Tyne and Wear

Contents

Figures

Tables

Boxes

Introduction

Juan Martos Pérez, Pedro M. González, María Llorente Comí and Carmen Nieto

There is no doubt one of the objects of greatest interest to the human being throughout history has been the understanding of himself. This interest is, in turn, one of the defining characteristics of our enigmatic and elusive nature. We believe that this book is a modest contribution to this arduous, costly and passionate task of understanding. As has been indicated on other occasions (Hobson 2002), the understanding of the mind not only includes the study of those processes which we consider to be normal, but also the study of those processes which produce discomfort, as they may provide us with an understanding equally as enriching.

Some of the terms used to describe human nature, such as 'enigmatic' or 'elusive', are also applicable to many of its variations. One example of a dysfunction of human conduct clearly deserving of such terms is autism. Since the psychiatrist Leo Kanner (1943) and the paediatrician Hans Asperger ([1944] 1991), both Austrian, first documented the syndrome which we today know as autism in the scientific literature, this disorder has come to represent one of the principal themes of developmental psychopathology. Both of those articles, but above all the first, have become key references each and every time one reflects on autism. To not mention those authors, aside from being quite difficult (in the specialized literature they are the most frequently cited authors), would be like travelling to Madrid without passing through the Prado, or visiting London without seeing Buckingham Palace.

There remains no doubt that autism is fascinating for many reasons, some of which we will approach in this introduction.

Since its first definition in 1943, and more intensely since the latter half of the 1980s, a lot of effort has been made to understand autism. This effort is manifested in a large number of publications, in specialized scientific journals as well as in books, which approach diverse aspects of the clinical picture of autism, from its genetic bases to overt behaviours, from psychological theories to intervention procedures. It is certain that we have advanced in our understanding, and have made great improvements to the treatment and quality of life of people who suffer from the disorder and of their families. However, we must admit that autism resists us still. Uta Frith and Elisabeth Hill (2004) have been able to put into words a sentiment that many of us feel: the more we know about autism, the more questions we ask.

In our opinion, a second reason which justifies the great interest awakened in many professionals by this disorder is the strange combination of the elements of which it is composed. There is no doubt that autism constitutes a syndrome, a covariation of simultaneously altered behaviours, such as alterations of: (a) social interaction, (b) communication, and (c) symbolic activity. These three 'elements' are what have been termed Wing's triad (Wing and Gould 1979). The question remains, why are these three types of behaviours altered simultaneously in this developmental disorder which we call autism? Specifically, why would a child with important limitations in social interaction be incapable of using and understanding symbols? Why would someone who cannot utilize symbols be highly inflexible and live attached to a series of routines which, on occasion, govern their behaviour? In short, what relationship exists between these three elements of Wing's triad? The answer to this question would have immediate theoretical and practical implications. For example, if reduced social isolation follows a greater capacity for symbolization, at least two implications arise. First, the intervention should be directed to favour the motivation for interaction with others. Second, does this mean that the symbol has its origins in human social interactions?

We permit the reader one last link in this chain of thought. If, on the one hand, the fundamental element of the construction of the mind is the capacity to symbolize, and that capacity in turn has its origins in social interaction, and, on the other hand, that which drives the establishment and maintenance of social interaction is emotion, the question would be: what role do emotions play in the construction of the mind?

None of these questions are new to psychology, yet it may be interesting to recall them from time to time, as the search for statistically significant results may lead us to forget, as suggested by Karmiloff-Smith (1992), that the final objective of this line of research is not to demonstrate a certain result in hypothesis testing, but to understand autism, and, by extension, human development.

A question which constitutes a powerful reason to understand the interest in the disorder (indeed, there are many, but this introduction can only cover so much) is what is the psychological capacity (or capacities) which, when altered during the process of ontogenetic construction, may give rise to a person with psychometrically normal intelligence, intact visuospatial and logical/mathematical reasoning skills, grammatically correct language and even with the potential to attain great professional success, such as Temple Grandin, Richard Borcherds, the winner of the 1998 Fields medal in mathematics (Baron-Cohen 2003), or even Wittgenstein himself (Fitzgerald 2004)? At the same time, these people show incredible deficits in other areas, such as a difficulty in understanding what a friend is (Hobson 1993), the significance of a joke or irony (Rivière 1997) or subtleties of non-verbal communication (American Psychiatric Association 2000). Therefore, it is understandable that when we interact with a person who meets the above described psychological profile we go home with our heads full of questions, and we return over and over again to the word 'enigma' as the only word which describes what has happened. What we intend by this last phrase is that perhaps the fundamental reason why autism fascinates us is precisely because it appears to contradict the logic which governs our conception of the human being and its development.

All those readers with an interest in such questions may consult here reasoned reflections on these and other issues. This book is composed of a series of chapters, the majority of which are unedited, and were written expressly for the Association of Parents of People with Autism (Asociación de Padres de Personas con Autismo, APNA) in celebration of the IV International Symposium on Autism which took place in Madrid on 4–6 May 2005 under the title *Autism: The Future is Today* (*Autismo: el futuro es hoy*). The texts are not presentations but scientific articles produced exclusively for APNA, with the objective of putting the book together which you now hold in your hand.

Important and useful practical applications are derived from these reflections. Kurt Lewin (1978) said that there is nothing more practical than a good theory. We agree with this idea, but we also believe that a good theory must be based on practice and daily experience. For that reason we have not only collected interesting aspects of autistic spectrum disorders (ASDs), such as their genesis, early manifestations or psychological or neurobiological substrates, but we have also asked each author to extract practical applications for the therapeutic approach to the wide variety of ASDs which they discuss. Our objective is to advance the construction of the necessary bridges between theory and practice (Howlin and Jordan 1997). To that end, this book may also be of interest to those who, in one way or another, must confront the complex behaviours shown by a person with ASD on a daily basis.

In Chapter 1, Eric Fombonne undertakes an exhaustive review of the epidemiology of ASD. The detailed analyses show, among other things, that they are important not only qualitatively, in that to study ASDs it is important to understand the normal developing mind, but also quantitatively, in terms of figures; something which must be taken into account in providing services. In Chapter 2, Juan Martos Pérez, Pedro M. González, María Llorente Comí and Carmen Nieto have focused on early manifestations of the profile. Questions such as at what age do the first symptoms of autism commence? What are they? And to what psychological domain do they belong? are responded to for a number of reasons including aiding early detection and diagnosis. In Chapter 3, Catherine Lord approaches the diagnosis and its temporal stability. Within ASDs there are different groups of diagnoses. It may happen that a child meets criteria for Kanner disorder, and some years later their behaviour is better described by Asperger syndrome. Just what key behaviours should direct our attention in these borderline cases is also approached by Lord. In Chapter 4, Laura Grofer Klinger, Mark R. Klinger and Rebecca L. Pohlig describe a new deficit which they themselves have identified: the alteration of implicit learning. This type of incidental and effortless knowledge acquisition occurs during the normal interaction of the child and its environment. According to the data presented by these authors, it would seem that this type of learning is altered in subjects with an autistic spectrum disorder. In Chapter 5, Peter Mundy and Danielle Thorp literally dissect the capacity of joint attention. It is surprising that a behaviour shown by children at the end of their first year of life is so complex and important for the development of later capacities exclusive to humans. The analysis of Mundy and Thorp is complex, passionate and provides neuropsychological consistency to such abstract and profound concepts such as identification and movement in the adoption of emotional and epistemological perspectives, so elegantly discussed by Peter Hobson in Chapter 6. This author undertakes an inclusive analysis of the questions posed in this introduction, such as the role of emotion and social interaction in the construction of thought. Later, the theory of the extreme form of the masculine brain is exposed, heir of the now classic idea of a deficit of theory of mind purported by Simon Baron-Cohen. It is his close collaborator, Sally Wheelwright, who presents this focus in Chapter 7. This theory has its roots in the psychology of differences between man and woman. It is a daring, risky and very thought-provoking theory. In Chapter 8, Sally Ozonoff, Mikle South and Sherri Provencal take the wheel and lead us on an interesting, lucid and coherent journey through executive function. If someone has not done any reading on this theoretical approximation and would like to begin, or has not been able to keep up with recent advances in research on the superstars of current neuropsychology – the frontal lobes – this chapter is ideal. We believe that this chapter constitutes one of the finest existing revisions of autism and executive function.

Language and autism are like two inseparable friends. In Chapter 9, Isabelle Rapin describes alterations of language, whose study has been of great import for the understanding of ASD, among other disorders. In Chapter 10, Susan Leekam presents a longitudinal study of a large group of subjects with ASD. Through this chapter, the author submerges us in her profound reflections and reaches such interesting conclusions as that all the disorders which fall under the diagnostic categories for ASD, such as Asperger or Kanner syndrome, are differentiated by their severity but not their quality, meaning that the dysfunctions produced are dimensional and not categorical, quantitative rather than qualitative.

In the twenty-first century we have no doubt that the brain is the organ of the mind. Once Cartesian dualism is discarded, we understand the mind as a property emerging from the brain and, consequently, we understand that cognition occurs through the complex processes of neurotransmission. For this reason, in Chapter 11, Margaret L. Bauman and Thomas L. Kemper undertake a revision of the differences which have been found in the brains of people with autism. Among other anomalies, these subjects have fewer Purkinje cells, neural hyperdensity in the limbic system and recently anomalies in the minicolumns have been indicated, which is treated in detail in the following chapter by one of the authors who took part in that discovery, Manuel F. Casanova. Minicolumns are units of circuits encapsulated in radial structures in the width of a single cell. These structures contain between 80 and 250 cells, depending on the area of interest. Differences occur in the total number of minicolumns, in the horizontal space which separates them and in their internal structure (a relative dispersion of the cells).

In the same way, we are ever more sure of the implication of some genes in the origin of autism, which is lucidly described by Ángel Díez-Cuervo in Chapter 13. His analysis of genetic studies presents us with keys for understanding the relationship between the double helix and autism.

Finally, Hilde de Clercq and Theo Peeters present, in Chapter 14, the necessary collaboration between parents and professionals. De Clercq and Peeters do not only write about this collaboration, but actually speak from experience: the first author is the mother of a child with autism and a great professional, and the second is a recognized professional.

Last, but certainly not least, a final acknowledgement must be made. The Symposium which took place in Madrid in May of 2005, as well as the edition of a book such as this, is the result of exceptional dedication, effort and sacrifice. All of this has been made possible by the memory of our admired and beloved professor, Ángel Rivière, present among all the professionals of the APNA. Despite his sudden death in the spring of 2000, he still remains present through the intellectual legacy which he planted in his students and collaborators. We think that a job well done is the best way to keep his memory alive. We hope to have achieved that.

REFERENCES

American Psychiatric Association (2000) *Diagnostic and Statistical Manual of Mental Disorders* (4th edn, revised) (DSM-IV-R). Washington, DC: American Psychiatric Association.

Asperger, H. [1944] (1991) '"Autistic Psychopathy" in childhood.' In U. Frith (ed.) *Autism and Asperger Syndrome*, pp. 37–92. Cambridge: Cambridge University Press.

Baron-Cohen, S. (2003) *The Essential Difference: Men, Women and the Extreme Male Brain*. London: Penguin Press.

Fitzgerald, M. (2004) *Autism and Creativity: Is There a Link between Autism in Men and Exceptional Ability?* London: Brunner-Routledge Press.

Frith, U. and Hill, E. (2004) *Autism: Mind and Brain*. Oxford: Oxford University Press.

Hobson, P. (2002) *The Craddle of Thought*. London: Macmillan.

Hobson, R. P. (1993) *Autism and the Development of Mind*. London: Lawrence Erlbaum Press.

Howlin, P. and Jordan, R. (1997) Editorial. *Autism 1*, 9–11.

Kanner, L. (1943) 'Autistic disturbances of affective contact.' *Nervous Child 2*, 217–250.

Karmiloff-Smith, A. (1992) *Beyond Modularity: A Developmental Perspective on Cognitive Science*. Cambridge, MA: MIT Press. (Spanish translation: Más allá de la modularidad. Madrid: Alianza, 1994.)

Lewin, K. (1978) *Teoría de campo en la ciencia social*. Buenos Aires: Paidós.

Rivière, A. (1997) *La mirada mental*. Buenos Aires: Aique.

Wing, L. and Gould, J. (1979) 'Severe impairments of social interaction and associated abnormalities in children: epidemiology and classification.' *Journal of Autism and Developmental Disorders 9*, 11–29.

Chapter 1

Epidemiology of Pervasive Developmental Disorders

Eric Fombonne

Epidemiological surveys of autism started in the mid-1960s in England (Lotter 1966) and have since been conducted in many countries. This chapter provides an up-to-date review of the methodological features and substantive results of published epidemiological surveys and it updates a previous review (Fombonne 2003a). This chapter addresses the following questions:

1   What is the range of prevalence estimates for autism and related disorders?

2   What are the other correlates of autistic spectrum disorders?

SELECTION OF STUDIES

The studies were identified through systematic searches from the major scientific literature databases (MEDLINE, PSYCINFO) and from prior reviews (Fombonne 1999, 2003a; Wing 1993). Only studies published in the English language were included. Surveys that relied on a questionnaire-based approach to define whether a subject was a case or not a case were also excluded because the validity of the diagnosis is unsatisfactory in these studies. Overall, 42 studies published between 1966 and 2003 were selected that surveyed pervasive developmental disorders (PDDs) in clearly demarcated, non-overlapping samples. Of these, 36 studies provided information on rates of autistic disorder, three studies only provided estimates on all PDDs combined, and three studies provided data only on high-functioning PDDs.

SURVEY DESCRIPTIONS

Surveys were conducted in 14 countries, and half of the results have been published since 1997. Most studies were conducted in predominantly urban or mixed areas with only two surveys (Studies 6 and 11) carried out in predominantly rural areas. The proportion of children from immigrant families was generally not available and very low in five surveyed populations (Studies 11, 12, 19, 23 and 26). Only in Studies 4, 34 and 38 was there a substantial minority of children with either an immigrant or different ethnic background living in the area. The age range of the population included in the surveys is spread from birth to early adult life, with an overall median age of 8.0. Similarly, in 39 studies, there is huge variation in the size of the population surveyed (range: 826–4,590,000), with a median population size of 63,860 subjects (mean = 255,000).

STUDY DESIGNS

A few studies have relied on existing administrative databases (i.e. Croen *et al*. 2002a; Gurney *et al*. 2003) or on national registers (Madsen *et al*. 2002) for case identification. Most investigations have relied on a two-stage or multistage approach to identify cases in underlying populations. The first screening stage of these studies often consisted of sending letters or brief screening scales requesting school and health professionals to identify possible cases of autism. Each investigation varied in several key aspects of this screening stage. First, the coverage of the population varied enormously from one study to another. In some studies (3, 17, 20, 24, 33), only cases already known from educational or medical authorities could be identified. In other surveys, investigators achieved extensive coverage of the entire population, including children attending normal schools (Studies 1, 25, 40) or children undergoing systematic developmental checks (Studies 13, 19, 22, 32, 36). Second, the type of information sent out to professionals invited to identify children varied from simple letters including a few clinical descriptors of autism-related symptoms or diagnostic checklists rephrased in nontechnical terms, to more systematic screening based on questionnaires or rating scales of known reliability and validity. Third, participation rates in the first screening stages provide another source of variation in the screening efficiency of surveys. Although there is no consistent evidence that parental refusal to cooperate is associated with autism in their offspring, a small proportion of cases may be missed in some surveys as a consequence of non-cooperation at the screening stage.

Similar considerations about the methodological variability across studies apply to the intensive assessment phases. Participation rates in these second-stage assessments were not always available, either because they had simply not been calculated, or because the design and/or method of data collection did not lead easily to their estimation. When available (Studies 1, 5, 8, 12, 13, 15, 22, 23, 25, 29, 30, 32, 36), they were generally high, ranging from 76.1 per cent (Study 12) to 98.6 per cent (Study 25). The information used to determine final diagnostic status usually involved a combination of informants and data sources, with a direct assessment of the person with autism in 21 studies.

The assessments were conducted with various diagnostic instruments, ranging from a classical clinical examination to the use of batteries of standardized measures. The Autism Diagnostic Interview (Le Couteur *et al.* 1989) and/or the Autism Diagnostic Observational Schedule (Lord *et al.* 2000) were used in the most recent surveys. The precise diagnostic criteria retained to define caseness vary according to the study and, to a large extent, reflect historical changes in classification systems. Thus, Kanner's criteria and Lotter's and Rutter's definitions were used in Studies 1–8 (all conducted before 1982), whereas DSM-based definitions took over thereafter as well as ICD-10 since 1990. The heterogeneity of diagnostic criteria used across surveys is somewhat mitigated by reliance on expert clinical judgment for final case determination. It is furthermore difficult to assess the impact of a specific diagnostic scheme or of a particular diagnostic criterion on the estimate of prevalence since other powerful method factors confound between-studies comparisons of rates.

CHARACTERISTICS OF AUTISTIC SAMPLES

Data on children with autistic disorders were available in 36 surveys (1–36; see Table 1.1). In total, 7,514 subjects were considered to suffer from autism; this number ranged from six (Studies 18 and 25) to 5,038 (Study 34) across studies (median: 48; mean: 209). An assessment of intellectual function was obtained in 21 studies. These assessments were conducted with various tests and instruments; furthermore, results were pooled together in broad bands of intellectual level that did not share the same boundaries across studies. As a consequence, differences in rates of cognitive impairment between studies should be interpreted with caution. Despite these caveats, some general conclusions can be reached (Table 1.1). The median proportion of subjects without intellectual impairment is 29.6 per cent (range: 0 per cent to 60 per cent). The corresponding figures are 29.3 per cent (range: 6.6 per cent to 100 per cent) for mild-to-moderate intellectual impairments, and 38.5 per cent (range: 0 per cent to 81.3 per cent) for severe-to-profound mental retardation. Gender repartition among subjects with autism was reported in 32 studies totalling 6,963 subjects with autism, and the male/female sex ratio varied from 1.33 (Study 7) to 16.0 (Study 4), with a mean male:female ratio of 4.3:1. Thus, no epidemiological study ever identified more girls than boys with autism, a finding that parallels the gender differences found in clinically referred samples (Lord, Schopler and Revecki 1982). Gender differences were more pronounced when autism was not associated with mental retardation. In 13 studies (865 subjects) where the sex ratio was available within the normal band of intellectual functioning, the median sex ratio was 5.5:1. Conversely, in 12 studies (813 subjects), the median sex ratio was 1.95:1 in the group with autism and moderate-to-severe mental retardation.

Table 1.1 Prevalence surveys of autistic disorder

Study no.	Author, year	Area	Size of target population	Age (years)	Number of subjects with autism	Diagnostic criteria	% with normal IQ	Gender ratio (M:F)	Prevalence rate/ 10,000
1	Lotter 1966	Middlesex, UK	78,000	8–10	32	Rating scale	15.6	2.6 (23/9)	4.1
2	Brask 1970	Aarhus County, Denmark	46,500	2–14	20	Clinical	—	1.4 (12/7)	4.3
3	Treffert 1970	Wisconsin, US	899,750	3–12	69	Kanner	—	3.06 (52/17)	0.7
4	Wing et al. 1976	Camberwell, UK	25,000	5–14	17[1]	24 items rating scale of Lotter	30	16 (16/1)	4.8[2]
5	Hoshino et al. 1982	Fukushima-Ken, Japan	609,848	0–18	142	Kanner's criteria	—	9.9 (129/13)	2.33
6	Bohman et al. 1983	County of Västerbotten, Sweden	69,000	0–20	39	Rutter criteria	20.5	1.6 (24/15)	5.6
7	McCarthy et al. 1984	East Ireland	65,000	8–10	28	Kanner	—	1.33 (16/12)	4.3
8	Steinhausen et al. 1986	West Berlin, Germany	279,616	0–14	52	Rutter	55.8	2.25 (36/16)	1.9
9	Burd et al. 1987	North Dakota, US	180,986	2–18	59	DSM-III	—	2.7 (43/16)	3.26
10	Matsuishi et al. 1987	Kurume City, Japan	32,834	4–12	51	DSM-III	—	4.7 (42/9)	15.5
11	Tanoue et al. 1988	Southern Ibaraki, Japan	95,394	7	132	DSM-III	—	4.07 (106/26)	13.8

Continued on next page

Table 1.1 cont.

Study no.	Author, year	Area	Size of target population	Age (years)	Number of subjects with autism	Diagnostic criteria	% with normal IQ	Gender ratio (M:F)	Prevalence rate/10,000
12	Bryson et al. 1988	Part of Nova-Scotia, Canada	20,800	6–14	21	New RDC	23.8	2.5 (15/6)	10.1
13	Sugiyama & Abe 1989	Nagoya, Japan	12,263	3	16	DSM-III	—	—	13.0
14	Cialdella & Mamelle 1989	1 département (Rhône), France	135,180	3–9	61	DSM-III like	—	2.3	4.5
15	Ritvo et al. 1989	Utah, US	769,620	3–27	241	DSM-III	34	3.73 (190/51)	2.47
16	Gillberg et al. 1991[4]	South-West Gothenburg and Bohuslän County, Sweden	78,106	4–13	74	DSM-III-R	18	2.7 (54/20)	9.5
17	Fombonne & du Mazaubrun 1992	4 régions and 14 départements, France	274,816	9 & 13	154	Clinical ICD-10 like	13.3	2.1 (105/49)	4.9
18	Wignyosumarto et al. 1992	Yogyakarita (SE of Jakarta), Indonesia	5,120	4–7	6	CARS	0	2.0 (4/2)	11.7
19	Honda et al. 1996	Yokohama, Japan	8,537	5	18	ICD-10	50.0	2.6 (13/5)	21.08
20	Fombonne et al. 1997	3 départements, France	325,347	8–16	174	Clinical ICD-10-like	12.1	1.81 (112/62)	5.35
21	Webb et al. 1997	South Glamorgan, Wales, UK	73,301	3–15	53	DSM-III-R	—	6.57 (46/7)	7.2
22	Arvidsson et al. 1997	Mölnlycke, Sweden (West coast)	1,941	3–6	9	ICD-10	22.2	3.5 (7/2)	46.4

23	Sponheim & Skjeldal 1998	Akershus County, Norway	65,688	3–14	34	ICD-10	47.1[3]	2.09 (23/11)	5.2
24	Taylor et al. 1999	North Thames, UK	≅490,000	0–16	427	ICD-10	—	—	8.7
25	Kadesjö et al. 1999	Karlstad, Sweden (Central)	826	6.7–7.7	6	DSM-III-R/ICD-10 Gillberg's criteria (Asperger syndrome)	50.0	5.0 (5/1)	72.6
26	Baird et al. 2000	South-East Thames, UK	16,235		50	ICD-10	60	15.7 (47/3)	30.8
27	Powell et al. 2000	West Midlands, UK	25,377		62	Clinical/ICD-10/DSM-IV	–	—	7.8
28	Kielinen et al. 2000	North (Oulu et Lapland), Finland	152,732		187	ICD-8/ICD-9/ICD-10	49.8	4.12 (156/50)	12.2
29	Bertrand et al. 2001	Brick Township, New Jersey, US	8,896		36	DSM-IV	36.7	2.2 (25/11)	40.5
30	Fombonne et al. 2001	England and Wales	10,438	5–15	27	DSM-IV/ICD-10	55.5	8.0 (24/3)	26.1
31	Magnusson & Saemundsen 2001	Whole Island, Iceland	43,153	5–14	57	Mostly ICD-10	15.8	4.2 (46/11)	13.2
32	Chakrabarti & Fombonne 2001	Staffordshire, UK (Midlands)	15,500	2.5–6.5	26	ICD-10/DSM-IV	29.2	3.3 (20/6)	16.8
33	Davidovitch et al. 2001	Haiffa, Israel	26,160	7–11	26	DSM-III-R/DSM-IV	—	4.2 (21/5)	10.0

Continued on next page

Table 1.1 cont.

Study no.	Author, year	Area	Size of target population	Age (years)	Number of subjects with autism	Diagnostic criteria	% with normal IQ	Gender ratio (M:F)	Prevalence rate/ 10,000
34	Croen et al. 2002a	California DDS, US	4,950,333	5–12	5,038	CDER (Full syndrome)	62.8[5]	4.47 (4116/921)	11.0
35	Madsen et al. 2002	National register, Denmark	63,859	8	46	ICD-10	—	—	7.2
36	Chakrabarti & Fombonne 2005	Staffordshire, UK (Midlands)	10,903	4–7	24	ICD-10/DSM-IV	33.3	3.8 (19/5)	22.0

Notes

1 This number corresponds to the sample described in Wing and Gould (1979)

2 This rate corresponds to the first published paper on this survey and is based on 12 subjects amongst children aged 5 to 14 years

3 In this study, mild mental retardation was combined with normal IQ, whereas moderate and severe mental retardation were grouped together

4 For the Gothenburg surveys by Gillberg et al. (Gillberg 1984; Steffenburg and Gillberg 1986; Gillberg et al. 1991) a detailed examination showed that there was overlap between the samples included in the three surveys; consequently only the last survey has been included in this table

5 This proportion is likely to be overestimated and to reflect an underreporting of mental retardation in the CDER evaluations

PREVALENCE ESTIMATIONS FOR AUTISTIC DISORDER

Prevalence estimates ranged from 0.7/10,000 to 72.6/10,000 (Table 1.2). Prevalence rates were negatively correlated with sample size (Spearman r = -0.73; p<0.01); small-scale studies tended to report higher prevalence rates.

When surveys were combined in two groups according to the median year of publication (1994), the median prevalence rate for 18 surveys published in the period 1966 to 1993 was 4.7/10,000, and the median rate for the 18 surveys published in the period 1994 to 2004 was 12.7/10,000. Indeed, the correlation between prevalence rate and year of publication reached statistical significance (Spearman r=0.65; p<0.01); and the results of the 22 surveys with prevalence rates over 7/10,000 were all published since 1987. These findings point towards an increase in prevalence estimates in the past 15 to 20 years. To derive a best estimate of the current prevalence of autism, it was therefore deemed appropriate to restrict the analysis to 28 surveys published since 1987. The prevalence estimates ranged from 2.5 to 72.6/10,000 (average 95 per cent CI [Confidence Interval] width: 14.1), with an average rate of 16.2/10,000 and a median rate of 11.3/10,000. Similar values were obtained when slightly different rules and time cutpoints were used, with median and mean rates fluctuating between 10 and 13 and 13 and 18/10,000 respectively. From these results, a conservative estimate for the current prevalence of autistic disorder is most consistent with values lying somewhere between 10/10,000 and 16/10,000. For further calculations, we arbitrarily adopted the midpoint of this interval as the working rate for autism prevalence; that is, the value of 13/10,000.

UNSPECIFIED PERVASIVE DEVELOPMENTAL DISORDERS

Different labels have been used to characterize these conditions, such as the triad of impairments involving impairments in reciprocal social interaction, communication and imagination (Wing and Gould 1979). These groups would be overlapping with current diagnostic labels such as atypical autism and pervasive developmental disorders not otherwise specified (PDD-NOS). Fourteen of the 36 surveys yielded separate estimates of the prevalence of these developmental disorders, with ten studies showing higher rates for the non-autism disorders than the rates for autism. The ratio of the rate of non-autistic PDDs to the rate of autism was on average 1.6, which translates into an average prevalence estimate of 20.8/10,000 if one takes 13/10,000 as the rate for autism. This group has been much less studied in previous epidemiological studies, but progressive recognition of its importance and relevance to autism has led to changes in the design of more recent epidemiological surveys. They now include these less typical children in the case definition adopted in surveys. It should be clear from these figures that they represent a substantial group of children whose treatment needs are likely to be as important as those of children with autism.

ASPERGER SYNDROME AND CHILDHOOD DISINTEGRATIVE DISORDER

The reader is referred to recent epidemiological reviews for these two conditions (Fombonne 2002, 2005; Fombonne and Tidmarsh 2003). Epidemiological studies of Asperger syndrome (AS) are sparse, probably because it was acknowledged as a separate diagnostic category only recently in both ICD-10 and DSM-IV. Only two epidemiological surveys have specifically investigated its prevalence (Ehlers and Gillberg 1993; Kadesjö, Gillberg and Hagberg 1999). Only a handful (N<5) of cases were identified in these surveys, with the resulting estimates of 28 and 48/10,000 being extremely imprecise. By contrast, other recent autism surveys have consistently identified smaller numbers of children with AS than those with autism within the same survey. In Studies 23–27 and 32 (reviewed in Fombonne and Tidmarsh 2003) and Study 36, the ratio of autism to AS rates in each survey was above unity, suggesting that the rate of AS was consistently lower than that for autism (Table 1.2). How much lower is difficult to establish from existing data, but a ratio of 5:1 would appear to be an acceptable, albeit conservative, conclusion based on this limited available evidence. Taking 13/10,000 as the rate for autism, this translates into a rate for AS that would be 2.6/10,000 for AS, a figure which is used for subsequent calculations.

CHILDHOOD DISINTEGRATIVE DISORDER

Few surveys have provided data on childhood disintegrative disorder (CDD), also known as Heller syndrome, disintegrative psychosis (ICD-9), or late-onset autism (see Volkmar 1992). In addition to the four studies (9, 23, 31, 32) of our previous review (Fombonne 2002), another survey has provided new data on CDD (Study 36). Taking the five studies into account (Table 1.3), prevalence estimates ranged from 1.1 to 9.2/100,000. The pooled estimate based on seven identified cases and a surveyed population of 358,633 children was 1.9/100,000. The upper-bound limit of the associated confidence interval (4.15/100,000) indicates that CDD is a rare condition, with one case occurring for every 65 cases of autistic disorder.

PREVALENCE FOR COMBINED PDDs

Taking the aforementioned conservative estimates, the prevalence for all PDDs is at least 36.4/10,000 (the sum of estimates for autism (13/10,000), PDD-NOS (20.8/10,000) and AS (2.6/10,000)). This global estimate is derived from a conservative analysis of existing data. However, six out of eight recent epidemiological surveys yielded even higher rates (Table 1.4). The two surveys that did not show higher rates might have underestimated them. In the Danish investigation (Study 35), case finding depended on notification to a National Registry, a method that is usually associated with lower sensitivity for case finding. The Atlanta survey (Study 38) by the Centers for Disease Control and Prevention (CDC) was based on a very large population (which typically yields

Table 1.2 Asperger syndrome (AS) in recent autism surveys

Author, year	Size of population	Age group	Informants	Instruments	Diagnostic criteria	Autism		Asperger syndrome		
						N	Rate/ 10,000	N	Rate/ 10,000	Autism/ AS ratio
Sponheim & Skjeldal 1998	65,688	3–14	Parent, Child	Parental interview + direct observation, CARS, ABC	ICD-10	32	4.9	2	0.3	16.0
Taylor et al. 1999	490,000	0–16	Record	Rating of all data available in child record	ICD-10	427	8.7	71	1.4	6.0
Kadesjö et al. 1999	826	6.7–7.7	Child Parent Professional	ADI-R, Griffiths Scale or WISC, Asperger Syndrome Screening Questionnaire	DSM-III-R/ICD-10 Gillberg's criteria (Asperger syndrome)	6	72.6	4	48.4	1.5
Powell et al. 2000	25,377	1–4.9	Records	ADI-R, Available data	DSM-III-R, DSM-IV, ICD-10	54	—	16	—	3.4
Baird et al. 2000	16,235	7	Parent Child Other data	ADI-R, Psychometry	ICD-10, DSM-IV	45	27.7	5	3.1	9.0
Chakrabarti & Fombonne 2001	15,500	2.5–6.5	Child Parent Professional	ADI-R, 2 wks' multidisciplinary assessment, Merrill-Palmer, WPPSI	ICD-10, DSM-IV	26	16.8	13	8.4	2.0
Chakrabarti & Fombonne 2005	10,903	2.5–6.5	Child Parent Professional	ADI-R, 2 wks' multidisciplinary assessment, Merrill-Palmer, WPPSI	ICD-10, DSM-IV	24	22.0	12	11.0	2.0
Overall						614		123		5.0

Table 1.3 Surveys of childhood disintegrative disorder (CDD)

Author, year	Country (Region/State)	Size of target population	Age group	Assessment	N	M/F	Prevalence estimate (/100,000)	95% CI (/100,000)
Burd et al. 1987	US (North Dakota)	180,986	2–18	Structured parental interview and review of all data available – DSM-III criteria	2	2/–	1.11	0.13; 3.4
Sponheim & Skjeldal 1998	Norway (Akershus County)	65,688	3–14	Parental interview and direct observation (CARS, ABC)	1	?	1.52	0.04; 8.5
Magnusson and Saemundsen 2001	Iceland (whole island)	85,556	5–14	ADI-R, CARS and psychological tests – mostly ICD-10	2	2/–	2.34	0.3; 8.4
Chakrabarti & Fombonne 2001	UK (Staffordshire, Midlands)	15,500	2.5–6.5	ADI-R, two weeks' multidisciplinary assessment, Merrill-Palmer, WPPSI – ICD-10/DSM-IV	1	1/–	6.4	0.16; 35.9
Chakrabarti & Fombonne 2005	UK (Staffordshire, Midlands)	10,903	2.5–6.5	ADI-R, two weeks' multidisciplinary assessment, Merrill-Palmer, WPPSI – ICD-10/DSM-IV	1	1/–	9.2	0–58.6
Pooled estimates		358,633			7	6/–	1.9	0.87–4.15

Table 1.4 Newer epidemiological surveys of PDDs

Study no.	Author	Age	Autism			PDD-NOS + AS			All PDDs
			Rate/ 10,000	Male/Female ratio	% IQ normal	Rate/ 10,000	Male/Female ratio	% IQ normal	Rate/ 10,000
26	Baird et al. 2000	7	30.8	15.7	60	27.1	4.5	—	57.9
29	Bertrand et al. 2001	3–10	40.5	2.2	37	27.0	3.7	51	67.5
32	Chakrabarti & Fombonne 2001	4–7	16.8	3.3	29	44.5	4.3	94	61.3
35	Madsen et al. 2002	8	7.7	—	—	22.2	—	—	30.0
36	Chakrabarti & Fombonne 2005	4–7	22.0	4.0	33.3	35.8	8.7	91.6	58.7
37	Scott et al. 2002	5–11	—	—	—	—	—	—	58.3[a]
38	Yeargin-Allsopp et al. 2003	3–10	—	—	—	—	—	—	34.0
39	Gurney et al. 2003	6–11	—	—	—	—	—	—	52.0

Note

a   Computed by the author

lower prevalence, as described earlier) and age-specific rates were in fact in the 40 to 45/10,000 range in some birth cohorts (Fombonne 2003b). The common design features of the four other epidemiological inquiries (Studies 26, 29, 32, 36) that yielded higher rates are worthy of mention. First, the case definition chosen for these investigations was that of a pervasive developmental disorder (PDD) as opposed to the narrower approach focusing on autistic disorder. Second, case-finding techniques employed in these surveys were proactive, relying on multiple and repeated screening phases, involving both different informants at each phase and surveying the same cohorts at different ages, which certainly maximized the sensitivity of case identification. Third, assessments were performed with standardized diagnostic measures (Autism Diagnostic Interview – Revised [ADI-R] and Autism Diagnostic Observation Schedule [ADOS]), which match well the dimensional approach retained for case definition. Finally, these samples comprised young children around their fifth birthday, thereby optimizing sensitivity of case-finding procedures. Furthermore, the size of targeted populations was reasonably small (between 9,000 and 16,000), probably allowing for the most efficient use of research resources. Conducted in different regions and countries by different teams, the convergence of estimates is striking. Two further results are worth noting. First, in sharp contrast with the prevalence for combined PDDs, the separate estimates for autistic disorder and PDD-NOS vary widely in studies where separate figures were available. It appears that the reliability of the differentiation between autistic disorder and PDD-NOS was mediocre at that young age, despite the use of up-to-date standardized measures. Second, the rate of mental retardation was, overall, much lower than in previous surveys of autism. Although this should not be a surprise for children in the PDD-NOS/AS groups, this trend was also noticeable within samples diagnosed with autistic disorder. To what extent this trend reflects the previously mentioned differential classification issues between autism and PDD-NOS or a genuine trend over time towards decreased rate of mental retardation within children with autistic disorder (possibly as a result of earlier diagnosis and intervention) remains to be established.

In conclusion, the convergence of recent surveys around an estimate of 60/10,000 for all PDDs combined is striking, especially when coming from studies with improved methods. This estimate appears now to be the best estimate for the prevalence of PDDs currently available.

CORRELATES OF ASD
Medical conditions

Rates of medical conditions associated with autism were reported in 15 surveys. Conditions such as congenital rubella, PKU, neurofibromatosis, cerebral palsy and Down syndrome account for very few cases of autism. For fragile-X, the low rate available in epidemiological studies is almost certainly an underestimate because fragile-X was not recognized until relatively recently and the most recent surveys did not always include systematic screening for fragile-X. In line with prior reports (Smalley *et al.* 1992), tuberous sclerosis (TS) has a consistently high frequency among autistic samples. Assuming a population prevalence of 1/10,000 for TS, it appears that the rate of TS is about 100 times higher than that expected under the hypothesis of no association. Overall, the proportion of cases of autism that could be causally attributed to known medical disorders therefore remains low (about 5–6 per cent).

Immigrant status and ethnicity

Some investigators have mentioned the possibility that rates of autism might be higher among immigrants (Gillberg 1987; Gillberg, Steffenburg and Schaumann 1991; Gillberg, Schaumann and Gillberg 1995; Wing 1980). Five of the 17 children with autism identified in the Camberwell study were of Caribbean origin (Study 4; Wing 1980), and the estimated rate of autism was 6.3/10,000 for this group compared with 4.4/10,000 for the rest of the population (Wing 1993). However, the wide confidence intervals associated with rates from this study indicate no statistically significant difference. Only one child was born from British-born Afro-Caribbean parents in a recent UK survey (Study 21; Webb *et al.* 1997), providing little support to this particular hypothesis. Similarly, the findings from the Gothenburg studies paralleled an increased migration flux in the early 1980s in this area (Gillberg 1987); they, too, were based on relatively small numbers (19 children from immigrant parents). In the same geographic area, Arvidsson *et al.* (1997; Study 22) had five children out of nine in their sample with either both parents (N=2) or one parent (N=3) having immigrated to Sweden. However, there were no systematic comparisons with rates of immigrants in the population. A positive family history for developmental disorders was reported in three such cases and a chromosomal abnormality in one further case. In the Icelandic survey (Study 31), 2.5 per cent of the autism parents were from non-European origin compared to a 0.5 per cent corresponding rate in the whole population, but it was unclear if this represented a significant difference. In Study 23, the proportion of children with autism and a non-European origin was marginally but not significantly raised compared with the population rate of immigrants (8 per cent vs. 2.3 per cent), but this was based on a very small sample (two children of non-European origin). A UK survey found comparable rates in areas with contrasting ethnic composition (Powell *et al.* 2000). In the Utah survey, where a clear breakdown by race was achieved (Ritvo *et al.* 1989; Study 15, Table 1), the autism parents showed no deviation from the racial distribution of this state. The proportion of non-Whites in this study and state was, however, noticeably low, providing little power to detect departures from the null hypothesis. Other studies have not systematically reported the proportion of immigrant or ethnic groups in the areas surveyed. In four studies where the proportions of immigrant groups were low (11, 12, 19, 21), rates of autism were in the upper range of rates. Conversely, in studies of other populations (14, 17 and 20) where immigrants contributed substantially to the denominators, rates were in the rather low band. The analysis of a large sample (N=4,356) of

Californian PDD children showed a lower risk of autism in children of Mexico-born mothers and a similar risk for children of mothers born outside the United States compared with California-born mothers (Croen, Grether and Selvin 2002b). In this study, the risk of PDD was raised in African American mothers with an adjusted rate ratio of 1.6 (95 per cent CI: 1.5 to 1.8); by contrast, the prevalence was similar in White, Black, and other races in the population-based survey of Atlanta (Yeargin-Allsopp *et al.* 2003), where case ascertainment is likely to be more complete than in the previous study.

Taken altogether, the combined results of these reports should be interpreted in the specific methodological context of these investigations. Most studies had low numbers of identified cases, and especially small numbers of autistic children born from immigrant parents, and many authors in these studies relied on broadened definitions of autism. Statistical testing was not rigorously conducted, and doubts could be raised in several studies about the appropriateness of the comparison data that were used. In addition, studies sampling children through services or clinical sources may be biased because ethnicity, race and social class are likely to differentially affect access to these settings. Moreover, studies were generally poor in their definition of immigrant status, with unclear amalgamation of information on country of origin, citizenship, immigrant status, race and ethnicity. Moreover, it is unclear what common mechanism could explain the putative association between immigrant status and autism, since the origins of the immigrant parents (especially in Study 16; see also Gillberg and Gillberg 1996) were diverse and represented in fact all continents. With this heterogeneity in mind, what common biological features might these immigrant families share and what would be a plausible mechanism explaining the putative association between autism and immigrant status? The possibility of an increased vulnerability to intrauterine infections in non-immunized immigrant mothers was raised but not supported in a detailed analysis of 15 autistic children from immigrant parents (Gillberg and Gillberg 1996). These authors instead posited that parents, and in particular fathers, affected with autistic traits would be inclined to travel abroad to find female partners more naïve to their social difficulties. This speculation was based, however, on three observations only, and assessment of the autistic traits in two parents was not independently obtained.

The hypothesis of an association between immigrant status or race and autism, therefore, remains largely unsupported by the empirical results. Most of the claims about these possible correlates of autism were derived from post hoc observations of very small samples and were not subjected to rigorous statistical testing. Large studies have generally failed to detect such associations.

AUTISM AND SOCIAL CLASS

Twelve studies provided information on the social class of the families of autistic children. Of these, four studies (1, 2, 3 and 5) suggested an association between autism and social class or parental education. The year of data collection for these four investigations was before 1980 (Table 1.1), and all studies conducted thereafter provided no evidence for the association. Thus, the epidemiological results suggest that the earlier findings were probably due to artefacts in the availability of services and in the case-finding methods, as already shown in other samples (Schopler, Andrews and Strupp 1979; Wing 1980).

CONCLUSION

Epidemiological surveys of autism and PDDs have now been carried out in several countries. Methodological differences in case definition and case-finding procedures make between-survey comparisons difficult to perform. Despite these differences, some common characteristics of autism and PDDs in population surveys have consistently emerged. Autism is associated with mental retardation in about 70 per cent of the cases and is overrepresented among males (with a male/female ratio of 4.3:1). Autism is found in association with some rare and genetically determined medical conditions, such as tuberous sclerosis. Overall, the median value of about 5.5 per cent for the combined rate of medical disorders in autism derived from this review is consistent with the 5 per cent (Tuchman, Rapin and Shinnar 1991) to 10 per cent (Rutter *et al.* 1994) figures available from other investigations. A majority of surveys has ruled out social class as a risk factor for autism, a result once supported by studies of clinical, that is, less representative, samples. The putative association of autism with immigrant status or race is, so far, not borne out by epidemiological studies. The conclusion of a lack of variation in the incidence of autism according to race or ethnicity is reached, however, from a weak empirical base and future studies might address this issue more efficiently. In fact, epidemiological studies of autism and PDDs have generally been lacking sophistication in their investigation of most other risk factors. Currently, the best estimate available for the prevalence of all PDDs combined is around 60/10,000 or 0.6 per cent. This figure is higher than that for Down syndrome, cystic fibrosis and other serious medical conditions affecting children. These figures carry straightforward implications for service planning.

REFERENCES

Arvidsson, T., Danielsson, B., Forsberg, P., Gillberg, C., Johansson, M. and Kjellgren, G. (1997) 'Autism in 3–6-year-old children in a suburb of Goteborg, Sweden.' *Autism 2*, 163–173.

Baird, G., Charman, T., Baron-Cohen, S., Cox, A., Swettenham, J., Wheelwright, S. and Drew, A. (2000) 'A screening instrument for autism at 18 months of age: a 6-year follow-up study.' *Journal of the American Academy of Child and Adolescent Psychiatry 39*, 694–702.

Bertrand, J., Mars, A., Boyle, C., Bove, F., Yeargin-Allsopp, M. and Decoufle, P. (2001) 'Prevalence of autism in a United States population: the Brick Township, New Jersey, investigation.' *Pediatrics 108*, 1155–1161.

Bohman, M., Bohman, I. L., Björck, P. O. and Sjöholm, E. (1983) 'Childhood psychosis in a northern Swedish county: some preliminary findings from an epidemiological survey.' In M. H. Schmidt and H. Remschmidt (eds) *Epidemiological Approaches in Child Psychiatry*. New York and Stuttgart: George Thieme Verlag, pp. 164–173.

Brask, B. H. (1970) 'A prevalence investigation of childhood psychoses.' *Nordic Symposium on the Care of Psychotic Children*. Oslo: Barnepsychiatrist Forening.

Bryson, S. E., Clark, B. S. and Smith, I. M. (1988) 'First report of a Canadian epidemiological study of autistic syndromes.' *Journal of Child Psychology and Psychiatry 4*, 433–445.

Burd, L., Fisher, W. and Kerbeshan, J. (1987) 'A prevalence study of pervasive developmental disorders in North Dakota.' *Journal of the American Academy of Child and Adolescent Psychiatry 26*, 5, 700–703.

Chakrabarti, S. and Fombonne, E. (2001) 'Pervasive developmental disorders in preschool children.' *Journal of the American Medical Association 285*, 24, 3093–3099.

Chakrabarti, S. and Fombonne, E. (2005) 'Pervasive developmental disorders in preschool children: high prevalence confirmed.' *American Journal of Psychiatry 162*, 1133–1141.

Cialdella, P. and Mamelle, N. (1989) 'An epidemiological study of infantile autism in a French department.' *Journal of Child Psychology and Psychiatry 30*, 1, 165–175.

Le Couteur, A., Rutter, M., Lord, C., Rios, P., Robertson, S., Holdgrafer, M. *et al.* (1989) 'Autism diagnostic interview: a standardized investigator-based instrument.' *Journal of Autism and Developmental Disorders 19*, 363–387.

Croen, L. A., Grether, J. K., Hoogstrate, J. and Selvin, S. (2002a) 'The changing prevalence of autism in California.' *Journal of Autism and Developmental Disorders 32*, 3, 207–215.

Croen, L. A., Grether, J. K. and Selvin, S. (2002b) 'Descriptive epidemiology of autism in a California population: who is at risk?' *Journal of Autism and Developmental Disorders 32*, 3, 217–224.

Davidovitch, M., Holtzman, G. and Tirosh, E. (2001) 'Autism in the Haifa area: an epidemiological perspective.' *Israeli Medical Association Journal 3*, 188–189.

Ehlers, S. and Gillberg, C. (1993) 'The epidemiology of Asperger syndrome: a total population study.' *Journal of Child Psychology and Psychiatry 34*, 1327–1350.

Fombonne, E. (1999) 'The epidemiology of autism: a review.' *Psychological Medicine 29*, 769–786.

Fombonne, E. (2002) 'Prevalence of childhood disintegrative disorder (CDD).' *Autism 6*, 2, 147–155.

Fombonne, E. (2003a) 'Epidemiological surveys of autism and other pervasive developmental disorders: an update.' *Journal of Autism and Developmental Disorders 33*, 4, 365–382.

Fombonne, E. (2003b) 'The prevalence of autism.' *Journal of the American Medical Association 289*, 1, 1–3.

Fombonne, E. (2005) 'Epidemiological studies of pervasive developmental disorders.' In F. Volkmar (ed.) *Handbook of Autism and PDD* (3rd edn). New York: Wiley and Sons, pp. 42–69.

Fombonne, E. and du Mazaubrun, C. (1992) 'Prevalence of infantile autism in 4 French regions.' *Social Psychiatry and Psychiatric Epidemiology 27*, 203–210.

Fombonne, E. and Tidmarsh, L. (2003) 'Epidemiological data on Asperger disorder.' *Child and Adolescent Psychiatric Clinics of North America 12*, 15–21.

Fombonne, E., du Mazaubrun, C., Cans, C. and Grandjean, H. (1997) 'Autism and associated medical disorders in a large French epidemiological sample.' *Journal of the American Academy of Child and Adolescent Psychiatry 36*, 11, 1561–1566.

Fombonne, E., Simmons, H., Ford, T., Meltzer, H. and Goodman, R. (2001) 'Prevalence of pervasive developmental disorders in the British nationwide survey of child mental health.' *Journal of the American Academy of Child and Adolescent Psychiatry 40*, 7, 820–827.

Gillberg, C. (1984) 'Infantile autism and other childhood psychoses in a Swedish region: epidemiological aspects.' *Journal of Child Psychology and Psychiatry 25*, 35–43.

Gillberg, C. (1987) 'Infantile autism in children of immigrant parents. A population-based study from Göteborg, Sweden.' *British Journal of Psychiatry 150*, 856–858.

Gillberg, C. and Gillberg, C. (1996) 'Autism in immigrants: a population-based study from Swedish rural and urban areas.' *Journal of Intellectual Disability Research 40*, 24–31.

Gillberg, C., Steffenburg, S. and Schaumann, H. (1991) 'Is autism more common now than ten years ago?' *British Journal of Psychiatry 158*, 403–409.

Gillberg, C., Schaumann, H. and Gillberg, I. C. (1995) 'Autism in immigrants: children born in Sweden to mothers born in Uganda.' *Journal of Intellectual Disability Research 39*, 141–144.

Gurney, J. G., Fritz, M. S., Ness, K. K., Sievers, P., Newschaffer, C. J. and Shapiro, E. G. (2003) 'Analysis of prevalence trends of autism spectrum disorder in Minnesota [comment].' *Archives of Pediatrics and Adolescent Medicine 157*, 7, 622–627.

Honda, H., Shimizu, Y., Misumi, K., Niimi, M. and Ohashi, Y. (1996) 'Cumulative incidence and prevalence of childhood autism in children in Japan.' *British Journal of Psychiatry 169*, 228–235.

Hoshino, Y., Yashima, Y., Ishige, K., Tachibana, R., Watanabe, M., Kancki, M. *et al.* (1982) 'The epidemiological study of autism in Fukushimaken.' *Folia Psychiatrica et Neurologica Japonica 36*, 115–124.

Kadesjö, B., Gillberg, C. and Hagberg, B. (1999) 'Autism and Asperger syndrome in seven-year-old children: a total population study.' *Journal of Autism and Developmental Disorders 29*, 4, 327–331.

Kielinen, M., Linna, S. L. and Moilanen, I. (2000) 'Autism in Northern Finland.' *European Child and Adolescent Psychiatry 9*, 162–167.

Lord, C., Schopler, E. and Revecki, D. (1982) 'Sex differences in autism.' *Journal of Autism and Developmental Disorders 12*, 317–330.

Lord, C., Risi, S., Lembrecht, L., Cook, E., Leventhal, B., DiLavore, P. *et al.* (2000) 'The Autism Diagnostic Observation Schedule-Generic: a standard measure of social and communication deficits associated with the spectrum of autism.' *Journal of Autism and Developmental Disorders 30*, 205–223.

Lotter, V. (1966) 'Epidemiology of autistic conditions in young children: I. Prevalence.' *Social Psychiatry 1*, 124–137.

McCarthy, P., Fitzgerald, M. and Smith, M. A. (1984) 'Prevalence of childhood autism in Ireland.' *Irish Medical Journal 77*, 5, 129–130.

Madsen, K. M., Hviid, A., Vestergaard, M., Schendel, D., Wohlfahrt, J., Thorsen, P. *et al.* (2002) 'A population-based study of measles, mumps, and rubella vaccination and autism.' *New England Journal of Medicine 347*, 19, 1477–1482.

Magnusson, P. and Saemundsen, E. (2001) 'Prevalence of autism in Iceland.' *Journal of Autism and Developmental Disorders 31*, 153–163.

Matsuishi, T., Shiotsuki, M., Yoshimura, K., Shoji, H., Imuta, F. and Yamashita, F. (1987) 'High prevalence of infantile autism in Kurume City, Japan.' *Journal of Child Neurology 2*, 268–271.

Powell, J., Edwards, A., Edwards, M., Pandit, B. S., Sungum-Paliwal, S. R. and Whitehouse, W. (2000) 'Changes in the incidence of childhood autism and other autistic spectrum disorders in preschool children from two areas of the West Midlands.' *UK Developmental Medicine and Child Neurology 42*, 624–628.

Ritvo, E. R., Freeman, B. J., Pingree, C., Mason-Brothers, A., Jorde, L., Jenson, W.R. *et al.* (1989) 'The UCLA–University of Utah epidemiologic survey of autism: prevalence.' *American Journal of Psychiatry 146*, 2, 194–199.

Rutter, M., Bailey, A., Bolton, P. and Le Couteur, A. (1994) 'Autism and known medical conditions: myth and substance.' *Journal of Child Psychology and Psychiatry 35*, 311–322.

Schopler, E., Andrews, C. E. and Strupp, K. (1979) 'Do autistic children come from upper-middle-class parents?' *Journal of Autism and Developmental Disorders 9*, 2, 139–151.

Scott, F. J., Baron-Cohen, S., Bolton, P. and Brayne, C. (2002) 'Brief report: prevalence of autism spectrum conditions in children aged 5–11 years in Cambridgeshire, UK.' *Autism 6*, 3, 231–237.

Smalley, S. L., Tanguay, P. E., Smith, M. and Gutierrez, G. (1992) 'Autism and tuberous sclerosis.' *Journal of Autism and Developmental Disorders 22*, 339–355.

Sponheim, E. and Skjeldal, O. (1998) 'Autism and related disorders: epidemiological findings in a Norwegian study using ICD-10 diagnostic criteria.' *Journal of Autism and Developmental Disorders 28*, 217–222.

Steffenburg, S. and Gillberg, C. (1986) 'Autism and autistic-like conditions in Swedish rural and urban areas: a population study.' *British Journal of Psychiatry 149*, 81–87.

Steinhausen, H.-C., Göbel, D., Breinlinger, M. and Wohlloben, B. (1986) 'A community survey of infantile autism.' *Journal of the American Academy of Child Psychiatry 25*, 2, 186–189.

Sugiyama, T. and Abe, T. (1989) 'The prevalence of autism in Nagoya, Japan: a total population study.' *Journal of Autism and Developmental Disorders 19*, 87–96.

Tanoue, Y., Oda, S., Asano, F. and Kawashima, K. (1988) 'Epidemiology of infantile autism in Southern Ibaraki, Japan: differences in prevalence in birth cohorts.' *Journal of Autism and Developmental Disorders 18*, 155–166.

Taylor, B., Miller, E., Farrington, C., Petropoulos, M.-C., Favot-Mayaud, I., Li, J. and Wright, P. (1999) 'Autism and measles, mumps, and rubella vaccine: no epidemological evidence for a causal association.' *The Lancet 353*, 2026–2029.

Treffert, D. A. (1970) 'Epidemiology of infantile autism.' *Archives of General Psychiatry 22*, 431–438.

Tuchman, R. F., Rapin, I. and Shinnar, S. (1991) 'Autistic and dysphasic children: II. Epilepsy.' *Pediatrics 88*, 1219–1225.

Volkmar, F. R. (1992) 'Childhood disintegrative disorder: issues for DSM-IV.' *Journal of Autism and Developmental Disorders 22*, 625–642.

Webb, E., Lobo, S., Hervas, A., Scourfield, J. and Fraser, W. I. (1997) 'The changing prevalence of autistic disorder in a Welsh health district.' *Developmental Medicine and Child Neurology 39*, 150–152.

Wignyosumarto, S., Mukhlas, M. and Shirataki, S. (1992) 'Epidemiological and clinical study of autistic children in Yogyakarta, Indonesia.' *Kobe Journal of Medical Sciences 38*, 1, 1–19.

Wing, L. (1980) 'Childhood autism and social class: a question of selection?' *British Journal of Psychiatry 137*, 410–417.

Wing, L. (1993) 'The definition and prevalence of autism: a review.' *European Child and Adolescent Psychiatry 2*, 61–74.

Wing, L. and Gould, J. (1979) 'Severe impairments of social interactions and associated abnormalities in children: epidemiology and classification.' *Journal of Autism and Developmental Disorders 9*, 1, 11–29.

Wing, L., Yeates, S. R., Brierly, L. M. and Gould, J. (1976) 'The prevalence of early childhood autism: comparison of administrative and epidemiological studies.' *Psychological Medicine 6*, 89–100.

Yeargin-Allsopp, M., Rice, C., Karapurkar, T., Doernberg, N., Boyle, C. and Murphy, C. (2003) 'Prevalence of autism in a US metropolitan area.' *Journal of the American Medical Association 289*, 1, 49–55.

Chapter 2

Early Manifestations of Autistic Spectrum Disorder During the First Two Years of Life

Juan Martos Pérez, Pedro M. González, María Llorente Comí and Carmen Nieto

INTRODUCTION

Autism is a developmental disorder which is detected before three years of age. It appears defined in this way in the criteria of diagnostic manuals, in the DSM-IV-TR (American Psychiatric Association 2000) as well as the ICD-10 (World Health Organization 1993): 'the disturbance must be identified before three years of age'. We could say that practically no one questions the fact that the profile appears before three years of age; but when does it first appear and why? Are there different patterns which may develop into different configurations of the disorder? Susan Leekam, in Chapter 10 of this same volume, presents a magnificent study which analyses the presence of subgroups within the autistic spectrum. Is the useful and suggestive concept of the continuum, without precise limits, applicable to the apparition of the profile?

The knowledge and understanding of the genesis of autism is certainly a challenge for current research and entails important implications not only for practice, but also for theory, which in itself may orient future research in various areas of autistic spectrum disorders.

It is indubitable that early identification of autistic spectrum disorders makes early intervention plans, as well as access to specific and individualized specialized treatment services, possible which, according to the experimental evidence, leads to a better prognosis. The earlier treatment is initiated, the better the results of the intervention (Howlin 1997), thus making the age at initiation of treatment an extrinsic factor which determines the prognosis of children with ASD (Rivière 1997). Nonetheless, it may be questioned whether this affirmation is independent of the age at which the first signs are detected, meaning that we could question whether a late manifestation of the profile is associated with a more or less favourable prognosis. The signs of alert or alarm which may be identified early are the first and necessary steps towards an immediate diagnostic assessment (Filipek *et al.* 1999; Hernández *et al.* 2005) and, by extension, to the determination of the needs of intervention of the child and the family. Yet, would these first signs, which may permit immediate intervention, also permit the establishment of a differential diagnosis with respect to other developmental difficulties such as mental retardation?

The introduction of early intervention programmes counts on cerebral plasticity. The existence of the so-called critical periods has been widely accepted and demonstrated, from the point of view of neurobiology as well as from a perspective more strictly psychological (Rivière 1997). If determined synaptic connections are not made early in development, it is improbable that they will be made later. Some experiments have clearly shown how early experiences modify the way in which the brain interconnects and how these changes are maintained in adult life (Knudsen 1998). Rivière (2000) put forward the idea that development is a dynamic process in which important psychological functions incorporate diverse functional systems over time and are lost when this incorporation is not possible.

If understanding and early identification are important for ASD in terms of practice, then they are no less important for theory. However, this importance is characterized by the necessity to provide scientific answers to the great number of questions which remain unaddressed. Investigation into the early signs of autism and their course over the first years of life could permit us to follow its developmental trail, or even to penetrate to its psychological substrates, in addition to being a research strategy in harmony with the ontogenetic nature of the disorder.

Nonetheless, research in early manifestations confront some aspects which make it diametrically opposed to research in cognitive processes in populations with different diagnostic characteristics. One of the unique elements of the identification of autism in an early phase of development is the complexity of its early manifestations. Subjects with autism, in contrast to other disorders such as Down syndrome, do not show phenotypic traits which aid early detection. Furthermore, the first indicators are so subtle that the majority of cases remain undetected throughout the first year. In fact, as we will see over the course of this review, there are still no conclusive data on the presence of signs in the first year of life. We are attempting to approach the study of these first signs – but how? How do we select a sample? Many methods have been applied such as observation of home videos, retrospective interviews with the parents, or longitudinal studies. Confronted with this variety, we feel it is important to dedicate a first section of this review to the description and analysis of the type of methodologies used in different studies, which would permit the analysis of those methods in terms of different contributions of the results for the age of manifestation, specific signs, etc.

Once we have presented the type of study, we go on to analyse three fundamental questions: (a) At what age are the first signs detected? (b) What are these signs? and (c) Can specificity be identified in the observed signs?

STUDIES OF EARLY MANIFESTATIONS OF AUTISTIC SPECTRUM DISORDERS: METHODOLOGICAL ASPECTS

Before beginning our revision, we feel it appropriate to refer to Leo Kanner (1943), who, in his seminal article, sketched out some answers for the first two years of life, despite the fact that all but one of the children in that study were first seen in practice after three years of age. It is difficult to extract common guidelines for the early clinical manifestations in the Kanner study sample, except those which became pathognomonic signs, although we may indicate that all the children had difficulty in establishing affective links and showed abnormal verbal and non-verbal communication. Of the 11 cases, three of them (cases 2, 7 and 8) had some complication at birth, one was born in breech position, by caesarean section, and two others were born prematurely, one of those also by caesarean. In relation to psychomotor development, the acquisition of motor skills such as cephalic control, sitting and independent movement was normal, except in the cases of Herbert B. and John F., who began to walk at 24 and 20 months, respectively. For her part, Elaine C. (case 11) stood at seven months and walked before her first birthday. Kanner frequently referred to the difficulties shown in eating, given that more than half of the cases (cases 1, 4, 5, 7, 8 and 10) presented problems in this area, which was the principal reason for seeking help in case 10, John F. Other data which draws attention when reading this preliminary report is the abundance of the suspicion of hearing impairment, present in nearly half of the sample (cases 3, 5, 6, 7 and 11). In other children (cases 8, 9 and 10) reference is made to delayed development, to a lack of anticipatory behaviour in postural adjustment or to being picked up (cases 2 and 3). At the same time, there exists a clear allusion to the presence of regression. Specifically, in case 3, Richard M., Kanner (1943) cited the words of the mother: 'I can't be sure of when he stopped imitating the sounds of words. It seems like he had gone backwards mentally, gradually during the last two years.'

In our revision we include the most relevant studies published since 1975. In total, 39 articles were reviewed. Table 2.1, chronologically ordered, collects author information, the number of subjects (N) and the data collection method used by the authors.

As we see in Table 2.1, it is clear that the studies under revision have used heterogeneous research methods and data collection procedures. In general, to obtain data on early manifestations, the following strategies have been used: (1) analysis of retrospective information provided by parents, via specifically designed questionnaires and interviews which frequently use other instruments or rating scales; (2) analysis of home videos with different situations, ages and codification systems; (3) clinical assessment at the moment of diagnosis using various tests or instruments which, in some studies, were followed up (some studies have carried out assessment based on experimental tasks);

Table 2.1 Year, author, number of subjects and data collection method

Year, author	Subjects (N)	Data collection method
1975, Harper, J. and Williams, S.	131 subjects with autism	Questionnaires, interviews, assessments
1975, Massie, H.	2 subjects with autism	Analysis of home videos
1977, Ornitz, E. *et al.*	74 subjects with autism 38 subjects with normal development	Parent questionnaires
1978, Massie, H.	10 clinical subjects (heterogeneous group: autism, schizophrenia, psychosis) 10 subjects with normal development	Analysis of home videos
1980, Rosenthal, J. *et al.*	14 subjects with autism and childhood psychosis 14 subjects with normal development	Analysis of home videos
1985, Volkmar, F. *et al.*	129 subjects with one of three DSM-III diagnoses: childhood infantile autism, generalized atypical developmental disorder and early childhood psychosis	Analysis of reports/files
1987, Hoshino, Y. *et al.*	80 subjects with autism (DSM-III)	Parent interviews
1987, Ohta, M. *et al.*	141 subjects with autism (DSM-III) 33 subjects with mental retardation	Parent questionnaires
1989, Dahlgren, S. and Gillberg, C.	26 subjects with autism (DSM-III) 17 subjects with mental retardation 22 subjects with normal development	Parent questionnaires
1990, Lösche, G.	8 subjects with autism (DSM-III) 8 subjects with normal development	Analysis of home videos
1990, Rogers, S. and Dilalla, D.	26 subjects with autism 13 subjects with PDD-NOS (DSM-III)	Analysis of reports/files
1990, Gillberg, C. *et al.*	28 subjects referred for possible autism (DSM-III-R)	Clinical assessment, interview and follow-up
1991, Adrien, J. *et al.*	9 subjects with autism 3 subjects with generalized atypical developmental disorder (DSM-III)	Analysis of home videos
1991, Sparling, J.	Single case study	Follow-up of a single case from birth to four years
1992, Kurita, H. *et al.*	18 subjects with CDD 196 subjects with autism (DSM-III)	Analysis of reports/files, assessment by scales

Year, author	Subjects (N)	Data collection method
1992, Burack, J. and Volkmar, F.	30 low-functioning subjects with autism 30 high-functioning subjects with autism 30 low-functioning subjects without autism 30 high-functioning subjects without autism and developmentally disabled (DSM-III)	Study of the developmental sequence at the moment of assessment Questions from the Vineland for parents
1993, Adrien, J. *et al.*	12 subjects with autism 12 subjects with normal development	Analysis of home videos
1994, Osterling, J. and Dawson, G.	11 subjects with autism (DSM-III-R) 11 subjects with normal development	Analysis of home videos
1995, Lord, C.	25 boys and 9 girls referred for 'possible autism' (ADI-R)	Follow-up from two to four years, assessment and standardized tests
1996, Baron-Cohen, S. *et al.*	Administration of the CHAT to 16,000 subjects	Routine check-up at 18 months
1998, Dawson, G. *et al.*	20 subjects with PDD (13 with autism, 7 with PDD-NOS) (DSM-III-TR) 19 subjects with Down syndrome 20 subjects with normal development	Individual assessment with orientation and shared attention tasks
1998, Hadwin, J. and Hutley, G.	8 subjects with autism and IQ less than 50 (DSM-IV) 8 without autism and IQ less than 50	Teacher questionnaire
1998, Mars, E. *et al.*	10 subjects with autism 15 subjects with PDD-NOS (DSM-IV) 25 subjects with normal development	Analysis of home videos
1998, Vostanis, P. *et al.*	39 subjects with autism 13 subjects with Asperger syndrome 14 subjects with semantic pragmatic disorder 20 subjects with learning disabilities 20 subjects with other disorders (ICD-10)	Parent questionnaire
1998, Bernabei, P. *et al.*	7 subjects with autism 3 subjects with PDD-NOS (DSM-IV)	Analysis of home videos
1998, Martos, J. and Rivière, A.	22 subjects with autism 22 subjects with developmental delay and autistic traits 22 subjects with normal development (DSM-IV)	Parent questionnaire

Continued on next page

Table 2.1 cont.

Year, author	Subjects (N)	Data collection method
1999, Baranek, T.	11 subjects with autism 10 subjects with developmental disabilities 11 subjects with normal development (DSM-IV and CARS)	Analysis of home videos
1999, Maestro, S. *et al.*	16 subjects with autism 10 subjects with PDD-NOS	Analysis of home videos
1999, Stone, L. *et al.*	65 referred for assessment (DSM-IV and CARS)	Clinical assessment Clinician questionnaire
2000, Werner, E. *et al.*	15 subjects (8 with autism, 7 with PDD-NOS) (DSM-III-R) 15 subjects with normal development	Analysis of home videos
2000, Bailey, D. *et al.*	13 groups of three formed of one subject with autism, one subject with fragile-X and one subject with autism and fragile-X (DSM-IV and CARS)	Three scales
2000, Baird, G. *et al.*	16,235 children at 18 +/-2 months.	Follow-up study with CHAT (Checklist for Autism in Toddlers)
2000, Rivière, A.	100 subjects with autism (DSM-III-R)	Analysis of reports/files
2000, Stone, L. *et al.*	40 subjects with autism (DSM-IV) 33 subjects with normal development	Validation of the STAT (Screening Tool for Autism in Two-Year-Olds)
2000, Wimpory, D. *et al.*	10 subjects with autism (DSM-IV and CARS) 10 subjects with developmental delay	Parent information via the DAISI (Detection of Autism by Infant Sociability Interview)
2005, Zwaigenbaum, L. *et al.*	65 siblings of subjects with autism 23 subjects with normal development	Follow-up study from birth to 24 months with the AOSI (Autism Observation Scale for Infants)
2004, Martos, J. and Ayuda, R.	42 subjects with autism 41 subjects with specific language disorder (DSM-IV)	Form for retrospective parent information
2004, Wetherby, M. *et al.*	18 subjects with ASD 18 subjects with developmental delay 18 subjects with normal development	CSBS DP (Communication and Symbolic Behaviour Scales Developmental Profile)
2005, Receveur, C. *et al.*	18 subjects with autism, divided in two groups (IQ more or less than 50)	Analysis of home videos Examination video at 4 years

(4) validation of specific instruments; and (5) longitudinal studies of cases of ASD or cases of high risk, such as siblings of children with ASD.

One relevant question at this point is related to the use of diagnostic criteria. The times in which the revised studies were done reflect the changes introduced by internationally accepted diagnostic criteria. In studies from between 1975 and 1985 no diagnostic criteria were specified, using instead groups of subjects with mixed diagnosis or diagnostic labels with doubtful validity (e.g. psychosis, schizophrenia, etc.). In general, that decade was dominated by psychodynamic conceptions, such that some of the results, as we will see, should be taken with caution. In the five years following, until 1990, the DSM-III (APA 1980) criteria were employed. Between 1990 and 1998 the DSM-III-R (APA 1987) criteria were used and since approximately 1998 diagnoses were based on the DSM-IV (APA 1994). Some studies have used the ICD-10 criteria of the World Health Organization (1993). It must be mentioned that some studies have also used criteria based on rating scales or diagnostic lists such as the CARS (Schopler *et al.* 1980), or the ABC (Gillberg *et al.* 1990). Still other studies did not even mention the criteria employed for the assignation of diagnoses to the participants. Clearly, this panorama complicated the comparing and contrasting of the results obtained in this broad variety of studies.

With the objective of making a more profound analysis of the revised studies, and also with the objective of making that analysis more didactic and understandable, we have considered the characteristics of each of the strategies used to collect data on early manifestations of ASD in more detail, lending special attention to the directions and research marked by each one of the strategies and their obtained results.

ANALYSIS OF RETROSPECTIVE INFORMATION PROVIDED BY THE FAMILY

The methodological validity has to be questioned in studies which have used this strategy, in that the information obtained is based on memory and is therefore subject to inaccuracies or distortions or which may have difficulties in accurately locating the relevant information in time. Osterling and Dawson (1994) allude to some of these methodological problems. It has also been indicated that other variables which may bias the information may come into play in this type of study, such as the expectations and emotions of the parents, contradictions and disagreement in the provided information, the possible influence of the number of children in the family which may serve as a source of comparison or the acceptance of irrational causal attributions. When the information is extracted from the analysis of reports or medical histories relevant information is not always found, as the appropriate questions relating to a possible early presentation of symptoms have been unclear or have remained unasked.

Nonetheless, some authors may be found which support the use of retrospective family information. Ohta *et al.* (1987) consider that, despite the limitations of these retrospective reports, parents are capable of perceiving the nature or character of autistic symptoms. For their part, Ornitz, Guthrie and Farley (1977) carried out a small study to find support for this methodology and compared the rate of coincidence between the information provided by the parents of children with normal development with the norms established on the Bayley Scale of Infant Development (BSIS). These authors considered their results to defend the use of this methodology.

The studies which have analysed this retrospective information have had the following lines of research as their objective:

1   possible relationship between the time of onset and prognosis of the disorder, as well as the influence of variables such as IQ, language and educational variables (Dahlgren and Gillberg 1989; Harper and Williams 1975; Hoshino *et al.* 1987; Volkmar, Stier and Cohen 1985)

2   presentation of related disorders (Harper and Williams 1975; Hoshino *et al.* 1987; Ornitz *et al.* 1977)

3   moment at which the parents noticed that something was wrong and the symptoms they described (Hoshino *et al.* 1987; Martos and Ayuda 2004; Martos and Rivière 1998; Ohta *et al.* 1987; Ornitz *et al.* 1977; Rivière 2000)

4   presence of regression (Hoshino *et al.* 1987; Kurita *et al.* 1992)

5   use of instruments such as developmental rating scales and questioners (Bailey *et al.* 2000; Dahlgren and Gillberg 1989; Hadwin and Hutley 1998; Martos and Rivière 1998; Ornitz *et al.* 1977; Stone, Coonrod and Ousley 2000; Vostanis *et al.* 1998; Wetherby *et al.* 2004)

6   differentiation of symptoms and other variables with different control groups (Bailey *et al.* 2000; Dahlgren and Gillberg 1989; Kurita *et al.* 1992; Martos and Ayuda 2004; Ohta *et al.* 1987; Rivière 2000; Volkmar *et al.* 1985; Vostanis *et al.* 1998; Wetherby *et al.* 2004)

7   study of developmental sequences (Burack and Volkmar 1992).

The most relevant conclusions extracted from the above-cited studies are collected together in the following summary.

Summary of results of studies of retrospective information

- A clear and consistent relationship between the time of onset, prognosis and course of the disorder cannot be established, nor is there a clear relationship between the age of onset and symptom severity or between the age of onset and variables such as IQ or the educational level of the parents. However, it is possible that the age at onset may be related to different subtypes of autism.

- The age of observation of symptoms is variable and oscillates between six months and three and a half years. Nonetheless, the majority of parents notice the first symptoms between six months and two and a half years. Parents of children with mental retardation notice the first symptoms much earlier than the parents of children with autism.

- In the majority of cases of autism a normal course of development is identified which extends to the end of the first year or year and a half of life. A clear qualitative alteration of development is then observed which tends to coincide with the development of language.

- The most frequently described initial symptoms of autism are: language delay, supposed hearing impairment, poor response to others, isolation, not playing with other children, absence of pointing behaviour, scarce eye contact, passivity.

- Passivity and the absence of pointing behaviour by the end of the first year are signs of alert for autism.

- A characteristic absence of intentioned communication, in asking as well as declaring, is observed between 9 and 17 months.

- Autism, in contrast to mental retardation, is associated with less motor delay and fewer medical and neurological problems. A significant item which may differentiate autism from mental retardation is the abnormal response to sound. Children with childhood disintegrative disorder (CDD) are even more affected than autistics without language. Children with autism present an unbalanced profile and are more affected in social and communication domains when compared to children with fragile-X without autism. Children with fragile-X and autism are more affected than children with autism only. Parents of children with semantic pragmatic disorder indicated that they have social deficits which reflect something beyond a communication disorder. Significant differences were found between children with autism and children with severe learning disorders. Stereotypias, isolation and scarce eye contact are the most differential symptoms between autistics and children with language disorders.

- The data does not support the hypothesis of a similar developmental structure, although certain support is found for the hypothesis that a similar developmental sequence may exist with respect to communication skills.

ANALYSIS OF HOME VIDEOS

The studies which have analysed home videos recorded by the parents constitute a valuable source of data for the early manifestations of autistic spectrum disorder. Some articles have made arguments in support of the use of this method (Adrien *et al.* 1991). However, methodological problems may be readily detected in the difficulty to find relevant situations and the possibilities of similarities in the comparison of the chosen control groups. Frequently the videos show anecdotal or artificial situations, or may be under the influence of uncontrolled variables. Also, it is not always possible to assess specific segments of age. The usually small sample sizes are frequently criticized.

The studies which analyse home video information have led to the following lines of research:

1   analysis of social interaction (Massie 1978; Receveur *et al.* 2005)

2   recognition of initial signs, analysis of symptoms and behaviour (Adrien *et al.* 1991; Massie 1978)

3   study of the sensory-motor stage and sensory processing (Baranek 1999; Lösche 1990; Rosenthal, Massie and Wulf 1980)

4   use of codification systems specifically designed to assess different behaviours, construction of instruments and specific scales for observation (Adrien *et al.* 1993; Bernabei, Camaioni and Levi 1998; Mars, Mauk and Dowrick 1998; Osterling and Dawson 1994; Werner *et al.* 2000)

5   analysis of daily sequences and play situations (Maestro *et al.* 1999)

6   analysis of imitation (Receveur *et al.* 2005).

The most relevant results of the above cited studies are summarized below.

Results of studies analysing home videos

- Passivity and problems with eye contact are frequently observed.

- Factors such as conjoint attention are the most important markers: eye contact, showing objects, indicating objects with the eyes, pointing and not orienting when called are discriminative behaviours signifying pervasive developmental disorder (PDD). The face may become an important predictor for autism but not for PDD not otherwise specified (PDD-NOS). Within the autism group there are no differences between subjects with or without mental retardation.

- Subjects with autism show fewer sensory-motor behaviours. The differences (compared to children with normal development) increase over development and are more evident when the children begin to walk. Between 31 and 42 months, children with normal development spend much more time inventing new ends and new means, while autistic children employ more time in repeating the same actions. In autistic subjects, goal-directed behaviours were reduced and continuous action increased, while normal children developed multiple actions. Sensory-motor variables, in addition to social variables, have been shown to be useful for the identification of autism, although more research is required to determine any deficits in sensory processing as precursors of other difficulties before 12 months.

- In general, the differences from the normal controls begin to be observed clearly from a year and a half onwards. Before the first year is completed the differences are few. Only the social variables may be differentiated in children of less than one year. Different types of presentations and trajectories are described: the first and most frequent is the regressive type in which the children show a period of normal development lasting until 12–18 months. Progressive and fluctuating types are also described.

- The behaviours observed were found to coincide with diagnostic categories, with the addition of observed difficulties in attention. Five types of difficulties were described: alterations of visual behaviour, alterations of expression or understanding of emotional behaviours, alterations of social conduct, alterations of motor tone and behaviour and strange behaviours.

- Delay and deficit in the development of imitation is suggested and appears to decrease over development.

- The earliest signs appear before the parents are aware that something is wrong. It was observed that the adults developed compensatory behaviours for these deficits.

STUDIES BASED ON CLINICAL ASSESSMENT

Studies which carried out a clinical assessment at the moment of diagnosis, which in some cases was followed up, have some advantages such as the use of standardized tests and instruments or even diagnostic precision. In some cases specific experimental tasks have been used. However, frequently the children in these studies are over one year old and the course of previous development must be reconstructed.

The studies reviewed in this section contribute results which are essentially related to diagnostic aspects, from symptom identification to the stability of the diagnosis (Gillberg *et al.* 1990; Stone *et al.* 1999). The work of Dawson *et al.* (1998) constructed an assessment situation of orientation tasks to social and non-social stimuli. The results of this type of study are summarized below.

Results of studies based on clinical assessment

- A precise identification of ASD can be made before three years of age. The stability of the diagnosis is high and greater in autism than in PDD-NOS. The DSM-IV criteria for two years old are essentially social (differences in the use of non-verbal communication and lack of socio-emotional reciprocity).

- The recognition of autism in infancy is centred on speech problems, abnormal perceptive responses and various social dysfunctions. The most common symptoms are abnormal play, autistic aloneness and peculiarities in visual and auditory orienting.

- A dysfunction of orienting towards social stimuli may constitute one of the first signs of autism. The alterations of shared attention may be understood as a consequence of a deficit to attend to social stimuli. Children with ASD, compared to normal development and Down syndrome, perform poorly in orientation tasks and the failure is greater when using social stimuli.

LONGITUDINAL STUDIES

We discuss the results of three studies, although some studies from the previous section may also be included here. Sparling (1991) reported a longitudinal study of a single case from birth to four years, combining several observational measures. Lord (1995) carried out a study of children from two to four years of age, completing a re-assessment 12 to 15 months following. Zwaigenbaum *et al.* (2005) developed a study of high-risk children (having a sibling with autism) from 6 to 36 months using children with normal development as control and taking advantage of several instruments, scales and tests for assessment. The results of these works are summarized below.

Results of longitudinal studies

- Presence of sensory and perceptual anomalies.

- The diagnosis was shown to be stable from two to three years in the majority of the cases, although a greater diagnostic differentiation was produced at three years. Diagnosis at an early age may be precise. The diagnostic criteria must be adapted to encompass formulations which account for the particularities of early ages. Some items such as 'directs the attention of another person' and 'pays attention to voice' have been shown to be discriminative.

- Positive markers are found at 12 months which are related to eye contact and visual tracking, orientation to their name, imitation, smiling and social reactivity and sensory-motor behaviours. At approximately 12 months more intense and frequent distress was detected in temperament, centred in objects or parts of objects during prolonged periods of time, less capacity of inhibitory control and reduced affective response. Differences in receptive and expressive language were also found.

STUDIES OF VALIDATION OF INSTRUMENTS AND OTHER DETECTION SCALES

Early detection via instruments or scales which have been shown to be effective, with high sensitivity and specificity, has also guided some studies related to early manifestations of ASD. Here we cite works such as those of Baron-Cohen *et al.* (1996) and Baird *et al.* (2000) in reference to the CHAT (checklist for autism in toddlers), the work of Stone *et al.* (2000), on the validation of the STAT (screening tool for autism in two-year-olds), the use of the DAISI (detection of autism by infant sociability interview) by Wimpory *et al.* (2000), and the study by Wetherby *et al.* (2004) on the CSBS DP (communication and symbolic behaviour scales developmental profile). The general conclusions extracted from this type of study on screening instruments, interviews and scales are summarized below.

Results of studies of instrument validation

- The errors in the combination of shared attention and symbolic play at 18 months may be good indicators of autism according to the CHAT.

- Having acceptable levels of sensibility and specificity, the STAT contains selected items which are adequate for two-year-olds, but not for later ages.

- The person–person communicative interaction and the establishment of triangular person–person–object relations are differential items on the DAISI.

- High values of sensitivity and specificity were found on the CSBS DP. Significant differences were found between ASD and retardation and between ASD and normal development on: (a) lack of appropriate looking, (b) absence of demonstrations of affection, expressions of happiness with looking, (c) absence of shared happiness or interest, (d) does not respond to own name, (e) lack of coordination between looking, facial expression, gesture and sound, (f) absence of indicating movements, (g) unusual prosody, (h) repetitive movements or positions of the body, arms, hands or fingers, and (i) repetitive movements with objects.

IN RESPONSE TO SOME QUESTIONS

Once the different methodologies used in the studies have been analysed, as we have previously mentioned, we now proceed to extract information in response to three questions:

1 At what age are the first signs of disorder found?

2 What are these signs?

3 Are these first signs specific to autism, permitting differential identification from other developmental disorders?

At what age are the first signs of the disorder found?

In this section we make reference only to those works which cover very early ages. Specifically, 11 of the 39 revised studies allude in one way or another to the presence of some abnormality during the first year of life. In this way, focusing only on the first 12 months, the studies which find subtle signs during this period are (in chronological order): Massie (1975), Ornitz *et al.* (1977), Gillberg *et al.* (1990), Rogers and Dilalla (1990), Sparling (1991), Adrien *et al.* (1993), Osterling and Dawson (1994), Bernabei *et al.* (1998), Rivière (2000), Werner *et al.* (2000) and Zwaigenbaum *et al.* (2005).

Of these 11 studies, five specifically identify the presence of anomalies before 12 months. Massie (1975) referred to the age of three months in one of the two case studies presented. Gillberg *et al.* (1990) reported that 90 per cent of the surveyed mothers (28) noticed that something was wrong by the end of the first year, and five mothers detected some anomaly before eight months (specifically, at 1, 4, 7, 7 and 8 months). Osterling and Dawson (1994) found that 80 per cent of parents noticed some type of developmental difficulty in the first year of life of their children. It must be said that these results (such high percentages of suspicion of problems in the first year) are contrasted by those found in other studies. Rivière (2000), for example, reported that only 25 per cent of parents were worried during the first year. Ornitz *et al.* (1977) alluded to the presence of some delay in motor development at six months, which again contrasts with other studies which specifically report no motor delay (Rivière 2000). Werner *et al.* (2000) focus on turning towards the sound of one's name, where at 8–10 months 75 per cent of children with normal development turn, while only 37 per cent of autistic children do the same. Finally, the case study presented by Sparling (1991) reported slight differences at three months, which appears confusing as this sometimes does not fall outside the range of normality. The remaining studies did not specify ages earlier than 12 months, with the exception of the work of Zwaigenbaum *et al.* (2005) which specifically reports no differences at six months and confirms their presence by 12 months.

During the second year of life, the number of differences in behaviour found is significantly increased. In this respect, we highlight that, in the majority of cases of autism, a period of normal development is reported which extends into the first year to year and a half, which terminates with the appearance of a qualitative alteration of development usually coinciding with the phase of the development of language. Ángel Rivière (2000) found, in contrast to the above-mentioned studies, that the clear interruption of development occurs in the second year. At the same time, Baron-Cohen *et al.* (1996) indicated 18 months as the age at which signs of pathological development could be identified, specifically referring to the absence of protodeclarative behaviours, fiction games and gaze monitoring.

We can extract as preliminary conclusions that at least one-third of the studies found that the first year of life is not marked by normal development, although the signs of that abnormality are subtle, that there exists a sizeable amount of interindividual variability between cases and that in no case are these signs sufficient for such an early identification of the disorder. As an extension of these conclusions, we must learn with certainty to what point these subtle manifestations are specific to autism – a question that is addressed in the following section.

What are the first signs?

One of the first signs described in the first year is what could be generally termed passivity. This sign is addressed by Rivière (2000), and hypoactivity and poor social reactivity is discussed in Massie (1975) and Zwaigenbaum *et al.* (2005). For their part, Adrien *et al.* (1993) and Massie (1975) report the presence of low muscle tone. Aside from passivity, other studies discuss irritability or low tolerance to frustration (Rogers and Dilalla 1990; Sparling 1991). Irritability is also mentioned in other studies, although at later ages, such as that of Maestro *et al.* (1999).

Other signs frequently repeated in the literature are anomalies of eye contact. We could include those anomalies in a broad category of 'social dysfunctions', but we find it appropriate to treat them separately because of their repeated mention in the literature. In the first year, anomalies of eye contact are reported by Gillberg *et al.* (1990), Massie (1975), Osterling and Dawson (1994), Sparling (1991) and Zwaigenbaum *et al.* (2005). At two years they are collected by Adrien *et al.* (1991) and Mars *et al.* (1998). These anomalies of eye contact may be related to alterations of shared attention, direction of attention, visual tracking and engagement and failure in alternative glances. Adrien *et al.* (1993) and Zwaigenbaum *et al.* (2005) report the presence of difficulties in the direction of attention and visual tracking and engagement. The same is found somewhat later in Dawson *et al.* (1998) and Lord (1995). For their part, Osterling and Dawson (1994) and Bernabei *et al.* (1998) found difficulties in taking turns at 12 months, while at two years, Mars *et al.* (1998) found failures in alternative glances. Finally, we also mention the work of Rogers and Dilalla (1990), who discuss a loss of eye contact at approximately one-and-a-half to two years.

Under the general term 'social dysfunctions' fall such behaviours as isolation (Bernabei *et al.* 1998 in the first year; and Adrien *et al.* 1993, Gillberg *et al.* 1990, Maestro *et al.* 1999 and Rogers and Dilalla 1990, around two years); poor interaction (Adrien *et al.* 1993, Sparling 1991 and Zwaigenbaum *et al.* 2005); lack of reaction to strangers and resistance to separation (Rogers and Dilalla 1990); altered social smiling (at 12 months in Adrien *et al.* 1993, Massie 1975 and Zwaigenbaum *et al.* 2005; and later, around two years, in Maestro *et al.* 1999). We also find here examples of the loss of apparently normal social behaviour (Rogers and Dilalla 1990).

In reference to early communication patterns, the presence of generic alterations in the first year have been reported by Ornitz *et al.* (1977), Sparling (1991) and Adrien *et al.* (1993); failures to indicate and show objects at one year (Osterling and Dawson 1994) and at two years in the investigation of Mars *et al.* (1998), Kurita *et al.* (1992) and Vostanis *et al.* (1998). At two years Maestro *et al.* (1999) discuss a lack of effort in communication and problems in vocalizations at a year and a half. Mars *et al.* (1998) and

Gillberg *et al.* (1990) also identify problems with speech and language at two years. In the same way, we find a lack of appropriate gestures in Adrien *et al.* (1993) and Maestro *et al.* (1999), absence of behaviours such as reaching out to be picked up before the first year in Massie (1977) and a lack of what are called 'expressive postures' at around two years (Adrien *et al.* 1993 and Lord 1995).

Another important block is that reserved for the abnormal response to sensory stimulation. It is common to find the term 'apparent paradoxical hearing impairment' or 'the lack of response and orientation to name' in some studies reporting on those over 12 months of age (Osterling and Dawson 1994; Werner *et al.* 2000; Zwaigenbaum *et al.* 2005). We may find studies which allude to an abnormal response to visual and proximal stimulation (Baranek 1999) and others which report auditory alterations beyond the lack of response to name (Gillberg *et al.* 1990; Maestro *et al.* 1999; Ornitz *et al.* 1977). Within this block we must also cite the tendency to focus on isolated parts of objects, identified at 12 months by Zwaigenbaum *et al.* (2005) and the presence, from two years, of stereotypical sensory-motor activity (Maestro *et al.* 1999; Massie 1978).

In relation to this peculiar information processing identified in the first years, we find signs which could be interpreted as rigidity or lack of flexibility, for example at 12 months Zwaigenbaum *et al.* (2005) discuss the presence of stress given various stimuli and reduced capacity of inhibitory control and anticipation. Also in line with executive functions, at 13 months Lösche (1990) identified problems with the use of means–ends, and Rogers and Dilalla (1990) find a loss of initiative at two years.

Finally, we must comment on signs of alteration reported in relation to play and imitation. Bernabei *et al.* (1998) reported problems in the first year, while Gillberg *et al.* (1990) and Vostanis *et al.* (1998) found them somewhat later. Maestro *et al.* (1999) allude to difficulty in the use of objects around two years. In relation to imitation skills, Zwaigenbaum *et al.* (2005) again situated the first manifestations of difference at 12 months. It is also important to underscore the existence of a study which reported exactly the contrary, showing no differences in play or imitation during the first two years (Lord 1995).

It may be seen that social, interpersonal and intersubjective factors appear to constitute the first signs of autism. Shared attention skills, eye contact, showing objects, pointing, responding to name, etc., appear to be important markers to be taken into account. Poor social and affective reactivity, as well as the presence of passivity, are quite frequent and appear relatively early. Information provided by the majority of the instruments and early detection scales appear to point towards social symptoms as the most relevant and salient. At the same time, although with less frequency but certainly not of less importance, other aspects related to sensory or perceptual anomalies (e.g. reduced capacity for inhibitory control and difficulties in changing the focus of attention, centring in objects or parts of objects during prolonged periods of time) have been indicated, yet require further study.

Nonetheless, assuming that signs exist in the first year, are they specific to autistic disorder? This is addressed in the following section.

Are these first signs specific to autism, permitting differential identification from other developmental disorders?

In the first place, we believe it important to mention that the reviewed studies, especially those carried out before the latter half of the 1980s, frequently do not include comparison groups. However, since the latter half of the 1980s and above all in the 1990s, control groups were indeed included, yet practically no study includes a sample which permits the comparative study of (at least) mental retardation, language disorders and autism, and the age of the samples tends to be quite elevated for the study of early indicators. Aside from these inconveniences, we will analyse the work available to approach the question of the specificity of early signs.

We find a group of studies which only include children with autism or possible autism. Lord (1995) completed a follow-up study of children from two to four years of age with possible autism. Given the results, the author suggests that a reliable diagnosis may be made at two years of age, at the same time reporting that standardized tests such as the ADI may erroneously detect autism in subjects with severe cognitive deficits, which is to say that there is a relatively high probability of false positives. By three years of age, the reliability and stability of the diagnosis is greater, in addition to being the age established by the diagnostic manuals.

A second group of work approaches the differences between PDDs. The most recent study is that of Volkmar, Stier and Cohen (1985) which addresses three diagnostic criteria from the DSM-III (childhood autism, PDD in early childhood and atypical PDD). The fundamental conclusion reached by these authors is that there exist many difficulties between these categories, above all between early childhood PDD and childhood autism. Kurita *et al.* (1992) carried out a similar study working with only two groups, autistic disorder and childhood disintegrative disorder. The conclusion reached was similar to the previous study: in initial states there are few differences in the manifestations. More recently, Mars *et al.* (1998) included three subject groups, children with autism, with PDD-NOS and a third group of subjects with normal development. Their results clearly lead to the idea of the continuum. They describe a series of differences which are distributed with greater or lesser severity between PDD and autism. The altered behaviours consisted of following verbal orientations, looking at faces, showing objects, alternating the glance, looking at people, indicating with the glance, expressing words and imitating verbalizations. These authors also report results which confirm how difficult it is to differentiate limits, in that 40 per cent of the PDD-NOS group were initially diagnosed as having an autistic disorder. What is certain is that the results of this study are not surprising – the idea of the spectrum clearly addresses these limitations. Yet, can we differentiate ASD from mental retardation?

Hadwin and Hutley (1998) worked with two groups of children, one with autism and another with mental retardation. Baranek (1999), Dahlgren and Gillberg (1989) and Rivière (2000) included a third comparison group composed of children with normal development. Hadwin and Hutley (1998) found differences between the two groups, specifically the children with autism showed less conjoint attention, less eye contact, less functional and symbolic play and stereotypic behaviour, interests and activities. It would seem as if it is more a question of degree than of quality. Rivière (2000) centred on early signs, specifically in the first and second years of life. The results of that study show that 75 per cent of parents of children with mental retardation suspected that something was wrong with their child's development during the first year, versus only 25 per cent of children with autism and without mental retardation. Nonetheless, this data is not confirmed by other studies. Gillberg *et al.* (1990) reported that nearly 90 per cent of the mothers knew that something was wrong during the first year. Osterling and Dawson (1994) found that 80 per cent of parents noticed some type of developmental difficulty within the first year. In relation to 'passivity', Rivière (2000) found no differences between the autism and mental retardation groups, where both groups presented levels superior to that of normal development. In reality, the sign which this author seems to emphasize as the most differential between the two groups is the existence of delay in motor development in the group of children with mental retardation. In the same way, Gillberg *et al.* (1990) also found that 85 per cent of a group of children with autism had an acceptable state of motor development.

Dahlgren and Gillberg (1989) centred on the age of two, collecting information about this period by interviewing parents of children up to 15 years old. The parents were asked to recall information about their children when they were two years old. They found that the items which best discriminated between the three groups were 'apparent isolation from the environment' and 'does not play with other children'. They also reported that the items which discriminated between autism and the other two groups were 'does not attempt to grab the attention of the adult' and 'vacant look'. The results of Baranek (1999), instead of supporting these discoveries, appear to be contrary, as they identify fewer affective responses in the mental retardation group than in the autism group. Children with mental retardation showed a more stereotypic play with objects, looked less at the camera and more frequently had an unusual posture than the children with autism. The autistic children showed an unusual response to visual and proximal sensory stimulation and turned less when they were called by their name.

Finally, the study by Bailey *et al.* (2000), in which they analysed fragile-X and autism, included a third group of children formed of children which met the requirements for both groups. The most interesting conclusion reached was that the children with autism showed an irregular profile and more severe impairment in social and communication domains compared to children with fragile-X without autism. As may be expected, the existence of the combination of both disorders increases the severity of the profile. Again appears the question of degree, although the subjects with autism have a performance profile much more irregular.

CONCLUSIONS

One of the great difficulties which we have found in producing this review was to organize the information extracted from each one of the studies. The different methodologies employed, the existence of diverse control groups, the breadth of the age groups, the diagnostic criteria and other factors have made the structuring of this chapter extraordinarily difficult. For that reason, we have carefully selected the question–answer format to address the conclusions.

At what age are the first symptoms observed?

Although there is great variability extending from six months to three and a half years, the first symptoms are generally observed by the parents (Gillberg *et al.* 1990; Osterling and Dawson 1994) between one-and-a-half and two years. It may be, however, that the earliest symptoms appear before the parents are conscious that something is wrong. In many cases compensation strategies are initiated as difficulties arise. In children who show mental retardation, the first signs of retardation are generally observed before those of autism and tend to have different characteristics (Rivière 2000). One relevant conclusion which may be extracted is that currently, in accordance with the reviewed studies, it is difficult to observe or detect symptoms before the close of the first year.

What are the first symptoms?

Social, interpersonal and intersubjective factors appear to constitute the first symptoms of autism (Adrien *et al.* 1993; Bernabei *et al.* 1998; Maestro *et al.* 1999). Conjoint attention skills such as eye contact, looking at the face, object indicating behaviours, pointing, orienting to name, etc., are important markers to be taken into account. In general, failures and differences in orientation to social stimuli are detected (Dawson *et al.* 1998) and may be understood, together with differences in shared attention, as a consequence of a possible deficit to attend to social stimuli. Poor social and affective reactivity and the presence of passivity are relatively frequent and are often shown early (Massie 1975; Rivière 2000). Information provided by the greater part of the instruments and early detection scales also shows social symptoms as the most relevant and salient (Baron-Cohen *et al.* 1996; Wimpory *et al.* 2000).

Some aspects associated with sensory and perceptive anomalies, such as reduced capacity for inhibitory control and difficulties in changing the focus of attention, centring on objects or parts of objects over prolonged periods of time, have also been shown as early symptoms, although with somewhat less frequency but by no means of less importance (Baranek 1999; Werner *et al.* 2000). These require further investigation.

To what point is retrospective parent information accurate and objective?

From the analysis of the obtained results it may not be deduced that the information provided by the families is necessarily inaccurate or not objective (Osterling and Dawson 1994). Moreover, certain evidence may be found, in the information provided by other sources (such as development scales), which supports information provided by the parents (Ornitz *et al.* 1977).

How is the disorder presented and what is its course?

Different types of presentation and trajectory have been described (Hoshino *et al.* 1987). The first, and most frequent, to be observed in the majority of children with autism is the regressive type, in which the children experience a period of normal development until approximately a year to a year-and-a-half (Rivière 2000). A progressive and a fluctuating type has also been described (Maestro *et al.* 1999). The data obtained do not support the hypothesis of a similar structure of development, although it does appear to support the hypothesis of a similar developmental sequence, at least with respect to communication skills (Burack and Volkmar 1992).

Can a relationship be established between time of onset and prognosis?

The obtained results do not establish a clear and consistent relationship between time of onset and prognosis of the disorder. Neither is a clear relationship established between age at presentation and the severity of symptoms or between the age at presentation and other variables such as IQ and educational level of the parents (Hoshino *et al.* 1987).

What are the differential aspects when comparing autistic disorder to normal controls or other disorders?

In general, the differences from normal controls are clearly observed from the first year-and-a-half and beyond. Before the end of the first year the differences are few, where social variables, as has been mentioned, differentiate between younger children (Dahlgren and Gillberg 1989). The differences increase over development and are more evident when the children begin walking, being especially noticeable between 31 and 42 months in which children with normal development spend much more time inventing new means for new ends, while autistic children spend more time repeating the same actions. Moreover, in children with autism, goal directed behaviours are reduced and continuous action is increased, while children with normal development develop multiple actions–means (Lösche 1990). It is therefore important to extract sensory-motor variables, in addition to social variables, as useful for the detection of autism (Maestro *et al.* 1999; Massie 1978).

In autistic disorder, compared to normal development, more failures in orientation tasks are observed (Osterling and Dawson 1994) and the failure is greater with social stimuli (Dawson *et al.* 1998). Differences are also found in temperament and receptive and expressive language.

When comparing autism with other disorders, autism is associated with less motor delay and a lesser degree of medical and neurological alteration than mental retardation (Gillberg *et al.* 1990; Rivière 2000). One significant item which may differentiate between autism and mental retardation is the unusual response to sounds. Children with childhood disintegrative disorder are more affected than even children with autism with an absence of language, although there are practically no differences in clinical signs in early manifestations (Kurita *et al.* 1992; Volkmar *et al.* 1985). Compared to children with fragile-X (without autism), children with autism show an unbalanced profile and are more greatly affected in social and communication domains (Bailey *et al.* 2000). On the other hand, children with autism and fragile-X are more clinically impaired than children with autism alone. The parents of children with semantic pragmatic disorder reported that their children had altered social behaviours which reflect something more than a communication disorder. Stereotypias, isolation and scarce eye contact are the most differential symptoms between children with autism and children with language disorders (Martos and Ayuda 2004). Significant differences have also been found between children with autism and children with severe learning disabilities.

Curiously, within the autism group itself, no differences are found between children with or without mental retardation with respect to early manifestations.

What are the implications for diagnosis?

The behaviours found coincide with diagnostic criteria and also show difficulties in attention. Four types of difficulties have been observed: of visual conduct; of expression, understanding and emotional responses; of social conduct; and in strange behaviours.

Diagnosis at an early age may be precise, although diagnostic criteria may have to be adapted to take into account the particularities of early ages (e.g. social and shared attention items). The stability of the diagnosis is high, and greater for autism than for PDD-NOS. That stability is produced between two and three years in the majority of cases, although greater diagnostic differentiation is produced at three years (Lord 1995).

What current psychological explanations are related to early manifestations of the disorder?

The revision of work on early manifestations of autistic disorder show that the most relevant and consistent early signs are related to deficits and difficulties in social development. This supports psychological explanations which emphasize autism as a developmental disorder in which the establishment of social, interpersonal and, specifcally, intersubjective competencies are affected. These competencies are characteristics of normal human development and are observable by the second semester of life and especially by the last trimester of the first year. We find ourselves before evidence which clearly recalls the initial position of Kanner and the importance given to social aspects of the disorder. Nonetheless, contrary to the clinical impression of Kanner which assumed the manifestation of autism 'from the beginning of life', the data extracted from the analysed studies shows that in the majority of cases the onset of the disorder begins after at least the first year of life. We have no other option here but to recur to the incisive reflections of Rivière (1997), relating this typical pattern of apparition to processes of normal development, therefore understanding their alteration in terms of normal processes. As was shown by Rivière, the moment at which autism may be clearly manifested is a critical period for development in which occur the emergence and gradual consolidation of relevant psychological functions such as the beginning of representative and symbolic intelligence and the development of self-consciousness and the internalization of social standards, making possible the evaluation of one's own behaviour. Also at this time, the first combining structures and rudimentary forms of conversation appear in the development of language, and fictional play and patterns which imply specifically human forms of representation, known as 'metarepresentations', are initiated. From a neurobiological framework, this period implies transition and important changes (e.g. the number of neurons and synapses in many brain areas is maintained at very high levels during the entire period of development extending between 18 months and 5–6 years). Autism may be understood, consequently, as 'the shadow left on development which makes it difficult or impossible to establish certain psychological functions whose critical period for acquisition extends between one-and-a-half and 5 or 6 years' (Rivière 1997, p.40).

REFERENCES

Adrien, J. L., Faure, M., Perrot, A., Hameury, L., Garreau, B., Barthelemy, C. and Sauvage, D. (1991) 'Autism and family home movies: preliminary findings.' *Journal of Autism and Developmental Disorders* 21, 43–49.

Adrien, J. L., Lenoir, P., Martineau, J., Perrot, A., Hameury, L., Larmande, C. and Sauvage, D. (1993) 'Blind ratings of early symptoms of autism based upon family home movies.' *Journal of the American Academy of Child and Adolescent Psychiatry 32*, 617–626.

American Psychiatric Association (APA) (1980, 1987, 1994, 2000) *Diagnostic and Statistical Manual of Mental Disorders*, 4th edn. Washington, DC: American Psychiatric Association.

Bailey, D. B., Hatton, D. D., Mesibov, G., Ament, N. and Skinner, M. (2000) 'Early development, temperament and functional impairment in autism and fragile-X syndrome.' *Journal of Autism and Developmental Disorders 30*, 49–59.

Baird, G., Charman, T., Baron-Cohen, S., Cox, A., Swettenham, J., Wheelwright, S. and Drew, A. (2000) 'A screening instrument for autism at 18 months of age: a 6-year follow-up study.' *Journal of American Academy of Child and Adolescent Psychiatry 39*, 694–702.

Baranek, T. G. (1999) 'Autism during infancy: a retrospective video analysis of sensory motor and social behaviour at 9–12 months of age.' *Journal of Autism and Developmental Disorders 29*, 213–224.

Baron-Cohen, S., Cox, A., Baird, G., Swettenham, J., Nightingale, N., Morgan, K. *et al.* (1996) 'Psychological markers in the detection of autism in infancy in a large population.' *British Journal of Psychiatry 168*, 158–163.

Bernabei, P., Camaioni, L. and Levi, G. (1998) 'An evaluation of early development in children with autism and pervasive developmental disorders from home movies: preliminary findings.' *Autism 2*, 243–258.

Burack, J. A. and Volkmar, F. R. (1992) 'Development of low and high functioning autistic children.' *Journal of Child Psychology and Psychiatry 33*, 607–616.

Dahlgren, S. O. and Gillberg, C. (1989) 'Symptoms of autism in the first two years of life.' *European Archives of Psychiatry and Neurological Sciences 238*, 169–174.

Dawson, G., Meltzoff, A. N., Osterling, J., Rinaldi, J. and Brown, E. (1998) 'Children with autism fail to orient naturally occurring social stimuli.' *Journal of Autism and Developmental Disorders 28*, 479–485.

Filipek, P. A., Accardo, P., Baranek, G.T., Cook, E.H., Dawson, G., Gordon, B. (1999) 'The screening and diagnosis of autistic spectrum disorders.' *Journal of Autism and Developmental Disorders 29*, 6, 439–484.

Gillberg, C., Ehlers, S., Schaumann, H., Jakopson, G., Dalhgren, S., Lindblom, R. *et al.* (1990) 'Autism under 3 years: a clinical study of 28 cases referred for autistic symptoms in infancy.' *Journal of Child Psychology and Psychiatry 31*, 921–934.

Hadwin, J. and Hutley, G. (1998) 'Detecting features of autism in children with severe learning difficulties: a brief report.' *Autism 2*, 269–280.

Harper, J. and Williams, S. (1975) 'Age and type of onset as critical variables in early infantile autism.' *Journal of Autism and Childhood Schizophrenia 5*, 25–36.

Hernández, J. M., Artigas-Pallarés, J., Martos Pérez, J., Palacios Antón, S., Fuentes Biggi, J., Benlinchón Carmona, M. *et al.* (2005) 'Guía de buena práctica para la detección temprana de los trastornos del espectro autista.' *Revista de Neurología 41*, 4, 237–245.

Hoshino, Y., Kaneko, M., Yashina, Y., Kumashiro, H., Volkmar, F. and Cohen, J. D. (1987) 'Clinical features of autistic children with setback course in their infancy.' *Japanese Journal of Psychiatry and Neurology 41*, 237–246.

Howlin, P. (1997) 'Prognosis in autism: do specialist treatments affect long-term outcome?' *European Child and Adolescent Psychiatry 6*, 55–72.

Kanner, L. (1943) 'Autistic disturbances of affective contact.' *Nervous Child 2*, 217–250.

Knudsen, E. (1998) 'Capacity for plasticity in the adult auditory system expanded by juvenile experience.' *Science 27*, 1531–1533.

Kurita, H., Kita, M. and Miyake, Y. (1992) 'A comparative study of development and symptoms among disintegrative psychosis and infantile autism with and without speech loss.' *Journal of Autism and Developmental Disorders 22*, 175–188.

Lord, C. (1995) 'Follow-up of two-year-olds referred for possible autism.' *Journal of Child Psychology and Psychiatry 36*, 1365–1382.

Lösche, G. (1990) 'Sensorimotor and action development in autistic children from infancy to early childhood.' *Journal of Child Psychology and Psychiatry 31*, 749–761.

Maestro, S., Casella, C., Milone, A., Muratori, F. and Palacio-Espasa, F. (1999) 'Study of the onset of autism through home movies.' *Psychopathology 32*, 292–300.

Mars, E. A., Mauk, E. J. and Dowrick, W. P. (1998) 'Symptoms for pervasive developmental disorders as observed in prediagnostic home videos of infants and toddlers.' *The Journal of Paediatrics 132*, 500–504.

Martos, J. and Ayuda, R. (2004) 'Desarrollo temprano: algunos datos procedentes del autismo y los trastornos del lenguaje.' *Revista de Neurología 38* (Supl. 1).

Martos, J. and Rivière, A. (1998) 'Relación entre indicadores pronósticos y desarrollo a largo plazo en sujetos autistas.' In *Actas V Congreso Internacional de Autismo-Europa. La esperanza no es un sueño*, pp.247–255. Barcelona: Escuela Libre.

Massie, H. (1975) 'The early natural history of childhood psychosis.' *American Academy of Child Psychiatry 14*, 683–707.

Massie, H. (1977) 'Patterns of mother–infant behaviour and subsequent childhood psychosis.' *Child and Psychiatry and Human Development 7*, 211–230.

Massie, H. (1978) 'The early natural history of childhood psychosis.' *American Academy of Child Psychiatry 17*, 29–45.

Ohta, M., Nagai, Y., Hara, H. and Sasaki, M. (1987) 'Parental perception of behavioural symptoms in Japanese autistic children.' *Journal of Autism and Developmental Disorders 17*, 549–563.

Ornitz, E. M., Guthrie, D. and Farley, A. H. (1977) 'The early development of autistic children.' *Journal of Autism and Childhood Schizophrenia 3*, 207–229.

Osterling, J. and Dawson, G. (1994) 'Early recognition of children with autism: a study of the first birthday home videotapes.' *Journal of Autism and Developmental Disorders 24*, 247–257.

Receveur, C., Lenoir, P., Desombre, H., Roux, S., Barthelemy, C. and Malvy, J. (2005) 'Interaction and imitation deficits from infancy to 4 years of age in children with autism: a pilot study based on videotapes.' *Autism 9*, 69–82.

Rivière, A. (1997) 'Tratamiento y definición del espectro autista: relación social y comunicación.' In A. Rivière and J. Martos (eds) *El tratamiento del autismo. Nuevas perspectives*. Madrid: Imserso-Apna.

Rivière, A. (2000) 'Cómo aparece el autismo? Diagnóstico temprano e indicadores precoces del trastorno autista.' In A. Rivière and J. Martos (eds) *El niño pequeño con autismo*. Madrid: APNA y Ministerio de Trabajo y Asuntos Sociales.

Rogers, S. and Dilalla, D. (1990) 'Age of symptom onset in young children with pervasive developmental disorders.' *Journal of American Academy of Child and Adolescent Psychiatry 29*, 863–872.

Rosenthal, J., Massie, H. and Wulf, K. (1980) 'A comparison of cognitive development in normal and psychotic children in the first two years of life from home movies.' *Journal of Autism and Developmental Disorders 10*, 433–444.

Schopler, E., Reichler, R. J., DeVilles, R.F. and Daly, K. (1980) 'Towards Objective Classification of Childhood Autism: Childhood Autism Rating Scale (CARS).' *Journal of Autism and Developmental Disorders 10*, 91–103.

Sparling, J. W. (1991) 'Brief report: a prospective case report of infantile autism from pregnancy to four years.' *Journal of Autism and Developmental Disorders 21*, 229–235.

Stone, L. W., Coonrod, E. E. and Ousley, O. Y. (2000) 'Brief report: screening tool for autism in two years old (STAT): development and preliminary data.' *Journal of Autism and Developmental Disorders 30*, 157–162.

Stone, W. L., Lee, E. B., Ashford, L., Brassie, J., Hepburn, S. L., Coonrod, E. E. and Weiss, B. H. (1999) 'Can autism be diagnosed accurately in children under 3 years?' *Journal of Child Psychology and Psychiatry 40*, 219–226.

Volkmar, F. R., Stier, D. M. and Cohen, D. J. (1985) 'Age of the recognition of pervasive developmental disorder.' *American Journal of Psychiatry 142*, 1950–1952.

Vostanis, P., Smith, B., Sungum-Paliwal, R., Edwuards, A., Gilgell, K., Golding, R. *et al.* (1998) 'Parental concerns of early development in children with autism and related disorders.' *Autism 2*, 229–242.

Werner, E., Dawson, G., Osterling, J. and Dinno, N. (2000) 'Brief report. Recognition of autism spectrum disorder before one year of age: a retrospective study based on home videos.' *Journal of Autism and Developmental Disorders 30*, 157–162.

Wetherby, M. A., Woods, J., Allen, L., Cleary, J., Dickinson, H. and Lord, C. (2004) 'Early indicators of autism spectrum disorders in the second year of life.' *Journal of Autism and Developmental Disorders 5*, 473–493.

Wimpory, D., Hobson, P., Williams, M. and Nash, S. (2000) 'Are infants with autism socially engaged? A study of recent retrospective parental reports.' *Journal of Autism and Developmental Disorders 30*, 525–536.

World Health Organization (1993) *Mental Disorders: A Glossary and Guide to their Classification in Accordance with the 10th Revision of the International Classification of Disease (ICD-10).* Geneva: World Health Organization.

Zwaigenbaum, L., Bryson, S., Rogers, T., Roberts, W., Brian, J. and Szatmari, P. (2005) 'Behavioural manifestations of autism in the first year of life.' *International Journal of Developmental Neuroscience 3*, 143–152.

Chapter 3

Early Assessment of Autistic Spectrum Disorders

Catherine Lord

Autism spectrum disorders are behavioral diagnoses that are based on the presence of difficulties in three areas: social reciprocity, communication, and restricted and repetitive behaviors and interests. In addition, the diagnosis of autism (the most commonly studied and well understood spectrum disorder) requires abnormal or impaired development prior to age three years (American Psychiatric Association 1994). Most important to early assessment is the rule that this can be manifested by delays or abnormal functioning in any of the three areas: (1) social interaction, (2) language as used in social communication, or (3) symbolic or imaginative play. Thus, a child does not have to meet formal diagnostic criteria for autism under age three in order to be considered to have the disorder (see Box 3.1). In addition, autism is only diagnosed if the child's symptoms are not better accounted for by Rett's disorder, which is a rare neurological disorder seen primarily in girls or childhood disintegrative disorder (CDD). CDD, as shown in Box 3.2, involves features much like autism across the same three domains, but requires that the child has had normal development up to age two and has lost receptive language and social skills. Many children with CDD also lose adaptive skills, which is not common in autism. In general, CDD is a very rare phenomenon often associated with an outcome of severe autism and severe mental retardation.

As shown in Box 3.3, Asperger syndrome is another disorder much like autism which has a variety of different definitions, associated with different researchers and clinics. In DSM-IV and ICD-10, it is defined by having social deficits like autism, circumscribed interests, and sometimes other repetitive behaviors associated with autism and any absence of language or cognitive delay. Theoretically, cases of children who have diagnoses of autism are supposed to be excluded from this category, but often this has not been the case because it leaves the category with no cases (Ozonoff, South and

Miller 2000; Szatmari 2000). There has been controversy over whether individuals with Asperger disorder have gross motor or visual spatial deficits in addition to their defining characteristics. In the preschool years, several experts have proposed that there is relatively little point in discriminating Asperger disorder from high-functioning autism (Gillberg 1998).

**Box 3.1 DSM-IV/ICD-10
definition of autistic disorder**

Qualitative impairment in social interaction

Restricted, repetitive behaviors and/or interests

Abnormal or impaired development prior to age three manifested by delays or abnormal functioning in at least one of the following areas: (1) social interaction, (2) language as used in social communication, or (3) symbolic or imaginative play

---

Box 3.2 Features of child disintegrative disorder

Features much like autism (three domains)

Diagnosed first if child meets criteria for autism as well

Must have normal development to two years

Must lose receptive language and social skills

May lose motor and adaptive skills

Box 3.3 Features of Asperger syndrome

Social deficits like autism

Circumscribed interests and sometimes other repetitive behaviors like autism

May have gross motor or visual-spatial deficits

By exclusion

- Not autism
- Not language-delayed
- Not mentally handicapped in DSM-IV/ICD

Similarly, atypical autism and/or pervasive developmental disorder, not otherwise specified (PDD-NOS) are often used to refer to atypical autism (at least in North America). These disorders involve social deficits like autism, but often milder with either or both communication and/or repetitive behaviors similar to autism (see Box 3.4; Towbin 1997). This diagnosis (PDD-NOS/atypical autism) is primarily made by exclusion in that it is used to apply to children who are subthreshold on all three domains of autism or children who meet criteria in two areas (including social), but not the third, or children who meet criteria in all areas, but have late onset. Most recently, an argument has been made that this category might best be used to refer to children who do not have restricted and repetitive behaviors, although this is not yet a point of view yet widely shared (Walker *et al.* 2004).

Box 3.4 Features of PDD-NOS/atypical autism

Must have social deficits like autism

Must have either or both communication or repetitive behaviors like autism

- By exclusion
- Not autistic
- May meet two criteria but not the third, or may fall subthreshold on all three domains
- May have late onset

In fact, there is evidence from a number of sources that autistic spectrum disorders (ASDs), or at least some aspects of ASDs, fall in continuous dimensions, as shown in Figure 3.1. We are forced to categorize these dimensions in order to yield definable groups either for research or for clinical work. Discriminating ASDs from other disorders is easiest for school-age children with some language, but who are not yet fluent speakers. As we move down in age and as we move up or down in levels of mental retardation and language delay, discriminations become more difficult. This is in part because ASDs are developmental disorders, which means that they are both affected by development and that having these disorders affects development. In this context, discriminating autism from other disorders is made more difficult when a child has very minimal skills across most areas, because identification of specific social and/or communication deficits is limited. Conversely, for children who have strong skills in many areas, questions arise about the role of compensation and discrepancies in diagnosis. Should a child who has superior non-verbal skills and vocabulary, but is very socially awkward, be diagnosed as having ASD because of the size of discrepancy?

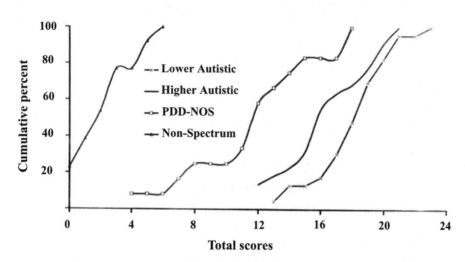

Figure 3.1 Continuous dimensions of ASD

ASDs can be diagnosed reliably in children as young as two years of age up through adulthood by experienced clinicians or researchers using standardized instruments. Historically, 70–85 percent of the cases of autism have been described as also having mental retardation, but the statistic has now been questioned as newer epidemiological studies with much higher prevalence rates have suggested that closer to 50 percent of children with ASDs do not have mental retardation (see Figure 3.2; Chakrabarti and Fombonne 2001). Similarly, our own longitudinal data suggested that, by age nine, about 85 percent of the children with autistic spectrum disorders will be speaking in some way with about 40 percent speaking fluently (Lord and Risi 2004).

We also have a much better understanding that the diagnosis of autism is determined not only by the presence of positive (abnormal) behaviors, but also the absence or limited presence of typical behaviors. This means that developmental level and contextual features (such as in what kind of circumstances does the child behave this way?) can both have significant effects on diagnostic judgment. The implication is that in making a diagnosis of autism one needs to consider what is appropriate for a child of that developmental level and/or that chronological age in that circumstance.

The last ten years have seen very significant changes occurring in the ages and rates of referral of young children with ASDs. In the over 30 years that I have been working with children with ASD, the typical age of referral, at least in tertiary care centers in the US, has gone from age five or six years, down to age two years (Siegel *et al.* 1988). In the last few years, we have had an influx of information about the assessment of very

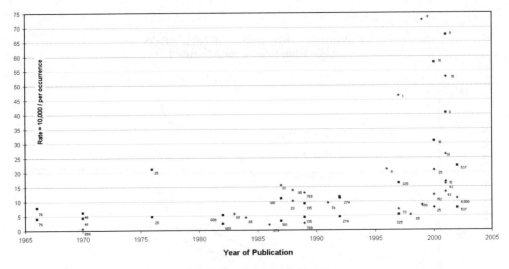

Figure 3.2 Prevalence rates of autism

young children. We have the advantage of numerous studies describing behaviors of young preschool children, particularly those aged four years and under, but still only limited knowledge from treatment or epidemiological studies, with children this age.

Descriptive studies of the behavior of preschool children with ASD have been very important in contributing to what would comprise a 'state of the art' assessment. Studies of joint attention, response to name, imagination, and beginning language development have all had quite practical effects on the ways in which we assess very young children (see Box 3.5; Mundy, Sigman and Kasari 1990). Numerous studies have suggested that the clearest discriminators of children with autism or ASD from other children with other disorders at young ages may be rather different than the same children at later ages. In our first follow-up study, in which we looked at consecutive referrals to a Canadian autism clinic of children under two years, we found that the clearest discriminators at age two of children who would have stable diagnoses of autism later on were based on parent report, children's attention to someone talking to them, and whether the children ever spontaneously directed others' attention in any way, either through eye contact or pointing (see Box 3.6; Lord 1995). These were a much more restricted set of features than we found at age three, when attention to voice continued to be one of the most powerful discriminators, but joined with pointing to express interest, hand and finger mannerisms, and the use of someone else's body as a tool, as shown in Box 3.7. In fact, from our observational data, using the Autism Diagnostic Observation Schedule (ADOS) to build further on this finding, by the time children are using simple sentences, a failure to respond to their names and the use of other people's bodies as tools become very rare even in children with autism and so are no longer important unique features.

**Box 3.5 Topics of investigation
in preschool-age children**

Joint attention: response to/initiation

Looking at faces; gaze

Response to name

Pretending

**Box 3.6 Clearest discriminators
from Canadian study (at age 2)**

Attention to voice (not name)

Child spontaneously directing other's attention (in any way)

**Box 3.7 Clearest discriminators
from Canadian study (at age 3)**

Attention to voice (but still not name)

Pointing to express interest

Hand and finger mannerisms

Use of other's body as a tool

In language development, we see similar developmental distinctions that are useful in assessment. At age two, a child who understood no words out of context had a worse prognosis than other children had. By age three, a child who had no meaningful spontaneous expressive words similarly had much less of a chance of developing language. Even in that brief period between two and three, different features predicted later outcome.

Just over ten years ago, we undertook another prospective longitudinal study in which we began to follow all the children under age three referred to several regions in North Carolina through the TEACCH Program and then in Chicago. Our goal was to use methods beyond a parent report, which was what we had used originally in Canada, with a larger sample and broader recruitment. These children most recently received a comprehensive assessment at age nine to ten years. We are now carrying out a study in which we send parents and teachers questionnaires and talk to them on the telephone every four months. We have managed to retain about 160 of the original 231 subjects in this study. At age nine we directly assessed about 170 of these children. As shown in Table 3.1, their mean age when we began to see them was between 28 and 29 months. Diagnoses of autism made at age two were very stable up to nine years of age (see Table 3.2). Of the children who had a diagnosis of autism at age two, 84 percent had autism diagnoses at age nine; 15 percent had diagnoses of PDD-NOS at age nine; and only one child (less than 1 percent) did not have a diagnosis on the spectrum, as shown in Figure 3.3. Conversely, of children who had a diagnosis of autism at age nine, 71 percent of them had been diagnosed as having autism at age two and 27 percent had diagnoses of PDD-NOS at age two, as shown in Figure 3.4 (Lord *et al.* submitted).

Table 3.1 Participants with data at age 9

	Race (B/W) %	Gender (M/F) %	Mean age in months at 1st test (SD)	Mean age in months at last test (SD)	Mean VIQ, age 9 (SD)	Mean NVIQ, age 9 (SD)
N Carolina N = 102	39/58	77/23	28.7 (4.8)	122.0 (8.3)	52.4 (39.3)	67.2 (23.6)
Chicago N = 68	8/86	85/15	29.3 (5.6)	98.2 (10.9)	55.6 (37.6)	74.3 (18.1)

Table 3.2 Best estimate diagnoses at 2 (vertical) and 9 (horizontal) (NC and Chicago)

	Autism	PDD-NOS	Non-spectrum
Autism	76	13	1
PDD-NOS	27	11	6
Non-spectrum	2	9	34

As shown in Figure 3.5, diagnoses of PDD-NOS or atypical autism at age two were much less stable. In fact, the majority of children with these diagnoses (61%) had diagnoses of autism at age nine. A quarter of them had diagnoses of PDD-NOS at age nine. Most of the children who had had consistent diagnoses of PDD-NOS from age two to age nine, in fact, had quite mild difficulties and were in regular mainstream programs with minimal services at age nine, even though their parents were still often quite concerned about their social development. About 14 percent of the children who had had a diagnosis of PDD-NOS at age two had diagnoses outside of the spectrum at age nine.

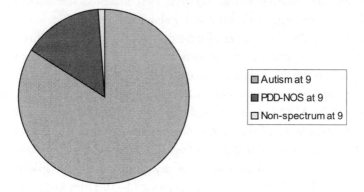

Figure 3.3 Diagnosis at age 9 of children with autism diagnosis at age 2

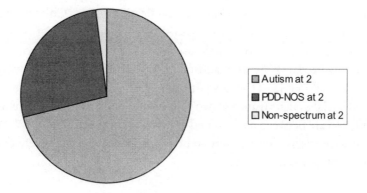

Figure 3.4 Diagnosis at age 2 of children with autism diagnosis at age 9

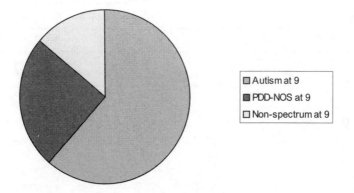

Figure 3.5 Diagnosis at age 9 of children with PDD-NOS diagnosis at age 2

They were the children whose progress best matched the 'recovery' that has been described, for example, in response to behavioral research.

Looking at the trajectories of development for various groups of children categorized by their diagnoses at age two and at age nine (for example, children with autism–autism classifications, or autism–PDD-NOS classifications) in Figure 3.6, on the whole, groups were quite stable in terms of social communication scores on various modules of the ADOS measured in direct observation. Children with autism diagnoses (1–1) at both points had the highest scores although they did show a slight decrease in scores between three and five years of age. Children who were never judged to be in the spectrum (3–3) had the lowest scores of any group except the children whose diagnoses went from PDD-NOS to outside the spectrum (2–3). These children showed consistent changes from age two to age three, from age three to age five, remaining consistently outside the spectrum from age five to age nine. Children whose diagnoses went from autism to PDD-NOS also showed their most dramatic improvements between ages two and three, and three and five, but continued to show improvements between ages five and nine in their decreasing social-communication scores. Children who consistently had diagnoses of PDD-NOS (2–2) also showed changes primarily between ages two and three, and three and five, which resulted in their scores being equivalent at age nine to children who had gone from autism to PDD-NOS and children with non-spectrum diagnoses. Children (2–1) who went from PDD-NOS to autism tended to have a flat profile of social deficits from age two to age nine. Thus, the greatest number of diagnostic changes were between age two and age five, as shown in Figure 3.7. During this time children were slightly more likely to be judged to have more severe diagnostic conditions than they had at age two.

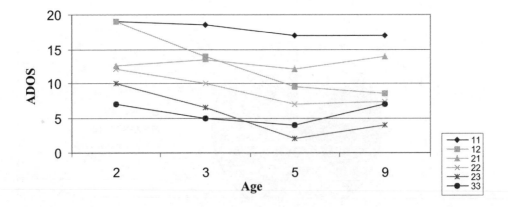

Figure 3.6 PL-ADOS/ADOS algorithm scores from age 2 to age 9 years, according to diagnoses at ages 2 and 9 (NC)

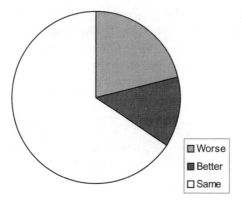

Figure 3.7 Diagnostic changes between ages 2 and 5

To our surprise, looking at change in verbal IQ (VIQ) for the same groups of children in Figure 3.8, verbal IQs remained quite stable for children who had consistent diagnoses of autism and children whose diagnoses were outside the spectrum at ages two and nine. Increases in verbal IQ particularly between ages five and nine (but less noticeably between ages two and three, and three and five) occurred for children whose diagnoses shifted from autism to PDD-NOS, for children whose diagnoses remained PDD-NOS, and for children whose diagnoses shifted from PDD-NOS outside the spectrum. All three of these groups had similarly high verbal IQs by age nine. One thing to remember here is that the children in the spectrum who made the greatest progress tended to be

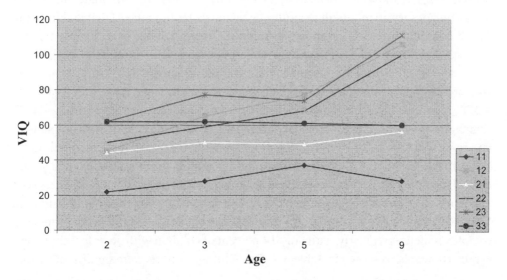

Figure 3.8 Ratio verbal IQs from age 2 to age 9 years, grouped by diagnoses at ages 2 and 9 (NC)

children with average to above average skills, which made them different from the children outside the spectrum in the study who were predominantly mentally retarded. Investigation of changes in non-verbal IQ (NVIQ) indicated that none of the groups changed significantly between ages two and nine (see Figure 3.9). On the whole, scores were remarkably consistent during this time.

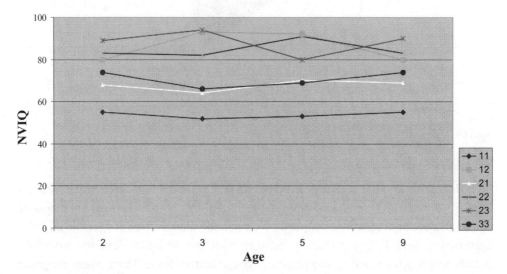

Figure 3.9 Ratio non-verbal IQs from age 2 to age 9 years, grouped by diagnoses at ages 2 and 9 (NC)

When we looked at which two-year-old measures best predicted having an autistic spectrum diagnosis at age nine, if we included the clinician's best estimate diagnosis (with the ADI-R and ADOS) available, the best estimate diagnosis accounted for a high proportion of the variance with repetitive behavior scores from the ADI-R and from the ADOS contributing as well, as shown in Table 3.3. If we excluded best estimate diagnoses, then the ADOS social communication score also contributed (see Table 3.4). When we looked at predicting having autism (so the more narrow diagnosis), again, best estimate diagnoses were the greatest contributor to variance (see Table 3.5). Again, the ADOS repetitive behavior scores contributed as did performance IQ and the ADI-R communication score. Without clinical diagnoses, again the ADOS social communication score was a predictor, as well as the ADOS repetitive score, ADI-R communication, and verbal IQ (see Table 3.6). What these findings suggest in the assessment of a young child is that attention needs to be paid particularly to social features that can be observed in a brief observation, repetitive behaviors, and level of communication impairment. When we predicted 'outcome' at age nine, 40 percent of the sample were producing complex sentences regularly, with only 14 percent of children with no or few consistent expressive words, as shown in Table 3.7. Our Chicago cohorts were significantly more

Table 3.3 Two-year-old measures predicting ASD at 9, including best estimate diagnosis (est. R^2 = 0.63; TPV = 92%)

	OR	se	z	p
Best estimate diagnosis	0.05	0.04	−4.38	0.001
ADI-R repetitive behavior	2.28	0.56	3.38	0.001
PL-ADOS repetitive behavior	1.68	0.36	2.45	0.014

Table 3.4 Two-year-old measures predicting ASD at 9, excluding best estimate diagnosis (est. R^2 = 0.52; TPV = 89%)

	OR	se	z	p
ADI-R repetitive behavior	2.15	0.42	3.89	0.001
PL-ADOS social-communication	1.26	0.06	4.78	0.001
PL-ADOS repetitive behavior	1.47	0.23	2.49	0.01

Table 3.5 Two-year-old measures predicting autism diagnoses at 9, including best estimate diagnosis (est. R^2 = 0.53; TPV = 85%)

	OR	se	z	p
Best estimate diagnosis	0.12	0.04	−5.68	0.001
PL-ADOS repetitive behavior	1.71	0.24	3.75	0.001
Ratio performance IQ	0.98	0.04	−3.33	0.001
ADI-R communication	1.13	0.07	1.93	0.05

Table 3.6 Two-year-old measures predicting autism diagnoses at 9, excluding best estimate diagnosis (est. R^2 = 0.42; TPV = 81%)

	OR	se	z	p
PL-ADOS repetitive behavior	1.17	0.20	4.54	0.001
ADI-R communication	1.16	0.07	2.40	0.02
PL-ADOS social-communication	1.12	0.05	2.37	0.02
Ratio verbal IQ	0.77	0.01	−2.06	0.04

Table 3.7 Estimates of expressive language level at age 9 – percentage of 151 participants

	Chicago	North Carolina
Complex sentences (ADOS module 3)	40.9	39.6
Sentences but not fluent (ADOS module 2)	35.3	28.9
Words but not sentences (ADOS module 1; ADI-R = 1)	10.5	16.8
No or few consistent words (ADI-R = 2)	14.3	14.4

likely to use simple sentences than the North Carolina group, where more children seemed to plateau at a level of using words.

When we looked at peer relations at age nine, as judged by teachers, a number of the ADOS scores from age two accounted for a significant amount of the variance. From the ADOS, requests, response to joint attention, and the initiating of joint attention all predicted the amount of peer interaction that children had. Requests also predicted the degree to which the teacher judged the child as being 'disconnected' from peers (see Figure 3.10). We found no relationship in this large group to amount of treatment, but this study was not designed to measure the effects of treatment, as shown in Table 3.8. Our measures of intervention were quite rudimentary and not controlled in any way (Schmidt, Risi and Lord, in preparation).

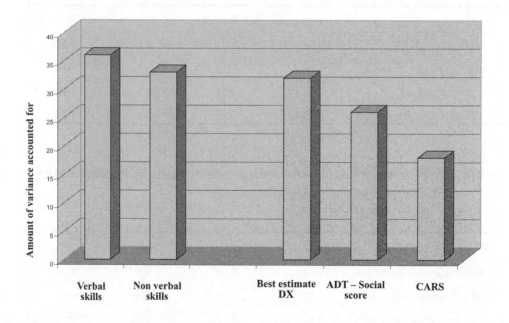

Figure 3.10 Predictors of change in Vineland scores from age 2 to age 5

Table 3.8 Percentage of children with intensive treatment (ABA plus preschool) in representative diagnostic categories

Diagnostic categories	%
Best outcome	14
Diagnosis moved to PDD-NOS (1/11)	9
Diagnosis moved to autism (5/29)	18
Stable diagnosis of autism (15/76)	20

We also found that a high proportion of children with ASD diagnoses could have been identified (based on the parents' retrospective report) prior to age two by a small number of variables. These included children who used fewer than five different words a day, but who were walking, children who did not attend when someone started speaking to them unless what they said was of very high interest, children whose parents spontaneously expressed concerns about them 'being in another world', or aloof, and children who were judged by their parents to have unusual eye contact. When parents were asked generally if they had any concerns about their child's social development, in fact, the majority of parents of typical children responded that they were concerned. They gave a variety of examples that did not have much to do with autism, for example that a child was very shy or was particularly aggressive.

Because developmental level plays such an important part, both in the diagnosis of autism in young children, and also in developing interventions for them, it is crucial to have appropriate developmental measures used in any assessment of a young child. Ideally, this assessment would be repeated fairly comprehensively in a year or two, even though full re-assessments may be spread out much further as the child gets older. Depending on how broadly PDD-NOS was used, there is evidence from some sites that diagnoses of PDD-NOS at young ages (under the age of two or three) were quite unstable and so really needed to be followed closely.

Assessments of developmental level should yield separate scores in non-verbal problem solving and in receptive and expressive language. Recently, a number of the collaborations in the United States and in the United Kingdom have begun using the Mullen Scales of Early Learning, which gives standard scores and age equivalents in gross motor skills, fine motor skills, non-verbal problem solving (visual reception), expressive language, and receptive language (Chawarska *et al.* in press). This test has the advantages of computing scores separately in these domains. Its materials are not quite as attractive to children as the Bayley Scales, and in the non-verbal problem-solving area it begins to rely on black-and-white line drawings for items above the age of three. A number of children with autism do not have much interest in these drawings and so it can be frustrating to see them scoring slightly lower as they grow bigger because of lack of interest. Nevertheless, the advantages of the Mullen's age equivalents and separate scores in different areas over the Bayley are significant.

For the same reason, the Differential Ability Scales (DAS), an American version of the British Ability Scales, has also become a favorite for a number of researchers and clinicians in the United States (Joseph, Tager-Flusberg and Lord 2002). This scale offers tasks that are rather more differentiated into language and non-language tasks than the Wechsler Tests. For preschool-age children it has a verbal comprehension test on which children with autism tend to do particularly poorly, but which is probably more related to functional receptive language, at least in children at age two than most other language tests. It only assesses naming vocabulary as an expressive language item so that it should be accompanied by some kind of language measurement that includes a standardized language sample. Speech and language testing in English is possible with very young children with minimal verbal skills using the Sequenced Inventory of Communication Development (SICD-R), the Mullen Scales or DAS, the Vineland Adaptive Behavior Scales, and the Preschool Language Scales. The Preschool Language Scales have recently been revised with more interesting material and more items at the lower end and so is probably the best omnibus language assessment for very young children.

For direct observation, the Autism Diagnostic Observation Schedule has three modules that are appropriate for young children (Lord *et al.* 1999; Lord *et al.* 2000). Module 1 is used for children who are non-verbal or who have only very few words to say. Module 2 is for children who have some language but where the syntax is not fluent. Module 3 is for older children and young adolescents who are verbally fluent. Items on Module 1 were reliable with children down to 12 months of age (as long as they were walking), but there seemed to be consistent floor effects for children between the non-verbal mental ages of between 12 and 18 months or so. Similarly, the ADI-R becomes quite over-diagnostic for children who do not have a non-verbal mental age of at least 18 months, and sometimes more like two years of age.

Factors outside the specific tests are relevant in assessing young children with suspected autistic or autistic spectrum disorders. There is no way to do this quickly. It is important to see the child in a situation in which they are relaxed and interested and not feeling rushed. Generally, young children should be seen with their parents in the room unless their parents feel they would do better without the parents. In many ways, diagnostic assessments of young children, for example the ADOS, and the cognitive testing is as important, because they elicit examples of the child's behavior, as they are in terms of providing hard and fast diagnoses or scores. It is critical that the examiner is sufficiently experienced with the tests that she or he does not need to be reading the manual, and that a pace can be set (sometimes quite a rapid pace for children who are interested in the materials) that fits the child's needs. There should be access to toys and other materials that the child may like and freedom from distraction by toys that the child may like so much that they cannot focus on the assessment. The examiner should very concretely experiment with how they want a room set up so that they can reach sufficient numbers of test materials to go quickly from task to task, but are not constantly barricading off areas from the child. With very small children, using a seat that clips on to a table or a high chair can be very effective in increasing the degree to which the child focuses his or her attention. For older children, they spend much of their energy trying to get out of the seat and so it might not be terribly helpful.

Along the same line, particularly in Module 1 of the ADOS, space is used as a way to look for attention and organization in the children. For this age child, it may be very helpful just to get the child up and away from the table in order to try new activities, or even to try the activities in bits and pieces somewhere else and move the child toward the table for the final version. Taking breaks for the young child may also be helpful. Often these breaks can actually be carried out right at the table where the child is working and be accomplished by giving the child something to play with and just moving the examiner's chair back. If it is difficult to get the child to sit at a table it is often possible to organize several activities and then wait until the child is interested in something in the room, then sit him down and sit beside him with the materials. Giving parents clear directions of when you expect them to help you and when you do not want them to help or coach is also helpful. It is quite difficult to watch a child not do something that they are able to do at home. Asking parents to bring a favorite toy and/or a favorite food can also be helpful if the child begins to get overwhelmed by the circumstance.

Overall, our ability to assess and define autism and other developmental disorders in preschool children has improved immensely in the last 10–15 years, as shown in Box 3.8. It is now possible to make a standardized diagnosis of a child with autism as low as 24 months and be relatively confident of its stability (in that this child is more likely to change diagnosis than are other children). Ways of observing children and of getting information from the parents and ways of reducing all this into standard diagnostic algorithms have been well-established. Developmental levels are relatively easily obtainable across four separate areas. All of this can contribute directly to a functional program for the child and future access to services.

Box 3.8 Conclusions

1 Diagnoses of autism made at two were remarkably stable up to age nine.

2 Most of the diagnostic change in children referred for possible autism at two occurred before age five.

3 The most common outcome for children classified at age two with PDD-NOS was autism, but there was great variation.

4 There was little evidence of 'complete' recovery. One child changed from an autism diagnosis at two to a non-spectrum categorization at nine.

5   However, a significant minority of our sample (about one out of six children referred for possible autism) are doing quite well. They are in mainstream school classes with no or minimal support, have IQs in the normal range, and score below autism cut-offs on diagnostic measures.

6   There were considerable improvements in verbal IQs from five to nine years. These changes were associated with changes in diagnosis from autism to PDD-NOS between age two and five years.

7   Although measures of repetitive behavior on the ADOS and ADI-R were not considered crucial for a diagnosis of autism at age two, they were important predictors of diagnostic status at age nine.

8   However, children suspected of having autism at age two are rarely without difficulties later.

9   'Small' differences in developmental level may affect how autism is manifested in the preschool years.

10   At age two, children late diagnosed as autistic are *not* aloof. Most do *not* show odd behaviors or fail to respond to separation.

11   At age two, children later diagnosed as autistic do fail to respond to someone speaking to them in a neutral fashion and do not try to direct others' attention in ordinary, unstructured situations.

12   A higher proportion of children had complex language and spontaneous phrases at age nine than expected from previous estimates. This is particularly encouraging because this was a sample identified at a young age in most cases because of severe language delays.

13   Getting children and families started in intervention programs, with appropriate goals and methods, is the purpose of diagnosis and assessment.

REFERENCES

American Psychiatric Association (1994) *Diagnostic and Statistical Manual of Mental Disorders* (4th edn). Washington, DC: American Psychiatric Association.

Chakrabarti, S. and Fombonne, E. (2001) 'Pervasive developmental disorders in preschool children.' *Journal of the American Medical Association 285*, 24, 3093–3099.

Chawarska, K., Klin, A., Paul, R. and Volkmar, F. (in press) 'Diagnostic and developmental profiles of 2-year-olds with Autism Spectrum Disorders.' *Journal of Autism and Developmental Disorders.*

Gillberg, C. (1998) 'Asperger syndrome and high-functioning autism.' *British Journal of Psychiatry 172*, 200–209.

Joseph, R. M., Tager-Flusberg, H. and Lord, C. (2002) 'Cognitive profiles and social-communicative functioning in children with autism spectrum disorder.' *Journal of Child Psychology and Psychiatry and Allied Disciplines 43*, 6, 807–821.

Lord, C. (1995) 'Follow-up of two-year-olds referred for possible autism.' *Journal of Child Psychology and Psychiatry and Allied Disciplines 36*, 8, 1365–1382.

Lord, C. and Risi, S. (2004) 'Trajectory of language development in autistic spectrum disorders.' In M. Rice (ed.) *Developmental Language Disorders: From Phenotypes to Etiologies*, pp.8–29. Mahwah, NJ: Erlbaum.

Lord, C., Rutter, M., DiLavore, P. and Risi, S. (1999) *Autism Diagnostic Observation Schedule-Generic.* Los Angeles, CA: Western Psychological Services.

Lord, C., Risi, S., Lambrecht, L., Cook, E. H., Leventhal, B. L., DiLavore, P. C. *et al.* (2000) 'The Autism Diagnostic Observation Schedule-Generic: a standard measure of social and communication deficits associated with the spectrum of autism.' *Journal of Autism and Developmental Disorders 30*, 3, 205–223.

Lord, C., Risi, S., DiLavore, P., Shulman, C., Thurm, A. and Pickles, A. (submitted) 'Autism from two to nine.' *Archives of General Psychiatry.*

Mundy, P., Sigman, M. and Kasari, C. (1990) 'A longitudinal study of joint attention and language development in autistic children.' *Journal of Autism and Developmental Disorders 20*, 1, 115–128.

Ozonoff, S., South, M. and Miller, J. N. (2000) 'DSM-IV-defined Asperger syndrome: cognitive, behavioral and early history differentiation from high-functioning autism.' *Autism: Special Issue: Asperger syndrome 4*, 1, 29–46.

Schmidt, H., Risi, S. and Lord, C. (in preparation) 'Peer interaction at age 9 in ASD.'

Siegel, B., Pliner, C., Eschler, J. and Elliott, G. R. (1988) 'How children with autism are diagnosed: difficulties in identification of children with multiple developmental delays.' *Journal of Developmental and Behavioral Pediatrics 9*, 4, 199–204.

Szatmari, P. (2000) 'Perspectives on the classification of Asperger Syndrome.' In A. Klin (ed.) *Asperger Syndrome*, pp. 403–407. New York, NY: The Guilford Press.

Towbin, K. E. (1997) 'Pervasive developmental disorder not otherwise specified.' In D. J. Cohen and F. R. Volkmar (eds) *The Handbook of Autism and Other Pervasive Developmental Disorders* (2nd edn), pp. 123–147. New York, NY: John Wiley and Sons.

Walker, D. R., Thompson, A., Zwaigenbaum, L., Goldberg, J., Bryson, S. E., Mahoney, W. J. *et al.* (2004) 'Specifying PDD-NOS: a comparison of PDD-NOS, Asperger syndrome, and autism.' *Journal of the American Academy of Child and Adolescent Psychiatry 43*, 2, 172–180.

Chapter 4

Implicit Learning Impairments in Autism Spectrum Disorders

Implications for Treatment

Laura Grofer Klinger, Mark R. Klinger and Rebecca L. Pohlig

Our research goal is to understand how people with autism spectrum disorders (ASDs) learn about and understand their world. It is becoming increasingly evident that people with ASD think differently from those without the disorder. In this chapter, we propose that studying the cognitive impairments present in persons with ASD may offer an insight into the neurobiological abnormalities present in ASD, has the potential to explain some of the behavioral symptoms that characterize ASD, and may provide information regarding appropriate intervention strategies. Specifically, we suggest that cognitive impairments are the intermediary link between the neuroanatomical abnormalities found in persons with ASD and the behavioral symptoms of ASD. That is, we believe that the neuroanatomical abnormalities cause the unusual cognitive processing abilities observed in persons with ASD, and that these cognitive impairments cause the social and communication impairments that characterize the disorder (see Figure 4.1). Understanding the social and communication symptoms that are a result of cognitive impairments will help explain why individuals with ASD engage in these behaviors and will suggest appropriate intervention strategies. Thus, we believe that this type of research offers potentially important information to researchers, clinicians, parents, and teachers working with people who have ASD.

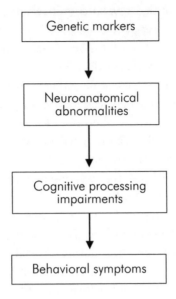

Figure 4.1 Cognitive processes as an intermediary between neurobiology and autism spectrum disorder symptomatology

LEARNING DISABILITIES IN AUTISM SPECTRUM DISORDER

Some of the most eloquent insights into the way that people with ASD think come from the writings of individuals with high-functioning autism. Temple Grandin, an adult with high-functioning autism, describes herself as having an unusual style of concept formation in which she memorizes visual images of different examples of a concept rather than integrating information across examples. For example, she writes that when she asks people to think of a church steeple or cat, many people report that they visualize a 'generic, generalized outline of a church steeple or a cat.' However, she writes that 'my cat or church steeple concept is based on a series of "videos" of different cats or churches that I have experienced. There is no generalized cat concept' (Grandin 1995, p.142). Donna Williams, another adult with autism, also describes herself as having difficulties understanding her world. She reports that she does not understand all of the 'rules' that people use for each situation that they encounter. She writes: 'My behavior puzzled others, but theirs puzzled me, too. It was not so much that I had no regard for their rules as that I couldn't keep up with many rules for each specific situation' (Williams 1992, p.69). Both authors seem to indicate that they have trouble integrating information across contexts, and instead try to memorize individual rules or visual details from each situation that they encounter. Both authors clearly describe themselves as having unusual cognitive abilities.

Recent research has identified several cognitive impairments in persons with an ASD. For example, we know that people with ASD have difficulties disengaging and shifting their attention (Casey *et al.* 1993; Townsend, Courchesne and Egaas 1996). That is, they tend to get 'stuck' on a particular object or topic and have difficulty refocusing their attention. We also know that people with ASD have trouble understanding that other people can have a different perspective from their own. That is, they have an impaired 'theory of mind' (see Baron-Cohen 2001 for a review). As a result, a child with ASD may not understand that other children may not share his fascination in particular topics (i.e. electrical cords, clocks, maps, etc.) or experience the same anxiety about particular situations (i.e. being in Wal-Mart or walking on asphalt). We also know that individuals with ASD have a weak central coherence (Frith and Happe 1994; Jolliffe and Baron-Cohen 1997). That is, they tend to focus on specific aspects or parts of the situation without recognizing the 'bigger picture.' For example, a child with ASD may focus on a person's mouth instead of their eyes during a social interaction (Klin *et al.* 2002). Whether this weak central coherence is due to an enhanced perceptual processing ability (Mottron and Burack 2001) or a focus on uniqueness rather than similarity among features (Plaisted 2001) remains unclear. Finally, we know that persons with ASD have impairments in executive function (Ciesielski and Harris 1997; Ozonoff and Jensen 1999; Ozonoff and McEvoy 1994). That is, they have impaired problem solving, particularly in their ability to think flexibly when trying to solve a dilemma. Although we describe these impairments in attention, theory of mind, central coherence, and executive function as impairments in separate cognitive skills, they are clearly linked. For example, weak central coherence is conceptually related to impairments in disengaging and shifting attention. Individuals with difficulty disengaging and shifting attention may tend to focus on only one aspect of an object without noticing the whole object. Indeed, integrating across these cognitive theories, there is a developing picture of the cognitive impairments in ASD as leading to a rigid, narrow focus of attention that prevents individuals from considering the larger picture, including another person's perspective.

This increasing evidence that people with ASD 'think differently' from people without ASD suggests that individuals with ASD have a type of pervasive learning disability that affects their ability to attend to and integrate information in the environment. This comparison of ASD with other types of learning disabilities suggests that, like other learning disabilities, there is an underlying neuroanatomical cause. Although we may not know the exact neuroanatomical differences in the brains of individuals with dyslexia or a writing disability, we clearly recognize that these difficulties are caused by some underlying difference in brain organization. Similarly, in ASD, there is increasing evidence that brain abnormalities are present (see Klinger, Dawson and Renner 2003 for a review). Several areas of the brain have been implicated in ASD including the cerebellum (Courchesne *et al.* 1988; Courchesne *et al.* 1994), the limbic system (Bachevalier 1991 and 1994; Bauman and Kemper 1988), and the cerebral cortex (Piven *et al.* 1990; Piven *et al.* 1996). In ASD, these abnormalities in brain development are thought to result from an underlying genetic predisposition to the disorder (rather than an environmental insult such as a head injury). Thus, we conceptualize ASD as involving a type of learning disability that is caused by abnormal brain development.

Identification of the particular pattern of cognitive strengths and weaknesses of persons with ASD should offer insights into appropriate interventions. Using a learning disability model, we propose that there are two different approaches to treating the cognitive weaknesses in ASD. First, interventions can use a compensation approach that capitalizes on the strengths and avoids the weaknesses. Second, interventions can use an approach that focuses on strengthening or ameliorating the weaknesses. Research clearly suggests that the earlier the intervention, the better the outcome for children with ASD (see Dawson and Osterling 1997). As a result, there has been an increasing emphasis on earlier identification of ASD so that treatment can begin as early as possible. Identification of very early developing cognitive impairments may provide one mechanism for early diagnosis. Our research has focused on identifying very early developing cognitive impairments in ASD that may lead to subsequent learning difficulties and some of the behavioral symptoms of ASD.

EARLY SYMPTOMS OF AUTISM SPECTRUM DISORDERS

If, as we propose, the behavioral symptoms of ASD are a result of differences in cognition and thinking about the world, then the cognitive differences must predate the behavioral symptoms. Recent research and clinical evidence suggests that the behavioral symptoms of ASD are evident within the first two years of life. Indeed, difficulties in understanding the world are commonly described by parents of very young children with autism. Catherine Maurice (1993) wrote about her two-year-old daughter's difficulties in understanding her environment:

> It wasn't just that she didn't understand language. She didn't seem to be aware of her surroundings. She wasn't figuring out how her world worked, learning about keys that fit into doors, lamps that turned off because you pressed a switch, milk that lived in the refrigerator. Daniel, even as a year-old baby, had tried to put the nipple onto the top of his bottle. Had Anne-Marie ever demonstrated that she understood, remembered, carried over from day to day, such a simple aspect of the world she inhabited? We could see almost no evidence of that kind of learning. If she was focusing on anything, it was on minute particles of dust or hair that she now picked up from the rug, to study with intense concentration. Worse, she didn't seem to be picking up anyone's feelings. (p.32–33)

Several studies have identified behavioral symptoms of autism within the first 18 months of life (Baron-Cohen *et al.* 1996; Osterling and Dawson 1994; Osterling, Dawson and Munson 2002). These early symptoms include a failure to look toward another person's face, failure to respond when their name is called, failure to share interests with others using gaze, showing or pointing gestures, and delayed pretend play. It is unclear when these symptoms first develop in infants and toddlers with ASD. However, Osterling and colleagues (Osterling and Dawson 1994; Osterling *et al.* 2002) reported that these early symptoms were present by 12 months of age. In typically developing infants, these skills are developing from very early on. For example, infants are typically born with a preference for the human face. Between six and nine months of age, infants typically begin to turn when their name is called and are able to follow another person's gaze. Between nine and twelve months of age, typically developing infants are able to share their interests by showing objects to others and by pointing to interesting objects (Butterworth 1995). Thus, delays in these skills strongly suggest that the symptoms of autism are present prior to nine months of age and perhaps are present at birth. If these behavioral symptoms are a result of differences in learning about and understanding the world, then these cognitive difficulties are likely present prior to nine months of age. Therefore, any attempt to identify early developing cognitive difficulties in children with ASD must examine thinking skills that typically develop within the first six months of life.

EARLY DEVELOPING COGNITIVE IMPAIRMENTS IN AUTISM SPECTRUM DISORDERS
Attention

Research examining the orienting and shifting of attention in persons with ASD has received a great deal of discussion. In typical development, the ability to orient toward a visual stimuli (e.g. follow a squeaky toy that moves across their field of vision) is present at birth (see Ruff and Rothbart 1996 for a review of the development of attention). By three to four months of age, infants are able to disengage their attention and shift it toward another stimulus (e.g. shift from looking at one squeaky toy to another squeaky toy; Atkinson *et al.* 1992; Johnson, Posner and Rothbart 1991). Thus, impairment in the ability to orient or the ability to shift attention in persons with ASD would represent a very early developing cognitive impairment. Several researchers have found evidence for a slowed orienting response in children and adults with ASD although it is unclear whether this slowed response is due to difficulties in disengaging attention or difficulties in shifting attention (Casey *et al.* 1993; Pascualvaca *et al.* 1998; Townsend, Harris and Courchesne 1996). More recently, several researchers have specifically investigated the very early developing, automatic forms of attention (i.e. exogenous orienting) in persons with ASD. Their results have been mixed, with some researchers finding evidence for impaired automatic attention orienting (Renner *et al.* 2003) and other researchers finding that these early developing automatic forms of attention shifting are intact, but the more later developing controlled types of attention shifting are impaired (Iarocci and Burack 2004; Leekam and Moore 2001). Additionally, it has been argued that early developing automatic forms of attention orienting are more impaired when the stimulus is social, involving a human face or voice, than when the stimulus is non-social (Dawson *et al.* 1998; Leekam and Moore 2001). Thus, while there is converging evidence that individuals with ASD have difficulty controlling the focus of their attention, it is unclear whether these difficulties are due to impairments in the early developing automatic form of attention or whether these difficulties are due to more later developing impairments in the more controlled, conscious aspects of attention. If the attention impairments are later developing, then they cannot explain some of the early symptoms of ASD that develop during the first year of life.

Implicit learning

Another early-developing, automatic cognitive process is implicit learning. During the first year of life, most learning occurs implicitly without conscious awareness. For example, by two years of age most toddlers are able to create short sentences that follow the rules of their native language. In English, children learn to say 'I want cookie' instead of 'cookie want I.' This knowledge of the underlying grammatical rules of their native language does not occur explicitly. That is, a two year old cannot tell you that the rule in English is that the object (e.g. 'cookie') typically follows the verb (e.g. 'want'). Instead, young children seem to have an intuitive or implicit understanding of the grammatical rules that underpin their native language. This implicit learning occurs after being exposed to many examples of their native language. Thus, implicit learning is a type of learning that seems to occur relatively automatically and involves the 'acquisition of knowledge that takes place largely independently of conscious attempts to learn and largely in the absence of explicit knowledge about what was acquired' (Reber 1993). In addition to the incidental learning of complex information, implicit learning often involves the ability to apply that information to new contexts (Hoffman and Koch 1998). For example, children who understand the grammatical rules of their culture (i.e. verb before object in English) will be able to apply this knowledge to new situations. That is, an English-speaking child hearing the Spanish word 'helado' for the first time, is likely to say 'I want helado' because he is automatically generalizing his grammatical knowledge of English to this new word for 'ice cream.'

Implicit learning contrasts with explicit learning in which there is a conscious attempt to learn specific information. Explicit learning occurs when children 'figure out' and use a set of rules about how to solve a certain problem. For example, children learning to spell often learn specific rules about letter combinations that are followed in their native language. In English, children learn that the letter 'i' comes before 'e' in a word except after the letter 'c.' Learning and applying this type of rule is not automatic or implicit and, instead, takes conscious effort.

Reber (Reber 1993; Reber, Walkenfeld and Hernstadt 1991) proposed an evolutionary theory of learning in which implicit learning systems are thought to have evolved prior to conscious, explicit learning systems. According to this perspective, implicit learning should (1) develop early in life and be consistent across the lifespan; and (2) be independent of intellectual ability. In contrast, explicit learning should change over the lifespan and should be influenced by intellectual ability. The majority of developmental research supports Reber's theory. Studies comparing implicit learning tasks from childhood through adulthood have typically shown equivalent levels of performance across chronological age (e.g. Hayes and Taplin 1993; Lee *et al.* 2000; Meulemans, Van der Linden and Perruchet 1998; Saffran *et al.* 1997). Studies examining the relationship between implicit learning tasks and intellectual level suggest that implicit learning is IQ-independent throughout the range of normal intelligence (Maybery, Taylor and O'Brien-Malone 1995; McGeorge, Crawford and Kelly 1997; Reber *et al.* 1991) and non-specific mild to moderate mental retardation (Atwell, Conners and Merrill 2003). In contrast, explicit learning has been shown to improve with both age (McGeorge *et al.* 1997) and intelligence (McGeorge *et al.* 1997; Reber *et al.* 1991).

IMPAIRED IMPLICIT LEARNING IN AUTISM SPECTRUM DISORDERS

We propose that persons with ASD have impairments in implicit learning. Implicit learning occurs both when individuals learn that there are relationships between different parts of stimuli and when individuals learn that there are relationships across experiences. For instance, when learning the concept of a cat, individuals must learn the relationships among different parts of a cat (e.g. the shape of the nose, size of the ears, and length of the tail) and individuals must combine their knowledge across multiple experiences with different cats to see which parts are unique to cats. It is our theory that persons with ASD have difficulty learning in situations that require perceiving relationships among different parts and perceiving relationships across multiple experiences. This theory is related to several other theories of cognitive impairment in ASD. Courchesne and colleagues (see Courchesne *et al.* 1994) reported that persons with ASD have difficulty disengaging and shifting their attention. This difficulty would prevent persons with ASD from attending to and noticing relationships between different parts of a stimulus. Similarly, Lovaas, Koegel and Schreibman (1979) reported that persons with ASD show 'stimulus overselectivity' characterized by a tendency to attend to idiosyncratic, irrelevant parts of stimuli during learning. This would result in persons not attending to relevant parts and thereby not noticing relationships between these parts. Frith and Happe (1994) hypothesized that people with ASD have impaired central coherence abilities and thus tend to perceive stimuli as separate pieces rather than an integrated whole (Frith and Happe 1994). This theory suggests that persons with ASD don't integrate pieces of stimuli, an implicit learning problem, though implicit learning also suggests difficulties integrating across separate experiences which is not part of central coherence theory. Plaisted (2001) proposed that persons with ASD focus on unique features of the environment and do not see the similarities across stimuli. This theory suggests that persons with ASD don't compare current experiences to past experiences in the same way as typical persons. This theory focuses on difficulties integrating separable experiences (the past and present) rather than integrating parts of a single experience as in central coherence theory. Our theory of impaired implicit learning encompasses these other theories that describe impairments in integrating features within a single object (e.g. central coherence) and theories that describe impairments integrating information across experiences or stimuli (e.g. Plaisted 2001).

COMPENSATING WITH EXPLICIT PROCESSES

We further hypothesize that an impairment in implicit learning leads persons with ASD to use a more effortful, explicit approach to tasks that appear effortless for typically developing (TD) children. This notion of impaired implicit processes that are compensated for by intact explicit processes has recently been proposed as a cognitive processing style that characterizes persons with obsessive-compulsive disorder (OCD; Rauch *et al.* 1997). This was supported by PET scan findings showing that when performing an implicit learning task, persons with OCD showed heightened medial temporal lobe activation (a region of the brain associated with explicit processing), whereas the control group showed heightened inferior striatal activation (a region of the brain associated with implicit processing). Evidence for this type of compensation in ASD comes from researchers who have commented on the fact that persons with ASD seem to use more explicit problem-solving approaches to tasks that are typically solved intuitively (Bowler, Matthews and Gardiner 1997; Happe 1995; Klinger and Dawson 1995). For example, Happe (1995) found that persons with ASD needed a higher verbal mental age to pass theory of mind tasks than TD children. She hypothesized that the children with ASD needed higher vocabulary skills to pass this task because they used more verbally mediated, effortful processes than TD children. The hypothesis that persons with ASD rely on explicit rule-based approaches to theory of mind tasks is also supported by researchers who have successfully taught children with autism to pass theory of mind tasks (Ozonoff and Miller 1995; Hadwin *et al.* 1996). These researchers used very explicit approaches to solving theory of mind tasks. However, in these studies theory of mind improvements did not generalize to other social skills. Hadwin and colleagues hypothesized that failure to generalize indicated that persons with autism learned to pass the tasks by applying a set of explicitly learned rules without implicitly understanding the concepts behind the task.

Several studies have provided evidence for the hypothesis that persons with ASD rely on explicit rule-based learning strategies. For example, Hermelin and O'Connor (1986) reported that the ability to calculate past and present calendar dates exhibited by some persons with ASD is due to an excellent ability to deliberately apply a set of complex rules. Additionally, several researchers (Berger *et al.* 1993; Klinger and Dawson 2001) have found intact rule-based categorization in persons with ASD.

APPLICATIONS OF IMPLICIT LEARNING TO SOCIAL AND LANGUAGE DEVELOPMENT

Implicit learning has been linked to the development of social and language skills (Gomez and Gerken 1999; Lieberman 2000; Saffran *et al.* 1997). There are many subtle, unspoken rules that govern social interaction and language. Presumably, implicit learning is used by infants to make sense out of these complex, unspoken rules that govern social and language development. The ability to automatically abstract information across experiences allows persons to understand these rules without requiring the ability to consciously describe these rules (Lewicki and Hill 1987). This implicit learning of the rules of social interaction leads to the development of social intuition (Lieberman 2000) and prevents young children from becoming overwhelmed by the complexity of their environments (Markman 1989). Additionally, implicit learning is vital to language development, including an understanding of the grammar and semantic relationships that underlie the language of the infant's culture. Young children implicitly learn the rules of their language and the unspoken implications of messages long before they are able to verbalize those rules (Gomez and Gerken 1999; Saffran, Aslin and Newport 1996; Saffran *et al.* 1997). This implicit understanding of social interactions and language use continues across the lifespan.

Finally, an impairment in implicit learning may explain some of the unusual symptoms that characterize ASD. We hypothesize that impaired implicit learning may cause social interactions and language to be difficult for persons with ASD because of the non-explicit, unpredictable information that is inherent in these types of stimuli (Klinger and Dawson 1992). For example, Ferrara and Hill (1980) reported that children with autism displayed more withdrawn behaviors when placed in unpredictable, novel situations. In contrast, they found that children with autism engaged in more play behaviors when placed in a situation where social and non-social events were predictable. Additionally, Dawson and colleagues found that children with autism tended to be more socially responsive and show a higher level of social ability when placed in a highly predictable social situation (Dawson and Galpert 1990; Klinger and Dawson 1992). We also hypothesize that the repetitive behaviors and restricted interests that characterize persons with ASD may be an attempt to make their environment more predictable and explicitly understood. This link between ritualistic behaviors and explicit processing is supported by Rauch *et al.*'s (1997) hypothesis that the ritualistic behaviors observed in adults with obsessive-compulsive disorder may be linked to an over-reliance on explicit rather than implicit learning. If persons with ASD use explicit processes to compensate for implicit learning impairments, future interventions will need to either find a method to teach individuals with ASD how to understand implicit information or, more likely, focus on providing them with explicit rules that facilitate their understanding of social and linguistic information.

RESEARCH RELATING IMPLICIT LEARNING TO AUTISM SPECTRUM DISORDERS

Our research has examined whether individuals with ASD are indeed impaired in their implicit learning. Furthermore, we have studied whether individuals with ASD compensate for impaired implicit learning by using explicit processes. Finally, we have examined whether implicit learning ability is related to the diagnostic symptoms that characterize ASD. Each of these research questions are addressed in more detail below.

Is implicit learning impaired in persons with autism spectrum disorders?

Our first goal was to test whether persons with ASD are impaired in their implicit learning ability. This was initially done using a category learning task (Klinger and Dawson 2001).

PROTOTYPE CATEGORY LEARNING

Much of category learning takes place implicitly (Ashby *et al.* 1998). There is substantial evidence that when persons encounter 'fuzzy,' natural categories, they learn by abstracting a best example (a prototype) of the category (Franks and Bransford 1971; Posner and Keele 1968). Posner and Keele (1968) argued that prototypes are created by computing a mental average of previously-experienced category members. In typical prototype formation experiments, participants are shown members of a category (e.g. a pretend species of animal) that vary on features (e.g. length of legs, size of tail, etc.) (see Figure 4.2). Following this familiarization, participants easily discriminate between and prefer the category prototype (i.e. an animal that is composed of the average of all the previously seen features) compared to novel category members. In studies with infant participants (some within a few hours of birth), infants respond as if the prototype was more familiar than novel category members (Bomba and Siqueland 1983; Strauss 1979; Walton and Bower 1993; Younger 1985).

We conducted a prototype learning task with children with ASD (Klinger and Dawson 2001). Participants included children with ASD and TD. Participants ranged in age from 5 to 21 years. Participants were matched on verbal mental age using the Peabody Picture Vocabulary Test – Revised (Dunn and Dunn 1981). Standard scores ranged from 40 to 87 for children with ASD, representing a fairly broad range of functioning although few children were in the average range. Mean standard scores were 56.8 and 99.9 for children with ASD and TD, respectively. Because they were matched on the basis of verbal mental age, children with ASD had higher chronological ages (M = 14 years, 5 months) than TD children (M = 6 years, 8 months).

The stimuli consisted of drawings of imaginary animals from different animal categories. Within each category, features varied along quantitative dimensions (e.g. length of leg, size of tail, etc.). Each dimension varied along five discrete values. Children participated in two conditions: an explicit rule learning condition and an implicit proto-type learning condition. During the rule condition, familiarization trials consisted of eight members of an animal category with each example composed of a different com-bination of feature values. However, each animal had a distinctive feature (e.g. a long neck) that determined category membership. In the rule condition, children were not told that there was a rule that determined category membership and were expected to figure out the rule during the familiarization trials. The test trials consisted of two alter-native forced-choice comparisons between two animals that varied only on the feature that determined category membership. Children were asked to choose which animal belonged to the category. Both diagnostic groups chose the animal that followed the rule significantly more often than chance (75–86 percent of trials compared to the chance level of 50 percent).

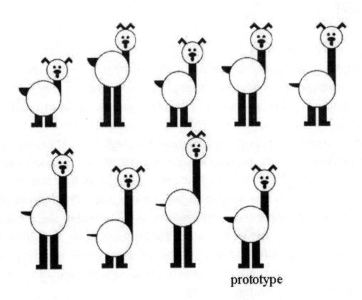

Figure 4.2 Sample stimuli for the prototype task: eight familiarization stimuli animals and the prototype animal

During the prototype condition, children were shown eight examples of an animal category in which there was no rule or combination of rules that determined category membership. During the test trials, children were given two alternative forced-choice comparisons between a novel animal composed of familiar features (e.g. features that were seen during the familiarization trials but were arranged in a new combination) and the prototype animal (e.g. features that were the mathematical average of all previously seen features). Results indicated that TD children chose the prototype at a rate much greater than chance (79 percent where chance equals 50 percent). In contrast, children with ASD chose the prototype at chance levels (54%).

This result provided strong initial evidence that persons with ASD may possess implicit learning impairments. This stands in sharp contrast to their explicit learning of rule-based categories, in which they learned the categories just as well as TD participants. It is important to note that participants in this research possessed relatively young mental ages (*M* = 6 years, 6 months) and that the ASD participants in this study, for the most part, were relatively low-functioning. It was unclear whether these implicit learning deficits would be apparent in persons with ASD who had older mental ages and were higher functioning.

ARTIFICIAL GRAMMAR LEARNING IN HIGH-FUNCTIONING CHILDREN WITH AUTISM SPECTRUM DISORDERS

We conducted a second study to test whether mentally older, high-functioning children with ASD show impaired implicit learning (Klinger *et al.* 2001). We used a different measure of implicit learning in this study, an artificial grammar learning task (Reber 1989). In this task, sequences of shapes are generated by a complex set of rules that determine the order in which shapes can appear (see Figure 4.3). In this task, participants are first shown examples of sequences generated from the grammar but are not told that the sequences were generated by a set of rules. Following this familiarization, participants easily discriminate between and prefer the sequences that follow the grammar rules compared to sequences that contain a rule violation. This demonstrates that even though they cannot explicitly describe the rules of the grammar, they have learned the rules implicitly (Reber 1989). Studies have shown that this implicit learning is developing early with infant participants responding to grammatical sequences as if they were more familiar than sequences with a rule violation (Gomez and Gerken 1999). Additionally, studies show that artificial grammar learning is developmentally stable with five- to six-year-olds showing similar amounts of learning as college students (Lee *et al.* 2000) and that artificial grammar learning is unrelated to IQ with mentally retarded adults learning as well as typical adults (Atwell *et al.* 2003).

In our experiment participants were asked to memorize 15 sequences of shapes generated by an artificial grammar. During the test trials, children were given two alternative forced-choice comparisons between a sequence generated from the grammar and a sequence that contained a violation of the rules. Learning was indicated by showing a higher rate of choosing the grammatical sequences. This indicates that participants have learned the rules even though the rules are difficult to learn consciously. Participants in this experiment were 12 children with ASD and 12 children with TD. Participants were both older and higher functioning (IQ range 92–128, mental age M = 11 years, 6 months) than in the previous, prototype study.

Results indicated that both TD children and children with ASD chose the grammatical sequences at a rate greater than chance (TD *M* = 67 percent, ASD *M* = 70 percent where chance performance equals 50 percent correct). These data suggest that older, high-functioning children may not differ from TD children in implicit learning.

However, we believe that it is likely that participants in this study were able to figure out some of the rules explicitly. Thus, we examined whether artificial grammar learning was linked to explicit learning ability for each group. Explicit learning was measured by performance on the matrices task of the Kaufman Brief Intelligence Test (Kaufman and Kaufman 1990) which is considered a measure of fluid intelligence. This measure of explicit learning was correlated with artificial grammar learning for the ASD group (r=+0.45), but not for the TD group (r = +0.13). That is, those children with ASD who had lower explicit learning ability did not choose the grammatical sequences at greater than chance levels, but those children with ASD and higher explicit learning ability were successful on this task.

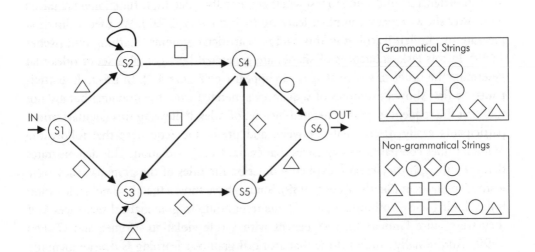

Figure 4.3 Example of an artificial grammar: three grammatical sequences and three non-grammatical sequences

This study found that implicit learning may not be impaired in an older, high-functioning population of persons with ASD. However, there was some evidence that persons with ASD may achieve this equivalent performance by using different learning processes from persons with TD. Similar to other studies, this study found for participants with TD implicit learning was, at most, weakly related to explicit learning ability. However, for participants with ASD implicit learning was strongly related to explicit learning ability.

Do persons with ASD compensate for implicit deficits by using explicit processes?

At this point our data were mixed; one set of results showed implicit learning impairments in persons with ASD (Klinger and Dawson 2001) and one set of results showed intact implicit learning (Klinger *et al.* 2001). However, our results suggested that persons with ASD may compensate for implicit learning deficits by using explicit learning processes. That is, they may not implicitly learn and understand subtle relationships as well as persons with TD and, instead, may compensate by attempting to learn and understand a set of explicit rules. Our second goal was to test this hypothesis. We conducted a study that used a large number of participants who varied substantially in their explicit learning capabilities. We also used multiple measures of implicit and explicit learning to test these ideas. This study included 100 participants, 50 each in the ASD and TD groups. All participants possessed IQs in the average to above average range (85–130). Participants ranged in age from 5 to 17 years old. This wide range was used to ensure that a wide range of explicit learning abilities was represented because explicit learning shows large developmental effects and is highly correlated with mental age. Participants were well matched on mental age though they differed slightly on IQ and chronological age.

Participants completed two implicit learning tasks: the prototype category learning task and the artificial grammar learning task. These tasks were virtually identical to those used in the previous studies. We first tested whether persons with ASD showed impairments on these two tasks across the full groups of participants. Children with ASD showed significantly less learning on both of these implicit learning tasks than children with TD (see Figure 4.4). Thus, our results suggest there is a reliable, replicable impairment in implicit learning for persons with ASD. This impairment holds across multiple measures of implicit learning and for participants who possess IQs in the normal range.

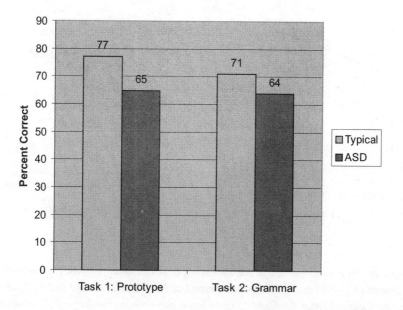

Figure 4.4 Mean correct prototype learning and artificial grammar learning for participants with typical development and autism spectrum disorder

However, we expected that not all children with ASD would show impairments in implicit learning performance. We hypothesized that if persons with ASD compensate for their implicit learning impairments by using explicit learning processes, then those children with ASD who have strong explicit learning skills ought to perform well on the implicit learning tasks. However, those with weaker explicit learning ought to do poorly on these implicit learning tasks. In this study we measured explicit reasoning using the matrix reasoning subtest from the KBIT and the Concept Formation test from the Woodcock-Johnson Test of Cognitive Abilities (Woodcock, McGrew and Mather 2001). The relationship between implicit and explicit learning was examined for each implicit learning task using a combined measure of explicit reasoning. It was expected that there would be little relationship between implicit and explicit learning in children with TD, but that implicit learning and explicit learning would be strongly related in children with ASD. For the prototype task there was a significant but relatively weak relationship between prototype learning and explicit learning for children with TD ($r = +0.31$). However, prototype learning was strongly related to explicit learning for children with ASD ($r = +0.69$) (see Figure 4.5a). Similar results were observed for the artificial grammar learning task. Artificial grammar learning was unrelated to explicit learning in children with TD ($r = +0.04$) but was strongly related in children with ASD ($r = +0.49$) (see Figure 4.5b).

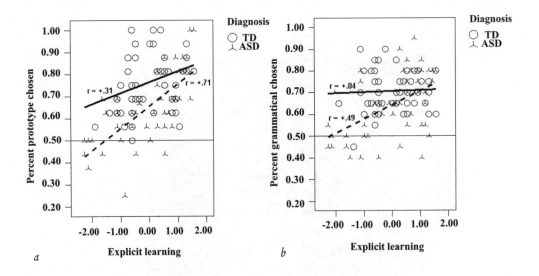

Figure 4.5 Scatterplot and regression line for implicit learning (a: percent prototype chosen; b: percent grammatical chosen) regressed on explicit learning. Data points represent individual participants. Solid lines display the regression lines for participants with typical development. Dashed lines display regression lines for participants with autism spectrum disorder

Both of these results showed a pattern in which explicit learning is weakly related or unrelated to implicit learning in typical children. This replicates the well established finding that implicit learning is weakly or unrelated to factors that affect explicit reasoning like chronological age or IQ in persons with typical development. This result supports the claim that implicit and explicit learning are largely independent cognitive processes in persons with typical development (Reber 1993; Reber *et al.* 1991). However, for children with ASD implicit learning was strongly related to explicit learning, suggesting that children with ASD use many of the same cognitive processes to complete implicit and explicit learning tasks. At the lowest explicit learning abilities, performance on both implicit learning tasks was near chance for the ASD children. Only once they developed improved explicit learning abilities were they able to perform well on the implicit tasks. These results support our hypothesis that children with ASD compensate for their impairment in implicit learning by using explicit learning processes to complete these tasks.

Is implicit learning related to the symptoms of autism spectrum disorders?

Our third and final goal was to examine whether implicit learning ability was related to the diagnostic symptoms of ASD. In our third study we included measures of symptoms in each of the three core areas that characterize ASD: social symptoms, communication symptoms, and restricted interest and repetitive behaviors. The measures of social symptoms included four theory of mind tasks, two subscales from the Childhood Social Behavior Questionnaire (CSBQ) (Luteijn *et al.* 2000), and two subscales from the Social Skills Rating Scale (Gresham and Elliott 1990). The measures of communication symptoms included two measures from the Test of the Reception of Grammar (Bishop 1982). The measures of restricted interests and repetitive behavior included two subscales from the Childhood Routine Inventory (Evans *et al.* 1997) and two subscales from the CSBQ. We constructed a composite measure of each core symptom area by standardizing and averaging across the measures in each symptom area. Additionally, we created a composite measure of implicit learning combining performance on the prototype and artificial grammar learning tasks.

Next, we looked at the relationship of implicit learning to the symptom measures for each diagnostic group. If implicit learning was a crucial cognitive process for understanding the symptoms of ASD, then implicit learning ought to be highly correlated with measures of the symptoms. We hypothesized that implicit learning would correlate especially highly with the social and communication symptoms. A great deal of other research has established that implicit learning is crucially important to understanding social and language information. We hypothesized that repetitive behaviors ought to be more weakly related to implicit learning because engaging in repetitive behaviors was seen as a coping strategy to help handle the discomfort of not understanding social and language information. Thus, repetitive behaviors ought to be linked to implicit learning but not as directly as social and communication processes. For ASD participants implicit learning performance was strongly related to both the social ($r = -0.53$, $p<0.001$) and communication ($r = -0.65$, $p<0.001$) symptoms. Implicit learning was also modestly related to repetitive behaviors ($r = -0.25$, $p<0.10$). These negative correlations indicate that those children with ASD who possessed better implicit learning performance showed fewer symptoms in all three areas. Those who performed poorly on the implicit learning tasks showed greater rates of symptoms, especially in the areas of social and communication impairments.

We also tested whether implicit learning performance was related to the symptom areas in children with TD. A similar, but weaker, pattern was expected for children with typical development given current thinking that ASD-like characteristics may represent a broad spectrum of symptoms. For children with TD, implicit learning was related, albeit more weakly, to social ($r = -0.19$, $p<0.20$), communication ($r = -0.29$, $p<0.05$), and repetitive behavior ($r = -0.33$, $p<0.05$) symptoms. These results support the claim that implicit learning is related to the symptoms seen in ASD.

In summary, our research supports the idea that individuals with ASD have impaired implicit learning, and as a result, they compensate by using explicit learning. Because implicit learning is a very early developing cognitive skill, we believe that impairments in implicit learning may underlie some of the behavioral symptoms that characterize ASD. In support of this notion, we have found that implicit learning is strongly correlated with the social and communication symptoms of ASD and modestly correlated with repetitive and restricted behaviors. If the behavioral symptoms of ASD are due to this implicit learning impairment, then this impairment should be considered when developing treatment and teaching approaches for affected individuals.

CLINICAL IMPLICATIONS OF IMPLICIT LEARNING DEFICITS IN ASD

Clinically, implicit learning may generally be described as 'picking up' on subtle stimulus cues and complex relationships between stimuli or situations. However, these cues and relationships are often so subtle that most individuals are not typically aware that they are gaining knowledge about them. For example, most people implicitly learn that if they smile at another person, that person is likely to smile at them in return. If individuals with ASD have impaired implicit learning, it is possible that the relationship between these two occurrences (i.e. smiling and being smiled at) is so subtle that they do not recognize it. This conceptualization of ASD leads to two broad options for treatment approaches: (1) demonstrate more salient complex relationships between stimuli and (2) teach the complex relationships between stimuli in an explicit manner.

Demonstrating more salient complex relationships between stimuli

The first broad treatment approach, demonstrating more salient complex relationships between stimuli, involves creating a learning environment that is more likely to facilitate implicit learning of complex relationships. In the same way that providing increased practice reading very simple words that have the same phonetic sounds (e.g. raw, saw, law) will improve phonetic decoding abilities in a child with a reading disability, maximizing the frequency and salience of complex relationships makes it more likely that individuals with ASD will learn them. The salience of complex relationships may be increased by increasing the frequency with which a relationship occurs and by isolating the relationship and displaying it without the presence of other environmental stimuli that may be distracting. For example, a child may learn to associate the word 'airplane' with airplanes by observing others point to them and say, 'airplane.' Typically, this pointing will exist amidst many other visual stimuli (e.g. clouds, trees, sun) and only on the rare occasions that an airplane is seen in the sky. To increase the visibility of this relationship between the actual vehicle and the word 'airplane,' extraneous stimuli could be removed (e.g. show an airplane with nothing else in sight) and the frequency of exposure to it could be increased (e.g. rather than naming an airplane when one happens to be in the sky, it could be named on a daily basis). Two existing treatment approaches for children with ASD that utilize these strategies are applied behavior analysis (ABA), as described by Ivar Lovaas (Lovaas and Smith 1989), and imitation therapy, as described by Klinger and Dawson (1992).

APPLIED BEHAVIOR ANALYSIS

Applied behavior analysis is a treatment approach based on learning theory (Lovaas and Smith 1989), and includes 'operant conditioning principles, such as shaping, chaining, discrimination training, and contingency management' (Smith *et al.* 1997, p.241). It has been the subject of many research studies and much debate among professionals (Lovaas, Smith and McEachin 1989; Smith and Lovaas 1997; Smith, McEachin and Lovaas 1993). Overall, ABA has had an enormous impact on the field and is considered here in terms of its theoretical utility. It is our suggestion that if ABA is an effective treatment, which it seems to be in some cases (Smith 1999), it is effective because it isolates stimuli and makes their complex or contingent relationships salient on a regular (frequent) basis.

ABA is typically conducted in a one-to-one setting with an extremely intensive time commitment (Smith *et al.* 1997). Early on, this treatment involves discrete trial training (DTT), in which a teacher presents a cue, prompts a response, and provides a consequence (Smith 2001). For example, the teacher may state the child's name and immediately bring a small tangible reinforcer (perhaps a small bit of food) to his or her eye level. When the child makes eye contact with the teacher, the reinforcer is immediately given to the child. After repeated, successful trials with this, chaining or shaping may be used to expand the response (i.e. eye contact). For example, the prompt (placing a reinforcer at eye level) may be delayed once the child begins making eye contact in response to their name alone (Maurice 1996). This isolated teaching of a specific skill (i.e. looking at someone when they call your name) makes the desired relation between a specific cue and a specific response very clear. At higher developmental levels, ABA may become more sophisticated, or complex, presumably because individuals with ASD are improving in their ability to learn in complex environments.

IMITATION THERAPY

Imitation therapy involves continuous imitation of a child's behavior to facilitate the child noticing and understanding the contingent relationship between their behavior and the behavior of others. Klinger and Dawson (1992) provide a step-by-step description of this treatment approach, noting that the purpose of the first phase 'is to help the child notice the similarity and contingent relationship between his or her actions and the adult's actions' (p.181). In short, imitation therapy involves a teacher or parent playing with a child using an identical set of toys (e.g. two matching pinwheels or two identical toy cars). As the child plays with his or her toy, the adult imitates the play with their toy. For example, if a child pats his pinwheel against a window, the adult should pat their pinwheel against the window. If the child stops this movement and puts his pinwheel on the floor, the adult puts their pinwheel on the floor right next to it. Whenever possible, the adult keeps their face at toy level to increase the chance of the child making eye contact with them during the play. As the child begins to notice that the adult is imitating him, he may begin to pause and watch for the adult to copy his actions. At this point, the adult tries to transition the play into a turn-taking game, which helps the child realize that other people's behavior is contingent upon theirs. For example, after the child begins pausing to watch for the adult to imitate his actions, the adult may initiate novel play with their toy to encourage the child to imitate their actions. Ideally, this type of imitation game could help children with ASD improve imitation skills, eye contact, and turn-taking skills, all of which involve complex relationships between stimuli.

Imitation therapy differs dramatically from ABA in several ways: (1) recommended time intensity (imitation therapy is recommended for 15–20 minutes a day, 5 times per week; ABA is typically recommended for 40 hours per week); (2) insistence on the child's cooperation (imitation therapy recommends terminating the session if the child cannot be easily redirected; ABA recommends insistence on the child's cooperation); and (3) focus of intervention (imitation therapy is primarily child-directed; ABA is a teacher-directed approach). However, in the context of this chapter, it is most interesting to consider the ways in which imitation therapy and ABA are similar to each other. We have included them in the same section of this chapter because they have several similar characteristics related to their creation of salient relationships between stimuli.

First, both imitation therapy and ABA recommend that therapy be conducted in a small, distraction-free environment, with a one-to-one student to teacher ratio. This results in both therapeutic techniques providing an isolated 'view' of contingent stimuli. We believe that recognizing the complex relationships between stimuli in a natural environment is particularly difficult for individuals with ASD. Thus, it seems reasonable that the isolation of such a relationship, which is a component of two different, yet effective therapy techniques, aids individuals with ASD in learning.

A second similarity between imitation therapy and ABA is the consistency and frequency with which one stimulus is presented in conjunction with another stimulus. Specifically, in imitation therapy, one action is always followed by a reciprocal, contingent action (e.g. every time a child taps their toy on a table, the adult also taps their toy on a table). Similarly, in ABA, a desired response is always reinforced (e.g. when teaching eye contact, the child is given a reward every time they look at the teacher). This is in stark contrast to the relatively infrequent and inconsistent presentation of contingent stimuli that occurs in the everyday world. As described earlier, with the example of a child learning the name for an airplane, most contingent relationships are not presented regularly or consistently every time the stimuli are present. However, just like distraction-free environments aid in identification of contingent relationships, more frequent and consistent presentation of the contingent relationship among stimuli should make it more salient. This new salience, in turn, should assist children with ASD in recognizing the relationship and committing it to memory.

According to our theoretical perspective, ABA and imitation therapy may be linked to two types of changes in learning. First, explicit learning may be more likely to occur because of the lack of extraneous stimuli and the increased repetitions that occur in DTT and imitation therapy. Second, if persons with ASD implicitly learn at a slower rate than persons with TD, the increased frequency and salience of the stimuli may facilitate implicit learning of complex relationships. That is, persons with ASD may simply require much more experience to show implicit learning that is similar to TD individuals.

Explicit teaching of the relation between contingent stimuli

The second broad treatment approach suggested by conceptualizing ASD as an impairment in implicit learning is to teach the relationship between specific stimuli in an explicit manner. This differs from the approach described above (i.e. making complex relationships between stimuli more salient) in that it is an explicit visual or verbal description of the relationship. Thus, rather than increasing the salience of the relationship between two stimuli or situations in hopes that it makes it easier for individuals with ASD to 'see' and implicitly learn relationships, this approach involves explicitly teaching individuals with ASD of the exact nature of the relationship. As increasing the salience of relationships between stimuli was compared to increased practice reading very simple words that have the same phonetic sounds, teaching the relationship between stimuli in an explicit manner can be compared to teaching reading to someone with a reading disability using a different approach (e.g. memorizing specific words using a whole language approach) rather than hoping the child will eventually learn to read using the typical approach. The existing treatment modality that best exemplifies this theoretical approach is the TEACCH (Treatment and Education of Autistic and other Communication handicapped CHildren) program, developed by Eric Schopler and Gary Mesibov (Schopler and Reichler 1971; Schopler *et al.* 1984; see also Ozonoff and Cathcart 1998, for a review of TEACCH treatment outcome studies). Other widespread treatment strategies focused on social skills interventions also fit in this category.

TEACCH

The TEACCH program involves explicitly demonstrating the organization and rules of a child's environment for them. This is accomplished through the use of visual systems that clearly depict what the child is supposed to do and what is going to happen in the environment. While this intervention was originally developed as a way to compensate for impairments in language and auditory processing in ASD by utilizing visual strategies (Schopler, Mesibov and Hearsey 1995), this approach also provides a mode of compensation for impairments in implicit learning. Specifically, the effective communication that is enabled by visual strategies creates a way to tell individuals with ASD about complex social and environmental relationships and processes.

One visual technique typically associated with the TEACCH approach is the use of schedules, which are visual systems for demonstrating what can be expected during a certain period of time. For developmentally young children, this may be in the form of a picture schedule of the sequence of their daily activities. For example, pictures of a book, a slide, and a cookie may be used to show a child that their morning will involve reading time, playground time, and snack time. This picture schedule not only demonstrates for the child which activity will follow another, but also teaches the contingency between tasks and activities in that one must be completed before the next may be started. Apart from a daily picture schedule, schedules for subsets of the day can be used to help children identify exactly what is expected of them in various settings. For example, a task-specific schedule for dressing may include pictures for pants, shirt, socks, and shoes.

Apart from schedules of specific tasks and activities, the TEACCH approach utilizes 'structured teaching.' A structured teaching program is a systematic way to teach children to remain at a table or work area and complete specific tasks. It can be used to prepare children for academic settings and, subsequently, to help children understand what is expected of them in such settings. Specifically, structured teaching involves arranging a set number of work tasks that will be followed by reinforcement (e.g. free time or a favorite toy). For developmentally young children this may include a table with three baskets lined up on it. The first two baskets contain specific work tasks (e.g. five shapes to insert into a shape sorter box, four beads to be strung onto a shoelace) and the third basket contains a favorite toy. The child is required to stay seated and complete the tasks in each basket, one at a time, before gaining access to the third basket and the play time that accompanies it. At a more complex level, this same system may be melded into a 'to do' list of several work tasks that the child must complete before being allowed time for recess. Essentially, this creates visual expectations for children's work and behavior that explicitly shows them what they are supposed to do. Additionally, structured teaching provides an environment that follows a set of fairly simple explicit rules and, thus, does not require a lot of implicit knowledge. This explicit demonstration of the way in which the child's environment operates is done visually (i.e. through picture schedules and 'to do' lists) because of the difficulty many children with ASD have in understanding the subtleties of language. Eventually, it is hoped that individuals with ASD will gain greater independence by learning to create their own schedules to provide structure and explicit rules for their activities.

SOCIAL SKILLS INTERVENTIONS

Social skills interventions in both individual and group format have become a common approach used in both clinical settings and schools. The goals of most of these interventions are to teach and rehearse specific social skills that individuals can use in everyday situations (see Barry *et al.* 2003 for a review). Various skills, such as greeting others, using eye contact during social interactions, giving and receiving compliments, and asking others appropriate questions, may be taught as step-by-step routines. Providing individuals with ASD-specific instructions about how to engage in social interaction is often done through explicit social rules and social scripts. For example, a script that can be used to demonstrate an appropriate way to greet someone may be:

1   turn your body toward the person

2   look at their eyes

3   smile

4   say, 'Hello.'

In addition to providing individuals with ASD a script like this, specific rules about when and where to use the script can be an important part of social skills training. For instance, it may be useful to create specific rules about using physical contact when greeting someone (e.g. it is okay to hug Grandma when you greet her, but it is not okay to hug the cashier at the store when you greet her).

Social Stories™ offer an additional technique for social skills interventions. Carol Gray (1998) describes Social Stories™ as 'short stories that describe social situations' (p.168). Her idea to use Social Stories™ as a way to inform individuals with ASD about the interchanges that occur in social situations has been a widely used teaching tool. In the context of this chapter, it is most important to note that Social Stories™ make the subtle nuances of specific social interactions and common occurrences explicit. For example, individuals with ASD may not automatically learn or understand the components of a social situation, such as shaking hands with someone else. While most children learn to engage in this common social ritual without being explicitly taught the components of the interaction, individuals with ASD may need explicit direction about how to engage in the interaction. An example of a Social Story™ that could explain this specific social interaction (i.e. shaking hands) comes from Gray (2000):

Learning to Shake Someone's Hand

When I meet new people, they sometimes hold out their hand. People do this as a way to say 'hello.' I can put my right hand toward theirs and tightly squeeze their hand. I will try to look at the person and smile. Sometimes they will smile back. After holding hands for a short time, each person may let go. I can learn to feel comfortable with this new way to say 'hello.' (Gray 2000, p.14, used by permission)

Stories like this fit into the category of treatment approaches that operate by explicitly teaching the complex, subtle relationship between contingent stimuli. Rather than isolating the interaction and prompting and reinforcing each of its components, as in ABA, the primary goal of the intervention is to explain the complete interaction in an explicit manner so that it can be purposefully used by persons with ASD.

The TEACCH approach, as well as the use of specific social skills interventions, help individuals with ASD to adapt to their environment. In short, rather than making environmental relationships more visible in the hopes that they will automatically 'see' them, these methods attempt to explicitly 'tell' individuals exactly what they should be looking at and 'seeing.'

According to our theoretical perspective, TEACCH and social skills interventions both seek to help persons with ASD compensate for their difficulties in implicitly understanding the world. By teaching a set of explicit rules, presumably persons with ASD are able to gain knowledge that most typically developing individuals have learned implicitly. Of course many of the social rules that govern our behavior are difficult to explicitly define. For instance, most individuals implicitly know when it is appropriate to greet an acquaintance with a hug and when a handshake is more appropriate. Explicit rules can be described that cover many situations, but it is difficult to explicitly describe the subtle nuances of social behavior in an explicit way. For instance, the rule 'It is appropriate to hug a relative but not someone who is not a relative' may be taught in social skills sessions. Unfortunately, in typical social settings there are many situations in which it is appropriate to hug someone who is not a relative. However, as persons with ASD develop and experience many different examples of social interactions, it is possible that they may be taught or can 'figure out' enough explicit rules to cover most social situations.

CONCLUSIONS

In this chapter, we proposed that studying the cognitive impairments present in persons with ASD may offer an insight into the neurobiological abnormalities in ASD, and may provide information regarding appropriate intervention strategies. That is, we suggest cognitive impairments are the intermediary link between the neuroanatomical abnormalities found in ASD and the behavioral symptoms of ASD. Using this model, we argued that because the behavioral symptoms of ASD are present by the end of the first year of life, the cognitive impairments in ASD must also be present by this time period. We then provided evidence from our research demonstrating that a typically early developing cognitive process, implicit learning, may be impaired in ASD. Furthermore, our research suggests that some persons with ASD are able to compensate for this impairment by using explicit, rule-based learning strategies. Finally, we provided evidence that impaired implicit learning may be related to poorer social skills, poorer language skills, and increased restricted and repetitive behaviors in persons with ASD. Using a learning disabilities model, we argue that these findings have significant implications for treatment. If implicit learning is simply slower in persons with ASD than in persons with TD, increasing the saliency and frequency of information should be effective. Alternatively, if implicit learning is a true 'deficit' for persons with ASD, a compensatory approach that explicitly teaches information that TD individuals learn implicitly should be the most effective. Future research is needed to determine whether impaired implicit learning represents a slower processing style or a true deficit.

REFERENCES

Ashby, F. G., Alfonso-Reese, L. A., Turken, U. and Waldron, E. M. (1998) 'A neuropsychological theory of multiple systems in category learning.' *Psychological Review 105*, 442–481.

Atkinson, J., Hood, B., Wattam-Bell, J. and Braddick, O. (1992) 'Changes in infants' ability to switch visual attention in the first three months of life.' *Perception 21*, 643–653.

Atwell, J. A., Conners, F. A. and Merrill, E. C. (2003) 'Implicit and explicit learning in young adults with mental retardation.' *American Journal of Mental Retardation 108*, 56–68.

Bachevalier, J. (1991) 'An animal model for childhood autism: memory loss and socioemotional disturbances following neonatal damage to the limbic system in monkeys.' In C. A. Tamminga and S. C. Schulz (eds) *Advances in Neuropsychiatry and Psychopharmacology: Vol. 1. Schizophrenia Research.* New York: Raven Press.

Bachevalier, J. (1994) 'Medial temporal lobe structures and autism: a review of clinical and experimental findings.' *Neuropsychologia 32*, 627–648.

Baron-Cohen, S. (2001) 'Theory of mind and autism: a review.' *International Review of Research in Mental Retardation 23*, 169–184.

Baron-Cohen, S., Cox, A., Baird, G., Swettenham, J., Nightingale, N., Morgan, K., Drew, A. and Charman, T. (1996) 'Psychological markers in the detection of autism in infancy in a large population.' *British Journal of Psychiatry 168*, 158–163.

Barry, T. D., Klinger, L. G., Lee, J. M., Palardy, N., Gilmore, T. and Bodin, S. D. (2003) 'Examining the effectiveness of an outpatient clinic-based social skills group for high-functioning children with autism.' *Journal of Autism and Developmental Disorders 33*, 685–701.

Bauman, M. and Kemper, T. (1988) 'Limbic and cerebellar abnormalities: consistent findings in infantile autism.' *Journal of Neuropathology and Experimental Neurology 47*, 369.

Berger, H., van Spaendonck, K., Horstink, M., Buytenhuijs, E., Lammers, P. and Cools, A. (1993) 'Cognitive shifting as a predictor of progress in social understanding in high-functioning adolescents with autism: a prospective study.' *Journal of Autism and Developmental Disorders 23*, 341–359.

Bishop, D. V. (1982) 'Comprehension of spoken, written and signed sentences in childhood language disorders.' *Journal of Child Psychology and Psychiatry 23*, 1–20.

Bomba, P. C. and Siqueland, E. R. (1983) 'The nature and structure of infant form categories.' *Journal of Experimental Child Psychology 35*, 294–328.

Bowler, D. M., Matthews, N. J. and Gardiner, J. M. (1997) 'Asperger's syndrome and memory: similarity to autism but not amnesia.' *Neuropsychologia 35*, 65–70.

Butterworth, G. (1995) 'Origins of mind in perception and action.' In C. Moore and P. Dunham (eds) *Joint Attention: Its Origins and Role in Development*. Hillsdale, NJ: Lawrence Erlbaum Associates.

Casey, B. J., Gordon, C. T., Mannheim, G. B. and Rumsey, J. M. (1993) 'Dysfunctional attention in autistic savants.' *Journal of Clinical and Experimental Neuropsychology 15*, 933–946.

Ciesielski, K. T. and Harris, R. J. (1997) 'Factors related to performance failure on executive tasks in autism.' *Child Neuropsychology 3*, 1–12.

Courchesne, E., Yeung-Courchesne, R., Press, G. A., Hesselink, J. R. and Jernigan, T. L. (1988) 'Hypoplasia of cerebellar vermal lobules VI and VII in autism.' *New England Journal of Medicine 318*, 1349–1354.

Courchesne, E., Townsend, J. P., Akshoomoff, N. A., Yeung-Courchesne, R., Press, G. A., Murakami, J. W. *et al.* (1994) 'A new finding: impairment in shifting attention in autistic and cerebellar patients.' In H. Broman and J. Grafman (eds) *Atypical Cognitive Deficits in Developmental Disorders: Implications for Brain Function*. Hillsdale, NJ: Lawrence Erlbaum Associates.

Dawson, G. and Galpert, L. (1990) 'Mothers' use of imitative play for facilitating social responsiveness and toy play in young autistic children.' *Development and Psychopathology 2*, 151–162.

Dawson, G. and Osterling, J. (1997) 'Early intervention in autism.' In M. J. Guralnick (ed.) *The Effectiveness of Early Intervention*. Baltimore, MD: Brookes.

Dawson, G., Meltzoff, A. N., Osterling, J., Rinaldi, J. and Brown, E. (1998) 'Children with autism fail to orient to naturally occurring social stimuli.' *Journal of Autism and Developmental Disorders 28*, 479–485.

Dunn, L. M. and Dunn, L. M. (1981) *Peabody Picture Vocabulary Test-Revised: Manual*. Circle Pines, MN: American Guidance Service.

Evans, D., Leckman, J., Carter, A., Reznick, S., Henshaw, D., King, R. and Pauls, D. (1997) 'Ritual, habit, and perfectionism: the prevalence and development of compulsive-like behavior in normal young children.' *Child Development 68*, 58–68.

Ferrara, C. and Hill, S. (1980) 'The responsiveness of autistic children to the predictability of social and non-social toys.' *Journal of Autism and Developmental Disorders 10*, 51–57.

Franks, J. J. and Bransford, J. D. (1971) 'Abstraction of visual patterns.' *Journal of Experimental Psychology 90*, 65–74.

Frith, U. and Happe, F. (1994) 'Autism: beyond "theory of mind".' *Cognition 50*, 115–132.

Gomez, R. L. and Gerken, L. (1999) 'Artificial grammar learning by one-year-olds leads to specific and abstract knowledge.' *Cognition 70*, 109–135.

Grandin, T. (1995) 'How people with autism think.' In E. Schopler and G. B. Mesibov (eds) *Learning and Cognition in Autism*. New York: Plenum Press.

Gray, C. (1998) 'Social stories and comic strip conversations with students with Asperger syndrome and high-functioning autism.' In E. Schopler, G. B. Mesibov and L. J. Kunce (eds) *Asperger Syndrome or High Functioning Autism?* New York: Plenum Press.

Gray, C. (2000) *The New Social Story Book*. Arlington, TX: Future Horizons Inc.

Gresham, F. M. and Elliott, S. N. (1990) *Social Skills Rating System (SSRS)*. Circle Pines, MN: American Guidance Service.

Hadwin, J. A., Baron-Cohen, S., Howlin, P. and Hill, K. (1996) 'Can we teach children with autism to understand emotions, belief, or pretence?' *Development and Psychopathology 8*, 345–365.

Happe, F. G. (1995) 'The role of age and verbal ability in the theory of mind task performance of subjects with autism.' *Child Development 66*, 843–855.

Hayes, B. K. and Taplin, J. E. (1993) 'Developmental differences in the use of prototype and exemplar-specific information.' *Journal of Experimental Child Psychology 55*, 329–352.

Hermelin, B. and O'Connor, N. (1986) 'Idiot savant calendrical calculators: rules and regularities.' *Psychological Medicine 16*, 885–893.

Hoffman, J. and Koch, I. (1998) 'Implicit learning of loosely defined structures.' In M. A. Stadler and P. A. Frensch (eds) *Handbook of Implicit Learning*. Thousand Oaks, CA: Sage Publications.

Iarocci, G. and Burack, J. A. (2004) 'Intact covert orienting to peripheral cues among children with autism.' *Journal of Autism and Developmental Disorders 34*, 257–264.

Johnson, M. H., Posner, M. I. and Rothbart, M. K. (1991) 'Components of visual orienting in early infancy: contingency learning, anticipatory looking, and disengaging.' *Journal of Cognitive Neuroscience 3*, 335–344.

Jolliffe, T. and Baron-Cohen, S. (1997) 'Are people with autism and Asperger syndrome faster than normal on the Embedded Figures Test?' *Journal of Child Psychology and Psychiatry 38*, 527–534.

Kaufman, A. S. and Kaufman, N. L. (1990) *Kaufman Brief Intelligence Test (K-BIT)*. Circle Pines, MN: American Guidance Service.

Klin, A., Jones, W., Schultz, R., Volkmar, F. and Cohen, D. (2002) 'Visual fixation patterns during viewing of naturalistic social situations as predictors of social competence in individuals with autism.' *Archives of General Psychiatry 59*, 809–816.

Klinger, L. G. and Dawson, G. (1992) 'Facilitating early social and communicative development in children with autism.' In S. F. Warren and J. Reichle (eds) *Causes and Effects in Communication and Language Intervention*. Baltimore, MD: Paul H. Brookes Publishing.

Klinger, L. G. and Dawson, G. (1995) 'A fresh look at categorization abilities in persons with autism.' In E. Schopler and G. B. Mesibov (eds) *Learning and Cognition in Autism*. New York: Plenum.

Klinger, L. G., and Dawson, G. (2001) 'Prototype formation in autism.' *Development and Psychopathology 13*, 111–124.

Klinger, L. G. Lee, J. M., Bush, D., Klinger, M. R. and Crump, S. E. (2001) 'Implicit learning in autism: artificial grammar learning.' Presented at the Biennial Meeting of the Society for Research in Child Development, Minneapolis, MN, April.

Klinger, L. G., Dawson, G. and Renner, P. (2003) 'Autistic disorder.' In E. J. Mash and R. A. Barkley (eds) *Child Psychopathology* (2nd edn). New York: The Guilford Press.

Lee, J., Klinger, L. G., Klinger, M. R. and Atwell, J. A. (2000) 'Implicit learning and children and adults: consistency across development.' Presented at the Biennial Meeting of the Conference on Human Development, Memphis, TN, April.

Leekam, S. and Moore, C. (2001) 'The development of attention and joint attention in children with autism.' In J. A. Burack, T. Charman, N. Yirmiya and P. R. Zelazo (eds) *The Development of Autism: Perspectives from Theory and Research*. Mahwah, NJ: Lawrence Erlbaum.

Lewicki, P. and Hill, T. (1987) 'Unconscious processes as explanations of behavior in cognitive, personality, and social psychology.' *Personality and Social Psychology Bulletin 13*, 355–362.

Lieberman, M. D. (2000) 'Intuition: a social cognitive neuroscience approach.' *Psychological Bulletin 126*, 109–137.

Lovaas, O. I. and Smith, T. (1989) 'A comprehensive behavioral theory of autistic children: paradigm for research and treatment.' *Journal of Behavior Therapy and Experimental Psychiatry 20*, 17–29.

Lovaas, O. I., Koegel, R. L. and Schreibman, L. (1979) 'Stimulus overselectivity in autism: a review of research.' *Psychological Bulletin 86*, 1236–1254.

Lovaas, O. I., Smith, T. and McEachin, J. J. (1989) 'Clarifying comments on the Young Autism Study: reply to Schopler, Short, and Mesibov.' *Journal of Consulting and Clinical Psychology 57*, 165–167.

Luteijn, E., Luteijn, F., Jackson, S., Volkmar, F. and Minderaa, R. (2000) 'The Children's Social Behavior Questionnaire for milder variants of PDD problems: evaluation and psychometric characteristics.' *Journal of Autism and Developmental Disorders 30*, 317–330.

McGeorge, P., Crawford, J. R. and Kelly, S. W. (1997) 'The relationships between psychometric intelligence and learning in an explicit and an implicit task.' *Journal of Experimental Psychology: Learning, Memory, and Cognition 23*, 239–245.

Markman, E. M. (1989) *Categorization and Naming in Children: Problems of Induction.* Cambridge, MA: MIT Press.

Maurice, C. (1993) *Let Me Hear Your Voice: A Family's Triumph Over Autism.* New York: Fawcett Columbine.

Maurice, C. (ed.) (1996) *Behavioral Intervention for Young Children with Autism.* Austin, TX: Pro-Ed.

Maybery, M., Taylor, M. and O'Brien-Malone, A. (1995) 'Implicit learning: sensitive to age but not IQ.' *Australian Journal of Psychology 47*, 8–17.

Meulemans, T., Van der Linden, M. and Perruchet, P. (1998) 'Implicit sequence learning in children.' *Journal of Experimental Child Psychology 69*, 199–221.

Mottron, L. and Burack, J. A. (2001) 'Enhanced perceptual functioning in the development of autism.' In J. A. Burack, T. Charman, N. Yirmiya and P. R. Zelazo (eds) *The Development of Autism: Perspectives from Theory and Research.* Mahwah, NJ: Erlbaum.

Osterling, J. and Dawson, G. (1994) 'Early recognition of children with autism: a study of first birthday home videotapes.' *Journal of Autism and Developmental Disorders 24*, 247–257.

Osterling, J. A., Dawson, G. and Munson, J. A. (2002) 'Early recognition of 1-year-old infants with autism spectrum disorder versus mental retardation.' *Development and Psychopathology 14*, 239–251.

Ozonoff, S. and Cathcart, K. (1998) 'Effectiveness of a home program intervention for young children with autism.' *Journal of Autism and Developmental Disorders 28*, 25–32.

Ozonoff, S. and Jensen, J. (1999) 'Brief report: specific executive function profiles in three neurodevelopmental disorders.' *Journal of Autism and Developmental Disorders 29*, 171–177.

Ozonoff, S. and McEvoy, R. E. (1994) 'A longitudinal study of executive function and theory of mind development in autism.' *Development and Psychopathology 6*, 415–431.

Ozonoff, S. and Miller, J. N. (1995) 'Teaching theory of mind: a new approach to social skills training for individuals with autism.' *Journal of Autism and Developmental Disorders 25*, 415–433.

Pascualvaca, D. M., Fantie, B. D, Papageorgiou, M. and Mirsky, A. F. (1998) 'Attentional capacities in children with autism: is there a general deficit in shifting focus?' *Journal of Autism and Developmental Disorders 28,* 467–478.

Piven, J., Berthier, M. L., Starkstein, S. E., Nehme, E., Pearlson, G. and Folstein, S. (1990) 'Magnetic resonance imaging evidence for a defect of cerebral cortical development in autism.' *American Journal of Psychiatry 147*, 734–739.

Piven, J., Arndt, S., Bailey, J. and Andreasen, N. (1996) 'Regional brain enlargement in autism: a magnetic resonance imaging study.' *Journal of the American Academy of Child and Adolescent Psychiatry 35*, 530–536.

Plaisted, K. C. (2001) 'Reduced generalization in autism: an alternative to weak central coherence.' In J. A. Burack, T. Charman, N. Yirmiya and P. R. Zelazo (eds) *The Development of Autism: Perspectives from Theory and Research.* Mahwah, NJ: Erlbaum.

Posner, M. I. and Keele, S. W. (1968) 'On the genesis of abstract ideas.' *Journal of Experimental Psychology 77*, 353–363.

Rauch, S. L., Savage, C. R., Alpert, N. M., Dougherty, D., Kendrick, A., Curran, T. *et al.* (1997) 'Probing striatal function in obsessive-compulsive disorder: a PET study of implicit sequence learning.' *Journal of Neuropsychiatry and Clinical Neurosciences 9*, 568–574.

Reber, A. S. (1989) 'Implicit learning and tacit knowledge.' *Journal of Experimental Psychology: General 118*, 219–235.

Reber, A. S. (1993) *Implicit Learning and Tacit Knowledge: An Essay on the Cognitive Unconscious.* New York: Oxford University Press.

Reber, A. S., Walkenfeld, F. F. and Hernstadt, R. (1991) 'Implicit and explicit learning: individual differences and IQ.' *Journal of Experimental Psychology: Learning, Memory, and Cognition 17*, 888–896.

Renner, P., Karatheodoris, L., Klinger, L. G., Klinger, M. R. and Dawkins, L. S. (2003) 'Exogenous versus endogenous orienting in high-functioning children with Pervasive Developmental Disorder.' Presented at the Biennial Meeting of the Society for Research in Child Development, Tampa, FL.

Ruff, H. A. and Rothbart, M. K. (1996) *Attention in Early Development: Themes and Variations.* New York: Oxford University Press.

Saffran, J. R., Aslin, R. N. and Newport, E. L. (1996) 'Statistical learning by 8-month-old infants.' *Science 274*, 1926–1928.

Saffran, J. R., Newport, E. L., Aslin, R. N., Tunick, R. A. and Barrueco, S. (1997) 'Incidental language learning: listening (and learning) out of the corner of your ear.' *Psychological Science 8*, 101–105.

Schopler, E. and Reichler, R. J. (1971) 'Parents as co-therapists in the treatment of psychotic children.' *Journal of Autism and Childhood Schizophrenia 1*, 87–102.

Schopler, E., Mesibov, G. B., Shigley, R. H. and Bashford, A. (1984) 'Helping autistic children through their parents: the TEACCH model.' In E. Schopler and G. B. Mesibov (eds) *The Effects of Autism on the Family.* New York: Plenum Press.

Schopler, E., Mesibov, G. B. and Hearsey, K. A. (1995) 'Structured teaching in the TEACCH system.' In E. Schopler and G. B. Mesibov (eds) *Learning and Cognition in Autism.* New York: Plenum Press.

Smith, T. (1999) 'Outcome of early intervention for children with autism.' *Clinical Psychology: Science and Practice 6*, 33–49.

Smith, T. (2001) 'Discrete trial training in the treatment of autism.' *Focus on Autism and Other Developmental Disabilities 16*, 2, 86–92.

Smith, T. and Lovaas, O. I. (1997) 'The UCLA young autism project: a reply to Gresham and MacMillan.' *Behavioral Disorders 22*, 202–218.

Smith, T., McEachin, J. J. and Lovaas, O. I. (1993) 'Comments on replication and evaluation of outcome.' *American Journal on Mental Retardation 97*, 385–391.

Smith, T., Eikeseth, S., Klevstrand, M. and Lovaas, O. I. (1997) 'Intensive behavioral treatment for preschoolers with severe mental retardation and pervasive developmental disorder.' *American Journal of Mental Retardation 102*, 238–249.

Strauss, M. S. (1979) 'Abstraction of prototypical information by adults and 10-month-old infants.' *Journal of Experimental Psychology: Human Learning and Memory 5*, 616–632.

Townsend, J., Courchesne, E. and Egaas, B. (1996) 'Slowed orienting of covert visual-spatial attention in autism: specific deficits associated with cerebellar and parietal abnormality.' *Development and Psychopathology 8*, 563–584.

Townsend, J., Harris, N. S. and Courchesne, E. (1996) 'Visual attention abnormalities in autism: delayed orienting to location.' *Journal of International Neuropsychology Society 2*, 541–550.

Walton, G. E. and Bower, T. G. R. (1993) 'Newborns form "prototypes" in less than one minute.' *Psychological Science 4*, 203–205.

Williams, D. (1992) *Nobody Nowhere: The Extraordinary Autobiography of an Autistic.* New York: Times Books.

Woodcock, R. W., McGrew, K. S. and Mather, N. (2001) *Woodcock-Johnson III.* Itasca, IL: Riverside Publishing.

Younger, B. (1985) 'The segregation of items into categories by ten-month-old infants.' *Child Development 56*, 1574–1583.

Chapter 5

Joint Attention and Autism

Theory, Assessment and Neurodevelopment

Peter Mundy and Danielle Thorp

Social impairments, along with problems with communication and repetitive behaviors, constitute a cardinal symptom domain of autism (APA 2000). Therefore, one important goal of research on autism is to fully describe the nature of the social impairments that are specific to autism. A second equally important goal is to describe neural systems that may be involved in the development of these social impairments. The latter is especially important because understanding the social neurodevelopment of autism may lead to insights about the types of behavioral and medical interventions that may work best with different groups of children with autism. It is also likely that a deeper understanding of the neural nature of autism will lead to better methods of diagnosis and a more complete appreciation of the complex system of genetic and environment interactions that contribute to this disorder.

Given the significance of inquiry in this arena it is not surprising that several different but complementary approaches have recently emerged in the literature with respect to identifying the neural systems involved in social behavior (Mundy 2003). One approach has been to identify anomalies in the neural functions of people with autism. Then researchers have attempted to relate these anomalies to the social behavior impairments of autism. Work on orienting difficulties and related cerebellar cell atypicalities in autism provide a seminal example of this approach (Carper and Courschesne 2000; Courschesne *et al.* 1994; Townsend *et al.* 2001).

Another approach begins with human and comparative studies that suggest that social perception, such as face recognition or interpreting the direction of gaze of a social partner, may be supported by a complex ventromedial 'social brain' circuit. This circuit involves the orbitofrontal cortex, temporal cortical areas including the superior temporal sulcus (STS) as well as superior temporal gyrus (STG), and subcortical areas such as the amygdala (Adolphs 2001; Brothers 1990; Elgar and Cambell 2001; Kawashima *et al.* 1999; LeDoux 1989; Wantanabe 1999). Behavioral deficits in social perception have long been recognized in autism (e.g. Hobson 1993; Sigman *et al.* 1992). Therefore, a major goal of this second approach is to examine the hypothesis that deficits in ventral 'social brain' systems give rise to fundamental impairments in the social perception and social behavior of children with autism (e.g. Baron-Cohen *et al.* 1999; Critchley *et al.* 2000; see Figure 5.1).

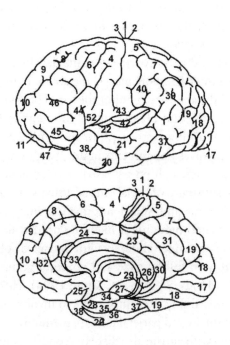

Figure 5.1 Lateral (top) and medial (bottom) illustrations of Brodmann's cytoarchitectonic areas of the cerebral cortex (adapted from Gazzagnia, Ivry and Mangun 1998). The dorsal medial-frontal cortex (DMFC) includes areas 8 and 9. The anterior cingulate is depicted as area 24. The ventral 'social brain' includes the orbitofrontal cortex (area 11), the amygdala (area 34), and the superior temporal gyrus (area 22) and the superior temporal sulcus (the division between areas 21 and 22)

A third and perhaps most expedient approach is to begin with the fundamental social symptoms of autism and attempt to work backward from behavior to the brain to understand the neural substrates of these pathognomic features of the syndrome. For example, one DSM-IV social impairment symptom of autism is 'a lack of spontaneously seeking to share experience with others' as manifest in impairments in joint attention behaviors such as showing or pointing. This type of disturbance reflects 'joint attention' impairment in autism (Mundy 1995). So, several research groups have begun to explore the neural and neuropsychological foundations of the development of this type of behavior

(Dawson *et al.* 2002; Griffith *et al.* 1999; Mundy, Card and Fox 2000). Research of this kind focuses on impairments in neural processes that may be involved in the *social output systems* that mediate the spontaneous organization, generation, and expression of social attention, behavior, and cognition (Klin *et al.* 2003; Minshew, Meyer and Goldstein 2002; Mundy 1995, Mundy and Neal 2001; Leslie 1987). Impairments in social output, or the flexible generation of adaptive social behaviors, are a hallmark of autism, and improvement in the flexible self-initiation of social-communication behaviors is a fundamental goal of intervention for autism (Mundy and Crowson 1997). Therefore, the study of neural output systems involved in the self-initiation of social behaviors and social attention is an important complement to 'social brain' research and its focus on perception or the *social input system.*

Another related tenet of this approach is that the development of functional social behavior involves at least three components: (1) the ability to monitor one's own social output (self-monitor), (2) the ability to monitor the social behavior of others (social perception or other monitoring), and (3) the ability to integrate information from self-monitoring and other monitoring systems (Frith and Frith 2001). Understanding the degree to which autism involves impairments in one, two, or all three of these components is an essential goal of research on pervasive developmental disorders.

Of course the neural substrates of social output systems may be different from those involved in social perception and social information integration systems. Thus, a complex, multi-process neural model will likely be needed to understand the social symptoms of autism. For example, children with autism display difficulty with the development of the ability to follow gaze and pointing gestures of others (Leekam, Lopez and Moore 2001; Mundy, Sigman and Kasari 1994). This is a type of responsive joint attention skill and this ability domain appears to involve primarily neural activity in the superior temporal sulcus and parietal lobes (e.g. Mundy *et al.* 2000; Vaughan and Mundy in press). Children with autism also display a robust disturbance of the tendency to initiate joint attention bids (e.g. show or point to object) to spontaneously share experience, and this ability domain appears to involve activity of the dorso-medial and orbito-medial frontal cortex, but relatively little input from the parietal and temporal cortex (Caplan *et al.* 1993; Dawson *et al.* 2002; Henderson *et al.* 2002; Mundy *et al.* 2000). Hence, impairments in different cortical systems may be involved in deficits in initiating and responding to the social communication bids of others. The cortical and subcortical regions involved in these systems are illustrated in Figure 5.1.

Understanding the neural systems that support the development of joint attention and early social communication skills provides new hypotheses about the nature of the social disturbance in autism. Examining these hypotheses will, it is hoped, lead to valuable insights about the nature of this disorder and how to improve methods for diagnosis and treatment. Therefore, in this chapter we will provide an overview of the literature on the neural substrates of joint attention development and consider what utility this information may offer for clinical research on autism. This discussion begins with a review of our understanding of the nature and significance of joint attention impairments in autism.

JOINT ATTENTION AND SOCIAL IMPAIRMENT IN AUTISM

The early social-communication disturbance of autism is exemplified by a robust developmental failure of joint attention skills development (Mundy and Sigman 1989). Joint attention skills refer to the capacity of individuals to coordinate attention with a social partner in relation to some object or event. In the first years of life this may only involve the social coordination of overt aspects of visual attention, such as when a toddler shows a toy to a parent. Theoretically, though, this capacity eventually becomes elaborated and integral to the social coordination of covert aspects of attention, as when social partners coordinate attention to psychological phenomena, such as ideas, intentions, or emotions (Tomasello 1995).

This capacity begins to emerge by at least six months of age (Scaife and Bruner 1975) and takes several different behavioral forms. One behavior involves an infant's ability to follow the direction of gaze, head turn, and/or pointing gesture of another person (Scaife and Bruner 1975). This behavior may be referred to as the skill of responding to joint attention (RJA) (Mundy, Hogan and Doehring 1996; Seibert, Hogan and Mundy 1982). Another type of skill involves the infant's use of eye contact and/or deictic gestures (e.g. pointing or showing) to spontaneously initiate coordinated attention with a social partner. The latter type of protodeclarative act (Bates 1976) may be referred to as the skill of initiating joint attention (IJA) (Mundy *et al.* 1996; Seibert *et al.* 1982). These behaviors, and especially IJA, appear to serve social functions. That is, the goal and reinforcement of these behaviors has been interpreted to revolve around sharing experience with others and the positive valence such early sharing has for the young child (Bates 1976; Mundy 1995). Alternatively, social attention coordination may also be used for less social but more instrumental purposes (Bates 1976). So, for example, infants and young children may use eye contact and gestures to initiate attention coordination with another person to elicit aid in obtaining an object or event. This may be referred to as a protoimperative act (Bates 1976) or initiating behavior request (IBR) (Mundy *et al.* 1996). Figure 5.2 provides illustrations of IJA, RJA, and IBR behaviors.

Joint attention skills are a critical milestone of early development and social learning (Bakeman and Adamson 1984; Baldwin 1995). Much of early language acquisition, for example, takes place in unstructured or incidental social-learning situations where: (a) the parent provides a learning opportunity by referring to a new object or event in the environment, but (b) the infant may need to discriminate among a number of stimuli in the environment in order to focus on the correct object/event to acquire the appropriate new word association. Thus, the infant is confronted with the possibility of referential mapping errors (Baldwin 1995). To deal with this problem infants may utilize the direction of gaze of the parent (i.e. use RJA skill) to limit the number of potential stimuli to attend to and increase the likelihood of a correct word learning experience (Baldwin 1995). Similarly, when an infant initiates bids for joint attention, the responsive caregiver may follow the child's line of regard and take advantage of the child's focus of attention to provide a new word in a context that maximizes the opportunity to learn (cf. Tomasello 1995). Hence, joint attention may be regarded as an early developing *self-organizing facility* that is critical to much of subsequent social and cognitive development (e.g. Baldwin 1995; Mundy and Neal 2001).

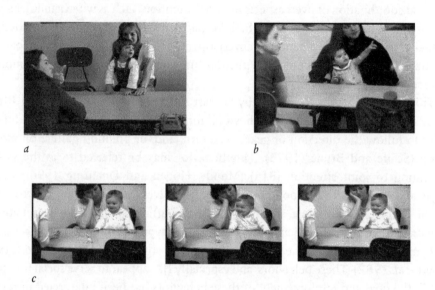

Figure 5.2 Examples of (a) responding to joint attention bids, (b) initiating joint attention with a point, and (c) initiating joint attention with alternating gaze, from the Early Social Communication Scales (ESCS; Seibert, Hogan and Mundy 1982; Mundy, Hogan and Doehring 1996). Reproduced from Cicchetti, D. and Cohen, D. J. (eds) (2006) Developmental Psychopathology, Theory and Method (2nd edn). Copyright © John Wiley & Sons, Inc. 2006. Reproduced by permission

Children with autism, unfortunately, display robust levels of impairments in joint attention development from at least as early as 12 to 18 months of age (Osterling, Dawson and Munson 2002; Swettenham *et al.* 1998). These impairments may be associated with a disruption of an early self-organizing process in social learning that contributes to the subsequent problems in behavioral, intellectual, and even the neural development of children with autism (Mundy and Crowson 1997; Mundy and Neal 2001).

Interestingly, though, young children with autism display dissociation in the development of joint attention skills. While children with autism display deficits in both IJA and RJA skills, they display less pronounced deficits in IBR or social attention coordination for instrumental purposes (Mundy *et al.* 1986). Moreover, young children with autism display basic gaze-following ability by two years of age (Chawarska, Klin and Volkmar 2003) and problems in RJA may remit among older children with autism or those with higher mental ages (Leekam *et al.* 2001; Mundy *et al.* 1994; Sigman and Ruskin 1999). The impairment in IJA, however, appears to be more robust with the expression of this impairment evident in older children (Mundy *et al.* 1994; Sigman and Ruskin 1999). Research also suggests that IJA but not RJA is related to individual differences in social symptom intensity in preschool children with autism (Mundy *et al.* 1994). Indeed, the chronic and fundamental nature of IJA impairment is emphasized by observations that differences in IJA among two- to six-year-old children with autism significantly predicted their tendency to spontaneously initiate social interaction with others seven to ten years later in life (Lord *et al.* 2003; Sigman and Ruskin 1999).

A dissociated pattern of IJA and RJA development is also observed in typical development and may occur because IJA and RJA reflect different integrations of social-cognitive and social-emotional processes (Mundy *et al.* 2000). IJA reflects the tendency to spontaneously initiate social attention coordination behavior, whereas RJA is a measure of the tendency to respond to another person's signal to shift attention. Hence, IJA may be more affected by executive and social-motivation processes involved in the generation and self-initiation of behavioral goals than RJA (Mundy 1995; Mundy *et al.* 2000). In particular, IJA appears to involve the tendency to spontaneously initiate episodes of sharing the affective experience of an object or an event with a social partner (Mundy, Kasari and Sigman 1992). Indeed, a significant component of IJA disturbance in autism may be explained in terms of an attenuation of the tendency to initiate episodes of shared positive affect with a social partner (Kasari *et al.* 1990).

This literature has led to the instantiation of joint attention disturbance, and especially IJA disturbance, as a central symptom of autism. For example, a 'lack of spontaneous seeking to share enjoyment, interests, or achievements with other people (e.g. by a lack of showing, bringing, or pointing out objects of interest)' is now one of four cardinal symptoms of the social impairment of autism in a current nosology (APA 2000, p.75). Thus, many of the current diagnostic and screening instruments for autism include measures of joint attention, including the 'gold standard' Autism Diagnostic Observation Schedule (ADOS) (Lord *et al.* 1999). The ADOS even reflects the notion of a developmental dissociation in joint attention. Measures used for diagnosis with the youngest children (Module 1) include both IJA and RJA assessments. Module 2 is designed for developmentally more advanced children and, although it includes measures of both IJA and RJA, only the information for IJA is included in the diagnostic scoring algorithm.

Thus, research suggests that both IJA and RJA impairments may be important components of the early development of autism. However, with development, dissociation appears to occur such that the intensity of RJA impairments decreases, but IJA impairments remaining robust. This dissociation in development suggests that the neural processes involved in IJA and RJA may diverge. Understanding this divergence and the neurodevelopment of IJA and RJA may provide insights into the neural nature of autism.

THE NEURAL SUBSTRATE OF RJA

Responding to joint attention is a complex behavior domain involving the perception and processing of social information from multiple aspects of behavior, such as the direction of gaze, head orientation, and/or pointing gestures of a social partner. Researchers may study responses to all of these behaviors displayed at the same time and we refer to this as RJA research. However, often researchers use less naturalistic, but more controlled paradigms to examine just the response to one behavior, especially responses to direction of gaze. This component of RJA may be referred to as 'gaze-following.'

Since RJA and gaze-following involve social perception, ventromedial 'social brain' circuits may support them. In particular the results of several studies converge to suggest that gaze-following and RJA may be mediated by part of this social brain circuit contained primarily within the superior temporal sulcus, superior temporal gyrus, and adjacent parietal areas (e.g. Brodmann's area (BA) 40 (see Figure 5.1)). These temporal and parietal areas of the brain are thought to contain neural networks that respond preferentially to faces, animate movement, and social spatial orientation including head, eye, and body orientation (e.g. Calder *et al.* 2002; Emery 2000).

Wicker *et al.* (2002) observed that neural groups in the posterior STS were activated in response to faces with direct or horizontally averted eye gaze, but not to faces with downward eye gaze. Wicker *et al.*, however, did not observe differences between direct and averted eye gaze conditions. Alternatively, Puce *et al.* (1998) reported that video of face stimuli with gaze moving horizontally from forward to averted gaze elicited greater posterior STS activation compared to faces with static forward gaze. Face-matching on the basis of direction of gaze also elicited activation of neurons in the left posterior STS, while identity-based face-matching elicited bilateral activation from the fusiform and inferior occipital gyri (Hoffman and Haxby 2000). Similarly, George, Driver and Dolan (2001) reported that direct gaze stimuli elicited more fusiform activation than averted gaze stimuli. Finally, Kingstone, Friesen and Gazzagnia (2000) reported data in two split-brain patients that were consistent with the notion that parietal as well as temporal subsystems specialized for face processing, and processing of information relevant to spatial orientation combine to support the development of gaze-following.

Mundy *et al.* (2000) have also reported observations linking RJA to parietal processes. In a study of 32 typically developing infants these authors examined the longitudinal relations between baseline EEG at 14 months and RJA at 18 months as measured on the Early Social Communication Scales (ESCS) (Mundy *et al.* 2003; Seibert *et al.* 1982). The ESCS is a structured, 20-minute observation instrument that provides quantitative measures of the development of RJA, IJA, and other non-verbal communication skills between 8 and 24 months of age. The EEG data were collected with a lycra cap with electrodes placed bilaterally at dorso-frontal, central, temporal, parietal, and occipital sites. RJA at 18 months was predicted by EEG indexes of left-parietal activation and right-parietal deactivation at 14 months. The location of the neural generators of EEG data was difficult to definitively delineate in this study. Nevertheless the EEG data were quite consistent with previous research (Emery 2000) that suggested that parietal areas specialized for spatial orienting and attention, along with adjacent temporal systems specialized for processing gaze, may contribute to gaze-following or related RJA skill development.

The results of these human imaging, electrophysiology, and neuropsychological studies are also consistent with earlier reports from comparative research that provide experimental evidence of temporal (i.e. STS) and adjacent parietal involvement in gaze-following (Emery 2000). In two studies pre-surgical monkeys demonstrated a clear ability to discriminate face stimuli on the basis of direction of gaze. After resection of the STS, however, the gaze discrimination abilities of the monkeys fell to chance (Cambell et al. 1990; Heyward and Cowley 1992). Eacott et al. (1993) compared two groups of monkeys, those with and without STS surgically induced lesions, on a task of discriminating pairs of eyes directed straight ahead or averted five or more degrees. The results indicated that the non-lesion monkeys were capable of discriminating targets involving horizontal eye gaze shifts of greater than five degrees, but the STS lesion animals were not. However, Eacott et al. also reported that the lesion animals performed worse than the non-lesion animals on a non-social task involving the discrimination between abstract forms.

The latter observation reminds us that, although research is beginning to pinpoint the systems involved in gaze-following and social perception, the specificity of these systems for social versus non-social processing has still to be definitively examined. One recent study, though, has addressed a related issue in imaging research on human gaze-following. Hooker (2002) used whole brain fMRI to compare neural activity in response to: (1) horizontal eye movement stimuli that provide directional information about where a visual stimulus would appear, or (2) arrow stimuli that provided equivalent directional information, or (3) eye movements that did not provide directional information. Hooker (2002) observed more activity in the STS in the first condition compared to either of the other conditions. Alternatively Hooker reported more activity in the fusiform gyrus and prefrontal cortex in the eye-motion control condition (condition 3) compared to the other conditions. These data were consistent with the notion that the STS may develop a specialization for processing gaze related, social-spatial orientation information.

One puzzling aspect of the imaging research on gaze-following has been noted by Calder et al. (2002). Theoretically, gaze-following behavior reflects aspects of social-cognitive processes (e.g. Baron-Cohen 1995). Recent imaging studies have suggested that, in addition to *ventral* 'social brain' activation, social-cognition is most consistently associated with activation of the *dorsal* medial frontal cortex (BA 8/9, Figure 5.1) and the anterior cingulate (Frith and Frith 1999, 2001; Mundy 2003). So why haven't studies of gaze-following revealed a link with frontal, dorsal medial activation? Calder *et al.* suggested that task difficulty needs to be considered in this regard. Most studies have examined passive gaze-following on tasks that did not require the perception or inference of intentions on the basis of eye gaze. These authors suggested that more complex presentations of sequences of gaze direction stimuli might elicit this type of processing, and provide evidence of more dorsal contributions to the neural substrate of gaze-following. To this end Calder *et al.* used Positron Emission Tomography (PET) to examine the neural responses of nine female volunteers to a relatively complex sequence of faces with varying gaze averted, gaze direct, and gaze down orientations. It wasn't completely clear from the methods described in this paper how these stimuli might have elicited more inferences of gaze related intentions than in previous studies. Nevertheless, the results provided evidence of activation in the dorsal medial frontal cortex (BA 8/9) and medial frontal cortex proximal to the anterior cingulate (BA 32), as well as areas of the STS, in response to horizontal gaze aversion.

Two other studies have more clearly indicated that, when the interpretation of intentions is an overt feature of the demands of a gaze processing task, activation of the dorsal medial frontal cortex appears to be involved. In an fMRI Baron-Cohen *et al.* (1999) presented six individuals with Asperger disorder and 12 typical controls with the 'eyes test' that requires inferring people's emotional states or gender from pictures of their eyes. The results of this study indicated that, in addition to activity in the orbito-frontal cortex, amygdala, and STS, activation of the left and right dorsal medial-frontal cortex was also a specific correlate of performance on this task in the typical sample. Interestingly, the autism group failed to display amygdala activation and may not have shown as much right dorsal medial activation in response to this gaze interpretation task. Russell *et al.* (2000) also employed the 'eyes test' (Baron-Cohen *et al.* 1999) in an fMRI study of the neural characteristics of individuals affected by schizophrenia. The control sample displayed relatively more activity in the medial-frontal lobe (BA 9 and 45) in association with performance on this task relative to the individuals with schizophrenia. In addition, more ventral 'social brain' components of the left inferior frontal gyrus (BA 44/45/47) and the left middle and superior temporal gyri (BA 21/22) contributed to clinical group differences on performance on this task.

Thus, the emerging literature on gaze-following indicates that the most consistent correlates of basic gaze-following and RJA skill appear to involve 'social brain' neural clusters in the STS and parietal lobes (see Table 5.1 for summary). However, when tasks involve interpretation of the meaning of direction of gaze (e.g. social cognitive inference of intentions) more dorsal-medial cortical systems may be brought to bear in processing gaze related stimuli. This difference across basic and more complex studies of RJA related behaviors is interesting because it is consistent with developmental studies that suggest that gaze-following may not initially reflect social-cognitive activity per se, but that it comes to do so over time (Brooks and Meltzoff 2002; Moore 1996; Woodward 2003). It is also consistent with the notion that elements of RJA may reflect an early developing, more reflexive posterior attention control system, but with experience and maturation it may become influenced by a more intentional anterior attention control system (Mundy *et al.* 2000).

Table 5.1 Summary of neurobehavioral research on gaze-following, joint attention, and related behaviors

Study	Participants	Measure/Method	Observations
Cambell *et al.* 1990	Primates	Gaze-following	STS involvement
Eacott *et al.* 1993		Neuro-lesion	
Heyward and Cowley 1992			
Hoffman and Haxby 2000	Adults	Gaze-following	STS involvement
Hooker 2002		Imaging	
Puce *et al.* 1998			
Wicker *et al.* 2002			
George *et al.* 2001	Adults	Direct vs. averted gaze Imaging	Fusiform involvement
Kingstone *et al.* 2000	Split-brain patients	Gaze-following Neuropsychology	Temporal-parietal involvement in face and gaze processing
Calder *et al.* 2002	Adults	Gaze-direction inferences Imaging	Dorsal medial frontal cortex
Caplan *et al.* 1993	Infants	IJA, RJA, IBR Imaging	Frontal involvement in IJA development
McEvoy *et al.* 1993 Griffith *et al.* 1999	Children with autism	IJA, RJA	Association with dorsolateral inhibition processes
Dawson *et al.* 2002	Children with autism	RJA and IJA Neuropsychology	Association with ventromedial reward perception and learning
Mundy *et al.* 2000	Infants	IJA, RJA, IBR Resting EEG	Dorsal medial frontal involvement with IJA, parietal involvement with RJA
Henderson *et al.* 2002	Infants	IJA, IBR pointing Resting EEG	Dorsal medial and ventromedial frontal involvement with IJA

In contrast to the emphasis on posterior temporal and parietal activation with RJA and related behaviors, research suggests that IJA may reflect the contribution of a more anterior and dorsal system to social development. This hypothesis is considered more completely in the next section of this chapter.

THE NEURAL SUBSTRATES OF IJA

The study of processes involved in the initiation of social behavior is as important but difficult than the study of processes involved in the perception of social behavior. This is because it is fairly straightforward to set up a controlled analogue of a social behavior (e.g. video of a face with moving eyes) that may be used in the study of the neural correlates of specific aspects of social perception. Alternatively, to study the initiation of a social behavior one typically needs a more interactive paradigm that provides individuals with ecologically valid contexts that motivate individuals to generate social goals and behaviors. The development of virtual environment paradigms may be one way to address this methodological difficulty (Eisenberger, Lieberman and Williams 2003). Currently, though, this methodological issue has limited the exploration of the neural correlates of self-initiated social behaviors such as IJA.

Nevertheless, important data in this regard have been provided in a study of the behavioral outcome of 13 infants who underwent hemispherectomies in an attempt to treat their intractable seizure disorders (Caplan *et al.* 1993). PET data were gathered prior to surgical intervention with the infants and the ESCS was used to assess the post-surgical development of IJA and RJA as well as the tendency for infants to initiate behavior requests. In addition to comparing IJA and RJA, IBR may also be important to consider in research on joint attention. Whereas IJA reflects the social use of attention directing behavior (e.g. directing attention to show or share interest in an object), IBR involves the instrumental use of attention directing behavior (e.g. directing attention to elicit aid in obtaining an object or event). Hence, by comparing IJA behaviors (e.g. showing a jar containing toys) with IBR behaviors (e.g. giving a jar containing toys to request aid in opening the jar), brain systems associated with the spontaneous initiation of 'social' joint attention bids versus 'instrumental' joint attention bids may be examined.

The results of the Caplan *et al.* (1993) study indicated that metabolic activity in the frontal hemispheres, and especially the left frontal hemisphere, predicted the development of initiating joint attention skill in this sample. However, the post-surgical development of the capacity of children to respond to joint attention bids, or initiate requesting bids, was not observed to relate to any of the PET indexes of cortical activity. Moreover, metabolic activity recorded from other brain regions, including ventral 'social brain' regions of the orbital, temporal, parietal, and occipital cortex, was not significantly associated with IJA or other social-communication skills in this study. Thus, dorsal anterior activity appeared to be specifically related to the development of the tendency to spontaneously initiate social joint attention bids to share experience with others.

Mundy *et al.* (2000) followed up on these observations with a study of the links between EEG activity and joint attention development in a longitudinal study of 14- to 18-month-olds. As previously noted, one result of this study was the observation that 14-month resting EEG activity at parietal sites predicted differences in RJA skill development at 18 months. Alternatively, individual differences in 18-month IJA were predicted by a different and complex pattern of 14-month resting EEG activity at left medial-frontal electrode sites, as well as indices of right central deactivation, left occipital activation, and right occipital deactivation. Although the source location of the EEG data could not be definitively determined in this study, the frontal correlates of IJA reflected activity from electrodes at F3 of the 10/20-placement system. These electrodes were positioned above a point of confluence of BA 8 and 9 of the medial-frontal cortex of the left hemisphere (Martin 1996). This area includes aspects of the frontal eye fields and supplementary motor cortex commonly observed to be involved in an anterior system of attention control (Posner and Petersen 1990).

Henderson *et al.* (2002) provided another important step in the study of the neural correlates of IJA. This research group also employed the ESCS to examine 14-month resting EEG data as predictors of 18-month joint attention development in 27 typically developing infants. However, to improve the spatial resolution of their EEG data, they used a higher-density array of 64 electrodes. Moreover, they reasoned that, since the total ESCS scores for measures of IJA and other domains used by Mundy *et al.* (2000) were composites of several behaviors, the exact nature of the associations with EEG activity observed in that study were unclear. To address this issue Henderson *et al.* compared the EEG correlates of only two types of ESCS behaviors, self-initiated pointing to share experience regarding an active mechanical toy (IJA pointing) and self-initiated pointing to elicit aid in obtaining an out of reach object (IBR pointing).

In this study no significant correlations were observed between any of the 14-month EEG data and IBR pointing at 18 months. With regard to IJA pointing, though, data in the 3–6 Hz band of 14-month resting EEG indicative of greater brain activity over the medial-frontal cortex was strongly associated with more 18-month pointing to share attention and experience with an adult social partner. These correlations involved electrodes that were placed above cortical regions corresponding to BA 8, 9, and 6. Henderson *et al.* (2002) also analyzed data from the 6–9 Hz band that revealed 15 significant correlations between 14-month resting EEG data and 18-month IJA pointing. Again, higher bilateral activity corresponding to the previously identified medial-frontal sites was a strong predictor of IJA pointing at 18 months. In addition, though, in this bandwidth IJA pointing at 18 months was also predicted by activity in this bandwidth from regions of the orbito-frontal, temporal, and dorsolateral frontal cortical regions. Thus, this study suggested that IJA development might reflect an integration of dorsal cortical functions (Mundy *et al.* 2000) with ventral 'social brain' and dorso-lateral functions identified in other studies (Dawson *et al.* 2002; Griffith *et al.* 1999; see below). However, there was no evidence for parietal involvement in IJA in this study.

The contribution of Henderson *et al.* (2002) also provided information about the social specificity of the link between IJA and dorsal cortical brain activity. As previously noted, the specific medial frontal cortical areas of involvement suggested by data from Mundy *et al.* (2000) and some of the data from Henderson *et al.* (2002) correspond to aspects of both the frontal eye fields and supplementary motor cortex associated with the control of saccadic eye movement and motor planning (Martin 1996). Therefore, these associations could simply reflect the motor control of the eye movements and/or gestural behaviors that are intrinsic to joint attention behavior. However, the simple elegance of the Henderson *et al.* study controls for this possible interpretation. The gross motor topography of IJA pointing and IBR pointing are virtually identical on the ESCS. Therefore, a neuro-motor explanation of the different cortical correlates of IJA and IBR appears unlikely. Instead, since IJA pointing and IBR pointing appear to serve different social-communicative functions, it is reasonable to assume that the difference in EEG correlates of these infant behaviors also reflects differences in the neurodevelopmental substrates of these social-communicative functions.

Several other neuropsychological studies have provided information on the functions and brain systems that may be involved with IJA. Two studies have reported that executive control, and especially the flexible inhibition of learned responses that may be associated with dorsolateral activity, is associated with both RJA and IJA performance in children with autism as well as those with typical development (Griffith *et al.* 1999; McEvoy, Rogers and Pennington 1993). However, there was little evidence in these studies that this component played a role in the joint attention deficits of children with autism that were also observed in this study. Dawson *et al.* (2002) have also reported a neuropsychological study that examined the hypothesis that IJA impairment in autism may be related to a disturbance in reward sensitivity and/or the ability to learn to flexibly associate rewards with elements in their environment (Dawson *et al.* 2002; Mundy 1995). To examine this hypothesis Dawson *et al.* observed the performance of children with autism and controls on a delayed non-matching to sample (DNMS) task that measures the ability of the child to learn to associate novel signs with the location of rewards in a forced choice task. Previous research indicates that DNMS performance is associated with functions of an orbito-frontal circuit that is involved in reward perception and learning (e.g. Diamond and Goldman-Rakic 1989; Rolls *et al.* 1994). Consistent with the involvement of reward responsiveness in joint attention, DNMS performance was significantly associated with performance on a combined measure of RJA/IJA in children with autism and typical development. However, while the children with autism displayed joint attention impairment they were not impaired on the DNMS measure. So it was not clear from this study whether reward responsiveness played a specific role on autistic joint attention impairment. Moreover, the joint attention measure used in this study was a composite of two RJA and one IJA measures and thus it was also unclear whether DNMS performance was related to IJA, RJA, or both skill domains.

Some clarification of the latter issue has been provided by a recent study of typically developing children (Nichols, Fox and Mundy 2005). Nichols *et al.* worked with 39 typically developing infants and examined the relations of DNMS task performance with measures of IJA and RJA in the 14 to 18 month period. However, since previous research had implicated the dorsal-medial cortex with IJA the authors also included a behavioral task that theoretically may be related to activity in this brain system. The dorsal-medial cortex appears to play a fundamental role in self-monitoring and self-awareness (Buch, Luu and Posner 2000; Craik *et al.* 1999; Frith and Frith 1999, 2001; Johnson *et al.* 2002; Stuphorn, Taylor and Schall 2000). So, for example, recent research indicates that the dorsal-medial frontal cortex plays a role in encoding and recalling words and actions that involve self-reference rather than those that do not involve self-reference (Craik *et al.* 1999; Johnson *et al.* 2002; see below). Therefore, Nichols *et al.* (2005) included a measure of infant self-recognition to examine the possible correlates of early self-awareness and self-monitoring with IJA. They hypothesized that if the data from Henderson *et al.* (2002) were correct then it was likely that variance in both an orbital frontal related behavior (DNMS) and a putative dorsal-medial related behavior (self-recognition) would make a unique contribution to the explanation of variance in IJA development. Consistent with these hypotheses both a composite of the DNMS and self-recognition tasks (combined 14-, 16-, and 18-month data) made significant contributions to a multiple regression for 18-month IJA. However, these measures did not contribute to the explanation of 18-month RJA data. Hence, consistent with the resting EEG data from Henderson *et al.* (2002) these behavioral data suggest that psychological functions associated both orbito-frontal and dorsal-medial frontal systems may make a contribution to IJA development. The integrated functioning of these two-brain systems may be critical not only for IJA development, but for later developing aspects of social engagement and social competence as well (Mundy and Acra 2006; Vaughan and Mundy in press).

Initiating joint attention, theory of mind, and the frontal cortex

Additional information pertinent to understanding the neural correlates of joint attention is provided by recent research on the brain systems involved in social cognition as measured with theory of mind (ToM) task performance. Several lines of theory suggest that, by the second year of development, the infant capacity for joint attention involves an elementary social cognitive understanding that others possess covert mental intentions that may be directed or shared (Tomasello 1999; Wellman 1993). Similarly, several researchers have suggested that deficits in both joint attention and theory of mind observed in children with autism reflect common social cognitive paths of disturbance (e.g. Baron-Cohen 1995; Mundy, Sigman and Kasari 1993). Surprisingly, little empirical data has been provided on the connections between joint attention and social cognitive development. One study, though, followed a sample of 13 typically developing infants from 20 to 44 months of age as part of a study on the early identification of autism (Charman *et al.* 2000). At 20 months, an alternating gaze measure was employed which involved children spontaneously initiating eye contact with a tester or parent after gazing at an interesting toy spectacle (see Figure 5.2c). Alternating gaze measures are often used as indexes of IJA (e.g. Mundy *et al.*1986; Tomasello 1995). After controlling for differences in IQ and language development, the 20-month IJA alternating gaze measure was observed to be a significant predictor of 44-month ToM performance.

If IJA in infants displays longitudinal continuity with ToM performance in preschool children, then imaging studies of ToM related task performance might provide information about the neural systems involved in IJA. Indeed, recent imaging research indicates that brain activity in the dorsal medial cortex (BA 8/9) and adjacent subcortical areas of the anterior cingulate is the most consistent correlate of ToM task performance (Frith and Frith 1999, 2001). This is true for both verbal (Fletcher *et al.* 1995; Goel *et al.* 1995) and non-verbal measures of social cognition (Brunet *et al.* 2000; Castelli *et al.* 2000; Gallagher *et al.* 2000). In addition, areas of the orbito-frontal and temporal cortices may also be involved in solving social cognitive tasks (see Mundy 2003). This pattern of activation has considerable overlap with the cortical areas that research suggests are involved in IJA. Indeed, since IJA and ToM abilities have long been linked theoretically, the imaging data on ToM task performance lends credence to observations of dorsal medial-frontal, as well as more orbito-frontal and temporal contributions to initiating joint attention.

IJA and functions of the anterior attention system

The foregoing research suggests that IJA is associated with a neural system involving the dorso-medial frontal cortex and anterior cingulate (DMFC/AC) which forms a significant component of what has been referred to as the anterior attention system (Rothbart and Posner 2001). This system becomes functional after the posterior parietal system, and that it makes numerous contributions to the planning, self-initiation, and self-monitoring of goal directed behaviors such as the intentional control of visual orienting (Mundy 2003; Rothbart, Posner and Rosicky 1994; Vaughan and Mundy in press). In particular, the anterior attention system plays a significant role in the capacity to share attention across dual tasks, or foci of attention (Stuss *et al.* 1995), especially with respect to the capacity to maintain and flexibly switch between goal representations in working memory (e.g. Birrell and Brown 2000; Rushworth *et al.* 2002). This anterior capacity likely contributes to the development of infants' ability to maintain representations of self, a social partner, and an interesting object spectacle while flexibly switching attention between these foci in initiating joint attention behaviors (Mundy *et al.* 2000). This attention switching facility of the anterior system makes a critical contribution to the supervisory attention system (SAS) (Norman and Shallice 1986) that function to guide behavior, especially attention deployment, *depending on the motivational context of the task* (e.g. Amador, Schlag-Rey and Schlag 2000; Buch *et al.* 2000). In this regard this system ultimately comes to participate in monitoring and representing the self, and directing attention to internal and external events (Faw 2003).

At least two lines of research link the DMFC/AC system with self-representation and self-monitoring. For example, Craik *et al.* (1999) and Johnson *et al.* (2002) have reported studies that reveal that self-referenced memory processes preferentially activate the dorsal medial frontal cortical component of this anterior system. With respect to self-monitoring, research has led to the observation that, when people make an erroneous saccadic response in an attention deployment task, there is a negative deflection in the stimulus and response locked ERP called the error-related negativity or ERN (Buch *et al.* 2000; Luu, Flaisch and Tucker 2000). Source location suggests the ERN emanates from an area of the DMFC proximal to the anterior cingulate cortex (Luu *et al.* 2000). Observations of the ERN suggest that there are specific cell groups within the DMFC/AC that are not only active in initiating a behavioral act, such as orienting to a stimulus, but also distinct cell groups involved in the processing of the positive or negative outcome of the response behavior (i.e. accuracy and reward or reinforcement information) (e.g. Amador *et al.* 2000; Holroyd and Coles 2002).

The ERN is thought to reflect a crucial component of the anterior cingulate's significant role in learning. In this regard Holroyd and Coles (2002) have suggested that distinct cortical areas control different adaptive motor output functions, such as searching for immediate reinforcement, inhibiting motor action in favor of delayed reinforcement, avoiding pain at all cost, and more complex behavior patterns such as navigating social encounters. The anterior cingulate is somatotopically connected to these distinct cortical motor control areas and acts as a selective switch that enables one or more of the cortical motor controllers to take command, at a particular time, to select and initiate goal directed behaviors that are most adaptive for a given set of environmental demands. This AC motor output regulatory function appears to be related to the SAS (Norman and Shallice 1986) which guides behavior, especially attention deployment, depending on the motivational context of the task. According to Holroyd and Coles the activity of the AC in this regard is most prominent in the earliest stages of learning and the AC itself is 'trained' to recognize which cortical control area(s) need to be given command per situation via reinforcement signals conveyed by a mesencephalic dopamine system. These reinforcement signals contribute to the error detection (and the ERN), which allows specific types of motor behavior to be shaped to its most effective and adaptive configuration depending upon reward and non-reward contingencies during motor activity. The AC also receives projections from limbic structures (e.g. amygdala), providing a pathway for emotional and motivation factors to influence AC cortical motor controller activation and inhibition (see Holroyd and Coles 2002 for additional details).

The nature of the distinct cortical motor controllers was not discussed in detail by Holroyd and Coles (2002). It may bear noting, though, that the term 'cortical motor controller' may have a limited connotation that needs to be recognized. Developmental theory suggests that with experience motor activity becomes internalized as representations, action sequences, or thought (Piaget 1952). So, ultimately, different cortical motor control areas also become associated with the mediation of different types of motor representation, or cognition. Faw (2003) has attempted to describe the distinct frontal motor-cognitive units and has suggested that the dorsal-medial/anterior cingulate system functions to represent the self in spatial temporal coordinates and direct attention to internal and external events. Related to this notion Frith and Frith (1999, 2001) have argued that the DMFC integrates proprioceptive information from the self (e.g. goal-directed motor behaviors) with exteroceptive perceptions processed by the STS about the goal-directed behaviors and emotions of others. This integrative activity may be facilitated by the abundance of connections between the DMFC, AC, and the STS (Morecraft, Guela and Mesulam 1993). Indeed, cell groups in and around BA 8/9 may be especially well connected to the STS (Ban, Shiwa and Kawamura 1991). We have described this putative facility for the integration of proprioceptive self-information with exteroceptive social perceptions as a social executive function (SEF) of the dorsal medial frontal cortex (Mundy 2003). Hypothetically this SEF utilizes the DMFC facility for the maintenance of representation of multiple goals in working memory to compare and integrate the actions of self and others. This integration gives rise to the capacity to infer the intentions of others by matching them with representations of self-initiated actions or intentions (Stich and Nichols 1992). Once this integration begins to occur in the DMFC, a fully functional, adaptive human social-cognitive system emerges with experience (Frith and Frith 1999, 2001).

According to the model of Holroyd and Coles (2002), though, this integrative development may not occur if early in development some disturbance in the motor control system occurs that prevents AC/DMFC 'learning' of the adaptive functions of social initiations such as directing visual attention to social partners or bidding for attention from social partners (e.g. IJA). Without social initiations it is difficult for the DMFC system to have the information required to develop a relational representation of self and other (Mundy and Neal 2001; Vaughan and Mundy in press). Although many details related to this process are unclear at this time, we have hypothesized that a developmental disturbance in control functions of the DMFC/AC system may make a significant contribution to the etiology of autism (Mundy 2003).

Several lines of research support this hypothesis. Most importantly, two recent studies have reported that individual differences in the fMRI and PET indicators of activity in the DMFC and anterior cingulate are specific correlates of the relative intensity of social symptom impairments displayed by children with autism (Haznedar et al. 2000; Ohnishi et al. 2000). Two studies (Castelli et al. 2002; Happé et al. 1996) have also observed that atypical DMFC/AC activation on social cognitive tasks is characteristic of some individuals with autism. Consistent with this possibility, Ernst et al. (1997) have observed a disturbance of dopaminergic activity in the dorsal medial-frontal cortex of children with autism. Morphometric studies have also revealed atypical gray matter density in components of the DMFC/AC system (i.e. anterior-cingulate, paracingulate sulcus, left superior frontal gyrus), as well as the amygdala, temporal lobe, left inferior parietal lobe, and cerebellum (Abell *et al.* 1999; Hardan *et al.* 2002). Finally, lesions or impairments of components of DMFC/AC complex have been observed to produce a variety of symptoms that are similar to those displayed by some people with autism including: akinetic mutism or a lack of will or motivation to generate behavior, excessive preoccupation with motor output and related ideation as in obsessive-compulsive disorder, inattention, dysregulation of autonomic functions, emotional instability, and variability in pain sensitivity (Buch *et al.* 2000; Holroyd and Coles 2002).

Clinical implications and applications

Behavioral research on early joint attention disturbance has had a positive impact on developing more effective diagnostic and intervention methods for children with autism. Therefore, one reasonable question to raise at this juncture is: does research on the neural correlates of joint attention add anything of significance to clinically relevant knowledge about the nature of autism? A complete answer to this question is not yet available because research on the neural development of joint attention has just begun and consequently interpretation of this research is highly speculative. Nevertheless, this literature begins to raise meaningful hypotheses about the neuropsychological functions involved in autism. These hypotheses, in turn, hold considerable promise for guiding future intervention related research and theory development with young children with autism. Examples of some of these hypotheses will be presented in the remainder of this chapter.

Autism and learning

First of all, the putative connections between IJA and functions of the DMFC/AC as described above are consistent with the notion that a disturbance of early neurodevelopmental learning processes may contribute to autism. Dawson, for example, has suggested that rule learning between stimuli and reward is critical to social development, including joint attention, and that an impairment in the capacity to connect stimuli and rewards plays a significant role in the development of social impairments in children with autism (Dawson *et al.* 2002). Related to this idea is the notion that children with autism may suffer from a specific deficit in their early sensitivity to the reward value of social stimuli (Mundy 1995; Panksepp 1979). A disturbance of learning functions of the DMFC/AC may contribute to either the more general stimulus reward association impairment (Dawson *et al.* 2002) or more specific social stimulus reward association impairment (Mundy 1995; Panksepp 1979).

In either case, problems with establishing and maintaining stimulus reward associations have long been recognized as a significant complication in intervention with children with autism (Dawson *et al.* 2001). It may be that work on the neural correlates of IJA will lead to a better understanding of the neural systems that underlie this general problem. For example, by linking the neural learning model of Holroyd and Coles (2002) to joint attention development, the possibility is raised that a disturbance in the relations between the mesencephalic dopamine system and the DMFC/AC may play a role in impairments in this domain and related social domains in autism. This possibility is quite consistent with ongoing research on drug treatments for autism that address the role of dopaminergic systems in the pathophysiology of autism (McDougle *et al.* 2001). Moreover, this model might clarify the types of effects that may be reasonably expected from pharmacological manipulations of dopamine related systems. Since activity of the AC is most prominent in the earliest stages of learning (Holroyd and Coles 2002), it may be that the most obvious effects of rectifying the dopaminergic system in autism would be revealed in the context of interventions designed to promote new learning. That is, it may be unreasonable to expect pharmacological interventions, by themselves, to have significant effects on the adaptive social behavior of children with autism, especially in short term trials (e.g. less than several months). However, if studied in conjunction with early interventions designed to facilitate social learning, it may be that dopaminergic intervention may augment the capacity of children with autism to appreciate stimulus-reward associations and, therefore, display enhanced speed and maintenance of learning within a behavioral intervention paradigm.

Intervention with RJA and IJA in autism

Given that pharmacological interventions may augment the ability of the child with autism to respond to behavioral intervention, the question then becomes what types of behavioral interventions may best address joint attention and related social developmental impairments in autism. Recall that research suggests that RJA and IJA are two distinct forms of joint attention skills that dissociate in the development of autism. Research also suggests that the neurodevelopment of joint attention may be described in terms of a dual process model (Mundy *et al.* 2003; Vaughan and Mundy in press). By the second year of life RJA may be primarily mediated by the posterior parietal attention system (Rothbart and Posner 2001) that is integrated with temporal circuits specific to social attention and social information processing (Vaughan and Mundy in press). Theoretically, one characteristic of the posterior attention system is that it is a relatively non-volitional system that automatically responds with shifts in attention to *external* biologically significant stimuli (Rothbart *et al.* 1994). Accordingly, posterior attention system behaviors such as RJA should be relatively open to modification through the manipulation of external stimulus conditions and stimulus contingencies. Alternatively, the link between IJA and the anterior attention system suggests that this type of behavior involves self-initiation and self-monitoring of goal-directed behaviors that may be under endogenous rather than exogenous motivational constraint (Mundy 1995; Mundy and Acra 2006; Mundy and Neal 2001). Hence, the contextual constraints that motivate a child with autism to initiate a social behavior like IJA may be different from those that may be effective in eliciting more responsive behaviors such as RJA. Let us consider these differences starting with RJA.

Research with normally developing children supports the notion that RJA is a highly responsive social behavior that may be relatively easily affected by exte rnal stimulus contingencies. Corkum and Moore (1998) worked with a sample of eight-month-old infants who displayed as many incorrect as correct responses to a gaze-following task. These researchers then established stimulus conditions for the infants such that whenever an infant displayed a correct gaze-following response they were 'rewarded' with an interesting event that occurred in their line of sight (i.e. a dark perspex box would be illuminated revealing an active, symbol clapping mechanical toy monkey). The results of this study indicated that infants who had not mastered gaze-following quickly acquired this skill under optimized conditions of contingent external reward. The study of Corkum and Moore is important for a number of reasons, not the least of which is that it suggests that it may be possible to develop intervention paradigms that manipulate stimulus reward contingencies that lead to the more rapid acquisition of RJA skill among children with autism.

Surprisingly, we know of no published intervention studies on the effects of manipulating external reward contingency as a specific intervention for RJA development in children with autism. Nevertheless, consistent with previous research (Mundy *et al.* 1994), Leekam *et al.* (2001) have reported that children with autism vary in their gaze-following RJA skill with better skill displayed by children with higher mental ages and IQs. Perhaps more important, Leekam *et al.* also reported that the performance of 40 percent of their sample of children with autism improved in gaze-following when illuminated targets like those in Corkum and Moore (1998) appeared in response to correct gaze shifts. This observation suggests a substantial number of children with autism may be sensitive to modifications of non-social external contingencies that facilitate RJA development.

This observation of improved performance on a gaze-following task is not well recognized in the intervention literature on autism, but may be very significant for several reasons. First, children do not only *learn to* control gaze-following RJA, but that they also *learn from* engagement in this pattern of motor behavior. That is, young children's own behavior becomes a critical source of information for subsequent executive and conceptual development (e.g. Piaget 1952). In this regard, consider the heuristic set of observations from comparative research reviewed by Calder *et al.* (2002). Different sets of cells in the STS of macaque monkeys appear to contribute to the processing of gaze direction versus the processing of the direction and orientation of limb movements (Perrett *et al.* 1992). However, a subset of limb movement cells appears to be modulated by activity of the gaze-following system (Jellema *et al.* 2000). Jellema *et al.* interpret these data to suggest that the *combined* analysis of direction of visual attention and body movements of others provides an important source of information that gives rise to the capacity to detect intentionality in others. Translated to human development, this suggests that gaze-following does not occur in isolation, but rather as an integrated element of processing of additional dimensions of social behavioral information about others. According to Jellema *et al.* this is consistent with the observation that, in addition to its social information processing specialization, the STS may also include polysensory areas involved in the attending to and processing information synchronously from multiple modalities. The integrated processing of others' direction of gaze, limb/postural direction, and vocal behavior ultimately may be an important, if not critical, source of information that enables the young child to learn about self, others, and social intentions. For example, with respect to gaze-following, Jellema *et al.* suggested that one major lesson learned from gaze-following is, 'Where the eyes go, behavior follows.' In this regard we have also suggested that neural connections between the posterior attention system and anterior attention system make it plausible that social and cognitive information that is gleaned as part of RJA development is fed forward to support the development of the self-initiation of critical social behaviors like IJA (Vaughan and Mundy in press). So the early facilitation of RJA may be an important goal for intervention targeting social cognitive disturbance in young children with autism.

RJA may also serve a self-organizing function that is specific to language development by reducing referential mapping errors and maximizing relevant social information processing in language-related incidental learning opportunities (Baldwin 1995). Observations consistent with the self-organizing role of RJA in the development of children with autism have been provided by Bono, Daley and Sigman (2004). These researchers examined the treatment responsiveness of 23 children with autism to varying intensities of intervention over a one-year period (6–43 hours per week). ESCS data were collected at baseline and the Reynell Language Development Scales were used to assess outcome. The results revealed that ESCS scores from both the IJA and RJA scales predicted individual differences in language outcome. Surprisingly, differences in intervention intensity were not associated with language outcomes. However, a significant interaction between intervention intensity and RJA was observed. Children with autism who more consistently responded correctly on RJA trials displayed more evidence of benefiting from higher intensities of intervention (i.e. more social learning opportunities) than did children with less consistent RJA skills.

These observations suggest that the adequate development of RJA may contribute to the capacity of the child with autism to profit from additional intervention. Moreover, recall that both behavioral research (Corkum and Moore 1998; Leekam *et al.* 2001) and research linking RJA development to the posterior attention system (e.g. Mundy *et al.* 2000) suggest that RJA skills may be sensitive to external rewards (cf. Leekam *et al.* 2001). Therefore, RJA appears to be a domain that is both pivotal to the development of the child with autism, and that can be targeted relatively easily. In contrast, as previously discussed, neural research on IJA is consistent with the notion that this domain of development may be more sensitive to endogenous motivation and executive constraints. Hence, effective intervention strategies for IJA-related aspects of development might be more complicated than those for RJA. However, considering the neurodevelopmental functions that may be associated with IJA development, it may be that effective intervention in this domain may be even more fundamental than intervention for RJA. We consider the implications of IJA development next.

Neurodevelopment, IJA, and the self-system in autism

In examining the development of behaviors displayed in Figure 5.2, researchers may ask at least two related but rather different questions: 'How are infants able to share attention and experience with others?' and 'Why do infants share attention and experiences with others?' The second question leads to reflection on the motivation factors and processes that contribute to the human tendency to share experience with others. For example, consider the following vignette. You are going to be part of the audience at an event that you are sure you will thoroughly enjoy (a play, a concert, a sporting event, etc.). You have a choice: you can go alone, or take a friend along. Many, if not most, people will choose the company of a friend. Moreover, during the event, there is a strong likelihood that you and your friend will exchange eye contact and experience a sense of relatedness at some point in response to your shared experience of an especially interesting or emotionally stimulating incident that occurs during the event. In that moment the two of you are socially engaged in joint attention, much like the infant in Figure 5.2c. Why do we, as infants, children, and adults, engage in this behavior even when viewing the event by ourselves would be pleasurable? Does the sharing of experience with others hold some positive reward value that motivates people to engage in acts of joint attention throughout the life span? Does this motivation system assist in bootstrapping the development of joint attention and its critical early self-organizing functions in human social development? Some would respond with an unequivocal 'yes' to these questions and go on to suggest that human beings have an intrinsic motivation for sharing of experience or intersubjectivity and this motivation is important for the early organization of social and cognitive development (e.g. Trevarthen and Aitken 2001). Extrapolating from this theory others have suggested that a disturbance of the intrinsic motivation for sharing experience or intersubjectivity with others makes a very significant contribution to IJA impairments and related components of the social developmental disorder of autism (Hobson 1993, 2002; Mundy 1995; Mundy and Neal 2001).

At least one study directly supports this hypothesis. Kasari and her colleagues (1990) integrated ESCS ratings of joint attention with systematic ratings of facial affect and made several important observations. First, in the typical control sample, infants conveyed positive affect significantly more often to social partners in the context of IJA bids compared to IBR or RJA behaviors. Alternatively, children with Down syndrome and autism did not display differences in affect across IJA and IBR measures, but for different reasons. The Down syndrome children displayed equally high rates of positive affect across both IJA and IBR bids, but the children with autism displayed equally low rates of positive affect in IJA and IBR. Positive affect was not a major component of RJA for any group. These results suggested that the sharing of positive affective experiences with others is a major component of IJA behavior in typical development, and that an attenuation of positive affect sharing may be an important component of IJA deficits in children with autism (Kasari *et al.* 1990).

Surprisingly few if any studies have been implemented to replicate and extend these important observations. Nevertheless, the basic observation that IJA involves affective sharing to a significantly greater degree than RJA or other forms of non-verbal communication in typical developing children has been replicated (Mundy *et al.* 1993) and appears to become codified in the behavioral repertoire of children between eight and ten months of age (Venezia *et al.* 2004). The data from these studies may be interpreted to suggest that IJA assessments provide an operational definition of the development of secondary intersubjectivity, or the tendency of children to initiate episodes of positive affective sharing with a social partner (see Figure 5.2c). Also, evidence consistent with the notion that intrinsic factors affect IJA has been presented by Vaughan *et al.* (2003) who have observed that individual differences in IJA development are specifically sensitive to temperamental factors associated with emotional reactivity in infants. Just because intrinsic factors may be involved in IJA development, however, does not mean that IJA is not sensitive to environmental factors. Indeed in this regard research suggests that relative to RJA, IBR, or other social communication skills, IJA is specifically sensitive to a complex system of factors involved in the degree of nurturing and positive social emotional caregiving experienced by young children (e.g. Claussen *et al.* 2002; Kroupina *et al.* 2003; Wachs and Chan 1986).

Trevarthen and Aitken (2001) suggest that the development of intersubjectivity is affected by motivation systems theoretically mediated by orbital-frontal and temporal brain systems involved in the perception of social stimuli (e.g. facial affect) and the association of these stimuli with positive reward value. According to this model, sensitivity to the reward value of these stimuli is inherent to human beings and possibly mediated by a neuropeptide based endogenous social reward system (Panksepp 1979). The identification of these brain systems in this regard is consistent with some of the neurodevelopment data and theory on IJA and its disturbance in autism (Dawson *et al.* 2002; Henderson *et al.* 2002; Mundy 1995). However, the social reward system involved in joint attention likely goes beyond the ventral brain systems to include more dorsal cortical regions including the anterior cingulate (Eisenberger *et al.* 2003; Mundy 2003). Moreover, the empirical connections between IJA and the DMFC also raises the hypothesis that, in addition to affective systems, the disturbance of this domain in autism reflects a disruption of the functions of the self-system. Specifically, IJA and related social impairments may reflect a disturbance in one or more of the DMFC facilities for: (a) self-monitoring, and/or (b) monitoring others, and/or (c) the capacity to monitor the relations between self and other behavior (Mundy *et al.* 1993; Mundy 2003; also see Faw 2003; Frith and Frith 2001). Problems in these putative DMFC functions may contribute to what some have described as a core disturbance in the propensity of people with autism to perceive and identify with the bodily expressed psychological attitudes of other people (Hobson 1993, 2002), and others describe as a fundamental impairment in the capacity to simulate the behavior of others (Frith and Frith 2001; Mundy 2003).

This literature affords a view of the characteristics of successful interventions with autism. For example, it is consistent with those who have recognized that optimal intervention programs with autism will need to target the motivational substrates of the tendency to initiate social behaviors (Koegel, Koegel and McNeary 2001). In addition, the hypothesis that autism may involve a self-monitoring and/or self–other monitoring disturbance may also help to explain why mirroring or imitation of the behavior of young children with autism has been observed to be a useful early intervention technique in bootstrapping social awareness and social behavior (Dawson and Adams 1984; Dawson and Galpert 1990; Field, Sanders and Nadel 2001). That is, in addition to a disturbance in orienting to others, young children with autism may be less aware of when other people are orienting to them. This problem, though, may be mitigated to some degree when social partners simplify their behavior and emphasize their own attention on a child through mirroring the behavior of that child.

Of course, neurological theory and research suggesting a biological attenuation of the basic social motivation system (Dawson *et al.* 2002; Hobson 1993; Mundy 1995) and/or difficulty in self-monitoring and apprehending the relations between self and other behavior (Hobson 1993; Mundy 2003) also point to the magnitude of the obstacles that need to be overcome in effective intervention with IJA-related social deficits in children with autism. Nevertheless, recent research on the responsiveness of IJA to nurturing and especially the affective tone of caregiving (Claussen *et al.* 2002; Kroupina *et al.* 2003; Wachs and Chan 1986) also provides some hope and direction for effective intervention development.

In programmatic efforts in this regard researchers and clinicians will need to identify a developmental sequence of techniques that have a positive impact on critical social behaviors, such as IJA. Several research groups have already begun to make headway with this (Kasari, Freeman and Paparella 2001; Yoder and Warren 2002). In this regard we believe it will be important to test the hypothesis that: (a) available techniques may be modified to provide effective intervention paradigms for RJA development in young children with autism (e.g. Leekam *et al.* 2001), (b) effective intervention with RJA will have a positive impact on children's social information processing and the capacity to perceive relations between self and others, and (c) improvement in these domains will facilitate subsequent language and social development, including IJA development, in a significant number of young children with autism.

It may also be important to develop methods to saturate the environment of children with autism with developmentally appropriate learning opportunities that magnify the salience of social-emotional responses to the child's behavior and increase the child's awareness of other people; parent training will be a critical component of any effective intervention. This will likely involve increasing the salience and frequency of caregiver positive affective responses to the behaviors of the child with autism in an attempt to compensate for biologically-based impairments in social perception, and/or social-reward sensitivity (Greenspan and Wieder 2000; Gutstein and Sheely 2002). Programmatic research here will need to provide evidence in support of this hypothesis (i.e. that increasing the salience and frequency of affective responses has a significant impact on development in young children with autism). It is also likely that optimally effective intervention of this kind will involve: (a) training parents to understand the nature and role of social motivation in developing the capacity for intersubjectivity in children with autism, and (b) providing parents with a developmentally sequenced system of technique that they can use in relatively natural interactions with their children throughout the day to optimize social emotional development and self–other awareness. Indeed, as is exemplified by relationship development intervention (RDI; Gutstein and Sheely 2002), creative and informed strides have already been made in developing such a manualized intervention system. However, like many new and promising intervention methods, RDI awaits thorough empirical examination before its effectiveness can fully be evaluated.

Of course, many would agree that it is unlikely that any one intervention modality will be sufficient to mitigate the complex developmental disturbances of autism. Rather, future effective intervention may need to combine both pharmacological and behavioral interventions to most effectively address the needs of children with autism. Understanding the biological substrates of early social-communication skills, such as IJA and RJA, may be critical to guiding the development of effective intervention strategies within both modalities.

Neurodevelopment and individual differences in autism

It is important to note that the neurodevelopmental research on joint attention may also contribute to an understanding of individual differences in social development and treatment responsiveness among children with autism. The research reviewed in this chapter suggests that the capacity to share experience with others (e.g. IJA skill) is a complex aspect of development that stems from the confluence of multiple neural systems (e.g. orbito-frontal, temporal/parietal, DMFC/AC systems) involved in learning, motivation, and affective processes, as well as intersubjectivity and self–other monitoring. It may be anticipated that individuals, including children with autism, display differences in the integrity and functioning of this array of neural systems. Some criterion level of dysfunction across these systems may give rise to autism. However, the pattern of dysfunction across systems, or the relative intensity of dysfunctions within systems, may vary among individuals with autism.

This variation may be manifest in the different types of social growth patterns that are exhibited by children with autism. Since the late 1970s, and before many of the contemporary forms of early intervention were available, it has been recognized that children with autism vary in their social presentation and outcomes with some children displaying a maximally aloof social style and others displaying an active but odd style that involves a relatively high frequency of attempts to initiate social interactions with others (Wing and Gould 1979). It seems likely that some aspects of these social individual differences in autism may be linked to variability in the functioning of the neural systems associated with joint attention and intersubjective processes in social development. For example, given what we are beginning to understand about the DMFC/AC it may well be that variation in the functioning of this system effects the capacity for social learning in autism. In some children this system may be moderately impaired but sufficiently intact to respond to concerted attempts to enrich their social-emotional environmental stimulation. For other children, however, the DMFC/AC system may be so impaired that all facets of learning are disrupted. These children may require a more structured sequence of intervention to establish even basic stimulus–reward mechanisms, as well as self-monitoring and self-regulatory functions.

Support for the notion that children with autism vary in the functioning of these neural systems is provided by previously noted research which observed that biological activity in the DMFC/AC brain system has been linked to variation in social symptom presentation in children with autism (Haznedar *et al.* 2000; Ohnishi *et al.* 2000). It is important to recognize, though, that the DMFC/AC system is not only associated with social development but is also strongly linked to basic learning and cognitive processes (Holroyd and Coles 2002). Indeed, this may be emphasized by developmental observations that link individual differences in infant joint attention to childhood intellectual outcomes in at-risk children (Neal *et al.* 2003; Ulvund and Smith 1996). The point here is that it would be a mistake to leave the reader with the impression that the neural systems which we believe to be involved in joint attention, intersubjectivity, and experience sharing disturbance in autism are only social-emotional systems. Rather we believe one value of the neurodevelopmental literature on joint attention is that it strongly suggests that the brain systems involved in this critical act of development, such as the DMFC/AC systems, are as integral to learning and cognition as they are to social development (Frith and Frith 2001; Holroyd and Coles 2002). Specifically, we believe the putative links between a behavioral marker of autism such as IJA disturbance and neural systems involving the functions of anterior cingulate (Holroyd and Coles 2002) raises an important hypothesis. That is that the relative function of the anterior cingulate and related cortical systems may contribute not only to the social deficits of autism, but also to the frequent association between autism and mental retardation. If so, one can well imagine why differences in intensity of DMFC/AC dysfunction may have a significant impact on the treatment responsiveness of children with autism.

Finally, we also believe that investigating the functional relations between anterior brain systems and social development may be important to understanding the wide range of phenotypic presentation in autism and related differences in the treatment responsiveness of these children. A recent study in our laboratory suggests that children with autism display individual differences in anterior cortical brain activity and that these are related to significant differences in the social symptoms, self-awareness, and cognitive style of older, higher-functioning children with autism (Sutton et al. 2004). The Sutton et al. (2004) study was based on an integration of research and theory that suggested that measures of resting anterior EEG asymmetry reflect complex brain processes associated with approach or avoidance motivation (e.g. Sutton and Davidson 1997), and that approach–avoidance motivation may be related to the development of the tendency to initiate and engage in social behaviors in children with autism (Mundy 1995). Basically the literature on EEG asymmetry suggests that individuals with more left anterior than right anterior resting cortical activity tend to have motivation tendencies associated with more behavioral activation and the initiation of more social interactions while a bias to right anterior activation is associated with behavioral inhibition and lower social interactive tendencies (Sutton and Davidson 1997). Early versions of this theory lead us to suggest that relative left frontal activation may be associated with social-emotional motivation in children with autism that is related to their tendency to initiate social interactions with others (Mundy 1995).

This integration of research and theory led to a study of the relations among resting anterior asymmetry, social impairment, and social anxiety in 23 high-functioning children with autism (HFA) and 20 verbal IQ and age matched controls (age range 9–14 years). Sutton et al. (2004) observed that these groups were significantly different on the measures of anterior asymmetry, social symptoms, and anxiety related measures. Moreover, HFA children who displayed right frontal asymmetry (RFA group) displayed more symptoms of social impairments and better visual analytic skills than did children who displayed left frontal asymmetry (LFA group). Alternatively, while the LFA group displayed fewer symptoms of social impairment they also reported greater levels of social anxiety, social stress, and lower satisfaction with interpersonal relations than did the RFA group (Sutton et al. 2004). These observations suggest that anterior EEG asymmetry may be a marker of motivation and emotion processes that refract the autism taxon into important individual differences in social ability and presentation in children with autism. Specifically, it raises the hypothesis that variation in left and right anterior brain systems, possibly including the DMFC/AC complex, is related to variation in the tendency of children to be motivated to interact with others and to be self-aware of their interactions with others. If this is correct those children with autism with greater biologically based social motivation and self-awareness may be expected to be responsive to different types of social interventions than those with a lower social motivation and self-awareness.

SUMMARY

Over the past few years several research groups, including our own, have been attempting to better understand the neural substrates of autism. For our own part we have started with observations on the nature of the critical early social behavioral difficulties of children affected by autism and then we have begun to try to identify the neural systems that may contribute to the developments in these critical behavior domains. From time to time, though, we ask ourselves what the immediate value of this line of inquiry is. As part of this chapter we have tried to address this question. The answer appears to be that integrating brain behavior research with developmental studies of joint attention can assist in revealing new perspectives and raising new hypotheses about the nature and treatment of autism. The research in this regard has just begun, hence the hypotheses that have been raised are clearly in their formative stage. Nevertheless, this approach is clearly heuristic and its immediate value lies in its potential to stimulate as well as corroborate new approaches to understanding treatment and individual differences in autism.

ACKNOWLEDGEMENT

The preparation of Chapter 5 was supported, in part, by NIH Grant HD38052, *Joint Attention and Developmental Outcome* (P. Mundy, P.I.) and by State of Florida funding for the University of Miami Center for Autism and Related Disabilities (UM-CARD).

REFERENCES

Abell, F., Krams, M., Ashburner, J., Passingham, R., Friston, K., Frackowiak, R. *et al.* (1999) 'The neuroanatomy of autism: a voxel-based whole brain analysis of structure scans.' *Neuroreport 10*, 1647–1651.

Adolphs, R. (2001) 'The neurobiology of social cognition.' *Current Opinion in Neurobiology 11*, 231–239.

Amador, N., Schlag-Rey, M. and Schlag, J. (2000) 'Reward predicting and reward detecting neuronal activity in the primate supplementary eye field.' *Journal of Neurophyisology 84*, 2166–2170.

American Psychiatric Association (APA) (2000) *Diagnostic and Statistical Manual-IV-Text Revision.* Washington, DC: American Psychiatric Association.

Bakeman, R. and Adamson, L. (1984) 'Coordinating attention to people and objects in mother–infant and peer–infant interaction.' *Child Development 55*, 1278–1289.

Baldwin, D. A. (1995) 'Understanding the link between joint attention and language.' In C. Moore and P. J. Dunham (eds) *Joint Attention: Its Origins and Role in Development.* Hillsdale, NJ: Lawrence Erlbaum.

Ban, T., Shiwa, T. and Kawamura, K. (1991) 'Cortico-cortical projections from the prefrontal cortex to the superior temporal sulcal area (STS) in the monkey studied by means of HRP method.' *Archives of Italian Biology 129*, 259–272.

Baron-Cohen, S. (1995) *Mindblindness*. Cambridge, MA: MIT Press.

Baron-Cohen, S., Ring, H., Wheelwright, S., Bullmore, E., Brammer, M., Simmons, A. *et al.* (1999) 'Social intelligence in the normal and autistic brain: an fMRI study.' *European Journal of Neuroscience 11*, 1891–1898.

Bates, E. (1976) *Language and Context: The Acquisition of Performatives.* New York, NY: Academic Press.

Birrell, J. and Brown, V. (2000) 'Medial-frontal cortex mediates perceptual attention set shifting in the rat.' *Journal of Neuroscience 20*, 4320–4324.

Bono, M., Daley, T. and Sigman, M. (2004) 'Relations among joint attention, amount of intervention, and language gain in early autism.' *Journal of Autism and Developmental Disorders 34*, 495–505.

Brooks, R. and Meltzoff, A. (2002) 'The importance of eyes: how infants interpret adult looking behavior.' *Developmental Psychology 38*, 958–966.

Brothers, L. (1990) 'The social brain: a project for integrating primate behavior and neurophysiology in a new domain.' *Concepts in Neuroscience 1*, 27–51.

Brunet, E., Sarfati, Y., Hardy-Bayle, M. C. and Decety, J. (2000) 'A PET investigation of the attribution of intentions with a non-verbal task.' *Neuroimage 11*, 157–166.

Buch, G., Luu, P. and Posner, M. (2000) 'Cognitive and emotional influences in the anterior cingulate cortex.' *Trends in Cognitive Science 4*, 214–222.

Calder, A., Lawrence, A., Keane, J., Scott, S., Owen, A., Christoffels, I. *et al.* (2002) 'Reading the mind from eye gaze.' *Neuropsychologia 40*, 1129–1138.

Cambell, R., Heywood, C., Cowey, A., Regard, M. and Landis, T. (1990) 'Sensitivity to eye gaze in prosopagnosic patients and monkeys with superior temporal sulcus ablation.' *Neuropsychologia 28*, 1123–1142.

Caplan, R., Chugani, H., Messa, C., Guthrie, D., Sigman, M., Traversay, J. *et al.* (1993) 'Hemispherectomy for early onset intractable seizures: presurgical cerebral glucose metabolism and postsurgical non-verbal communication patterns.' *Developmental Medicine and Child Neurology 35*, 582–592.

Carper, R. and Courchesne, E. (2000) 'Inverse correlation between frontal lobe and cerebellum sizes in children with autism.' *Brain 123*, 836–844.

Castelli, F., Happé, F., Frith, U. and Frith, C. (2000) 'Movement and mind: a functional imaging study of perception and interpretation of complex intentional movement patterns.' *Neuroimage 12*, 314–325.

Castelli, F., Frith, C., Happé, F. and Frith, U. (2002) 'Autism, asperger syndrome and brain mechanisms for the attribution of mental states to animated shapes.' *Brain 125*, 1839–1849.

Charman, T., Baron-Cohen, S., Swettenham, J., Baird, G., Cox, A. and Drew, A. (2000) 'Testing joint attention, imitation, and play infancy precursors to language and theory of mind.' *Cognitive Development 15*, 481–498.

Chawarska, K., Klin, A. and Volkmar, F. (2003) 'Automatic attention cuing through eye movement in 2-year-old children with autism.' *Child Development 74*, 1108–1123.

Claussen, A. H., Mundy, P. C., Malik, S. A. and Willoughby, J. C. (2002) 'Joint attention and disorganized attachment status in infants at risk.' *Development and Psychopathology 14*, 279–291.

Corkum, V. and Moore, C. (1998) 'The origins of joint visual attention in infants.' *Developmental Psychology 34*, 28–38.

Courchesne, E., Townsend, J., Akshoomoff, N., Yeung-Courchesne, G., Murakami, J., Lincoln, A. *et al.* (1994) 'A new finding: impairment in shifting attention in autistic and cerebellar patients.' In E. Broman and E. Grafman (eds) *Atypical Cognitive Deficits in Developmental Disorder: Implications for Brain Function*. Hillsdale, NJ: Erlbaum.

Craik, F., Moroz, T., Moscovich, M., Stuss, D., Winocur, G., Tulving, E. *et al.* (1999) 'In search of the self: a positron emission tomography study.' *Psychological Science 10*, 26–34.

Critchley, H., Daly, E., Bullmore, E., Williams, S., Van Amelsvoort, T., Robertson, D. *et al.* (2000) 'The functional neuroanatomy of social behavior: changes in the cerebral blood flow when people with autistic disorder process facial expressions.' *Brain 123*, 2203–2212.

Dawson, G. and Adams, A. (1984) 'Imitation and social responsiveness in autistic children.' *Journal of Abnormal Child Psychology 12*, 209–226.

Dawson, G. and Galpert, L. (1990) 'Mother's use of imitative play for the facilitation of social responsiveness and toy play in young autistic children.' *Development and Psychopathology 2*, 151–162.

Dawson, G., Osterling, J., Rinalidi, J., Carver, L. and McPartland, J. (2001) 'Brief report: Recognition memory and stimulus-reward associations: indirect support for the role of the ventromedial prefrontal dysfunction in autism.' *Journal of Autism and Developmental Disorders 31*, 337–341.

Dawson, G., Munson, J., Estes, A., Osterling, J., McPartland, J., Toth, K. *et al.* (2002) 'Neurocognitive function and joint attention ability in young children with autism spectrum disorder versus developmental delay.' *Child Development 73*, 345–358.

Diamond, A. and Goldman-Rakic, P. (1989) 'Comparison of human infants and rhesus monkeys on Piaget's AB task: evidence for the dependence on dorsolateral prefrontal cortex.' *Experimental Brain Research 74*, 24–40.

Eacott, M., Heywood, C., Gross, C. and Cowey, A. (1993) 'Visual discrimination impairments following lesions of the superior temporal sulcus are not specific for facial stimuli.' *Neuropsychologia 31*, 609–619.

Eisenberger, N., Lieberman, M. and Williams, K. (2003) 'Does rejection hurt? An fMRI study of social exclusion.' *Science 302*, 290–292.

Elgar, K. and Cambell, R. (2001) 'Annotation. The cognitive neuroscience of face recognition: implications for developmental disorders.' *Journal of Child Psychology and Psychiatry 6*, 705–717.

Emery, N. (2000) 'The eyes have it. The neuroethology, function and evolution of social gaze.' *Neuroscience and Biobehavioral Reviews 24*, 581–604.

Ernst, M., Zametkin, J., Matochik, J., Pascualvaca, D. and Cohen, R. (1997) 'Low medial prefrontal dopaminergic activity in autistic children.' *Lancet 350*, 638.

Faw, B. (2003) 'Prefrontal executive committee for perception, working memory, attention, long-term memory, motor control and thinking: a tutorial review.' *Consciousness and Cognition 12*, 83–139.

Field, T., Sanders, C. and Nadel, J. (2001) 'Children with autism display more social behaviors after repeated imitation sessions.' *Autism 5*, 3, 317–323.

Fletcher, P., Happé, F., Frith, U., Baker, S., Dolan, R., Frackowiak, R. *et al.* (1995) 'Other minds in the brain: a functional imaging study of "theory of mind" in story comprehension.' *Cognition 57*, 109–128.

Frith, C. and Frith, U. (1999) 'Interacting minds: a biological basis.' *Science 286*, 1692–1695.

Frith, U. and Frith, C. (2001) 'The biological basis of social interaction.' *Current Directions in Psychologic Science 10*, 151–155.

Gallagher, H., Happé, F., Brunswick, P., Fletcher, P., Frith, U. and Frith, C. (2000) 'Reading the mind in cartoons and stories: an fMRI study of "theory of mind" in verbal and nonverbal tasks.' *Neuropsychologia 38*, 11–21.

Gazzagnia, M., Ivry, R. and Mangun, G. (1998) *Cognitive Neuroscience.* New York, NY: Norton.

George, N., Driver, J. and Dolan, R. (2001) 'Seen gaze direction modulates fusiform activity and its coupling with other brain areas during face processing.' *Neuroimage 13*, 1102–1112.

Goel, V., Grafman, J., Sadato, N. and Hallett, M. (1995) 'Modeling other minds.' *Neuroreport 6*, 1741–1746.

Greenspan, S. and Wieder, S. (2000) 'A developmental approach to difficulties in relating and communication in autism spectrum disorders and related syndromes.' In A. Wetherby and B. Prizant (eds) *Autism Spectrum Disorders: A Transactional Developmental Perspective. Communication and Language Intervention Series, Vol 9*. Baltimore, MD: Paul Brookes Pub. Co.

Griffith, E. M., Pennington, B., Wehner, E. and Rogers, S. (1999) 'Executive functions in young children with autism.' *Child Development 70*, 817–832.

Gutstein, S. and Sheely, R. (2002) *Relationship Development Intervention with Young Children: Social and Emotional Development Activities for Asperger Syndrome, Autism, PDD, and NLD*. London, UK: Jessica Kingsley Publishers.

Happé, F., Ehlers, S., Fletcher, P., Frith, U., Johansson, M., Gillberg, C. *et al*. (1996) '"Theory of Mind" in the brain: evidence from a PET scan study of Asperger syndrome.' *Neuroreport 8*, 197–201.

Hardan, A., Minshew, N., Diwadkar, V., Yorbik, O., Sahni, S. and Keshavan, M. (2002) 'A voxel based morphometry study of grey matter in autism.' Paper presented at the International Meeting for Autism Research (IMFAR), Orlando, Florida, November.

Haznedar, M., Buchsbaum, M., Wei, T., Hof, P., Cartwright, C., Bienstock, C. *et al*. (2000) 'Limbic circuitry in patients with autism spectrum disorders studied with positron emission tomography and magnetic resonance imaging.' *American Journal of Psychiatry 157*, 1994–2001.

Henderson, L., Yoder, P., Yale, M. and McDuffie, A. (2002) 'Getting the point: electrophysiological correlates of protodeclarative pointing.' *International Journal of Developmental Neuroscience 20*, 449–458.

Heyward, C. and Cowley, A. (1992) 'The role of the "face cell" area in the discrimination and recognition of faces by monkeys.' *Philosophical Transactions of the Royal Society of London 335*, 31–38.

Hobson, R. P. (1993) *Autism and the Development of Mind*. Hillsdale, NJ: Lawrence Erlbaum.

Hobson, R. P. (2002) *The Cradle of Thought: Exploring the Origins of Thinking*. London, UK: Pan Macmillan.

Hoffman, E. and Haxby, J. (2000) 'Distinct representation of eye gaze and identity in the distributed human neural system for face perception.' *Nature Neuroscience 3*, 80–84.

Holroyd, C. and Coles, M. (2002) 'The neural basis of human error processing: reinforcement learning, dopamine and the error related negativity.' *Psychological Review 109*, 679–709.

Hooker, C. (2002) 'The neurocognitive basis of gaze perception: a model of social signal processing.' *Dissertation Abstracts International: Science and Engineering 63*, 2058.

Jellema, T., Baker, C., Wicker, B. and Perrett, D. (2000) 'Neural representation for the perception of intentionality of actions.' *Brain and Cognition 44*, 280–302.

Johnson, S., Baxyter, L., Wilder, L., Pipe, J., Heiserman, J. and Prigatano, G. (2002) 'Neural correlates of self reflection.' *Brain 125*, 1808–1814.

Kasari, C., Sigman, M., Mundy, P. and Yirmiya, N. (1990) 'Affective sharing in the context of joint attention interactions of normal, autistic, and mentally retarded children.' *Journal of Autism and Developmental Disorders 20*, 87–100.

Kasari, C., Freeman, S. and Paparella, T. (2001) 'Early intervention in autism: joint attention and symbolic play.' In Laraine Masters Glidden (ed.) *International Review of Research in Mental Retardation: Autism, Vol. 23*. San Diego, CA: Academic Press.

Kawashima, R., Sugiura, M., Kato, T., Nakamura, A., Hatano, K., Ito, K. *et al*. (1999) 'The human amygdala plays an important role in gaze monitoring: a PET study.' *Brain 122*, 779–783.

Kingstone, A., Friesen, C-K. and Gazzagnia, M. (2000) 'Reflexive joint attention depends on lateralized cortical functions.' *Psychological Science 11*, 159–166.

Klin, A., Jones, W., Schultz, R. and Volkmar, F. (2003) 'The enactive mind, or from actions to cognition: lessons from autism.' *Philosophical Transaction of the Royal Society of London 10*, 1–16.

Koegel, R., Koegel, L. and McNeary, E. (2001) 'Pivotal areas of intervention for autism.' *Journal of Community Psychology 30*, 19–32.

Kroupina, M., Kuefner, D., Iverson, S. and Johnson, D. (2003) *Joint Atention Skills of Post-institutionalized Children.* Poster presented at the Society for Research in Child Development, Tampa, Florida, April.

LeDoux, J. (1989) 'Cognitive–emotional interactions in the brain.' *Cognition and Emotion 3*, 267–289.

Leekam, S., Lopez, B. and Moore, C. (2001) 'Attention and joint attention in preschool children with autism.' *Developmental Psychology 36*, 261–273.

Leslie, A. (1987) 'Pretense and representation: the origins of "theory of mind".' *Psychological Review 94*, 412–426.

Lord, C., Risi, S., Lambrecht, L., Cook, E., Leventhal, B., DiLavore, P. *et al.* (1999) 'The Autism Diagnostic Observations Schedule-Generic: a standard measure of social and communication deficits associated with autism spectrum disorder.' *Journal of Autism and Developmental Disorders 30*, 205–223.

Lord, C., Floody, H., Anderson, D. and Pickles, A. (2003) 'Social engagement in very young children with autism: differences across contexts.' Paper presented at the Society for Research in Child Development, Tampa, FL, April.

Luu, P., Flaisch, T. and Tucker, D. (2000) 'Medial-frontal cortex in action monitoring.' *Journal of Neuroscience 20*, 464–469.

McDougle, C., Scahill, L., McCraken, J., Aman, M., Tierney, E., Arnold, E. *et al.* (2001) 'Research units on pediatric psychopharmacology (RUPP) Autism Network: background and rationale from an initial controlled study of risperidone.' *Child and Adolescent Psychiatric Clinics of North America 9*, 201–224.

McEvoy, R., Rogers, S. and Pennington, R. (1993) 'Executive function and social communication deficits in young autistic children.' *Journal of Child Psychology and Psychiatry 34*, 563–578.

Martin, J. (1996) *Neuroanatomy: Text and Atlas* (2nd edn). New York, NY: McGraw-Hill.

Minshew, N., Meyer, J. and Goldstein, G. (2002) 'Abstract reasoning in autism: a dissociation between concept formation and concept identification.' *Neuropsychology 16*, 327–334.

Moore, C. (1996) 'Theories of mind in infancy.' *British Journal of Developmental Psychology 14*, 19–40.

Morecraft, R., Guela, C. and Mesulam, M. (1993) 'Architecture of connectivity within the cingulo-frontal-parietal neurocognitive network for directed attention.' *Archives of Neurology 50*, 279–283.

Mundy, P. (1995) 'Joint attention and social-emotional approach behavior in children with autism.' *Development and Psychopathology 7*, 63–82.

Mundy, P. (2003) 'The neural basis of social impairments in autism: the role of the dorsal medial-frontal cortex and anterior cingulate system.' *Journal of Child Psychology and Psychiatry 44*, 793–809.

Mundy, P. and Acra, F. (2006) 'Joint attention, social engagement and the development of social competence.' In P. Marshall and N. Fox (eds) *The Development of Social Engagement: Neurobiological Perspectives.* New York, NT: Oxford University Press.

Mundy, P. and Crowson, M. (1997) 'Joint attention and early communication: implications for intervention with autism.' *Journal of Autism and Developmental Disorders 6*, 653–676.

Mundy, P. and Neal, R. (2001) 'Neural plasticity, joint attention and a transactional social-orienting model of autism.' *International Review of Mental Retardation 23*, 139–168.

Mundy, P. and Sigman, M. (1989) 'Specifying the nature of the social impairment in autism.' In G. Dawson (ed.) *Autism: New Perspectives on Diagnosis, Nature, and Treatment.* New York: Guilford Publications, Inc.

Mundy, P., Sigman, M., Ungerer, J. and Sherman, T. (1986) 'Defining the social deficits of autism: the contribution of nonverbal communication measures.' *Journal of Child Psychology and Psychiatry 27*, 657–669.

Mundy, P., Kasari, C. and Sigman, M. (1992) 'Joint attention, affective sharing, and intersubjectivity.' *Infant Behavior and Development 15*, 377–381.

Mundy, P., Sigman, M. and Kasari, C. (1993) 'The theory of mind and joint attention deficits in autism.' In S. Baron-Cohen, H. Tager-Flusberg and D. Cohen (eds) *Understanding Other Minds: Perspectives from Autism.* Oxford, UK: Oxford University Press.

Mundy, P., Sigman, M. and Kasari, C. (1994) 'Joint attention, developmental level, and symptom presentation in young children with autism.' *Development and Psychopathology 6*, 389–401.

Mundy, P., Hogan, A. and Doehring, P. (1996) *A Preliminary Manual for the Abridged Early Social-Communication Scales.* Coral Gables, FL: University of Miami (www.psy.miami.edu/faculty/pmundy).

Mundy, P., Card, J. and Fox, N. (2000) 'EEG correlates of the development of infant joint attention skills.' *Developmental Psychobiology 36*, 325–338.

Mundy, P., Delgado, C., Block, J., Venezia, M., Hogan, A. and Seibert, J. (2003) *A Manual for the Abridged Early Social Communication Scales (ESCS).* Available through the University of Miami Psychology Department, Coral Gables, Florida (pmundy@miami.edu).

Neal, R., Mundy, P., Claussen, A., Mallik, S., Scott, K. and Acra, F. (2003) 'The relations between infant joint attention skill and cognitive and language outcome in at-risk children.' Manuscript in submission.

Nichols, K., Fox, N. and Mundy, P. (2005) 'Joint attention, self-recognition and neurocognitive function in toddlers.' *Infancy 7*, 35–51.

Norman, D. and Shallice, T. (1986) 'Attention to action: willed and automatic control of behavior.' In R. Davidson, G. Schwartz and D. Shapiro (eds) *Consciousness and Self-Regulation.* New York, NY: Plenum.

Ohnishi, T., Matsuda, H., Hashimoto, T., Kunihiro, T., Nishikawa, M., Uema, T. *et al.* (2000) 'Abnormal regional cerebral blood flow in childhood autism.' *Brain 123*, 1838–1844.

Osterling, J., Dawson, G. and Munson, J. A. (2002) 'Early recognition of 1-year-old infants with autism spectrum disorder versus mental retardation.' *Development and Psychopathology 14*, 239–251.

Panksepp, J. (1979) 'A neurochemical theory of autism.' *Trends in Neurosciences 2*, 174–177.

Perrett, D., Heitenen, J., Oram, M. and Benson, P. (1992) 'Organization and functions of cells responsive to faces in the temporal cortex.' *Philosophical Transactions of the Royal Society of London 335*, 23–30.

Piaget, J. (1952) *The Origins of Intelligence in Children.* New York, NY: Norton.

Posner, M. and Petersen, S. (1990) 'The attention system of the human brain.' *Annual Review of Neuroscience 13*, 25–42.

Puce, A., Allison, T., Bentin, S., Gore, J. and McCarthy, G. (1998) 'Temporal cortex activation in humans viewing eye and mouth movements.' *Journal of Neuroscience 18*, 2188–2199.

Rolls, E., Hornak, J., Wade, D. and McGrath, J. (1994) 'Emotion related learning in patients with social and emotional changes associated with frontal lobe damage.' *Journal of Neurology, Neurosurgery and Psychiatry 57*, 1518–1524.

Rothbart, M. and Posner, M. (2001) 'Mechanism and variation in the development of attention networks.' In C. Nelson and M. Luciana (eds) *The Handbook of Developmental Cognitive Neuroscience.* Cambridge, MA: The MIT Press.

Rothbart, M., Posner, M. and Rosicky, J. (1994) 'Orienting in normal and pathological development.' *Development and Psychopathology 6*, 635–652.

Rushworth, M., Hadland, K., Paus, T. and Siplia, P. (2002) 'Role of the human medial frontal cortex in task switching: a combined fMRI and TMS study.' *Journal of Neurophysiology 87*, 2577–2592.

Russell, T., Rubia, K., Bullmore, E., Soni, W., Suckling, J., Brammer, M. *et al.* (2000) 'Exploring the social brain in schizophrenia: left prefrontal underactivation during mental state attribution.' *American Journal of Psychiatry 157*, 2040–2042.

Scaife, M. and Bruner, J. (1975) 'The capacity for joint visual attention in the infant.' *Nature 253*, 265–266.

Seibert, J. M., Hogan, A. E. and Mundy, P. C. (1982) 'Assessing interactional competencies: the Early Social Communication Scales.' *Infant Mental Health Journal 3*, 244–245.

Sigman, M. and Ruskin, E. (1999) 'Continuity and change in the social competence of children with autism, down syndrome, and developmental delay.' *Monographs of the Society for Research in Child Development 64*, 256, 1–108.

Sigman, M., Kasari, M., Kwon, J. and Yirmiya, N. (1992) 'Responses to the negative emotions of others by autistic, mentally retarded and normal children.' *Child Development 63*, 796–807.

Stich, S. and Nichols, S. (1992) 'Folk psychology: simulation versus tacit theory.' *Mind and Language 7*, 29–65.

Stuphorn, V., Taylor, T. and Schall, J. (2000) 'Performance monitoring by the supplementary eye field.' *Nature 408*, 857–860.

Stuss, D., Shallice, T., Alexander, M. and Picton, T. (1995) 'A multidimensional approach to anterior attention functions.' In J. Grafman, K. Holyoak, and F. Boller (eds) *Structure and Function of the Human Prefrontal Cortex. Annals of the New York Academy of Science, Vol. 769.* New York, NY: New York Academy of Sciences.

Sutton, S. and Davidson, R. (1997) 'Prefrontal brain asymmetry: a biological substrate of the behavioral approach and inhibition systems.' *Psychological Science 8*, 204–210.

Sutton, S., Burnette, C., Mundy, P., Meyer, J., Vaughan, A., Sanders, C. *et al.* (2004) 'Resting cortical brain activity and social behavior in higher functioning children with autism.' *Journal of Child Psychology and Psychiatry 45*, 211–222.

Swettenham, J., Baron-Cohen, S., Charman, T., Cox, A., Baird, G., Drew, A. *et al.* (1998) 'The frequency and distribution of spontaneous attention shifts between social and nonsocial stimuli in autistic, typically developing, and nonautistic developmentally delayed infants.' *Journal of Child Psychology and Psychiatry 39*, 747–753.

Tomasello, M. (1995) 'Joint attention as social cognition.' In C. Moore and P. Dunham (eds) *Joint Attention: Its Origins and Role in Development.* Hillsdale, NJ: Lawrence Erlbaum.

Tomasello, M. (1999) *The Cultural Origins of Human Cognition.* Boston, MA: Harvard University Press.

Townsend, J., Westerfield, M., Leaver, E., Makeig, S., Tzyy-Ping, J., Pierce, K. *et al.* (2001) 'Event-related brain response abnormalities in autism: evidence for impaired cerebello-frontal spatial attention networks.' *Cognitive Brain Research 11*, 127–145.

Trevarthen, C. and Aitken, K. (2001) 'Infant intersubjectivity: research, theory and clinical applications.' *Journal of Child Psychology and Psychiatry 42*, 3–48.

Ulvund, S. and Smith, L. (1996) 'The predictive validity of nonverbal communication skills in infants with perinatal hazards.' *Infant Behavior and Development 19*, 441–449.

Vaughan, A. and Mundy, P. (in press) 'Neural systems and the development of gaze-following and related joint attention skills.' To appear in R. Flom, K. Lee and D. Muir (eds) *The Ontogeny of Gaze Processing in Infants and Children.* Mahwah, NJ: Lawrence Erlbaum Associates.

Vaughan, A., Mundy, P., Block, J., Burnette, C., Delgado, C. and Gomez, Y. (2003) 'Child, caregiver and temperament contributions to infant joint attention.' *Infancy 4*, 603–616.

Venezia, M., Messinger, D., Thorp, D. and Mundy, P. (2004) 'Timing changes: the development of anticipatory smiling.' *Infancy 6*, 397–406.

Wachs, T. and Chan, A. (1986) 'Specificity of environmental action, as seen in environmental correlates of infants' communication performance.' *Child Development 57*, 1464–1474.

Wantanabe, M. (1999) 'Neurobiology: attraction is relative not absolute.' *Nature 398*, 661–663.

Wellman, H. (1993) 'Early understanding of mind: the normal case.' In S. Baron-Cohen, H. Tager-Flusberg and D. Cohen (eds) *Understanding Other Minds: Perspectives from Autism*. Oxford, UK: Oxford University Press.

Wicker, B., Michel, F., Henaff, M. and Decety, J. (2002) 'Brain regions involved in the perception of gaze.' *Neuroimage 8*, 221–227.

Wing, L. and Gould, J. (1979) 'Severe impairments of social interaction and associated abnormalities in children: epidemiology and classification.' *Journal of Autism and Developmental Disorders 9*, 11–29.

Woodward, A. (2003) 'Infants' developing understanding of the link between looker and object.' *Developmental Science 6*, 297–311.

Yoder, P. and Warren, S. (2002) 'The effects of prelinguistic milieu teaching and parent responsivity education on dyads involving children with intellectual disabilities.' *Journal of Speech, Language and Hearing 45*, 1158–1174.

Chapter 6

On Being Moved in Thought and Feeling

An Approach to Autism

Peter Hobson

INTRODUCTION

Suppose you are having coffee with a group of friends in one of the delightful cafés of Madrid. Out of the blue, one turns to you and asks: 'What *is* autism, anyway?' You could be forgiven for spilling your coffee into your lap. The answer should be so straight-forward, at least in outline. As someone who has read about, and probably spent time with, individuals with autism, you feel you should be able to articulate a response without hesitation. And yet beyond mumbling something about autism not really existing as such, given that there are only people who 'have' autism; then half-contra-dicting yourself, in offering the formulation that autism is a syndrome, that is, a set of clinical features that regularly go together; and finally, after giving some kind of sketch of what those features are in terms of impairments in social relations and communica-tion, creative symbolic thinking, and flexible relations with the world…you might well stumble to a faltering stop.

Then you realize how to rescue yourself from the ensuing silence. You start to tell stories of *what it is like* to be with one or another specific person with autism; how it felt to meet such a person for the first time; how some of the things that the person says are so strangely misplaced or 'concrete' in meaning; how difficult it is to engage with the person's own subjective experiences of the world in such a way as to make them one's own; how impervious to the influence of other people, at times, are the person's own ways of seeing or doing things; and at the same time, how touching and impressive the person can be.

Your friend is intrigued. But then she asks something else: 'What *causes* this syndrome, then?' At first this seems an easier question, because you can say it is a neurodevelopmental disorder (that should keep her quiet for a while), often with genetic underpinnings, which leads to the brain failing to function properly. You might add that, sometimes, specific medical conditions such as maternal rubella or tuberose sclerosis play a causative role. 'Ah,' says your friend, 'then these cause damage to one part of the brain that allows us to make social relations, another that allows us to communicate with each other, another to use language properly, and yet another to be flexible and well-ordered in our thinking and actions? I see.'

This makes you feel even worse. If only it were that straightforward! There is so little known about the areas of the brain that are malfunctioning in autism, and anyway, the areas probably differ in different individuals. Moreover, there are some serious complications to such a picture, for example where the *perceptual* impairments of congenital blindness appear to greatly increase the chances that an affected child will develop autism. Most important of all, you have not yet told your friend how only some of the features of autism will prove to be 'basic' to the disorder, and many aspects of the syndrome will turn out to be the developmental effects of these earlier-appearing but pivotal impairments...and by now, you already anticipate that your friend will still not be satisfied, and ask you the $64,000 question: 'Ok, then, what *is* basic to autism?'! Even that might not end the stream of questions, because there is a need to explain how brain damage of such extensiveness could sometimes leave an affected individual with a normal IQ, or how it could be that individuals with autism can change over development, or why it is that extensive brain damage after the earliest years of life does not cause autism.

I am going to break off my description of this imaginary encounter, to explain why I have followed the to-and-fro of the exchange. Of course this could be a conversation we have with ourselves. What it illustrates is how likely we are to become ensnared by some very understandable but mistaken presumptions about the nature of human psychology. In particular, we should not *presume* that we need to explain a person's difficulties in, say, using language or thinking flexibly, in terms of dysfunction of specific bits of the brain designed to 'compute' linguistic structure or to support the neurological activity that plans flexible actions. Instead we must take seriously the facts of development. Brain development depends as much on a person's experience as a person's experience depends upon the development of the brain. Moreover, in explaining psychological development, we often need an explanation in terms of the kinds of *experience* that are responsible for emergent social and cognitive abilities. In the case of autism, correspondingly, we may need to complement the usual 'external' perspectives from medicine or brain science or information-processing models of psychology, with an account of the children's experiences of the world. If children with autism experience the world differently, then how far do *their* experiences provide what is needed to establish relations with other people, to tap into the resources of cultural life, and to develop increasingly sophisticated concepts and flexible ways of dealing with the environment?

Such questions do not gainsay the importance of brain pathology in causing the syndrome of autism. They do not, emphatically not, prompt a return to so-called psychogenic theories of autism. Of course, brain disorders are responsible for many striking abnormalities in a person's experiences. Some abnormalities in experience are so exceptional that they occur more or less exclusively in the context of serious organic dysfunction (including severe perceptual impairments). Those that characterize autism are almost certainly of this kind. As Kanner's original account illustrated, there is no contradiction whatsoever in viewing autism as a biologically-based neurodevelopmental disorder, and seeing that one of the basic, core abnormalities lies in the children's limited or atypical experiences, and specifically, experiences of other people.

It might be a challenging task to explain all this to your friend in the café. It is even more challenging to argue the case with many researchers in the field of cognitive science. Yet now we come to another consideration that is even more radical, and even more controversial. Suppose we accept that what is common to the experience of young children with autism, or perhaps what is common to such children by way of lack in experience, might have important implications for subsequent development. There is a complication to this when we are considering *social* experience. In this domain, we may need to draw away from an exclusive concern with the individual child's psychology, and consider what happens *between* the child and others. In particular, we may need to focus upon a child's experience of the world *through* others. In other words, the story does not stop with how a child relates to others. It extends to the child's relations with others' relations with a shared world, or to put this differently, to the child's engagement with other people's experiences of the world. Very importantly, this world-as-related-to-by-others includes the child him- or herself.

Now, at last, I can explain the title of this chapter, 'On being moved in thought and feeling: an approach to autism', because I want to approach the question 'What is autism?' from a fresh starting-point, one that encompasses a particular view of typical development. The view is that early interpersonal experience is critically important for the acquisition of cognitive as well as social abilities. On the other side to this coin is a thesis about what makes autism 'autism'. The thesis is closely allied to Kanner's (1943, p.250) suggestion that the children have 'inborn disturbances of affective contact'. The story is one that focuses both on what individual children lack by way of the necessary equipment to achieve fully-fledged intersubjective engagement with others, and what follows by way of interference with the kinds of *inter*personal process that normally promote flexibility in children's thinking and attitudes.

The central idea is that *being moved by others* – and here I am talking about movement in subjective orientation, especially as these involve feelings and attitudes – is one of the most significant features of human social life. It is foundational for experiencing people *as* people with their own subjective orientations to the world, for evolving forms of self–other awareness, for the construction of increasingly sophisticated concepts about the mind ('theory of mind'), for self-reflection and aspects of executive functioning, and for the kinds of symbolic functioning and flexible stance in relation to the world that contribute so much to human creativity in thinking and action.

Of course it will not be possible for me to argue for each and every one of these claims. I have tried to do so in two books (Hobson 1993, 2002), of which the most recent (*The Cradle of Thought*) is intended to be reader-friendly to a wide audience. What I shall try to do in this contribution is to illustrate what I mean by 'being moved'. I shall do this by citing specific studies, mainly but not exclusively conducted in the Developmental Psychopathology Research Unit, Tavistock Clinic and University College London. En route, I shall offer some reflections on the implications of the findings for our notion of what is 'basic' to autism.

A CLINICAL PERSPECTIVE

Whenever I need to regain my bearings with regard to autism, I turn not to DSM-IV (American Psychiatric Association 1994], nor to some expensive textbook crammed with the latest novelties from experimental science, but to my much-thumbed and heavily underlined photocopy of Leo Kanner's (1943) paper in *Nervous Child*. Here is why: consider this single excerpt concerning Case 2, Frederick, attending Kanner's clinic for the first time at the age of six years:

> He was led into the psychiatrist's office by a nurse, who left the room immediately afterward. His facial expression was tense, somewhat apprehensive, and gave the impression of intelligence. He wandered aimlessly about for a few moments, showing no sign of awareness of the three adults present. He then sat down on the couch, ejaculating unintelligible sounds, and then abruptly lay down, wearing throughout a dreamy-like smile. When he responded to questions or commands at all, he did so by repeating them echolalia fashion [i.e. echoing back exactly what was said]. The most striking feature in his behavior was the difference in his reactions to objects and to people. Objects absorbed him easily and he showed good attention and perseverance in playing with them. He seemed to regard people as unwelcome intruders to whom he paid as little attention as they would permit. When forced to respond, he did so briefly and returned to his absorption in things. When a hand was held out before him so that he could not possibly ignore it, he played with it briefly as if it were a detached object. He blew out a match with an expression of satisfaction with the achievement, but did not look up to the person who had lit the match. (p.224)

I have just discovered that I cited this very excerpt (though other vignettes from Kanner's paper would do almost as well) in the APNA conference of five years ago. No wonder: each time I return to the description, I find something new in it. And it is heartening that now, five years on from the conference, I think I understand just a little more about *why* Frederick was echolalic; why objects, but not people, 'absorbed him easily'; why another person's hand was treated as a detached object; and why he failed to look up to the person who lit the match.

In order to convey what is involved in this shift in perspective, I need to turn from clinical description to systematic scientific research. I shall begin by revisiting three vintage studies ('vintage', it would be nice to think, in the *Shorter English Dictionary* sense of 'wine, especially of good or rare quality', and not merely 'used with reference to the age or year'), with which readers may already be familiar. Two of these studies were conducted by ourselves, and one by researchers at UCLA. My aim here is to see whether, setting off from our new starting-point, we may find that the results reflect how children with autism are relatively 'unmoved' by and to others' attitudes. I shall consider three settings, those involving person-to-person natural interactions, imitation, and person–person–world (so-called 'triadic') relations. I shall then turn to three very recent studies in each of the three settings, to see if these might reveal something more.

'NATURAL' PERSON-TO-PERSON INTERACTION

My colleague Tony Lee and I (Hobson and Lee 1998) studied children and adolescents between 8 and 23 years old, greeting and taking their leave from an unfamiliar person. In fact, I was the unfamiliar person, and Tony was the one with whom the children were already well-acquainted. Tony went to collect each individual in turn from their classroom or workshop, and explained that he would be taking them to meet someone else in another room. I was sitting there waiting, at a table about ten metres from and facing the door. A videocamera was positioned behind my shoulder pointing past my head towards the door so that the child's approach and departure were recorded.

As Tony led the child through the door, he said: '[Child's name], this is Peter.' I kept my eyes on the child's face, but remained silent as I counted two seconds under my breath, to give the child a chance to initiate a greeting. After the two seconds, I said 'Hello, [child's name]' and after a brief pause, indicated the free chair at the table. This was what we called the greeting episode.

We then spent ten minutes engaged in a simple task, and when this was concluded, I thanked the child and said: 'That's all, you can go now.' Tony, who was standing nearby, added: 'Let's go back to the classroom', and began to walk towards the door. The child stood up, and in some cases made a spontaneous communication of farewell. As he or she turned away to leave the table, I said: 'Goodbye.' This was what we called the farewell episode.

Finally, as the child approached the door, I called: 'Goodbye, [child's name]!'.

The videotapes were subsequently rated for the presence or absence of spontaneous or prompted gestures of greeting and farewell, and, in particular, for words and/or nods, for eye-to-face contact, and for smiles.

The results for the 'Hello' episode were that compared with age- and language-matched control children, there were about half as many participants with autism who gave spontaneous expressions of greeting. A substantial proportion of those with autism failed to respond even after prompting. By the end of this episode, almost all non-autistic participants had expressed a greeting to me which included verbal contact (or in the case of one child, a firm nod), all had made eye contact, and a substantial majority had smiled. Among the group with autism, on the other hand, seven of the 24 individuals had failed to acknowledge my presence with a verbal greeting or a nod, eight had failed to make eye contact, and only six had smiled.

The results for the farewell episode were broadly similar, and so I shall simply note that when we looked at how many participants made eye contact and said a goodbye (whether or not these were prompted), half of the non-autistic but only three individuals with autism did so. Of these, nine of the non-autistic but not a single autistic individual also smiled.

The final farewell episode took place as the participants were already heading out of the room. Nearly everyone made some response to my heavy prompt, in most cases a slightly impatient 'Goodbye!', but we noticed that over half the non-autistic but only six participants with autism waved. All these latter participants gave waves that were either ill-directed, or clumsy and limp.

We adopted a second approach to rating the videotapes. We asked our judges to look at the greeting episode up to the time the child sat down at the table. For each child, they were asked to respond to the following question: 'Over this period and prior to sitting down, to what degree did you feel that the child engaged with Peter?' The categories of response were deliberately crude: either strongly engaged, somewhat engaged, or hardly, if at all, engaged. It turned out that different judges who made these ratings independently were in good agreement with each other. The results were that 14 of the non-autistic children were judged to be strongly engaged, and only two hardly, if at all, engaged. In contrast, only two of the children with autism were judged to be strongly engaged, and 13 of them seemed hardly, if at all, engaged.

Now one important lesson from this study is that intersubjective engagement is something one can assess objectively. It occurs through, and is manifest in, such bodily expressions as eye contact, gestures and smiles, but it also has a 'subjective' dimension. Interpersonal engagement is felt as well as observed. Beyond this, however, one can consider how observations such as these reflect the degree to which one person is 'moved' not only to *behave* in new ways when engaging with someone else, but also to *shift in attitude* and stance as part and parcel of that engagement. This is so obvious that it hardly deserves comment: *of course* interpersonal engagement entails new kinds of attitude and stance, because that is what interpersonal engagement means. So when, on entering the room, the children without autism immediately gave gestures of greeting, established eye contact, and smiled, or when they communicated farewell, for example by waving, these bodily expressions were indeed expressive of interpersonal attitudes of greeting and taking leave from someone else. The very presence, and then the behaviour, of someone else in the room elicited such qualities of relatedness. So the point is self-evident: encounters with another person can and do lead to shifts in mental stance as one becomes intersubjectively engaged, and such engagement involves a special set of attitudes both to the person, and to the person's attitudes towards oneself. The very concepts of 'greeting' or 'taking one's leave from' someone else implicate the coordinated attitudes involved in establishing or breaking interpersonal contact. And these concepts also entail *movement* from one set of attitudes (when one is not engaged with someone else) to another (when one is). Again rather obviously, one could see clear changes in the way the participants without autism felt and communicated when becoming engaged with, and then departing from, the unfamiliar adult. In the case of the children with autism, the changes in attitude, as manifest in communicative bodily expressions but also detectable through the 'subjective judgements' of our raters, were much less striking.

It may be worth adding some reflections on two aspects of these findings. First, the participants without autism appeared to take it for granted that the unfamiliar adult would be oriented towards themselves and anticipate communication from them. They, too, appeared to expect communication from the adult. Not only did they expect to experience (and probably, share) experiences of being greeted, for example, but so, too, they expected the adult to expect such experiences. This correspondence between what participants felt in themselves, and what they anticipated in the adult, is not trivial. They must have come to recognize that, in certain respects, there exists a kind of 'identity' between themselves and others, as potential communicators and sharers of experience.

Second, what about those waves? Why should they have been so uncommon among the participants with autism, and so peculiarly ill-directed (often not towards the adult), uncoordinated and limp? From a communicative point of view, they were hardly the most convincing of gestures. The question arises: how do children *without* autism come to wave in such a recognizably adult-like way? As anyone who knows young children will testify, early waves are far from 'adult-like' in the details of action, yet they are directed towards the other, they are usually far from limp, and they are communicatively arresting. Presumably, something of the morphology of the wave, together with its communicative intent and directedness, are learned. If they are learned, they are learned from others who are observed to wave their hands (the morphology of waves involves more than hands, of course) in settings where they are taking leave of either the child or other people. Is it enough to suppose that mere 'copying' is involved here? Or are we witnessing a form of role-taking into the bodily-expressed, intersubjectively-coloured, communicatively-intended, message-sending act? In other words, might it be that typical children *identify with* others who wave? If this is so, then the strange waves of the individuals with autism might reflect how they have missed out on this kind of interpersonal, shaping experience. But is this plausible? The evidence that follows is relevant for addressing this question.

IMITATION

In a study conducted by Hobson and Lee (1999), matched groups of children with and without autism were tested for their ability to imitate a person demonstrating four novel goal-directed actions on objects in two contrasting 'styles'. For example, they saw the demonstrator press down the head of a toy policeman on wheels to make him move, where the demonstrator used either his wrist or two outstretched fingers to depress the head; another example is that they saw him 'strum' a wooden stick along another wooden object with slots in its edge (in fact, an old pipe-rack of mine), to make a staccato sound, either harshly or gently. Our aim was to see how far the children copied the *way* in which someone else carried out the actions, and we anticipated there would be a dissociation between two components of this ability. One sense of adopting another person's way of doing something is to copy the person's strategy of action to achieve a goal. Because such an ability might require only that the participants would need to observe the goal of the action and the means to achieve the goal, we predicted that those with autism would manage this well. A second sense of adopting another person's way of doing something is to imitate the 'style' with which the person conducts or expresses himself, for example whether he uses a harsh or gentle approach, even when this is irrelevant to achieving the goal.

The results confirmed our predictions. The children with autism copied the goal-directed aspect of the actions, but showed marked divergence from the control group insofar as very few adopted the demonstrator's style of acting upon the objects involved. Moreover, when the actions were 'self-orientated', as in the case of the pipe-rack that the demonstrator positioned against his own shoulder, most of the participants who did not have autism responded by positioning the pipe-rack against *their* own shoulder. Those with autism, by contrast, tended to ignore this aspect of the strumming episode, and simply laid the pipe-rack on the table in front of them.

We interpreted the results of this study in terms of a distinction between the children's ability to observe and copy actions per se, relatively intact in autism, and their propensity to identify with and thereby imitate a *person's* expressive mode of relating to the world. The participants with autism were not 'moved' to take the same bodily expressive mode of action that was demonstrated by the other person. Here it is of note that many aspects of imitation specifically impaired in autism concern the ability to copy facial, vocal and gestural expressions, or variants of these such as meaningless postures, which convey such 'expressive modes of relating' rather than strategies of goal-directed action. Children with autism appear to be less responsive to such expressive features of another person's actions (Hobson 1995). When one considers how such responsiveness applies to patterns of bodily configuration, rhythm, and flow that convey something of a person's emotional quality or tone (Stern 1985), one begins to appreciate a domain in which imitating a person's actions and responding to a person's feelings overlap. It is in this domain that the concept of identification fills an important gap in our theorizing about how children are 'moved' to adopt the stance of someone else.

PERSON–PERSON–WORLD (TRIADIC) RELATIONS

There is another respect in which children can be moved to adopt new attitudes through their engagement with the attitudes of others. This is when someone is observed to have an emotional reaction to objects and events in the environment. Marian Sigman and her colleagues (Sigman *et al.* 1992) explored whether children with autism show this kind of interpersonal coordination of affect. Participants were 30 young autistic children with a mean age of under four years, and closely matched non-autistic retarded and typically developing children. The technique was to code these children's behaviour when an adult pretended to hurt herself by hitting her finger with a hammer, simulated fear towards a remote-controlled robot, and pretended to be ill by lying down on a couch for a minute, feigning discomfort. In each of these situations, children with autism were unusual in rarely looking at or relating to the adult. When the adult pretended to be hurt, for example, children with autism often appeared unconcerned and continued to play with toys. When a small remote-controlled robot moved towards the child and stopped about four feet away, the parent and the experimenter, who were both seated nearby, made fearful facial expressions, gestures and vocalizations for 30 seconds. Almost all the non-autistic children looked at an adult at some point during this procedure, but fewer than half the children with autism did so, and then only briefly. The children with autism were not only less hesitant than the mentally retarded children in playing with the robot, but they also played with it for substantially longer periods of time. It seemed that they were less influenced by the fearful attitudes of those around them. Here again we find evidence that autistic children are relatively 'unengaged' not only in one-to-one interpersonal-affective transactions, but also with another person's emotional attitudes towards objects and events in the world.

These studies have inspired more recent investigations of 20-month-olds by Charman *et al.* (1997). Children's videotaped reactions to an investigator's feigned hurt revealed that only four out of ten children with autism but every one of the non-autistic children looked to the investigator's pained face. When a potentially anxiety-provoking toy was placed on the floor a short distance from the child, the children with autism very rarely switched their gaze between toy and adult to check out the toy (and see Bacon *et al.* 1998, for related results with somewhat older children). In each respect, these very young children seemed unconnected with the feelings of others.

Once again, therefore, we see how children with autism are relatively unmoved to adopt the attitudes of others, both towards others as individual people, and towards objects in the environment. Those meanings that other people find in the world, for example finding a toy frightening, are often meanings to which the children are oblivious. More often than not, they remain 'fixed' in their own position, with relatively little change in their own attitudes, and little change in the meanings they find in the world.

Now I turn to more recent studies that we have conducted in each of these three settings.

'NATURAL' PERSON-TO-PERSON INTERACTION

Here we cite a study that was built upon research we conducted and published some years ago (Lee and Hobson 1998). The research involved us interviewing children and adolescents with autism, along with closely matched participants without autism, to discover how they think about themselves. What emerged was that the two groups were very similar in the ways they described their physical characteristics, whether involving reference to their bodies or their abilities in activities like sport. More surprisingly, they were also similar in the numbers of their responses that made reference to psychological states, although the *quality* of the responses were different in the individuals with autism. They gave more emphasis to their preferences rather than their emotions or intellectual capacities, and there was a limited range of emotions expressed. The principal group difference was that very few of the statements made by the adolescents with autism referred to social relations, and many of those that did merely implied social awareness (for example, with reference to themselves as 'good' or 'nice'). Half as many of the adolescents with autism mentioned their families, but most striking of all, not a single individual with autism mentioned a friend except in passing (and even this happened only once), whereas 70 per cent of the non-autistic adolescents did so. Only a quarter of the adolescents with autism but as many as 90 per cent of those without autism made explicit social statements of other kinds, for example about helping others, being bullied by others and membership of social groups such as scouts.

Now these findings suggest that even within their own minds, individuals with autism rarely think about themselves in relation to other people who have attitudes towards them, and rarely take up a stance in which they think about others, think about themselves, and compare the two in relation to one another. Such forms of intrapsychic role-taking may well implicate being moved to the position of others, and then moving back to a focus on oneself. Whatever the case in this respect, we now wanted to see whether in this interview setting participants with autism could be distinguished in terms of differences in the patterns of mutual engagement (Garcia-Peréz 2003). With this in mind, a pre-selected standard three minutes of the videotaped interview were evaluated second-by-second for aspects of non-verbal communication by independent 'blind' raters.

The results were that the children and adolescents with and without autism were similar in some of these ratings (such as looking and smiling), but different in one important respect. When episodes of explicit affirmative replies to questions were excluded, the children with autism were observed to shake and nod their heads just as often as those in the comparison group when they were the ones speaking, but were significantly less likely to do so when listening to the other person (i.e. the interviewer) speak. This might appear a trivial finding, but it was in keeping with the results from a previous study by Capps, Kehres and Sigman (1998).

So one is led to enquire about the significance of such a phenomenon. Our own view is as follows. Most of us nod unselfconsciously when listening to someone else. If you watch people talking to one another, you will notice this happens a great deal. Sometimes, no doubt, one is deliberately giving support and encouragement to the other person. At other times, however, one is simply thinking about what the other is saying. So just as you nod according to yourself when you are the one speaking (again, watch other people nodding as they speak), perhaps when someone else is speaking you nod *according to yourself in identification with the other*, and with what the other is saying. If this is so, then the observed group difference might arise from the limited degree to which participants with autism identify with the interviewer.

With this hypothesis in mind, we made one further prediction. Given that identification is a reciprocal process, we predicted that the interviewer, too, would demonstrate a lack of identification with the person with autism. If this were the case, he should have a reduced propensity to shake and nod his head when the person with autism was talking. As predicted, the interviewer showed very similar numbers of shakes and nods when he was the one speaking, but a significantly reduced number when the participants with autism were doing the talking. If our interpretation of these findings is correct, then even in moment-to-moment interactions, in autism there is something amiss when it comes to being moved to the stance of the other. Indeed, there is a reciprocal something amiss: both for the children, and for those with whom the children interact, the process of mutually identifying with each other is conspicuous for its absence.

IMITATION

I have already mentioned in passing that one index of identification is the propensity to copy another person's self-orientated actions by transferring that 'self-orientation' to one's own case. In adopting what someone else does in relation to him- or herself, one does it in relation to oneself. In the following study (Meyer and Hobson 2004), we adopted a novel approach to testing this facet of identification in children with autism. We tested 32 children between the ages of 6 and 14 years, 16 with autism and 16 without autism but with learning difficulties or developmental delays. The children with and without autism were group-matched for chronological age, as well as language and fine-motor abilities.

Our procedure began with the tester and child seated on carpet squares on the floor, situated on opposite ends of a testing mat, directly across from each other at a distance of approximately 20 inches (50 cm). There were two straight lines of blue tape across the mat, one 5 inches (12.5 cm) in front of the experimenter and one at the same distance in front of the participant, leaving 10 inches (25 cm) between the two lines of tape. The lines of tape were employed to standardize the administration and coding of the orientation of the actions.

The actions involved stacking one box on top of another, strumming a stick along a wooden frog's serrated back to produce a croaking noise, rolling a small wheel with a metal handle and tapping a set of beanbags. These actions were presented in a fixed order, but with systematic variation in whether they were administered first in a self-orientated or other-orientated version. In each case, the investigator placed the object(s) for the test in specific locations with regard to herself, the participant and the centre area of the testing mat. She secured the child's attention by using his or her name and giving the instruction 'Watch this', and demonstrated an action on the object(s) that was orientated in movement in relation to the child or the examiner. This involved: (i) altering the position of the object(s) either towards the child or the examiner, and/or (ii) acting on the object(s) relative to her own and the child's positions. After demonstrating the action, the examiner returned the object(s) to the original position and instructed the child: 'Now you.' There was no explicit instruction to copy what the investigator had done. The children saw the investigator produce each action in one of two possible orientations – towards or close to herself, or towards or close to the child – for each of the four conditions in the first visit, and saw the alternative orientation for each condition in a second visit on another day.

The children's subsequent actions were scored as reflecting *identification* if the child copied the investigator's stance (i.e. the action in relation to self or other). For example, identification occurred when the children imitated the tester's close-to-self-orientation by rolling the wheel close to him- or herself (i.e. on the participant's side of his or her line of tape), or copied close-to-other-orientation by rolling the wheel close to the investigator. In those cases where the action was *not* characterized by identification with the other person's stance, we made a further categorization: was it simply that the response was out of keeping with identification, and perhaps without specific orientation, or did it take the form of an exact replication of the action, so that it resulted in a second run-through of the child's original view of what was done to the object(s)? In the latter case, we classified the response as being an instance of geometric repetition.

The only participants in either group who failed to copy all eight actions were one participant with autism and one child in the comparison group, who each copied all but one action. In accordance with our prediction, the children with autism were significantly less likely to imitate the self–other orientation of the actions. Thus any group differences were not determined by inattentiveness on the part of children with autism, nor were they affected by failure to perceive, recall and copy the actions demonstrated. On the contrary, all participants copied many essentials of each of the actions on almost every condition of the task.

The main findings were that while half of the children in the comparison group copied the self–other orientation of the actions on at least half of the eight trials, only 3 out of the 16 children with autism did so; and from a complementary perspective, six of the participants with autism imitated self–other orientation on fewer than two occasions, while only one participant in the comparison group did so as infrequently as this.

Then we examined the children's responses according to the most prevalent category of response, that is whether they primarily responded with *identification* on the one hand, or *geometric repetition* on the other, or whether there was no consistent orientation. Half of the children (eight in each group) fell into this latter category and displayed a lack of consistent orientation. Of the remaining eight children in the control group, *all* eight showed a predominant response of identifying with the investigator, and adopting her self–other orientation relative to themselves. Therefore not a single child in the comparison group used geometric repetition as a primary form of response. Of the remaining eight participants with autism, by contrast, five of the children showed a predominant response of geometric repetition, and only three that of identification.

Thus, the response strategy of geometric repetition – that is, responding so that the physical movements and locations of the objects acted-upon were replicated – was predominant among some (albeit a minority) of the children with autism, but none of the children in the control group. This result, reminiscent of instances of mimicry and echolalia reported in clinical accounts of autism, suggests either that these children had a natural propensity to be object- or stimulus-bound in their focus of attention, or perhaps more plausibly, given the sporadic nature of such responses, that they had developed this mode of apprehending and/or dealing with the world in the relative *absence* of the contrasting orientation towards other people's stance-in-acting. In either case, there was a group difference in the degree to which participants were moved to adopt the self/other-orientated stance that was demonstrated.

PERSON–PERSON–WORLD (TRIADIC) RELATIONS

This third novel study (Hobson, Lee and Meyer 2004) is an investigation of three things at once: person–person–world relations, imitation and communication. The kind of interpersonal exchanges we tested were intended to highlight several different aspects of the one essential element of social engagement that has been the subject of this chapter: 'being moved' to adopt and adjust to someone else's stance.

Two investigators met with children and adolescents who either did or did not have autism. While the first investigator demonstrated an action to the participant, the second investigator remained outside of the testing room. Prior to each demonstration, participants were instructed to 'Get Pete to do this' (where Pete was the second investigator not present during the demonstration). Participants were each presented with a series of eight actions, one at a time, in fixed order. Three actions involved goal-directed use of objects such as using a mechanical arm to place a cloth frog into a waste-bin, two were non-goal-directed involving the body such as raising one's hands above one's head, and three included a form of expressive style such as placing one's hands on one's hips in a proud, assertive stance.

Following the demonstration of each action, the second investigator was invited to re-enter the room, and the participant's task was to communicate to him what needed to be done. While the first investigator observed, the participant conveyed the message to the second investigator, who initially failed to execute the action accurately (using a standard set of conspicuous and mildly humorous errors), then made an improved but stylistically inaccurate attempt to provide a chance for the participant to give further feedback or assistance, and finally carried out the action accurately. The second investigator conveyed his fumbling struggles to understand what action he was supposed to do, often looking toward the participant and, if not given assistance, asking for feedback. The sessions were videotaped for later scoring by independent judges who were unaware of group membership.

All of the participants were attentive to the demonstrations of the actions by the first investigator. Indeed, the majority copied the actions of the first investigator when relaying the message to the second investigator most of the time, and all participants used copying at least once. As predicted, however, there were several group differences. The participants with autism had difficulty shifting from being in the role of learner, where the actions were shown to them, to the role of teacher in which it was important to not only show the action, but also be attentive and sensitive to the needs of their communicative partner as a learner. They were also significantly less likely to adopt the expressive style used by the first investigator in his demonstration (e.g. jumping vigorously onto a cloth frog). They were less emotionally engaged with the testers; for example, children in the comparison group reacted with expressions of humour and pride whereas those with autism were often rated as emotionally disconnected. Finally, they were limited in their propensity to engage in joint attention, for example in sharing the experience of the second investigator's humorous and successful attempts with the first investigator.

We consider that identification with someone else is a critical ingredient of each of these facets of social engagement. Role shifting, the imitation of expressive style, joint attention and emotional engagement each involve a special quality and intensity of engagement with another person's bodily-expressed attitudes. I shall conclude by distilling what this 'special quality and intensity of engagement' means.

CONCLUSIONS

I shall make these conclusions brief. I trust that in the research I have described, and our approach to interpreting the findings, it is apparent why colleagues and myself consider that individuals with autism are distinctive in having a lesser (but probably not absent) propensity to identify with other people. This is the process we consider to underlie those various and pervasive occasions when one person is moved in attitude and psychological orientation by and through another person. In our view, it is a basic and hugely important propensity of human beings, from early in life. It moves a child to engage with, empathize and share feelings with others, and to shift in attitude through engaging with others' relations towards the world. If we are correct that individuals with autism have a relative lack in the propensity to identify with others and to be moved in the ways I have described, it comes as no surprise that in their thoughts as well as feelings, they remain in a one-track, inflexible stance instead of shifting, shifting, and shifting again in accordance with the attitudes and actions of other people.

Most human beings enjoy the kind of social engagement in which one 'dwells in' the experiences of another person, in such a way that one feels something of those experiences not only for the other, but also for and within oneself. We are 'moved' by others. Individuals with autism may need sensitive and energetic help, if they are to share the pleasures and benefits of such forms of social engagement that come naturally to those of us who do not have autism.

ACKNOWLEDGEMENTS

I give sincere thanks to my colleagues Jessica Meyer, Tony Lee and Rosa Garcia-Peréz for sharing in the research work and thinking that went into this chapter, the final stages of which were completed while I was a Fellow at the Center for Advanced Study in the Behavioral Sciences, Stanford, US.

REFERENCES

American Psychiatric Association (1994) *Diagnostic and Statistical Manual of Mental Disorders* (4th edn, revised). Washington, DC: American Psychiatric Association.

Bacon, A. L., Fein, D., Morris, R., Waterhouse, L. and Allen, D. (1998) 'The responses of autistic children to the distress of others.' *Journal of Autism and Developmental Disorders 28*, 129–142.

Capps, L., Kehres, J. and Sigman, M. (1998) 'Conversational abilities among children with autism and children with developmental delays.' *Autism 2*, 325–344.

Charman, T., Swettenham, J., Baron-Cohen, S., Cox, A., Baird, G. and Drew, A. (1997) 'Infants with autism: an investigation of empathy, pretend play, joint attention, and imitation.' *Developmental Psychology 33*, 781–789.

Garcia-Peréz, R. (2003) *Conversational Non-verbal Communication in Autism*. Presentation at the biennial meeting of the Society for Research in Child Development, Tampa, Florida.

Hobson, R. P. (1993) *Autism and the Development of Mind*. Hove, Sussex: Lawrence Erlbaum.

Hobson, R. P. (1995) 'Apprehending attitudes and actions: separable abilities in early development?' *Development and Psychopathology 7*, 171–182.

Hobson, R. P. (2002) *The Cradle of Thought*. London: Macmillan.

Hobson, R. P. and Lee, A. (1998) 'Hello and goodbye: a study of social engagement in autism.' *Journal of Autism and Developmental Disorders 28*, 117–126.

Hobson, R. P. and Lee, A. (1999) 'Imitation and identification in autism.' *Journal of Child Psychology and Psychiatry 40*, 649–659.

Hobson, R. P., Lee, A. and Meyer, J. A. (2004) *Impaired Communication in Autism: The Case of Identification*. Presentation at the International Meeting for Autism Research, 7–8 May, Sacramento, CA.

Kanner, L. (1943) 'Autistic disturbances of affective contact.' *Nervous Child 2*, 217–250.

Lee, A. and Hobson, R. P. (1998) 'On developing self-concepts: a controlled study of children and adolescents with autism.' *Journal of Child Psychology and Psychiatry 39*, 1131–1141.

Meyer, J. A. and Hobson, R. P. (2004) 'Orientation in relation to self and other: the case of autism.' *Interaction Studies 5*, 221–244.

Sigman, M. D., Kasari, C., Kwon, J. H. and Yirmiya, N. (1992) 'Responses to the negative emotions of others by autistic, mentally retarded, and normal children.' *Child Development 63*, 796–807.

Stern, D. N. (1985) *The Interpersonal World of the Infant.* New York: Basic Books.

Chapter 7

Systemizing and Empathizing in Autism Spectrum Conditions

Sally Wheelwright

INTRODUCTION

Autism spectrum conditions (ASCs) are diagnosed when a child or adult has abnormalities in a 'triad' of behavioural domains: social development, communication, and repetitive behaviour/obsessive interests (APA 1994; ICD-10 1994). In the past, cognitive developmental theories of autism have not attempted to account for the whole triad; rather they have focused on one or two of its components. Here we present a new theory, empathizing–systemizing (E–S) theory, which does account for the whole triad. E–S theory evolved from the mindblindness theory of autism.

MINDBLINDNESS THEORY

The mindblindness theory of autism (Baron-Cohen 1995) proposed that in autism spectrum conditions, there are deficits in the normal process of empathizing, relative to mental age. These deficits can occur by degrees. Here we use the term 'empathizing' to encompass 'theory of mind', 'mind-reading', and taking the 'intentional stance' (Dennett 1987).

Empathizing involves two major elements: (a) the ability to attribute mental states to oneself and others, as a natural way to understand agents (Baron-Cohen 1994a, 1994b; Leslie 1995; Premack 1990), and (b) having an emotional reaction that is appropriate to the other person's mental state. In this sense, it includes what is normally meant by the term 'theory of mind' (the attributional component) but it goes beyond this, to also include having some affective reaction (such as sympathy).

Empathizing thus essentially allows us to make sense of the behaviour of another agent we are observing, predict what they might do next, and how they might feel.

And it allows us to feel connected to another agent's experience, and respond appropriately to them.

Since the first test of mindblindness in children with autism (Baron-Cohen, Leslie and Frith 1985), there have been more than 30 experimental tests. The vast majority of these have revealed profound impairments in the development of their empathizing ability. These are reviewed elsewhere (Baron-Cohen 1995; Baron-Cohen, Tager-Flusberg and Cohen 1993), but include deficits in the following:

- joint attention (Baron-Cohen 1989a)

- use of mental state terms in language (Tager-Flusberg 1993)

- production and comprehension of pretence (Baron-Cohen 1987; Wing and Gould 1979)

- understanding that 'seeing-leads-to-knowing' (Baron-Cohen and Goodhart 1994; Leslie and Frith 1988)

- distinguishing mental from physical entities (Baron-Cohen 1989b; Ozonoff, Pennington and Rogers 1990)

- making the appearance–reality distinction (Baron-Cohen 1989b)

- understanding false belief (Baron-Cohen *et al.* 1985)

- understanding beliefs about beliefs (Baron-Cohen 1989c)

- understanding complex emotions (Baron-Cohen 1991)

- showing concern at another's pain (Yirmiya *et al.* 1992).

Some children and adults with Asperger syndrome (AS) only show their empathizing deficits on age-appropriate adult tests (Baron-Cohen *et al.* 1997a, 1997b, 2001). This deficit in their empathizing is thought to underlie the difficulties such children have in social and communicative development (Baron-Cohen 1988; Tager-Flusberg 1993), and the development of imagination (Baron-Cohen 1987; Leslie 1987).

EMPATHIZING–SYSTEMIZING (E–S) THEORY

As explained above, we have defined empathizing so as to include both the recognition of mental states, and the appropriate emotional response to these. A deficit in empathizing might account for the social and communication abnormalities that are diagnostic of autism, but such a deficit has little if anything to contribute to our understanding of the third domain of abnormality in the triad: the repetitive behaviour and obsessions. For this reason, our view of autism is now broader, and suggests that alongside empathizing deficits, a different process is *intact or even superior*. This is what we call *systemizing*.

Systemizing is the drive to analyse the variables in a system, to derive the underlying rules that govern the behaviour of a system. Systemizing also refers to the drive to construct systems. Systemizing allows you to *predict* the behaviour of a system, and to control it.

A system is defined as something that takes inputs, which can then be operated on in *variable* ways, to deliver *different* outputs in a rule-governed way. There are at least six kinds of system, technical, natural, abstract, social, organizable and motoric, but all share this same underlying process which is monitored closely during systemizing:

Below, an example from each of the six types of system is given:

INPUT ⟶ OPERATION ⟶ OUTPUT

(A) An example of a *technical* system: a sail

INPUT	OPERATION	OUTPUT
Sail	Angle 10 degrees	Speed slow
Sail	Angle 30 degrees	Speed medium
Sail	Angle 60 degrees	Speed fast

(B) An example of a *natural* system: a flower

INPUT	OPERATION	OUTPUT
Rhododendron	Mildly alkaline soil	Light blue petals
Rhododendron	Strongly alkaline soil	Dark blue petals
Rhododendron	Acidic soil	Pink petals

(C) An example of an *abstract* system: a number

INPUT	OPERATION	OUTPUT
3	Squared	9
3	Cubed	27
3	Inverse	0.3

(D) An example of a *social* system: a constituency boundary

INPUT	OPERATION	OUTPUT
New York	Inner city	Small number of voters
New York	Whole city	Medium number of voters
New York	Whole state	Large number of voters

(E) An example of an *organizable* system: a CD collection

INPUT	OPERATION	OUTPUT
CD collection	Alphabetical	Order on shelf A–Z
CD collection	Date of release	Order on shelf 1980–2000
CD collection	Genre	Order on shelf: classical–pop

(F) An example of a *motoric* system: a tennis stroke

INPUT	OPERATION	OUTPUT
Hit ball	Top spin	Ball bounces left
Hit ball	Back spin	Ball bounces right
Hit ball	No spin	Ball bounces forward

As can be seen in the examples above, the process in systemizing is always the same. One of the three elements (typically the input) is treated as a *fixed* feature (i.e. it is held constant), whilst another of the three elements (typically the operation) is treated as a *variable* (i.e. it can vary: think of a dimmer on a light switch). Merely observing the consequences of these two elements delivers you important information: the output changes from Output 1, to Output 2, to Output 3. That is, you learn about the system. Systemizing works for phenomena that are indeed ultimately lawful, finite and deterministic. Note that the other way we systemize is when we are confronted by various outputs, and try to infer *backwards* from the output as to what the operation is that produces this particular output.

Systemizing is of almost no use when it comes to predicting the moment-by-moment changes in a person's behaviour. To predict human behaviour, empathizing is required. Systemizing and empathizing are very different kinds of processes. Empathizing involves attributing mental states to others, and responding with appropriate affect to the other's affective state. Empathizing covers not only what is sometimes called 'theory of mind', or 'mentalizing' (Morton, Frith and Leslie 1991), but also what is covered by the English words 'empathy' and 'sympathy'.

To see why you cannot systemize a person's behaviour with much predictive power, consider the next example:

INPUT	OPERATION	OUTPUT
Jane	Birthday	Relaxes
Jane	Birthday	Withdraws
Jane	Birthday	Laughs
Jane	Birthday	Cries

Why does the same input (Jane) have such different outputs (behaviour) when the same operation (her birthday) is repeated? Someone who relies on systemizing to predict people's behaviour would have to conclude that people are not clearly rule-governed. This is a correct conclusion, but there is nevertheless an alternative way of predicting and making sense of Jane's behaviour: via empathizing. During empathizing, the focus is on the person's *mental state* (including his or her emotion). Furthermore, during empathizing there is an appropriate emotional reaction in the observer to the other person's mental state. Without this extra stage, one could have a very accurate reading of the person's emotion, a very accurate prediction of the other's behaviour, but a psychopathic lack of concern about A's mental state.

To complicate matters further, during empathizing, the observer does not expect lawful relationships between the person's mental state and his or her behaviour. The observer only expects that the person's mental state will at least constrain their behaviour.

TESTING E–S THEORY

The E–S theory of autism makes clear predictions about how people with ASCs should score on tests of empathizing and systemizing, relative to people without ASCs: people with ASCs should find empathizing tasks more difficult, whilst matching or even out-performing people without ASCs on systemizing tasks. In fact, we can go further with our predictions relating to people without ASCs. The extreme male brain (EMB) theory of autism (Baron-Cohen and Hammer 1997) holds that the cognitive profile seen in people with ASCs is an extreme variation of that seen in non-affected males. So scores on tests of *empathizing* should follow this pattern:

People with an ASC   <   Non-ASC males   <   Non-ASC females

Whilst this picture is reversed for tests of *systemizing*:

People with an ASC   >   Non-ASC males   >   Non-ASC females

There is already some evidence for this predicted pattern of results. For example, in the 'Reading the Mind in the Eyes' Test, females score higher than males, and people with AS score even lower than males (Baron-Cohen *et al.* 1997b). In this empathizing test, participants have to choose the word that best describes what a person is thinking or feeling, just by looking at a picture of their eyes. In the embedded figures task (EFT), which is a systemizing test, participants are asked to find a simple shape in a much more complex, colourful design (Jolliffe and Baron-Cohen 1997; Shah and Frith 1983). On the EFT, males score higher than females, and people with AS or HFA score even higher than males. Note that this theory does not make any predictions about whether there will be a difference between how males and females with ASCs will score in comparison with each other.

The experiments presented here test the E–S theory using two approaches. In Experiment 1, we tested the E–S theory using two self-report questionnaires: the systemizing quotient (SQ) and the empathizing quotient (EQ). In Experiment 2, we tested E–S theory using two cognitive tests: the Physical Prediction Questionnaire (PPQ) and the Social Stories™ Questionnaire (SSQ) (Lawson, Baron-Cohen and Wheelwright 2004).

EXPERIMENT 1
Instruments

The SQ was designed to be short, easy to complete and easy to score. It is shown in Appendix 7.1. The SQ comprises 60 questions: 40 assessing systemizing and 20 filler (control) items. Approximately half the items were worded to produce a 'disagree' response, and half an 'agree' response, for the systemizing response. This was to avoid a response bias either way. Following this, items were randomized. An individual scores two points if they strongly display a systemizing response and one point if they slightly display a systemizing response. There are 20 filler items (items 2, 3, 8, 9, 10, 14, 16, 17, 21, 22, 27, 36, 39, 46, 47, 50, 52, 54, 58, 59), randomly interspersed throughout the SQ, to distract the participant from a relentless focus on systemizing. These questions are not scored at all. The final version of the SQ has a forced-choice format, can be self-administered, and is straightforward to score, since it does not depend on any interpretation in the scoring.

The EQ, shown in Appendix 7.2, has a very similar structure to the SQ, in that it also comprises 60 questions, broken down into two types: 40 questions tapping empathy and 20 filler items (items 2, 3, 5, 7, 9, 13, 16, 17, 20, 23, 24, 30, 31, 33, 40, 45, 47, 51, 53, 56). Each of the empathy items scores one point if the respondent records the empathic behaviour mildly, or two if strongly (see below for scoring each item). Like the SQ, approximately half the items were worded to produce a 'disagree' response, and half an 'agree' response for the empathic response, to avoid a response bias either way. Also, like the SQ, the EQ has a forced-choice format, can be self-administered and is straightforward to score.

Participants

Two groups of participants (all of whom had given informed consent) were tested:

Group 1 comprised n=88 adults with AS (41 males, 47 females). All participants in this group had been diagnosed by psychiatrists using established criteria for autism or AS (APA 1994). They were recruited via several sources, including the National Autistic Society (UK), specialist clinics carrying out diagnostic assessments and adverts in newsletters/web-pages for adults with AS or high-functioning autism (HFA). Their mean age was 34.9 years (sd=12.0). They had all attended mainstream schooling and were reported to have an IQ in the normal range. Their occupations reflected their mixed socio-economic status (SES).

Group 2 comprised n=278 normal adults (114 males, 164 females) taken from two sources: n=104 were drawn from the general public from the UK and Canada, and represented a mix of occupations, including professional, clerical and manual workers; n=174 were drawn from undergraduate students currently studying at Cambridge University or a local A Level college in Cambridge. Students from a variety of disciplines were targeted. An initial analysis found that there was no difference between the participants from the different sources so their results were pooled together. The students had a mean age of 20.5 years (sd=6.5) and the non-students had a mean age of 41.3 years (sd=12.7).

Method

Participants were sent the SQ and EQ by post or completed online versions of the questionnaires. Participants were instructed to complete the two questionnaires on their own, as quickly as possible, and to avoid thinking about their responses too long. They could choose for themselves in which order to complete the questionnaires. Participants in Group 2 had the option to remain anonymous.

Scoring

THE SQ

'Strongly agree' responses score two points, and 'slightly agree' responses score one point, on the following items: 1, 4, 5, 7, 13, 15, 19, 20, 25, 29, 30, 33, 34, 37, 41, 44, 48, 49, 53, 55. 'Strongly disagree' responses score two points, and 'slightly disagree' responses score one point, on the following items: 6, 11, 12, 18, 23, 24, 26, 28, 31, 32, 35, 38, 40, 42, 43, 45, 51, 56, 57, 60. The filler (control) questions score no points, irrespective of how the individual answers them. Nevertheless, responses on the filler items were analysed for any systematic bias.

THE EQ

'Strongly agree' responses score two points, and 'slightly agree' responses score one point, on the following items: 1, 6, 19, 22, 25, 26, 35, 36, 37, 38, 41, 42, 43, 44, 52, 54, 55, 57, 58, 59, 60. 'Strongly disagree' responses score two points, and 'slightly disagree' responses score one point, on the following items: 4, 8, 10, 11, 12, 14, 15, 18, 21, 27, 28, 29, 32, 34, 39, 46, 48, 49, 50.

Results

Mean SQ and EQ results are shown in Table 7.1. Figure 7.1 shows the distribution of SQ scores from the AS group, non-AS males and non-AS females, and Figure 7.2 shows the EQ distribution. Note that the curve from the AS/HFA group is only based on n=88, whilst the curves from the control males and females are based on n=278. The AS group is not split into males and females because of small numbers.

Table 7.1 Means and standard deviations for both groups on the SQ and EQ

Group		SQ score	EQ score
AS males (n = 47)	mean	38.9	16.6
	sd	13.9	8.0
AS females (n = 41)	mean	37.2	18.0
	sd	17.4	10.2
Combined AS group (n = 88)	mean	38.1	17.3
	sd	15.5	9.0
Non-AS males (n = 114)	mean	30.3	38.8
	sd	11.4	12.4
Non-AS females (n = 164)	mean	24.1	47.4
	sd	9.9	11.6
Combined non-AS group (n = 278)	mean	26.7	43.9
	sd	10.9	12.6

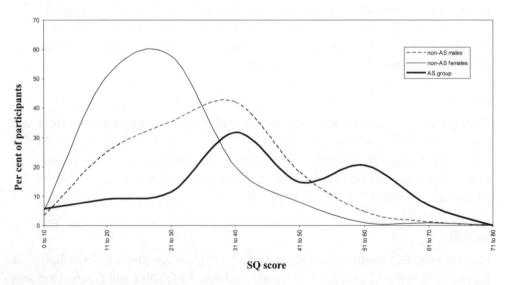

Figure 7.1 The distribution of SQ scores

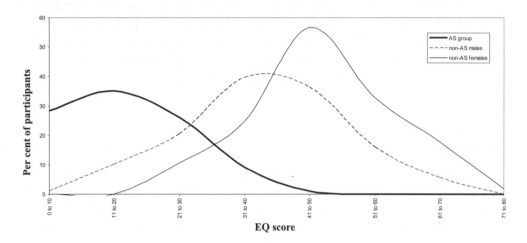

Figure 7.2 The distribution of EQ scores

Separate ANOVAs were conducted on the SQ and EQ scores with two between subject factors (group: AS vs. non-AS; and sex: males vs. females). For the SQ, there was a significant main effect of group, $F(1,362) = 54.9$, $p<0.0001$, with the AS group scoring higher than the non-AS group. There was also a significant main effect of sex, $F(1,362) = 7.1$, $p = 0.008$, with males scoring higher than females. Finally, the interaction between Group and Sex was not significant, $F(1,362) = 2.3$, $p = 0.128$. For the EQ, there was a significant main effect of group, $F(1,362) = 342.8$, $p<0.0001$, with the non-AS group scoring higher than the AS group. There was also a significant main effect of sex, $F(1,362) = 12.7$, $p.<0.0001$, with females scoring higher than males. Finally, the interaction between Group and Sex was significant, $F(1,362) = 6.7$, $p = 0.01$. Inspection of the means suggested that this interaction arose because the difference between the EQ scores of the male and female participants in the AS group was not significantly different. This was confirmed by a t-test, $t = -0.70$, $d = f86$, $p = 0.49$. This pattern of results was replicated when age was entered as a covariate.

Finally, the EQ and SQ were demonstrated to be significantly negatively correlated to each other, $r = -0.29$, $p<0.0001$.

Discussion

As predicted by E–S theory and EMB theory, people with AS scored highest on the SQ followed by non-AS males, with non-AS females scoring the lowest. These theories were also supported by the results from the EQ: non-AS females scored higher than non-AS males, with people with AS scoring the lowest.

Comparing males and females with AS, for the SQ there was a main effect of sex and no group by sex interaction, suggesting that, as in the non-AS group, males with AS score higher on the SQ than females with AS. However, this appears to be a statistical anomaly as there is just a 1.7 point difference in the scores for males and females with AS. Indeed, a t-test confirmed that there is no difference between males and females with AS on the SQ, $t = 0.5$, $df = 86$, $p = 0.62$. For the EQ, there was also a main effect of sex but the significant interaction between sex and group confirmed that there was no difference between males and females with AS on the EQ.

EXPERIMENT 2
Instruments

The Physical Prediction Questionnaire (PPQ) involves understanding physical systems but was designed to be challenging enough so as to reveal individual differences. It comprises 40 items taken from the Vincent Mechanical Diagrams Test (NIIP n.d.) in which participants study mechanical diagrams and predict the movement of two levers or bobs in response to the movement of a connected lever. The test was in multiple-choice format where participants had to choose one of five possible outcomes. An example of the questions is shown in Appendix 7.3.

The Social Stories™ Questionnaire (SSQ) contains ten short stories and involves utterances made by one character that could upset another character in the story. An example of a vignette is shown in Appendix 7.4. Each story is divided into three sections making 30 sections overall with at least four utterances in each section. Ten of the sections contained a blatant target utterance, ten contained a subtle target utterance and ten contained no target utterance. Each section contained several questions for the participant to answer. First, they had to judge whether the section contained a potentially upsetting utterance and where relevant underline the text in question. Second, they had to judge whether this utterance (if present) would have upset the character concerned. Each of the ten stories also included a control question and only those participants who answered all of these correctly were included in the analysis. Participants were scored according to the number of targets correctly identified. The erroneous identification of non-targets was not included in this paper although it is worth mentioning that no participants consistently answered 'yes' to every question. Decisions concerning whether specific utterances were blatant or subtle in nature were made by a mixed-sex panel of six judges, and only those in which there was unanimous agreement were included.

Participants

A total of 107 adult participants (over the age of 18 years) took part in the study: Group 1 contained 18 males with AS (AS males) diagnosed according to internationally recognized criteria (APA 1994; ICD-10 1994), Group 2 contained 44 males without Asperger syndrome (non-AS males) and Group 3 contained 45 females also without Asperger syndrome (non-AS females). Age and IQ information is summarized in Table 7.2.

Table 7.2 Summary of participant information for Experiment 2

	N	Mean age	sd	Mean IQ	sd	Range
AS males	18	36	11.3	117	6.7	47
Non-AS males	44	30	14.2	113	10.3	36
Non-AS females	45	28	13.1	112	8.3	36

IQ in Group 1 was measured using either the WASI (Wechsler 1999) or the short form WAIS-R (Wechsler 1997) and in the other groups by the NART (Nelson 1991). Although the use of different IQ scales is not ideal it has been argued that the two tests are highly comparable (Crawford *et al.* 1989). These test results serve as an index that all had an IQ in the normal range.

Group 1 consisted of individuals on a research database at the Autism Research Centre. They came from varied socio-economic and educational backgrounds. Groups 2 and 3 were respondents to a newspaper advertisement requesting 'volunteers for research into thinking styles'. The groups did not differ in terms of socio-economic and educational background.

Method

Participants were sent the two test booklets by post, along with a covering letter. As there was no way to control task order they were asked to complete the two booklets in which ever order they preferred. Participants were also instructed to take as long as was needed and to ensure that they were not helped in any way by anyone else. Completed booklets were then returned in person, at which time IQ measurements were taken.

Results

The results from the tests are summarized in Table 7.3 below.

Table 7.3 PPQ and SSQ mean results and standard deviations (sd)

	PPQ		SSQ	
	Mean	sd	Mean	sd
AS males	28.2	11.8	9.2	3.08
Non-AS males	28.0	10.9	12.0	2.98
Non-AS females	16.2	9.3	13.6	2.37

Results from the SSQ were distributed in an approximately gaussian way. The PPQ results, however, showed a bi-modal distribution that appeared to be caused by the differences between male and female scores. As the skewness and kurtosis statistics both fell within the standard 'acceptable range' (-2 to +2), no transformations of the data were carried out.

In response to the slight deviation from normality and the low numbers in the AS group, the results were first examined with a Mann-Whitney test. On the SSQ the non-AS females scored significantly higher than non-AS males ($z = -2.4$, $p<0.02$) who scored higher than the AS males ($z = -3.6$, $p<0.002$). On the PPQ the non-AS females scored significantly lower than their nearest group, the non-AS males ($z = -4.7$, $p<0.001$), but the AS males did not score significantly higher than the non-AS males ($z = -0.161$, $p<0.87$). The SSQ and PPQ scores were then examined using a multivariate analysis of covariance (MANCOVA) and post hoc test (Tukey HSD). In order to examine any possible role of age and IQ these variables were entered as covariates but were found to be non-significant (age, $p>0.171$ and IQ, $p>0.918$). On the SSQ, significant score differences were found between the three groups ($F = 12.21$, $df = 2$, $p<0.001$). Post hoc tests indicated that AS males performed significantly worse than non-AS males ($p<0.016$) who in turn performed worse than non-AS females ($p<0.017$). On the PPQ, once again significant differences were found between the three groups ($F = 15.31$, $df = 2$, $p<0.001$). Examination with post hoc tests indicated a significant difference between only two of the groups. Non-AS females performed significantly worse than non-AS males ($p<0.001$) and AS males ($p<0.006$). The male groups did not differ significantly from each other ($p>0.853$).

The data was also examined to see whether scores on the two tests were correlated but no significant correlation was found overall or within each group (all groups $r = 0.046$, $p>0.63$; females $r = 0.136$, $p>0.37$; non-AS males $r = 0.174$, $p>0.25$; AS males $r = 0.33$, $p>0.19$).

Discussion

This study employed two measures to test predictions from the E–S and extreme male brain models. On the empathizing task (SSQ), non-AS females, on average, performed better than non-AS males who in turn performed better than AS males. On the systemizing task (PPQ) the female group, on average, performed worse than both of the male groups. The two male groups did not differ significantly from each other on this task. These results support the idea that people with autism spectrum conditions demonstrate an empathizing deficit whilst having a level of systemizing skills that is, at least, in the normal range. They are also consistent with the extreme male brain theory of autism (Baron-Cohen 1999).

INDIVIDUAL DIFFERENCES IN EMPATHIZING AND SYSTEMIZING

The two experiments above support both E–S theory and EMB theory. In Experiment 1 there was a negative correlation between the EQ and SQ, suggesting that there could be a trade-off between empathizing and systemizing abilities. This was not supported by Experiment 2, but this could be partly due to sample size. Results from both these experiments were analysed with respect to groups of participants, but we can also consider individuals. There are individual differences in both empathizing and systemizing. According to the E–S theory, individuals in whom empathizing is more developed than systemizing are referred to as Type E, or extreme Type E if the discrepancy is particularly large. Similarly, individuals in whom systemizing is more developed than empathizing are called Type S, or extreme Type S if the discrepancy is particularly large. Individuals in whom systemizing and empathizing are both equally developed are called Type B (to indicate the 'balanced' brain).

E–S theory predicts that people with ASCs are more likely to be Type S or extreme Type S, non-ASC males will be Type B or Type S and non-ASC females will be Type B or Type E. We tested this prediction using the SQ and EQ data from Experiment 1, as this is the larger data set.

The SQ and EQ scores were standardized using the following formulae, $S = (SQ - \langle SQ \rangle)/80$ and $E = (EQ - \langle EQ \rangle)/80$ (i.e. we first subtracted the control population mean (denoted by $\langle \ldots \rangle$) from the scores, then divided by the maximum possible score, 80). The means were: 26.7 (SQ) and 43.9 (EQ). The original EQ and SQ axes were then rotated by 45°, essentially factor analysing S and E, to produce two new variables, D and C. We normalized by the factor of 0.5 as is appropriate for an axis rotation. These new variables are defined as follows: $D = (S - E)/2$ (i.e. the difference between the normalized SQ and EQ scores) and $C = (S + E)/2$ (i.e. the sum of the normalized SQ and EQ scores).

Because variable D is a measure of the difference between somebody's empathizing and systemizing ability, it allows us to determine an individual's brain type: a positive score indicates brain Type S, or extreme Type S, a negative score indicates brain Type E, or extreme Type E, and a score close to zero indicates brain Type B. In numerical terms, these brain types are assigned according to the percentiles of the combined non-AS males and non-AS females on the D axis. Table 7.4 shows the percentage of participants with each brain type and Figure 7.3 shows the results translated back into raw scores on the SQ and EQ tests so that individual brain types can be classified.

As predicted by E–S theory and EMB theory, the majority of people with AS have an extreme Type S brain, most non-AS males have brain Type S and most non-AS females have brain Type E.

Table 7.4 Percentage of participants with each brain type

Brain type	Percentile (per)	Brain boundary	Group		
			AS group (n=88)	Non-AS males (n=114)	Non-AS females (n=163)
Extreme Type E	per <2.5	D <-0.11	0	0	4.3
Type E	2.5 ≤ per <35	-0.11 £ D <0.0095	1.1	16.7	43.6
Type B	35 ≤ per <65	0.0095 ≤ D <0.085	6.8	22.8	35.6
Type S	65 ≤ per <97.5	0.085 ≤ D <0.27	27.3	54.4	16.6
Extreme Type S	per ≥ 97.5	D ≥0.27	64.8	6.1	0

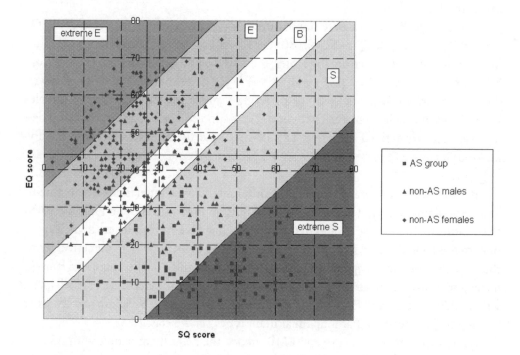

Figure 7.3 Experiment results translated back into raw scores on the SQ and EQ tests

GENERAL DISCUSSION

The results from both experiments support both E–S theory and EMB theory. People with AS are as good, if not better, than people without this condition at systemizing but are relatively impaired at empathizing. Males without AS are better at systemizing than empathizing and females without AS are better at empathizing than systemizing. It is worth stressing that these descriptions refer to groups of participants, and general patterns, and naturally assumptions about individuals should not be made. Nevertheless, about 92 per cent of people with AS have a Type S or extreme Type S brain. This means that their systemizing skills far outweigh their empathizing ability. In non-AS males, over 50 per cent have a Type S brain, about 23 per cent have a balanced brain (Type B) and about 17 per cent have a Type E brain. These results are roughly mirrored by the non-AS females. About 17 per cent of this group have a Type S brain, 36 per cent are Type B and 44 per cent are Type E.

These results suggest that the underlying neuro-cognitive mechanisms underlying empathizing and systemizing are independent, since some people are equally good at both. However, there does seem to be a trend for some trade-off between these two domains, suggesting that even if two independent mechanisms are involved, there may be a special relationship between the two. In terms of the brain basis of empathizing, a number of important brain regions have now been identified, specifically the orbito- and medial-frontal cortex, superior temporal sulcus, and the amygdala (Baron-Cohen and Ring 1994; Baron-Cohen *et al.* 1999, 2000; Frith and Frith 1999). Studies are currently investigating the brain basis of systemizing. Studies are also under way to identify the genes associated with systemizing and empathizing.

It is important to consider whether these results could be accounted for by alternative cognitive theories of autism. People with autism spectrum conditions show 'repetitive behaviour', a strong desire for routines, and a 'need for sameness'. The executive dysfunction theory (Ozonoff *et al.* 1994; Pennington *et al.* 1997; Russell 1997) paints an essentially negative view of this behaviour, assuming that it is a form of 'frontal lobe' perseveration or inability to shift attention.

We recognize that some forms of repetitive behaviour in autism, such as 'stereotypies' (e.g. twiddling the fingers rapidly in peripheral vision), are likely to be due to executive deficits. Moreover, we recognize that as one tests people with autism who have additional learning disabilities, executive deficits are more likely to be found (Russell 1997). However, although executive dysfunction theory would make no clear prediction about scores on tests of empathizing, it would predict impaired performance on tests of systemizing. Our results show that people with AS have preserved or superior systemizing talents. This suggests that executive dysfunction cannot be a core feature of autism spectrum conditions.

Moreover, the executive account has also traditionally ignored the *content* of 'repetitive behaviour'. Certainly, our study of obsessions suggests that these are not random with respect to content (which would be predicted by the content-free executive dysfunction theory), but that these tend to cluster in the domain of systemizing (Baron-Cohen and Wheelwright 1999).

An alternative cognitive theory of autism is the central coherence theory (CC) (Frith 1989; Happe 1996). This theory refers to the individual's preference for local detail over global processing. This has been demonstrated in terms of an autistic superiority on the Embedded Figures Task (EFT) and the Block Design Subtest (Jolliffe and Baron-Cohen 1997; Shah and Frith 1983, 1993). It has also been demonstrated in terms of an autistic deficit in integrating fragments of objects and integrating sentences within a paragraph (Jolliffe in press; Jolliffe and Baron-Cohen 2001). The faster and more accurate performance on the EFT and Block Design Test have been interpreted as evidence of good segmentation skills and superior attention to detail. The latter has also been demonstrated on visual search tasks (Plaisted, O'Riordan and Baron-Cohen 1998a, 1998b).

There is an overlap between systemizing and certain aspects of the central coherence theory. For example, both the E–S theory and the CC theory predict excellent attention to detail. However, the E–S and CC theories also make opposite predictions when it comes to an individual with autism being able to understand a whole system. The E–S theory predicts that a person with autism, faced with a new system to learn, will learn it faster than someone without autism, so long as there are underlying rules and regularities that can be discovered. In contrast, the CC theory predicts that they should fail to understand whole (global) systems or the relationships between parts of a system. In other words, CC theory would predict impaired performance for people with AS on our tests of systemizing, whereas the actual results showed preserved or superior performance.

Although E–S theory and EMB theory provide the best account of the results presented here, there are clearly some limitations associated with the present study. First, the conclusions drawn here are made from just two measures of empathizing and two measures of systemizing. More tasks need to be developed so that the theories can be tested more stringently. Also increasing the number of participants is important to ensure results are reliable. The current tests were designed for adults of average or above average intelligence. Future tests should be designed for people who are of below average intelligence. We are currently developing the tests for use with children. The work presented here was limited to people with AS so we need to check whether the results are replicated in people with other ASCs. Finally, it is important to invite other clinical groups to participate in the research to confirm that the results presented are specific to people with ASCs.

FINAL THOUGHTS

Superior systemizing depends on exactness in information processing. Systemizing does not entail a search for approximate answers to questions. Systemizing is searching for the exact answer. We surmise that the systemizing mechanism is an exactness mechanism. By this we mean that it is only concerned with absolute facts of the most well-specified kind. Good systemizing means that excellent detail is being detected. The benefit of this is that all potentially important input is being considered, and harnessed to the aim of predicting output.

A man with AS whom we met recently told us that he thought the question 'Where do you live?' was not a good question. 'What information are they after?' he asked. 'Do they want to know which country I live in, or which county I live in, or which city I live in, or which neighbourhood, or which street, or which house?' For him, a better question would have been 'Which city do you live in?' since that could only have one correct answer. Questions which could have multiple answers are unanswerable via systemizing, as they cannot be resolved. When this same man with AS was asked 'When did you leave home this morning?' he could only answer 'At 7.06 a.m.' It would have been incorrect to say 'At about 7 a.m.' when he knew the correct answer was '7.06 a.m.' When he was asked where he sat in the plane last year, he did not answer 'Near the front' but instead answered 'In seat 14B.'

This exactness is seen in the speech of people with autism or AS. Their speech is described as pedantic (Tager-Flusberg 1993). This can lead them to include far more detail in their answers than is needed for adequate communication. Here we see the interaction of an empathizing deficit (failing to appreciate what the other person needs to know) and a systemizing property (exactness). Their memories are described as astonishingly detailed, so that for example many adults with AS can recall not only the date they visited a place many years earlier, but an enormous amount of detail about the visit which most people would find both irrelevant but astonishing. If one asks people with AS about their obsessional interests, typically one uncovers the fact that the person has a collection of objects (e.g. CDs, videos, or even something unusual, like coffee mugs). The collection typically has hundreds of items, each of which can be recalled in precise detail, and may be stored in a very precise order. The adults with AS we have met in our clinic have all worked in occupations in which they could use their very precise mind in domains which are factual, rule-based and in which patterns can be identified. Science, engineering, maths and physics may be clear examples of these, but by no means define the limits of such domains. Linguistics is another one, as is history or law.

One of the disadvantages of having your exactness mechanism too highly tuned is that you cannot answer questions to which an exact answer is unavailable. It also takes longer to select an answer from the range of possible answers, since this involves a search of detail. Lastly, it means that you are overloaded with detail and, where there are no systematic laws to be uncovered, you could instead be left submerged with data. Textual comprehension, and estimation, are examples of skills that would be expected to suffer, since here good systemizing would not help. We speculate that this highly tuned exactness mechanism could even affect one's empathizing skills, in that in this domain answers are never exact ('What was John intending? He *probably* meant x').

Appendix 7.1 The SQ

1.	When I listen to a piece of music, I always notice the way it's structured.	strongly agree	slightly agree	slightly disagree	strongly disagree
2.	I adhere to common superstitions.	strongly agree	slightly agree	slightly disagree	strongly disagree
3.	I often make resolutions, but find it hard to stick to them.	strongly agree	slightly agree	slightly disagree	strongly disagree
4.	I prefer to read non-fiction than fiction.	strongly agree	slightly agree	slightly disagree	strongly disagree
5.	If I were buying a car, I would want to obtain specific information about its engine capacity.	strongly agree	slightly agree	slightly disagree	strongly disagree
6.	When I look at a painting, I do not usually think about the technique involved in making it.	strongly agree	slightly agree	slightly disagree	strongly disagree
7.	If there was a problem with the electrical wiring in my home, I'd be able to fix it myself.	strongly agree	slightly agree	slightly disagree	strongly disagree
8.	When I have a dream, I find it difficult to remember precise details about the dream the next day.	strongly agree	slightly agree	slightly disagree	strongly disagree
9.	When I watch a film, I prefer to be with a group of friends, rather than alone.	strongly agree	slightly agree	slightly disagree	strongly disagree
10.	I am interested in learning about different religions.	strongly agree	slightly agree	slightly disagree	strongly disagree
11.	I rarely read articles or web pages about new technology.	strongly agree	slightly agree	slightly disagree	strongly disagree
12.	I do not enjoy games that involve a high degree of strategy.	strongly agree	slightly agree	slightly disagree	strongly disagree
13.	I am fascinated by how machines work.	strongly agree	slightly agree	slightly disagree	strongly disagree

14.	I make it a point of listening to the news each morning.	strongly agree	slightly agree	slightly disagree	strongly disagree
15.	In maths, I am intrigued by the rules and patterns governing numbers.	strongly agree	slightly agree	slightly disagree	strongly disagree
16.	I am bad about keeping in touch with old friends.	strongly agree	slightly agree	slightly disagree	strongly disagree
17.	When I am relating a story, I often leave out details and just give the gist of what happened.	strongly agree	slightly agree	slightly disagree	strongly disagree
18.	I find it difficult to understand instruction manuals for putting appliances together.	strongly agree	slightly agree	slightly disagree	strongly disagree
19.	When I look at an animal, I like to know the precise species it belongs to.	strongly agree	slightly agree	slightly disagree	strongly disagree
20.	If I were buying a computer, I would want to know exact details about its hard drive capacity and processor speed.	strongly agree	slightly agree	slightly disagree	strongly disagree
21.	I enjoy participating in sport.	strongly agree	slightly agree	slightly disagree	strongly disagree
22.	I try to avoid doing household chores if I can.	strongly agree	slightly agree	slightly disagree	strongly disagree
23.	When I cook, I do not think about exactly how different methods and ingredients contribute to the final product.	strongly agree	slightly agree	slightly disagree	strongly disagree
24.	I find it difficult to read and understand maps.	strongly agree	slightly agree	slightly disagree	strongly disagree
25.	If I had a collection (e.g. CDs, coins, stamps), it would be highly organized.	strongly agree	slightly agree	slightly disagree	strongly disagree
26.	When I look at a piece of furniture, I do not notice the details of how it was constructed.	strongly agree	slightly agree	slightly disagree	strongly disagree
27.	The idea of engaging in 'risk-taking' activities appeals to me.	strongly agree	slightly agree	slightly disagree	strongly disagree
28.	When I learn about historical events, I do not focus on exact dates.	strongly agree	slightly agree	slightly disagree	strongly disagree
29.	When I read the newspaper, I am drawn to tables of information, such as football league scores or stock market indices.	strongly agree	slightly agree	slightly disagree	strongly disagree
30.	When I learn a language, I become intrigued by its grammatical rules.	strongly agree	slightly agree	slightly disagree	strongly disagree
31.	I find it difficult to learn my way around a new city.	strongly agree	slightly agree	slightly disagree	strongly disagree

32.	I do not tend to watch science documentaries on television or read articles about science and nature.	strongly agree	slightly agree	slightly disagree	strongly disagree
33.	If I were buying a stereo, I would want to know about its precise technical features.	strongly agree	slightly agree	slightly disagree	strongly disagree
34.	I find it easy to grasp exactly how odds work in betting.	strongly agree	slightly agree	slightly disagree	strongly disagree
35.	I am not very meticulous when I carry out D.I.Y.	strongly agree	slightly agree	slightly disagree	strongly disagree
36.	I find it easy to carry on a conversation with someone I've just met.	strongly agree	slightly agree	slightly disagree	strongly disagree
37.	When I look at a building, I am curious about the precise way it was constructed.	strongly agree	slightly agree	slightly disagree	strongly disagree
38.	When an election is being held, I am not interested in the results for each constituency.	strongly agree	slightly agree	slightly disagree	strongly disagree
39.	When I lend someone money, I expect them to pay me back exactly what they owe me.	strongly agree	slightly agree	slightly disagree	strongly disagree
40.	I find it difficult to understand information the bank sends me on different investment and saving systems.	strongly agree	slightly agree	slightly disagree	strongly disagree
41.	When travelling by train, I often wonder exactly how the rail networks are coordinated.	strongly agree	slightly agree	slightly disagree	strongly disagree
42.	When I buy a new appliance, I do not read the instruction manual very thoroughly.	strongly agree	slightly agree	slightly disagree	strongly disagree
43.	If I were buying a camera, I would not look carefully into the quality of the lens.	strongly agree	slightly agree	slightly disagree	strongly disagree
44.	When I read something, I always notice whether it is grammatically correct.	strongly agree	slightly agree	slightly disagree	strongly disagree
45.	When I hear the weather forecast, I am not very interested in the meteorological patterns.	strongly agree	slightly agree	slightly disagree	strongly disagree
46.	I often wonder what it would be like to be someone else.	strongly agree	slightly agree	slightly disagree	strongly disagree
47.	I find it difficult to do two things at once.	strongly agree	slightly agree	slightly disagree	strongly disagree
48.	When I look at a mountain, I think about how precisely it was formed.	strongly agree	slightly agree	slightly disagree	strongly disagree
49.	I can easily visualize how the motorways in my region link up.	strongly agree	slightly agree	slightly disagree	strongly disagree

50.	When I'm in a restaurant, I often have a hard time deciding what to order.	strongly agree	slightly agree	slightly disagree	strongly disagree
51.	When I'm in a plane, I do not think about the aerodynamics.	strongly agree	slightly agree	slightly disagree	strongly disagree
52.	I often forget the precise details of conversations I've had.	strongly agree	slightly agree	slightly disagree	strongly disagree
53.	When I am walking in the country, I am curious about how the various kinds of trees differ.	strongly agree	slightly agree	slightly disagree	strongly disagree
54.	After meeting someone just once or twice, I find it difficult to remember precisely what they look like.	strongly agree	slightly agree	slightly disagree	strongly disagree
55.	I am interested in knowing the path a river takes from its source to the sea.	strongly agree	slightly agree	slightly disagree	strongly disagree
56.	I do not read legal documents very carefully.	strongly agree	slightly agree	slightly disagree	strongly disagree
57.	I am not interested in understanding how wireless communication works.	strongly agree	slightly agree	slightly disagree	strongly disagree
58.	I am curious about life on other planets.	strongly agree	slightly agree	slightly disagree	strongly disagree
59.	When I travel, I like to learn specific details about the culture of the place I am visiting.	strongly agree	slightly agree	slightly disagree	strongly disagree
60.	I do not care to know the names of the plants I see.	strongly agree	slightly agree	slightly disagree	strongly disagree

(Baron-Cohen *et al.* 2003. Reproduced by permission.)

Appendix 7.2 The EQ

1.	I can easily tell if someone else wants to enter a conversation.	strongly agree	slightly agree	slightly disagree	strongly disagree
2.	I prefer animals to humans.	strongly agree	slightly agree	slightly disagree	strongly disagree
3.	I try to keep up with the current trends and fashions.	strongly agree	slightly agree	slightly disagree	strongly disagree
4.	I find it difficult to explain to others things that I understand easily, when they don't understand it first time.	strongly agree	slightly agree	slightly disagree	strongly disagree
5.	I dream most nights.	strongly agree	slightly agree	slightly disagree	strongly disagree
6.	I really enjoy caring for other people.	strongly agree	slightly agree	slightly disagree	strongly disagree
7.	I try to solve my own problems rather than discussing them with others.	strongly agree	slightly agree	slightly disagree	strongly disagree
8.	I find it hard to know what to do in a social situation.	strongly agree	slightly agree	slightly disagree	strongly disagree
9.	I am at my best first thing in the morning.	strongly agree	slightly agree	slightly disagree	strongly disagree
10.	People often tell me that I went too far in driving my point home in a discussion.	strongly agree	slightly agree	slightly disagree	strongly disagree
11.	It doesn't bother me too much if I am late meeting a friend.	strongly agree	slightly agree	slightly disagree	strongly disagree
12.	Friendships and relationships are just too difficult, so I tend not to bother with them.	strongly agree	slightly agree	slightly disagree	strongly disagree
13.	I would never break a law, no matter how minor.	strongly agree	slightly agree	slightly disagree	strongly disagree
14.	I often find it difficult to judge if something is rude or polite.	strongly agree	slightly agree	slightly disagree	strongly disagree

15.	In a conversation, I tend to focus on my own thoughts rather than on what my listener might be thinking.	strongly agree	slightly agree	slightly disagree	strongly disagree
16.	I prefer practical jokes to verbal humour.	strongly agree	slightly agree	slightly disagree	strongly disagree
17.	I live life for today rather than the future.	strongly agree	slightly agree	slightly disagree	strongly disagree
18.	When I was a child, I enjoyed cutting up worms to see what would happen.	strongly agree	slightly agree	slightly disagree	strongly disagree
19.	I can pick up quickly if someone says one thing but means another.	strongly agree	slightly agree	slightly disagree	strongly disagree
20.	I tend to have very strong opinions about morality.	strongly agree	slightly agree	slightly disagree	strongly disagree
21.	It is hard for me to see why some things upset people so much.	strongly agree	slightly agree	slightly disagree	strongly disagree
22.	I find it easy to put myself in somebody else's shoes.	strongly agree	slightly agree	slightly disagree	strongly disagree
23.	I think that good manners are the most important thing a parent can teach their child.	strongly agree	slightly agree	slightly disagree	strongly disagree
24.	I like to do things on the spur of the moment.	strongly agree	slightly agree	slightly disagree	strongly disagree
25.	I am good at predicting how someone will feel.	strongly agree	slightly agree	slightly disagree	strongly disagree
26.	I am quick to spot when someone in a group is feeling awkward or uncomfortable.	strongly agree	slightly agree	slightly disagree	strongly disagree
27.	If I say something that someone else is offended by, I think that that's their problem, not mine.	strongly agree	slightly agree	slightly disagree	strongly disagree
28.	If anyone asked me if I liked their haircut, I would reply truthfully, even if I didn't like it.	strongly agree	slightly agree	slightly disagree	strongly disagree
29.	I can't always see why someone should have felt offended by a remark.	strongly agree	slightly agree	slightly disagree	strongly disagree
30.	People often tell me that I am very unpredictable.	strongly agree	slightly agree	slightly disagree	strongly disagree
31.	I enjoy being the centre of attention at any social gathering.	strongly agree	slightly agree	slightly disagree	strongly disagree
32.	Seeing people cry doesn't really upset me.	strongly agree	slightly agree	slightly disagree	strongly disagree
33.	I enjoy having discussions about politics.	strongly agree	slightly agree	slightly disagree	strongly disagree

34.	I am very blunt, which some people take to be rudeness, even though this is unintentional.	strongly agree	slightly agree	slightly disagree	strongly disagree
35.	I don't tend to find social situations confusing.	strongly agree	slightly agree	slightly disagree	strongly disagree
36.	Other people tell me I am good at understanding how they are feeling and what they are thinking.	strongly agree	slightly agree	slightly disagree	strongly disagree
37.	When I talk to people, I tend to talk about their experiences rather than my own.	strongly agree	slightly agree	slightly disagree	strongly disagree
38.	It upsets me to see an animal in pain.	strongly agree	slightly agree	slightly disagree	strongly disagree
39.	I am able to make decisions without being influenced by people's feelings.	strongly agree	slightly agree	slightly disagree	strongly disagree
40.	I can't relax until I have done everything I had planned to do that day.	strongly agree	slightly agree	slightly disagree	strongly disagree
41.	I can easily tell if someone else is interested or bored with what I am saying.	strongly agree	slightly agree	slightly disagree	strongly disagree
42.	I get upset if I see people suffering on news programmes.	strongly agree	slightly agree	slightly disagree	strongly disagree
43.	Friends usually talk to me about their problems as they say that I am very understanding.	strongly agree	slightly agree	slightly disagree	strongly disagree
44.	I can sense if I am intruding, even if the other person doesn't tell me.	strongly agree	slightly agree	slightly disagree	strongly disagree
45.	I often start new hobbies but quickly become bored with them and move on to something else.	strongly agree	slightly agree	slightly disagree	strongly disagree
46.	People sometimes tell me that I have gone too far with teasing.	strongly agree	slightly agree	slightly disagree	strongly disagree
47.	I would be too nervous to go on a big roller-coaster.	strongly agree	slightly agree	slightly disagree	strongly disagree
48.	Other people often say that I am insensitive, though I don't always see why.	strongly agree	slightly agree	slightly disagree	strongly disagree
49.	If I see a stranger in a group, I think that it is up to them to make an effort to join in.	strongly agree	slightly agree	slightly disagree	strongly disagree
50.	I usually stay emotionally detached when watching a film.	strongly agree	slightly agree	slightly disagree	strongly disagree
51.	I like to be very organized in day to day life and often make lists of the chores I have to do.	strongly agree	slightly agree	slightly disagree	strongly disagree

52.	I can tune into how someone else feels rapidly and intuitively.	strongly agree	slightly agree	slightly disagree	strongly disagree
53.	I don't like to take risks.	strongly agree	slightly agree	slightly disagree	strongly disagree
54.	I can easily work out what another person might want to talk about.	strongly agree	slightly agree	slightly disagree	strongly disagree
55.	I can tell if someone is masking their true emotion.	strongly agree	slightly agree	slightly disagree	strongly disagree
56.	Before making a decision I always weigh up the pros and cons.	strongly agree	slightly agree	slightly disagree	strongly disagree
57.	I don't consciously work out the rules of social situations.	strongly agree	slightly agree	slightly disagree	strongly disagree
58.	I am good at predicting what someone will do.	strongly agree	slightly agree	slightly disagree	strongly disagree
59.	I tend to get emotionally involved with a friend's problems.	strongly agree	slightly agree	slightly disagree	strongly disagree
60.	I can usually appreciate the other person's viewpoint, even if I don't agree with it.	strongly agree	slightly agree	slightly disagree	strongly disagree

(Baron-Cohen *et al.* 2003. Reproduced by permission.)

Appendix 7.3 Example of a question from the PPQ

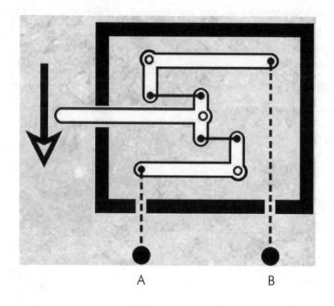

What is the outcome?

(1)   A ⇓   B ⇓

(2)   A ⇑   B ⇑

(3)   A ⇓   B ⇑

(4)   A ⇑   B ⇓

(5)   None of the above

Appendix 7.4 Example of a question from the SSQ

'Hello,' said Julie, 'do you have any vacancies at the moment?'

'Well my dear,' the woman replied thoughtfully, 'I've got a double room overlooking the meadow and that would be £50.00 for the two of you. Perhaps the room around the side would be closer to your price range though. Breakfast starts at 7.30 and you need to leave your room by 11.00.'

'Right,' replied Julie. 'Is it OK if we have a look at the rooms first?'

'No problem my dear,' said the woman, 'come on in.'

ACKNOWLEDGEMENTS

Parts of this chapter are reprinted, by permission, from:

Baron-Cohen, S., Richler, J., Bisarya, D., Gurunathan, N. and Wheelwright, S. (2003) 'The Systemising Quotient (SQ): an investigation of adults with Asperger Syndrome or High-functioning Autism and normal sex differences.' *Philosophical Transactions of the Royal Society, Series B, Special issue on 'Autism: Mind and Brain'* 358, 361–374.

Baron-Cohen, S., Wheelwright, S., Griffin, R., Lawson, J. and Hill, J. (2002) 'The exact mind: empathising and systemising in autism spectrum conditions.' In U. Goswami (ed.) *Handbook of Cognitive Development.* Oxford: Blackwells.

Lawson, J., Baron-Cohen, S. and Wheelwright, S. (2004) 'Empathising and systemising in adults with and without Asperger Syndrome.' *Journal of Autism and Developmental Disorders* 34, 301–310. Copyright © Springer Science and Business Media 2004.

REFERENCES

APA (1994) *DSM-IV Diagnostic and Statistical Manual of Mental Disorders* (4th edn). Washington, DC: American Psychiatric Association.

Baron-Cohen, S. (1987) 'Autism and symbolic play.' *British Journal of Developmental Psychology 5,* 139–148.

Baron-Cohen, S. (1988) 'Social and pragmatic deficits in autism: cognitive or affective?' *Journal of Autism and Developmental Disorders 18,* 379–402.

Baron-Cohen, S. (1989a) 'Joint attention deficits in autism: towards a cognitive analysis.' *Development and Psychopathology 1,* 185–189.

Baron-Cohen, S. (1989b) 'Are autistic children behaviourists? An examination of their mental–physical and appearance–reality distinctions.' *Journal of Autism and Developmental Disorders 19,* 579–600.

Baron-Cohen, S. (1989c) 'Thinking about thinking: how does it develop? Critical notice.' *Journal of Child Psychology and Psychiatry 30,* 931–933.

Baron-Cohen, S. (1991) 'Do people with autism understand what causes emotion?' *Child Development 62,* 385–395.

Baron-Cohen, S. (1994a) 'The development of a theory of mind: where would we be without the Intentional Stance?' In M. H. Rutter (ed.) *Developmental Principles and Clinical Issues in Psychology and Child Psychiatry.* Oxford: Basil Blackwell.

Baron-Cohen, S. (1994b) 'How to build a baby that can read minds: cognitive mechanisms in mindreading.' *Cahiers de Psychologie Cognitive/Current Psychology of Cognition 13,* 513–552.

Baron-Cohen, S. (1995) *Mindblindness: An Essay on Autism and Theory of Mind.* Boston: MIT Press/Bradford Books.

Baron-Cohen, S. (1999) 'The extreme male-brain theory of autism.' In H. Tager-Flusberg (ed.) *Neurodevelopmental Disorders.* Cambridge, MA: MIT Press.

Baron-Cohen, S. and Goodhart, F. (1994) 'The "seeing leads to knowing" deficit in autism: the Pratt and Bryant probe.' *British Journal of Developmental Psychology 12,* 397–402.

Baron-Cohen, S. and Hammer, J. (1997) 'Is autism an extreme form of the male brain?' *Advances in Infancy Research 11,* 193–217.

Baron-Cohen, S. and Ring, H. (1994) 'A model of the mindreading system: neuropsychological and neurobiological perspectives.' In P. Mitchell and C. Lewis (eds) *Origins of an Understanding of Mind.* Hove, E. Sussex: Lawrence Erlbaum Associates.

Baron-Cohen, S. and Wheelwright, S. (1999) 'Obsessions in children with autism or Asperger Syndrome: a content analysis in terms of core domains of cognition.' *British Journal of Psychiatry 175*, 484–490.

Baron-Cohen, S., Leslie, A. M. and Frith, U. (1985) 'Does the autistic child have a "theory of mind"?' *Cognition 21*, 37–46.

Baron-Cohen, S., Tager-Flusberg, H. and Cohen, D. (eds) (1993) *Understanding Other Minds: Perspectives from Autism.* Oxford: Oxford University Press.

Baron-Cohen, S., Jolliffe, T., Mortimore, C. and Robertson, M. (1997a) 'Another advanced test of theory of mind: evidence from very high functioning adults with autism or Asperger Syndrome.' *Journal of Child Psychology and Psychiatry 38*, 813–822.

Baron-Cohen, S., Wheelwright, S. and Jolliffe, T. (1997b) 'Is there a "language of the eyes"? Evidence from normal adults and adults with autism or Asperger syndrome.' *Visual Cognition 4*, 311–331.

Baron-Cohen, S., Ring, H., Wheelwright, S., Bullmore, E. T., Brammer, M. J., Simmons, A. *et al.* (1999) 'Social intelligence in the normal and autistic brain: an fMRI study.' *European Journal of Neuroscience 11*, 1891–1898.

Baron-Cohen, S., Ring, H., Bullmore, E., Wheelwright, S., Ashwin, C. and Williams, S. (2000) 'The amygdala theory of autism.' *Neuroscience and Behavioural Reviews 24*, 355–364.

Baron-Cohen, S., Wheelwright, S., Hill, J., Raste, Y. and Plumb, I. (2001) 'The "Reading the Mind in the Eyes" test revised version: a study with normal adults, and adults with Asperger Syndrome or High-Functioning Autism.' *Journal of Child Psychology and Psychiatry 42*, 241–252.

Baron-Cohen, S., Richler, J., Bisarya, D., Gurunathan, N. and Wheelwright, S. (2003) 'The Systemising Quotient (SQ): an investigation of adults with Asperger Syndrome or High-functioning Autism and normal sex differences.' *Philosophical Transactions of the Royal Society, Series B, Special issue on 'Autism: Mind and Brain' 358*, 361–374.

Crawford, J. R., Stewart, L .E., Cochrane, R. H., Foulds, J. A., Besson, J. A. and Parker, D. M. (1989) 'Estimating premorbid IQ from demographic variables: regression equations derived from a UK sample.' *British Journal of Clinical Psychology 28 (Pt 3)*, 275–278.

Dennett, D. (1987) *The Intentional Stance.* Cambridge, MA: MIT Press/Bradford Books.

Frith, C. and Frith, U. (1999) 'Interacting minds – a biological basis.' *Science 286*, 1692–1695.

Frith, U. (1989) *Autism: Explaining the Enigma.* Oxford: Basil Blackwell.

Happe, F. (1996) 'Studying weak central coherence at low levels: children with autism do not succumb to visual illusions. A research note.' *Journal of Child Psychology and Psychiatry 37*, 873–877.

ICD-10 (1994) *International Classification of Diseases* (10th edn). Geneva, Switzerland: World Health Organization.

Jolliffe, T. (in press) *Central Coherence Dysfunction in Autistic Spectrum Disorder.* University of Cambridge.

Jolliffe, T. and Baron-Cohen, S. (1997) 'Are people with autism or Asperger Syndrome faster than normal on the Embedded Figures Task?' *Journal of Child Psychology and Psychiatry 38*, 527–534.

Jolliffe, T. and Baron-Cohen, S. (2001) 'A test of central coherence theory: can adults with high-functioning autism or Asperger Syndrome integrate fragments of an object?' *Cognitive Neuropsychiatry 6*, 193–216.

Lawson, J., Baron-Cohen, S. and Wheelwright, S. (2004) 'Empathising and systemising in adults with and without Asperger Syndrome.' *Journal of Autism and Developmental Disorders 34*, 301–310.

Leslie, A. (1995) 'ToMM, ToBy, and Agency: core architecture and domain specificity.' In L. Hirschfeld and S. Gelman (eds) *Domain Specificity in Cognition and Culture.* New York: Cambridge University Press.

Leslie, A. M. (1987) 'Pretence and representation: the origins of "theory of mind".' *Psychological Review* *94*, 412–426.

Leslie, A. M. and Frith, U. (1988) 'Autistic children's understanding of seeing, knowing, and believing.' *British Journal of Developmental Psychology 6*, 315–324.

Morton, J., Frith, U. and Leslie, A. (1991) 'The cognitive basis of a biological disorder: autism.' *Trends in Neurosciences 14*, 434–438.

Nelson, H. E. (1991) *The National Adult Reading Test (NART)*. Windsor, Berkshire: NFER-Nelson.

NIIP, N.I.o.I.P. (n.d.) *Vincent Mechanical Diagrams Test*. Windsor, Berkshire: NFER Publishing.

Ozonoff, S., Pennington, B. and Rogers, S. J. (1990) 'Are there emotion perception deficits in young autistic children?' *Journal of Child Psychology and Psychiatry 31*, 343–363.

Ozonoff, S., Rogers, S., Farnham, J. and Pennington, B. (1994) 'Can standard measures identify subclinical markers of autism?' *Journal of Autism and Developmental Disorders 23*, 429–441.

Pennington, B., Rogers, S., Bennetto, L., Griffith, E., Reed, D. and Shyu, V. (1997) 'Validity Test of the Executive Dysfunction Hypothesis of Autism.' In J. Russell (ed.) *Executive Functioning in Autism*. Oxford: Oxford University Press.

Plaisted, K., O'Riordan, M. and Baron-Cohen, S. (1998a) 'Enhanced discrimination of novel, highly similar stimuli by adults with autism during a perceptual learning task.' *Journal of Child Psychology and Psychiatry 39*, 765–775.

Plaisted, K., O'Riordan, M. and Baron-Cohen, S. (1998b) 'Enhanced visual search for a conjunctive target in autism: a research note.' *Journal of Child Psychology and Psychiatry 39*, 777–783.

Premack, D. (1990) 'The infant's theory of self-propelled objects.' *Cognition 36*, 1–16.

Russell, J. (ed.) (1997) *Autism as an Executive Disorder*. Oxford: Oxford University Press.

Shah, A. and Frith, U. (1983) 'An islet of ability in autism: a research note.' *Journal of Child Psychology and Psychiatry 24*, 613–620.

Shah, A. and Frith, U. (1993) 'Why do autistic individuals show superior performance on the block design test?' *Journal of Child Psychology and Psychiatry 34*, 1351–1364.

Tager-Flusberg, H. (1993) 'What language reveals about the understanding of minds in children with autism.' In S. Baron-Cohen, H. Tager-Flusberg and D. J. Cohen (eds) *Understanding Other Minds: Perspectives from Autism*. Oxford: Oxford University Press.

Wechsler, D. (1997) *Wechsler Adult Intelligence Scale-III (WAIS-III)*. San Antonio, TX: The Psychological Corporation.

Wechsler, D. (1999) *Wechsler Abbreviated Scale of Intelligence (WASI)*. San Antonio, TX: The Psychological Corporation.

Wing, L. and Gould, J. (1979) 'Severe impairments of social interaction and associated abnormalities in children: epidemiology and classification.' *Journal of Autism and Developmental Disorders 9*, 11–29.

Yirmiya, N., Sigman, M., Kasari, C. and Mundy, P. (1992) 'Empathy and cognition in high-functioning children with autism.' *Child Development 63*, 150–160.

Chapter 8

Executive Functions in Autism

Theory and Practice

Sally Ozonoff, Mikle South and Sherri Provencal

INTRODUCTION

Executive function is the cognitive construct used to describe goal-directed, future-oriented behaviors thought to be mediated by the frontal lobes (Duncan 1986), including planning, inhibition of prepotent responses, flexibility, organized search, self-monitoring, and use of working memory (Baddeley 1986; Goldman-Rakic 1987; Pennington 1994). Executive dysfunction has been found in both individuals with autism and their family members, across many ages and functioning levels, on many different instruments purported to measure executive function. This chapter summarizes this still growing literature. We explore a number of issues that have emerged in the executive function literature as the field has matured, including the developmental trajectory of executive function, its relation to other cognitive abilities and features of autism, and its association with other neurodevelopmental disorders. We conclude the chapter with thoughts about future research directions, including new findings that executive dysfunction may be familial and suggestions for remediation.

EXECUTIVE FUNCTIONS IN AUTISM: A LITERATURE REVIEW
Initial studies

The first empirical investigation of the executive functions (EF) of people with autism was done by Rumsey (1985), who administered the Wisconsin Card Sorting Test (WCST), a measure of cognitive flexibility, to adult men with high-functioning autism. Relative to a sample of typical adults matched on age, individuals with autism demonstrated significant perseveration, sorting by previously correct rules, despite feedback that their strategies were incorrect. In a later study, Rumsey and Hamburger (1990) demonstrated that this perseveration was not a general consequence of learning or developmental disorders, as WCST impairment was specific to an adult sample with autism and was not apparent in matched controls with severe dyslexia.

Prior and Hoffmann (1990) were the first research team to administer the WCST to a pediatric sample with autism. Like adults with autism, the children in this study made significantly more perseverative errors than matched controls. They also performed significantly less well than controls on the Milner Maze Test, demonstrating deficits in planning and difficulty learning from mistakes. The authors noted that the autistic group 'perseverated with maladaptive strategies, made the same mistakes repeatedly, and seemed unable to conceive of a strategy to overcome their difficulties' (p.588).

The results of another study using the WCST with individuals with high-functioning autism were particularly interesting because deficits were found relative to a control group with attention deficit hyperactivity disorder (ADHD) and conduct disorder (Szatmari *et al.* 1990). As discussed later in this chapter, executive dysfunction may be associated with these syndromes as well (e.g. Chelune *et al.* 1986; Lueger and Gill 1990). Despite this conservative choice of control group, participants with autism still made significantly more perseverative errors and completed fewer categories on the WCST than the comparison sample. Ozonoff, Pennington and Rogers (1991) replicated this finding using a control group composed of children with learning and attention difficulties. They found not only significantly more perseveration by the group with autism but also significantly fewer failures to maintain set than the control group, a variable logically and conceptually opposite that of perseveration. Performance on another executive function measure, the Tower of Hanoi, a test of planning, correctly predicted diagnosis in 80 percent of subjects, while other neuropsychological variables (e.g. theory of mind, memory, emotion perception, spatial abilities) predicted group membership at no better than chance levels. Following the sample longitudinally, Ozonoff and McEvoy (1994) found that deficits on the Tower of Hanoi and WCST were stable over a 2.5-year period. Not only did executive function abilities not improve during the follow-up interval, they showed a tendency to decline relative to controls over time. Shu *et al.* (2001) reported significant deficits on WCST performance in a sample of 26 Taiwanese children with autism, relative to matched controls. Since these children were raised in a completely different culture and environment than the Western children who participate in most EF studies, the authors suggested that executive dysfunction may be a core impairment in autism.

In a review of the EF literature, Pennington and Ozonoff (1996) reported that 13 out of the 14 studies existing at the time of publication demonstrated impaired performance on at least one executive function task in autism, including 25 of the 32 executive tasks used across those empirical studies. The magnitude of group differences tended to be quite large, with an average effect size (Cohen's *d*) across all studies of 0.98, marked by especially large effect sizes for the Tower of Hanoi ($d = 2.07$) and the Wisconsin Card Sorting Test ($d = 1.04$).

More recent studies of EF and autism: component process analyses

Executive function is a multidimensional construct. The category includes a number of skills (flexibility, planning, inhibition, organization, self-monitoring, goal-setting, working memory) that appear to be, to some extent, dissociable. The tasks used in initial studies of executive function in autism were relatively imprecise, typically measuring several executive operations, with no method to examine variance in individual skills. For example, the Wisconsin Card Sorting Test, the most widely used measure of executive function in autism, is generally considered a test of cognitive flexibility, but other operations also appear to be required for successful performance, including attribute identification, categorization, working memory, inhibition, selective attention, and encoding of verbal feedback (Bond and Buchtel 1984; Dehaene and Changeux 1991; Ozonoff 1995; Perrine 1993; Van der Does and Van den Bosch 1992). To perform well on this task, subjects must be able to discriminate among stimuli, classify them according to abstract principles, inhibit previously reinforced responses, sustain attention to appropriate attributes of compound stimuli, and use verbal feedback, provided in the context of a social interaction, to change their behavior. When an individual receives a poor score on the WCST, it is difficult to determine which cognitive operations were responsible.

Ozonoff (1997) explored the utility of an information processing approach for examining individual components of executive function. The information processing approach focuses on understanding the sequence of mental operations involved in the performance of cognitive tasks (e.g. information input, encoding, transformation, selection, retrieval, and output). The information processing perspective is not a specific model or theory; rather, it is a broad framework for understanding cognition. It provides relatively theory-independent methods and specific experimental paradigms for understanding complex behavior (Anderson and Bower 1973; Ingram 1989). Thus, a variety of different cognitive models and constructs can be articulated and tested from within this framework. A central methodologic strategy of the information processing approach is component process analysis (Farah 1984; Friedrich and Rader 1996). The goal of component process analysis is decomposition of complex cognitive functions into the elementary operations that appear to underlie them, the time course and relationship of these component processes to each other, and the internal representations, schemas, or codes upon which they act (Friedrich and Rader 1996). The component process approach has been used for many years in the fields of experimental psychology and cognitive neuropsychology. This perspective has relevance for elucidating cognitive mechanisms of autism as well. The component process approach permits more detailed exploration of the specific role of EF in cognitive and social development in both normal and abnormal populations and may facilitate research into more precise interventions for individuals with autism spectrum disorders. This section summarizes recent research examining the component processes of EF most closely related to autism. Later in the chapter, the component process approach is applied to executive remediation efforts.

FLEXIBILITY AND INHIBITION

Two executive functions that are conceptually linked but often postulated to be separable are inhibition and flexibility. Some researchers have argued that autism involves a primary deficit in inhibitory control (Russell, Jarrold and Henry 1996; Russell *et al.* 1999b; Turner 1997, 1999), while others stress the central role of flexibility impairments in autism (Ozonoff and Jensen 1999). Many tasks confound the two cognitive operations and, even using a component process approach, it is difficult to design tasks that cleanly measure one or the other process. For example, the act of shifting attention has been postulated to require both inhibition of attention to previously relevant stimuli and movement of attention to new stimuli. Similarly, changing response patterns appears to require both inhibition of the previous motor program and switching to a new motor program (Luria 1966; Sandson and Albert 1984). By extension, flexibly shifting cognitive set (as in the WCST) would appear to confound these two processes as well, a problem that has complicated recent work to untangle the components of executive function and determine which are impaired in autism.

As an example of this problem, Ozonoff and McEvoy (1994) designed a novel Go–NoGo task to examine component skills that appear important to WCST performance. The task consisted of three test conditions with a hierarchy of processing demands: (a) a 'neutral inhibition' condition required subjects to respond to a neutral stimulus while simultaneously inhibiting responses to another neutral stimulus (this condition required no shifting of cognitive set); (b) a 'prepotent inhibition' condition required inhibition of a previously reinforced, well-learned response; and (c) a 'flexibility' condition necessitated frequent shifting from one response pattern to another, placing higher demands on cognitive flexibility. Individuals with autism performed as well as controls when inhibiting neutral responses, but were moderately impaired when inhibiting prepotent responses, and very deficient in shifting their response set. Interpretation of these results was complicated, however, by the confounding of the inhibition and flexibility conditions. Specifically, the prepotent inhibition condition also required flexibility (i.e. when shifting from the response pattern required in the neutral inhibition condition to the new response mode necessitated by the prepotent inhibition condition). Because the two constructs were not measured independently, it was difficult to determine which cognitive operation, inhibition or flexibility, contributed more to the poor performance of the prepotent inhibition condition.

Ozonoff and Strayer (1997) conducted a second study that isolated inhibition and flexibility operations more completely. Two inhibition tasks were administered to a group of high-functioning children with autism and a matched sample of typically developing children. In the Stop–Signal measure (Logan 1994; Logan, Cowan and Davis 1984), subjects were engaged in a simple task in which they categorized words as animals or objects by pressing keys on a two-choice response box. On a subset of trials, an auditory signal was presented to indicate that responses to the primary task should be inhibited on that trial. Thus, this task measured the ability to control a voluntary motor response and did not require any flexibility. The Negative Priming task (Tipper 1985) measured cognitive (rather than motor) inhibitory mechanisms (Neill, Lissner and Beck 1990). Participants saw a five-letter string (e.g. TVTVT) and were asked to judge whether the second and fourth letters were the same or different. On some trials, the target stimuli (letters 2 and 4) were the same as the distractor stimuli (letters 1, 3, and 5) from the immediately preceding trial. It has been demonstrated that when distractors from previous trials become targets on subsequent trials, performance is slower and less accurate than if the stimuli had not been previously seen (Tipper 1985). This disruption in performance, termed the *negative priming effect*, is thought to be due to the costs of actively inhibiting attention to the stimulus when it was a distractor in earlier trials. Thus, a weak negative priming effect indicates deficient cognitive inhibition (Neill *et al.* 1990).

Ozonoff and Strayer (1997) found that subjects with autism were unimpaired, relative to age- and IQ-matched normal controls, on both tests of inhibition. On the Stop–Signal task, no group differences were evident in the likelihood of responding on signal trials (i.e. when responses should have been withheld). On the Negative Priming task, both groups demonstrated an intact negative priming effect and there were no significant group differences in the magnitude of this effect. That is, when distractors on one trial became targets on subsequent trials, the act of previously ignoring these stimuli slowed reaction time and increased error rate to a similar extent in both groups. Thus, across tasks measuring both motor and cognitive components of inhibition, the inhibitory control of the autistic group was similar to that of matched typically developing controls. This effect was recently replicated using a different negative priming paradigm (Brian *et al.* 2003).

Consistent results have been found by other research teams employing different paradigms as well. Several groups have used a test from the Cambridge Neuropsychological Test Automated Battery (CANTAB) (Robbins *et al.* 1998) to tease apart the relative contributions of flexibility and inhibition in the performance deficits of individuals with autism. The Intradimensional–Extradimensional Shift Task (ID/ED) is a computerized set-shifting task that measures flexibility while controlling for other cognitive processes that might be important to task performance. A series of compound stimuli composed of colored shapes and lines are presented. Participants learn, through trial and error with computer-generated feedback, to respond to the shape; the line is effectively an irrelevant dimension. Once training to the shape is complete, the necessity to perform two kinds of shift takes place. In the first intradimensional shift, new shapes and lines are introduced, but shape remains the relevant response dimension. In the later extradimensional shift, the contingencies change, with the line becoming the salient stimulus and the previously trained shape now irrelevant. Only the extradimensional shift requires conceptual flexibility (that is, shifting from one concept or cognitive set to another); the intradimensional shift only requires perceptual flexibility, or shifting from one exemplar to another exemplar within the same cognitive set (e.g. shape). This task is functionally similar to the category shifts required by the Wisconsin Card Sorting Test, but conceptually simpler and with multiple manipulations built in to control for other sources of impairment, such as inhibitory dysfunction or discrimination learning deficits. Experiments on marmoset monkeys with prefrontal lesions suggest that both orbital and lateral regions of prefrontal cortex are involved in the extradimensional shift (Dias, Robbins and Roberts 1996).

Three recent investigations have used the CANTAB ID/ED subtest with individuals with autism spectrum disorders (Hughes, Russell and Robbins 1994; Ozonoff *et al.* 2004; Turner 1997). Relative to matched controls with mental retardation, individuals with autism and mental retardation demonstrated intact performance during the early phases of the task measuring discrimination learning, inhibitory control and intradimensional shifting, but impairment at the extradimensional shift (Hughes *et al.* 1994). The authors concluded that deficits in flexibility 'rather than low level motoric inhibition' were most prominent on this task (p. 488). Turner (1997) replicated the extradimensional shifting deficit in individuals with autism and mental retardation, but not in participants with autism of normal IQ, although small sample size and low power may have contributed to this result. In the most recent study, the ID/ED subtest was administered to 79 participants with autism and 70 well-matched typical controls recruited from seven universities who are part of the Collaborative Programs of Excellence in Autism (CPEA) network (Ozonoff *et al.* 2004). Significant group differences were found in ID/ED performance, with the autism group showing intact intradimensional shifting, but deficits in extradimensional shifting, relative to controls. Deficits were found in both lower- and higher-IQ individuals with autism across the age range of 6 to 47 years.

Another form of flexibility that has been investigated in autism is attention shifting. Courchesne *et al.* (1990, 1994) designed a task that examined the shifting of attention between sensory modalities. Subjects were told to monitor one modality (either auditory or visual) until an oddball target was detected and then shift to the other modality to find targets. 'False alarm' errors occurred when subjects failed to disengage from the first modality and inappropriately continued to respond to old targets, while 'misses' occurred when subjects failed to quickly move or reengage attention in the new channel, resulting in failure to detect new targets. Average IQ adults with autism performed as well as typical controls in the first phase of the task, which required no shifting. Performance was over six standard deviations below that of controls, however, during the phase that required rapid alternation of attention between auditory and visual channels. Results suggested that the deficit of the group with autism was primarily during the disengage operation, as evidenced by a high false alarm rate but a normal miss rate.

Another paradigm that has been used to study attention shifting in individuals with autism is the visuospatial orienting task of Posner (1980). In this task, two boxes are positioned on either side of a central fixation cross on a computer screen. Targets appear in one of the two boxes and subjects are instructed to respond to them as quickly as possible. A visuospatial cue is presented just before the target appears, indicating where attention should be directed. On valid cue trials, one of the boxes is brightened, followed by presentation of the target in that box. On invalid cue trials, one of the boxes is brightened, followed by presentation of the target in the opposite box. On neutral trials, both boxes brighten, rendering the cue uninformative. Typically, a validity effect is obtained, in which targets are processed more quickly on valid than on neutral trials and more slowly on invalid than on neutral trials. Using this paradigm, Wainwright-Sharp and Bryson (1993) found no validity effect for subjects with autism when the cue was presented very briefly (100 msec), but a robust validity effect when the cue was presented for longer duration (800 msec). This suggested that the participants with autism took longer than controls to disengage attention from the fixation cross and move it to the location indicated by the cue. Very similar results were obtained by others using the same paradigm (Casey *et al.* 1993), reinforcing the suggestion that the disengage/move component of attention is dysfunctional in autism.

Rinehart and colleagues also found deficits on an attention shifting task in a group of boys with high-functioning autism, compared to typically-developing controls matched on age, IQ, and sex (Rinehart *et al.* 2001). They used a global–local task, in which stimuli were large (global) digits composed of smaller (local) digits. Targets could appear at either the global or local level, necessitating shifting attention between stimulus levels on a trial-by-trial basis. The group with autism was significantly slower to find global targets when the previous stimulus was processed at the local level, suggesting delays in shifting between processing levels.

These studies, in aggregate, suggest that operations that require flexibility, including both shifting of cognitive set and shifting of attentional focus, are impaired in individuals with autism, while inhibitory functions appear relatively more intact. A recent study suggested that cognitive flexibility was a particularly good predictor of outcome (Berger *et al.* 2003), further highlighting its potential significance to autism. Specifically, it was found that performance on a set-shifting task was better able than tasks in other cognitive domains to predict social understanding and social competence in high-functioning adolescents and adults with autism.

WORKING MEMORY

Another component of executive function that has been explored in people with autism is working memory. This term refers to the ability to maintain information in an activated, on-line state to guide cognitive processing (Baddeley 1986). Initial interest in working memory in autism was driven by studies of performance on Tower tasks (Tower of Hanoi, Tower of London), which, as reviewed above, is typically quite poor in individuals with autism. Tower tasks are thought to measure planning and thus, at least intuitively, should require working memory (e.g. maintaining a representation of a potential move 'on-line' while considering its consequences). Bennetto *et al.* (1996) found that adolescents and adults with high-functioning autism were significantly impaired relative to age- and IQ-matched controls on several tests of verbal working memory (counting and sentence span tasks), while they performed similarly to controls on tests of declarative memory function, such as rote short-term, verbal long-term, and recognition memory.

In contrast, other studies have failed to find working memory deficits in autism. In an investigation by Russell and colleagues, a group with both autism and mental retardation did not differ from matched controls on three measures of verbal working memory capacity, a dice counting task, an odd-man-out task, and a sentence span test (Russell *et al.* 1996). Similarly, a case report of an individual with autism and mental retardation demonstrated deficits in flexibility, but normal working memory (Mottron *et al.* 1999). No group differences were found on the working memory index of the Wechsler Adult Intelligence Scale in a sample of high-functioning adults with autism spectrum disorders and matched controls (Lopez *et al.* 2005). And no group differences were found in a higher-functioning sample, relative to matched comparison groups with Tourette syndrome and typical development, on three tasks of working memory in a third study (Ozonoff and Strayer 2001). One hypothesis of this study was that performance would be more impaired on a task of verbal working memory (an n-back task, in which participants had to identify whether the digit on the computer screen was the same as or different from the digit either one or two trials previously) than on tasks of non-verbal working memory (a box search task, with penalties for returning to locations that had already been examined, and a spatial span task). This prediction was not borne out and the group with autism performed as well as both comparison groups on all tasks, despite having a non-significant but still substantial IQ disadvantage of approximately two-thirds of a standard deviation.

Thus, there is mixed evidence for working memory as an impaired component of executive function. This has prompted some reconsideration of Tower tasks as measures of working memory. A task analysis performed by Goel and Grafman (1995) suggests that Tower tasks measure planning functions less than they might appear, but are instead primary measures of the ability to resolve goal–subgoal conflicts. Tower tasks often require participants to perform moves that appear, at a superficial level, to be incorrect or opposite the goal state. Failure to appreciate this results in poorer task performance and lower planning efficiency scores, but for reasons more conceptually related to flexibility than to working memory. At the current time, it is not clear whether working memory is a specific difficulty for people with autism and more research is needed.

Section summary

This body of research begins to clarify the nature of executive dysfunction in autism. While tasks employed in initial research, such as the WCST, suggested impairments in flexibility, they were relatively imprecise measures that confounded a number of executive processes. Further work has refined our ability to examine specific executive components and their respective associations with autism. At the present time, this work suggests that inhibitory control and possibly working memory are relatively spared functions, while mental flexibility of a variety of types (set shifting, attention shifting) appears compromised (Hill and Russell 2002; Hughes 2002; Ozonoff and Jensen 1999).

EMERGING ISSUES

As the affected components of executive function in autism have been clarified, a number of additional interesting issues have emerged from the EF literature in recent years.

Developmental course of executive dysfunction

An important question related to the contribution of executive processes to autism centers on *when* deficits emerge. Historically, based primarily on work with adult patients, the frontal lobes were assumed to become functionally mature only in adolescence; however, both developmental research and animal models have shown that this brain region is operational, remarkably capable and adaptable throughout development (Duncan 2001; Hughes and Graham 2002). EF research on children and animals necessarily requires adapting tasks to appropriate levels; the resulting creativity and simplicity has been very beneficial for component process research (Dawson *et al.* 2002; Diamond *et al.* 1997; Hughes and Graham 2002).

Two research groups have tested age-related EF development in very young children with autism. The first investigation to examine executive functions in pre-school-age children with autism was conducted by McEvoy, Rogers and Pennington (1993). They used several developmentally simple measures of prefrontal function that were first designed for use with non-human primates and human infants (Diamond and Goldman-Rakic 1986). Their sample included young children with autism (mean age = 5 years 4 months) and matched developmentally delayed and typically developing control groups. In the spatial reversal task, an object was hidden in one of two identical wells outside of the subject's vision. The side of hiding remained the same until the subject successfully located the object on four consecutive trials, after which the side of hiding was changed to the other well. Thus, successful search behavior required flexibility and set shifting. Significant group differences were found, with the children with autism making more perseverative errors than children in either the mental- or chronological-age-matched groups. However, no group differences were evident on three other EF measures. It was suggested that these tasks may have been less developmentally appropriate for the sample.

However, in another investigation by the same research team (Griffith *et al.* 1999), studying even younger children with autism (mean age = 4 years 3 months), there were no differences in performance on any of eight executive tasks (including the spatial reversal task), compared to a developmentally delayed group matched on chronological age and both verbal and non-verbal mental age. Based on limited normative data (Diamond *et al.* 1997), both groups performed at levels lower than expected for their mental age, suggesting that EF impairment at this age may not be autism-specific, but rather a function of general developmental delay. Likewise, in a larger study (n = 72) of even younger children with autism (mean age = 3 years 8 months), Dawson *et al.* (2002) reported no significant differences on six EF tasks (again including spatial reversal), relative to developmentally delayed and typically developing control groups matched on mental age.

This work raises the possibility that differential EF deficits emerge with age and are not present (at least relative to other samples with delayed development) early in the pre-school range. Whether this is because of a general deficit, common to developmental delay, or whether there is no delay in autism early on is not certain. Since executive functions are just beginning to develop during the early preschool period in all children, a relative lack of variance across groups may explain this apparent developmental discontinuity. Differences in the way EF is measured at different ages may also contribute to this finding. The executive tests that have been administered to very young children with autism do not require the same use of arbitrary rules that those given to older individuals do. If arbitrary rule use is central to the EF performance deficits of autism (Biro and Russell 2001), then the discontinuity between earlier and later development may be due simply to measurement differences.

Further work, particularly longitudinal research, is needed to examine when during development specific executive difficulties emerge and what their developmental precursors may be. It has been argued, for example, that executive dysfunction is secondary to (and thus driven by) other earlier appearing symptoms, a topic to which we turn next. This timing argument has at times been used to determine which cognitive or psychological processes are core or 'primary' to autism. Emergence early in development does not necessarily indicate primacy, nor must development of an impairment over time imply that it is secondary. If autism is a disorder with multiple core deficits, as many researchers suspect, then it is plausible that different impairments may come on line at different points in development.

Relationship to other cognitive impairments and symptoms of autism

The relationship among executive functions, other cognitive and social-cognitive processes, and the development of autism is complex and has been explored in several recent studies. The explanatory power of executive dysfunction to autism would be greatest if individual differences in executive function predicted variations in other impairments or in symptoms of autism. In this section, we discuss the relationships among executive functions, social-cognitive processes, language, intelligence, and autistic symptoms.

EF AND SOCIAL PROCESSES

Prefrontal cortex appears to be involved not only in executive function performance, but also in the regulation of social behavior, emotional reactions, and social discourse (Dennis 1991; Grattan *et al.* 1990; Price *et al.* 1990; Stuss 1992), so relationships among these skills are not unexpected. Bennetto *et al.* (1996) provide a coherent model of how executive deficits could lead to social difficulties in autism, as effective social interaction depends on the ability to hold a variable stream of context-specific information in mind, including subtle verbal and non-verbal cues, then plan and respond to this ever-changing stream appropriately and flexibly. As mentioned above, significant correlations between performance on set-shifting tasks and social understanding tasks have been found (Berger *et al.* 2003), as have relationships between executive function and adaptive behavior (Gilotty *et al.* 2002).

One of the first studies to document a relationship between social and executive processes was conducted by McEvoy *et al.* (1993) who reported that performance on executive tasks was significantly correlated with measures of social interaction, including joint attention, in preschool-aged autism and control groups. This was an intriguing finding, as joint attention intuitively would appear to require rapid attention shifting and, by extension, intact executive function. In fact, a recent EEG study indicated that activity in the left frontal region was associated with the initiation of joint attention in typical infants (Mundy, Card and Fox 2000). Also examining very young children with autism, Griffith *et al.* (1999) replicated the finding of significant correlations between joint attention and executive functions. In contrast, Dawson *et al.* (1998, 2002) did not find a relationship between joint attention and executive performance in their sample of young children with autism, but instead found an association with a memory task, the delayed non-match to sample task. And Swettenham *et al.* (1998) found that young children with autism have more difficulty shifting attention between social than non-social stimuli, suggesting that the impairment is not simply in the shifting process, but interacts with the nature of the stimulus.

The relationship between executive dysfunction and theory of mind impairment has also been studied. Ozonoff *et al.* (1991) found significant correlations between performance on EF and false belief tasks and this finding has since been replicated several times (see Perner and Lang 1999, for a review). Several explanations for this association have been proposed: (1) the deficits are independent modular cognitive operations that are parallel central impairments of autism, (2) one ability is a prerequisite for the other, so that deficits in one cause deficits in the other, (3) both are driven by a third shared impairment, or (4) both share similar neural underpinnings (Hughes 2001; Ozonoff 1995; Rutter and Bailey 1993).

One way to examine these possibilities is to experimentally manipulate task requirements to see which ability contributes more to success or failure on the task. An early study of this type was performed by Russell and colleagues, using a task originally designed to examine strategic deception ability (Russell *et al.* 1991). Children with autism were taught to play a game in which they competed with an experimenter for a piece of candy. The candy was placed in one of two boxes with windows that revealed the contents of the box to subjects, but not to the experimenter. The objective of the task was to 'fool' the experimenter into looking for the candy in the empty box. It was explained that the strategy of pointing to the empty box would be successful in winning the candy, whereas pointing to the box that actually contained the chocolate would result in losing it. Even after many trials, however, the participants with autism were unable to point to the empty box, despite the consequences of this strategy. Russell *et al.* (1991) first attributed these results to a perspective-taking deficit that caused an inability to engage in deception. In a follow-up study, however, Hughes and Russell (1993) demonstrated that significant group differences remained even after the element of deception was removed from the task. Subjects were simply instructed to point to the empty box to get the candy. Even with no opponent present, the children with autism persisted in using the inappropriate strategy. Hughes and Russell (1993) attributed this pattern of performance to a deficit in disengaging from the object and using internal rules to guide behavior. This behavior is similar to the perseveration, inappropriate strategy use, and stimulus over-selectivity documented on the WCST and other tasks.

The work of Russell and Hughes led the way for several other studies that explored the hypothesis that some degree of executive control is necessary for successful performance on theory of mind tasks and, by extension, for the development of theory of mind (Moses 2001; Russell *et al.* 1999b). In one of the most recent studies of this kind, Perner and Lang (2002) reported a pair of large studies of typically developing preschool children in which the executive account of false belief was explicitly tested. As in previous studies, the false belief performance was strongly correlated ($r = 0.65$) with performance on a simple card-sorting task. However, against explicit predictions from the executive theory, the card-sorting task was just as strongly correlated ($r = 0.65$) with a verbal explanation task that was *not* dependent on executive abilities. Perner and colleagues also found intact theory of mind, but deficient executive functions, in young children at risk of ADHD, arguing against the theory that later theory of mind development is a consequence of improvements in executive control (Perner, Kain and Barchfeld 2002). Perner and Lang (2002), having, in their minds, discounted the strictly executive account of false belief and other mentalizing skills, concluded that there was still no clear explanation to account for the remarkably strong relationship between theory of mind and executive tasks.

Indeed, the story was not so simple and the opposite hypothesis, that some level of social awareness is necessary for executive function, has also received support. In the WCST, for example, feedback is provided by the examiner after each card is sorted; successful set shifting requires using this feedback to alter behavior. If, however, feedback supplied in a social context is less salient or more difficult to process for people with autism, they may perform poorly on EF tasks for primarily social reasons. A few studies have contrasted performance on executive tests when they are administered in the traditional manner, by human examiners, to performance when they are administered by computer. Ozonoff (1995) reported that the WCST was significantly easier for individuals with autism when it was given by computer, with group differences considerably smaller in the computer administration than the human administration conditions. In the group with autism, the number of perseverations was cut in half on the computerized version of the task, while performance did not differ across conditions in the typically developing control group (Ozonoff 1995). Two other research teams have found similar facilitation of performance on computer-administered executive tasks relative to standard (human) administration (Griffith 2002; Pascualvaca *et al.* 1998). This suggests that the format of the executive task, particularly the nature of the feedback (social v. non-social), may have a much greater impact on performance for people with autism than has previously been appreciated. This may even help explain the apparent developmental discontinuity of performance on executive tests discussed above. In the tasks used with very young children with autism (Griffith *et al.* 1999), feedback is supplied by the apparatus itself (e.g. a tangible reward under a cup or in a well) and not by a human. However, other studies have found executive deficits in individuals with autism when the task was fully computerized and all feedback was provided by machine, with no social interaction required, as in the CANTAB studies reported earlier (Ozonoff *et al.* 2004). And computerized tasks, in constraining the problem space, reduce the opportunity for rule violations and thus may be less sensitive to particular types of executive deficits (Brophy, Taylor and Hughes 2002). Thus, it has been difficult to tease apart the relative primacy of executive function and mentalizing or other social deficits in the chain of cognitive impairments that are involved in autism.

Another hypothesis is that executive function and theory of mind abilities share similar cognitive underpinnings, and impairments in this basic cognitive function drive both deficits. At a superficial level of analysis, executive function and theory of mind appear rather dissimilar. Focusing on the content of the domains may, however, obscure similarities that exist at a process level of analysis. Several writers have suggested that the operations involved in successful executive function and theory of mind task performance are similar (Carlson, Moses and Breton 2002; Hughes 1998; Perner and Lang 1999).

The Smarties task is a standard false-belief measure (Perner *et al.* 1989). Subjects are shown a box of Smarties (similar to M & Ms) and asked what it contains. After a response is given, the box is opened to reveal that it actually holds a pencil. Subjects are then asked to predict what the next subject, who has never seen the box, will think it contains. A pass is scored if the subject responds, 'Candy.' An analysis of this task (following Frye, Zelazo and Palfai 1995) suggests that successful performance requires consideration of two mental perspectives and two types of cognitive judgments. The subject must attend to two different perspectives about the contents of the box – his or her own perspective and that of the other person – and must also make two types of judgments – what *is thought to be* in the box and *what is really* in the box. As Frye *et al.* (1995) explain subjects must employ two recursive if–then rules to solve the problem correctly. Using only one or the other rule will result in an incorrect answer. Successful performance requires that the rules be considered in an embedded and sequential manner, for example 'If the question is about me, and if it is asking what the contents really are, then the answer is a pencil' versus 'If the question is about someone else, and if it is asking what the contents are thought to be, then the answer is candy.' Thus, a critical skill to successful solution of this false-belief task is *embedded use of if–then rules* (Frye *et al.* 1995).

The Tower of Hanoi is a standard executive function measure in which subjects must sequentially move disks among pegs to duplicate a goal state determined by the experimenter. To receive a high score on this task, subjects must predict intermediate disk configurations produced by different potential moves, consider their implications for future disk configurations, and evaluate their utility toward eventual attainment of the goal state (Harris 1993). Embedded rules, applied recursively, must again be used; for example, 'If I move the blue disk to peg 3, then it will leave peg 1 open for the yellow disk, thus freeing up the red disk' (etc.). This component process analysis suggests that Tower tasks are primary measures of rule-based reasoning and recursive rule use, as much as or more than they are measures of working memory (Goel and Grafman 1995). Furthermore, this analysis suggests that theory of mind and executive function tasks, which appear rather different at the content level, may be quite similar at the process level. Tasks in both domains appear to require recursive or sequential analysis of information and embedded rule use (Frye *et al.* 1995; Hughes and Russell 1993). The focus is not on *what type* of information is processed, but on *how* it is processed. Other impairments of autism that appear different at the macroanalytic, surface, or content level may be related at the microanalytic or process level.

The last hypothesis regarding the relationship between EF and theory of mind is that both abilities are subserved by neural networks in the same brain regions (Ozonoff *et al.* 1991). Imaging studies have, in fact, provided support for this hypothesis, both confirming the role of frontal cortex in executive functions (Baker *et al.* 1996; Dias *et al.* 1996) and demonstrating the involvement of frontal cortex in networks that are activated during social-cognition tasks (Baron-Cohen *et al.* 1999; Fletcher *et al.* 1995; Happe *et al.* 1996; Stone, Baron-Cohen and Knight 1998). Component process research has to date been very useful for suggesting and disproving theories and should continue to be fruitful over the next decade, particularly in combination with the new possibilities afforded by functional imaging techniques.

LANGUAGE AND IQ

The contribution of language development to EF ability has also received significant research attention. Hughes (1996) reported a simple set-shifting deficit in preschool children with autism, who had significant difficulty imitating a simple hand gesture after being primed with a different hand movement. She suggested that the deficit arose from a failure to use language to control thoughts and behavior. Russell *et al.* (1999a) explored this idea by devising an EF task that had no arbitrary or novel rules to follow and another that required only verbal response. There were no differences in performance between groups with autism, mixed developmental delay, and typical development. The authors theorized that the deficient performance on EF tests of people with autism arises primarily from failure to verbally encode rules and use them to drive behavior. When no such ability was required, performance was predicted to be unimpaired.

Liss *et al.* (2001) gave a battery of EF tests to children with high-functioning autism and a control group of children with developmental language disorders. The only group difference, more perserverative errors on the WCST by the autism group, disappeared when verbal IQ was statistically controlled. Likewise, significant relationships between EF performance and measures of autism symptom severity and adaptive behavior disappeared when controlling for IQ. Liss *et al.* concluded that EF deficits, while common in autism, are likely a function of more general cognitive impairments and should not be considered causal. Ozonoff has also identified significant contributions of IQ to EF performance in people with autism (Miller and Ozonoff 2000; Ozonoff and McEvoy 1994; Ozonoff and Strayer 2001).

REPETITIVE BEHAVIOR

Turner (1997, 1999) has suggested that executive dysfunction (e.g. perseveration, deficient inhibitory control, impaired generativity) may be responsible for the stereotyped, repetitive behaviors of autism spectrum disorders. Further, she hypothesized that different components of executive function would be associated with different types of repetitive behavior. In support of this, she reported that perseveration on a set-shifting task was correlated with more primitive stereotyped behaviors, such as hand flapping, while impoverished generativity was correlated with 'higher-level' repetitive behaviors such as circumscribed interests. A strong relationship between cognitive flexibility and repetitive behaviors was also recently reported by Lopez *et al.* (2005). In contrast, South, Ozonoff and McMahon (in press) found no significant correlations between any category of repetitive behavior and any executive function variable. For example, the correlations between the number of perseverations on the WCST and various forms of repetitive behavior ranged from a low of $r = 0.03$ for lifetime history of circumscribed interests to a high of $r = 0.16$ for lifetime history of unusual obsessions with objects. This sample was significantly older (mean age = 14 years) and more intellectually capable (mean VIQ = 111) than Turner's sample, so direct comparisons are difficult and further research is clearly needed.

Specificity to autism

No review of the executive function hypothesis would be complete without discussion of the so-called 'discriminant validity' problem (Pennington *et al.* 1996). For a causal mechanism to have explanatory power, it should be relatively specific to the disorder it is intended to explain (Pennington and Ozonoff 1991). Yet difficulties in executive function are seen in a wide variety of disorders, including ADHD (Chelune *et al.* 1986), conduct disorder (Lueger and Gill 1990), early-treated phenylketonuria (Welsh *et al.* 1990), obsessive-compulsive disorder (Head, Bolton and Hymas 1989), Tourette syndrome (Bornstein 1990), and schizophrenia (Axelrod *et al.* 1994; Beatty *et al.* 1994). If deficits in executive function generally distinguish 'normal' from 'abnormal,' but are not specific indicators that distinguish one syndrome from another, their explanatory power is diminished.

The discriminant validity problem may be 'more apparent than real' (Hughes 2001), however. Once the large construct of executive function is parsed into more unitary and functionally independent cognitive operations through component process analyses, it appears that different neurodevelopmental disorders are associated with different profiles of strength and weakness in executive function. For example, as discussed above, evidence suggests that inhibitory function may be intact in individuals with autism (Ozonoff and Strayer 1997). In contrast, performance on inhibition paradigms such as the Negative Priming and Stop–Signal tasks is deficient in both adults with schizophrenia and children with attention problems (Beech *et al.* 1989; Schachar and Logan 1990). Other dissociations are apparent in the domain of attention. The ability to sustain attention appears intact in autism, with several studies finding unimpaired performance on the Continuous Performance Test (Buchsbaum *et al.* 1992; Casey *et al.* 1993; Garretson, Fein and Waterhouse 1990). Deficits in sustained attention are a cardinal feature of ADHD (Douglas and Peters 1979) and are also prominent in Tourette syndrome (Comings and Comings 1987), schizophrenia (Bellak 1994; Cornblatt and Keilp 1994), and other disorders. Autism does appear to involve difficulty shifting attention, while this skill appears unimpaired in children with ADHD. Studies using Posner's (1980) paradigm have demonstrated difficulties in the disengage and move operations in children with autism (Casey *et al.* 1993; Courchesne *et al.* 1994; Wainwright-Sharp and Bryson 1993), but not children with ADHD (Swanson *et al.* 1991). Finally, selective associations of executive deficits with specific disorders have been demonstrated using CANTAB. On this battery's tower task, the Stockings of Cambridge, individuals with autism show clearly deficient performance (Ozonoff *et al.* 2004), while medicated children with ADHD (Kempton *et al.* 1999) and adults with OCD (Purcell *et al.* 1998) perform comparably to typical controls. Thus, considering EF as a multidimensional rather than a unitary construct has helped obtain more precision in the nature of the dysfunction associated with autism and has provided preliminary dissociations and evidence of distinct EF profiles in autism and other neurodevelopmental disorders.

Section summary

Although there remain many important questions to be answered, research regarding the component processes of executive dysfunction in autism has made many gains in recent years. Robust findings of EF deficits in older children and adults with autism, relative to appropriate clinical and normal controls, has been tempered by the discovery of more complex patterns of EF development in very young children with autism. It is likely that some important turning point is missed by children with autism sometime during the late preschool age; nonetheless, the specifics of this developmental milestone are not yet elucidated. There are indications of significant correlations between EF abilities and core symptoms of autism, beginning with very early social impairments and continuing throughout childhood and adulthood, but the causal directions and specific nature of these relationships are unknown. This section also reviewed associations between EF and other important characteristics of autism, including metacognitive mentalizing ability (e.g. theory of mind), IQ, language, and repetitive behaviors. In the next section, we explore new research that suggests exciting future directions for research on EF and autism.

FUTURE DIRECTIONS
EF and families: are EF deficits part of the broader autism phenotype?

Evidence exists that autism is inherited in a complex polygenic fashion, with up to a dozen genes possibly involved (Pickles *et al.* 1995; Risch *et al.* 1999). There is much interest in identifying the multiple susceptibility loci involved in causing the disorder. Research suggests that what is inherited is not autism itself, but an extended set of difficulties that are milder than but qualitatively similar to autism (Bailey *et al.* 1998; Piven and Palmer 1997). This broader autism phenotype, as it has come to be known, has been found in 15–45 percent of family members of people with autism in different samples (Bailey *et al.* 1998). New research, summarized in this section, suggests that cognitive difficulties, including executive dysfunction, may be part of the broader autism phenotype. It is hoped that specification of intermediate phenotypes may one day assist in gene localization efforts (Piven 2001). Examining the profiles of cognitive strengths and weaknesses in first-degree relatives of individuals with autism also provides an alternative strategy for identifying the core cognitive impairments of autism (Hughes 2001).

Ozonoff *et al.* (1993) found that siblings of probands with autism performed significantly less well than siblings of children with reading disabilities on the Tower of Hanoi, while the two groups performed equally on theory of mind tasks. Hughes, Plumet and Leboyer (1999) found deficient extradimensional shifting on CANTAB's ID/ED task in siblings of children with autism but not siblings of children with either delayed or typical development. The siblings of children with autism also performed more poorly than the comparison siblings on CANTAB's tower task once their significantly better performance on a spatial working memory subtest was statistically controlled.

Similar deficits in executive function have been reported for parents of children with autism, using tasks of set shifting, working memory, and planning (Hughes, Leboyer and Bouvard 1997; Koczat et al. 2002; Piven and Palmer 1997), although there are complex relationships with sex and clinical diagnosis. In one study, executive performance in the autism parent group was significantly positively correlated with pre-test clinical impressions of social oddity (Hughes et al. 1997), consistent with findings discussed above of significant correlations between set shifting and social behavior.

Other cognitive difficulties have also been reported in family members, including weak central coherence (Happe, Briskman and Frith 2001) and impaired theory of mind (Baron-Cohen and Hammer 1997). One study examined a variety of neuro-psychological functions in children diagnosed with either autism or dyslexia and all their parents and siblings (Ozonoff et al. 2002). Probands with autism demonstrated weaknesses in executive function and memory, but strengths in phonological decoding and visual–spatial function relative to probands with dyslexia. The very same cognitive profiles were found in both parents and siblings of the probands, with family members of children with autism demonstrating significantly inferior executive and memory functions, but significantly superior reading and visual–spatial skills, relative to the family members of children with dyslexia. Only 6 percent of the dyslexia families included at least one member with executive dysfunction, while 94 percent of the autism families did. Thus, while executive dysfunction is not the only cognitive diffi-culty that appears to be part of the inherited phenotype and that may be useful in gene localization efforts, its clear presence in family members, across multiple studies and lab-oratories, highlights its centrality to autism.

Remediation of executive dysfunction

Another new direction in executive function research is intervention. The component process approach to identifying relationships between specific cognitive deficits and behavioral symptoms of autism has clear implications for treatment. Almost no empiri-cal work has been done on remediation of executive deficits in autism, but there is a large literature on cognitive remediation of other disorders that may prove relevant to autism. Defined broadly, cognitive remediation is a systematic approach to teaching individuals to overcome cognitive deficits arising from brain dysfunction (Task Force on Head Injury 1984). It involves the identification of specific neuropsychological deficits and the design and implementation of a treatment program to retrain and/or compensate for deficits. Typically, cognitive remediation is only part of a more comprehensive program that includes other treatment modalities such as psychotherapy and organized social activities (Butler 1998). Typical targets of cognitive remediation are memory, attention, motivation, language, and executive functions. In this section, we describe the potential of cognitive remediation to address the executive deficits of autism described in the literature and highlight some key issues that will need to be addressed before this approach will be of use for persons with autism.

Much of what we know about the effectiveness of cognitive remediation is based on studies of adults with acquired brain injury or schizophrenia (Butler and Namerow 1988; Gianutsos 1991; Kurtz *et al.* 2001; Levine *et al.* 2000; Pilling *et al.* 2002). One of the more widely utilized approaches is the Attention Process Training (APT) program (Sohlberg and Mateer 1986). APT was originally developed for adults with brain injury. It contains modules for improving focused attention (the ability to respond to specific sensory information in the environment), sustained attention (the ability to maintain a behavioral response over time), selective attention (the ability to maintain a response in the presence of distracting or competing stimuli), alternating attention (the ability to shift focus of attention and demonstrate mental flexibility), and divided attention (the ability to respond simultaneously to more than one task or stimulus). The efficacy of APT has been demonstrated in adults with brain injury (Mateer, Sohlberg and Youngman 1990; Mateer 1992; Sohlberg and Mateer 1987) and schizophrenia (Kurtz *et al.* 2001).

The clinical application of cognitive remediation techniques to pediatric populations is fairly new. Several investigators have used the APT training package with some success with children with ADHD (Semrud-Clikeman *et al.* 1995; Stevenson *et al.* 2002; Williams 1989) and traumatic brain injury (Thomson 1994). Theoretical approaches underlying adult rehabilitation programs, however, may not fully apply to pediatric remediation efforts. Recognizing the need to address both developmental issues and the limited awareness and compromised reasoning skills of children with brain dysfunction, Kerns, Eso and Thomson (1999) modified APT to start at a more basic level and make tasks more child-friendly. Materials were made more interesting and engaging and stimuli were changed from abstract symbols to more familiar concepts, such as human features (hair, sex, clothing), family relationships (siblings, grandparents), and household items. In a small study of the efficacy of this program, called *Pay Attention!*, children with ADHD in the treatment group performed significantly better than matched controls on several measures of attention and academic performance.

Butler and Copeland (2002) developed a comprehensive cognitive rehabilitation program to remediate attention and executive processes in children suffering neurological impairments secondary to treatment for cancer (e.g. cranial irradiation). Their 20-session program included APT, training in metacognitive strategies, individual cognitive-behavioral therapy focused on self-monitoring and self-coaching skills and games and activities to promote generalization of new skills. A pilot study found that children in the treatment group improved their performance on measures of attention significantly more than no-treatment controls (Butler and Copeland 2002). No group differences were found on academic tests; however, suggesting generalization to other cognitive skills was not obtained. Nevertheless, this comprehensive therapeutic approach may be helpful in other populations of cognitively impaired children, including children and adolescents with autism spectrum disorders.

At first glance, the literature on the cognitive remediation of autism appears sparse. However, many comprehensive early treatment models, including applied behavioral analysis and TEACCH programs, fit into the broadest category of cognitive remediation. These approaches aim to improve skills within specific cognitive domains (e.g. expressive and receptive language, visual spatial abilities, etc.) by breaking down complex behaviors into basic components through a component process task analysis. Skill components are then taught in a hierarchical manner, with repeated practice. The TEACCH program also places emphasis on the development of compensatory strategies, which is another hallmark of cognitive remediation programs.

There are, however, few papers specifically addressing executive function remediation for people with autism (Ozonoff 1998). Bock (1994) reported an intervention that trained four children with autism on a tridimensional sorting task. Participants learned to sort the same set of objects into three different categories (color, shape, number). This required shifting cognitive set from one attribute of an object to another and is thus analogous to the Wisconsin Card Sorting Test and the ID/ED subtest of CANTAB. After training, children were tested using a different set of objects (cans of food) that they were asked to sort into new categorical sets (brand, size, food type). The study found that training on the categorization task increased sorting ability on the untrained item set and that gains were maintained two months post-intervention (Bock 1994).

Jepsen and von Thaden's report of a program called REHABIT (2002) suggested it may have efficacy for children with autism. This program was developed to teach a variety of cognitive skills, including executive functions, attention, memory, language, and academic achievement. Adolescents with mixed diagnoses, including autism, other developmental delays, and acquired neurological insults, were matched in a pairwise fashion on diagnosis, age, sex, and IQ and randomly assigned to either the REHABIT treatment group or the education-as-usual group. Pre-post test comparisons suggested significant group by time interaction effects, with adolescents in the treatment group demonstrating significantly more improvement than controls in planning, simultaneous processing, reading, and adaptive behavior (e.g. independent functioning, pre-vocational skills, self-direction, responsibility). While small sample size precluded diagnosis-specific analyses, the authors state that significant gains were made across diagnostic categories. Thus, it appears that the subgroup of children with autism who participated in this study benefited from this type of cognitive (including executive) remediation (Jepsen and von Thaden 2002).

Cognitive remediation of autism is faced with many of the same challenges that are common to other pediatric populations, including the poor fit that results from application of adult rehabilitation models to children, as noted above. Other challenges may be unique to autism spectrum disorders. Functional organization in the brain of individuals with a developmental disorder may be quite dissimilar from that of the typically developing brain. And most cognitive remediation programs have only a small component devoted to the particular cognitive difficulties of autism (e.g. shifting and divided attention, executive functions), suggesting that any efforts to use these packages with autism will require substantial modification or tailoring. Most cognitive rehabilitation programs are based on the assumption that the cognitive processes being trained were previously established and then damaged. Techniques are aimed at 'retraining' and strengthening neural connections through massed practice in order to restore mental functions and processing speed. This assumption is not likely to apply to a developmental disorder like autism and its impact on the efficacy of the approach is not known. Another issue is the problem of generalization of learned skills; as Butler and Copeland (2002) found, lack of generalization is not unique to children with autism. This imposes serious challenges to professionals developing and implementing cognitive remediation programs for individuals with autism spectrum disorders, who often have severe problems generalizing gains to other settings, materials, and teachers. Many cognitive remediation programs include some form of individual psychotherapy, usually focused on increasing awareness of deficits and teaching self-monitoring and compensatory strategies. Due to the limited self-awareness and insight of most people with autism spectrum disorders, however, the role that psychotherapy should play in the cognitive remediation of autism is not clear. In summary, cognitive remediation approaches may eventually prove useful in improving the executive functions of people with autism, but they will require modifications and careful thought to develop techniques appropriate for this population. This is an exciting new direction for future executive function research.

CONCLUSION

This chapter has reviewed the empirical literature on executive dysfunction in autism, from initial studies finding large group differences to more recent work specifying the nature of the affected component processes. An eventual goal of this research is to identify the executive profile or fingerprint of autism, which may someday assist in diagnosis, contribute to gene localization efforts, and improve remediation techniques. It has also explored issues that have emerged as executive function research has matured. With new studies have come new questions, most still unanswered, regarding the developmental course of executive dysfunction and its relationship to other symptoms of autism and to other neurodevelopmental disorders. Finally, this chapter has presented new research on the familiarity of executive dysfunction and the promise of newly developed remediation techniques. Over the past two decades, we have learned a great deal, only to find out how much more there is yet to know about this complex disorder and its many manifestations.

ACKNOWLEDGMENTS

Many thanks to the individuals with autism and their families who contributed to the work described here. This chapter was first presented as a paper at the APNA Simposium Internacional Sobre Autismo, in Madrid, Spain, in May 2005. I am grateful to Ms. Isabel Bayonas and Dr. Pedro González for organizing this congress. The research was supported by funding from the National Institutes of Health (R29-MH52229, F31-MH12566, P01-HD35476, R01-MH068398, and U19-HD35468). The chapter also appeared in *The Handbook of Autism and Pervasive Developmental Disorders, Volume 1, Diagnosis, Development, Neurobiology, and Behaviour, 3rd Edition*, edited by F. R. Volkmar, R. Paul, A. Klin and D. J. Cohen. Copyright © John Wiley and Sons, Inc. 2005. Reproduced by permission.

REFERENCES

Anderson, J. R. and Bower, G. H. (1973) *Human Associative Memory*. Hillsdale, NJ: Erlbaum.

Axelrod, B. N., Goldman, R. S., Tompkins, L. M. and Jiron, C. C. (1994) 'Poor differential performance on the Wisconsin Card Sorting Test in schizophrenia, mood disorder, and traumatic brain injury.' *Neuropsychiatry, Neuropsychology, and Behavioral Neurology 7*, 20–24.

Baddeley, A. D. (1986) *Working Memory*. Oxford: Clarendon Press.

Bailey, A., Luthert, P., Dean, A., Harding, B., Janota, I., Montgomery, M. *et al.* (1998) 'A clinicopathological study of autism.' *Brain 121*, 889–905.

Baker, S. C., Rogers, R. D., Owen, A. M., Frith, C. D., Dolan, R. J., Frackowiak, R. S. J. and Robbins, T. W. (1996) 'Neural systems engaged by planning: a PET study of the Tower of London task.' *Neuropsychologia 34*, 515–526.

Baron-Cohen, S. and Hammer, J. (1997) 'Parents of children with Asperger syndrome: what is the cognitive phenotype?' *Journal of Cognitive Neuroscience 9*, 548–554.

Baron-Cohen, S., Ring, H., Wheelwright, S., Bullmore, E., Brammer, M., Simmons, A. and Williams, S. (1999) 'Social intelligence in the normal and autistic brain: an fMRI study.' *European Journal of Neuroscience 11*, 1891–1898.

Beatty, W. W., Jocic, Z., Monson, N. and Katzung, V. M. (1994) 'Problem solving by schizophrenic and schizoaffective patients on the Wisconsin and California Card Sorting Tests.' *Neuropsychology 8*, 49–54.

Beech, A., Powell, T., McWilliam, J. and Claridge, G. (1989) 'Evidence of reduced "cognitive inhibition" in schizophrenia.' *British Journal of Clinical Psychology 28*, 109–116.

Bellak, L. (1994) 'The schizophrenic syndrome and attention deficit disorder: thesis, antithesis, and synthesis?' *American Psychologist 49*, 25–29.

Bennetto, L., Pennington, B. F. and Rogers, S. J. (1996) 'Intact and impaired memory functions in autism.' *Child Development 67*, 1816–1835.

Berger, H. J. C., Aerts, F. H. T. M., van Spaendonck, K. P. M., Cools, A. R. and Teunisse, J. P. (2003) 'Central coherence and cognitive shifting in relation to social improvement in high-functioning young adults with autism.' *Journal of Clinical and Experimental Neuropsychology 25*, 502–511.

Biro, S. and Russell, J. (2001) 'The execution of arbitrary procedures by children with autism.' *Development and Psychopathology 13*, 97–110.

Bock, M. A. (1994) 'Acquisition, maintenance, and generalization of a categorization strategy by children with autism.' *Journal of Autism and Developmental Disorders 24*, 39–51.

Bond, J. A. and Buchtel, H. A. (1984) 'Comparison of the Wisconsin card sorting test and the Halstead category test.' *Journal of Clinical Psychology 40*, 1251–1255.

Bornstein, R. A. (1990) 'Neuropsychological performance in children with Tourette's syndrome.' *Psychiatry Research 33*, 73–81.

Brian, J. A., Tipper, S., Weaver, B. and Bryson, S. (2003) 'Inhibitory mechanisms in autism spectrum disorders: typical selective inhibition of location versus facilitated perceptual processing.' *Journal of Child Psychology and Psychiatry 44*, 552–560.

Brophy, M., Taylor, E. and Hughes, C. (2002) 'To go or not to go: inhibitory control in "hard to manage" children.' *Infant and Child Development 11*, 125–140.

Buchsbaum, M. S., Siegel, B. V., Wu, J. C., Hazlett, E., Sicotte, N., Haier, R. *et al.* (1992) 'Attention performance in autism and regional brain metabolic rate assessed by positron emission tomography.' *Journal of Autism and Developmental Disorders 22*, 115–125.

Butler, R. W. (1998) 'Attentional processes and their remediation in childhood cancer.' *Medical and Pediatric Oncology 1*, 75–78.

Butler, R. W. and Copeland, D. R. (2002) 'Attentional processes and their remediation in children treated for cancer: a literature review and the development of a therapeutic approach.' *Journal of the International Neuropsychological Society 8*, 115–124.

Butler, R. W. and Namerow, N. S. (1988) 'Cognitive retraining in brain injury rehabilitation: a critical review.' *Journal of NeuroRehabilitation 2*, B1–B5.

Carlson, S. M., Moses, L. J. and Breton, C. (2002) 'How specific is the relation between executive function and theory of mind? Contributions of inhibitory control and working memory.' *Infant and Child Development 11*, 73–92.

Casey, B. J., Gordon, C. T., Mannheim, G. B. and Rumsey, J. M. (1993) 'Dysfunctional attention in autistic savants.' *Journal of Clinical and Experimental Neuropsychology 15*, 933–946.

Chelune, G. J., Ferguson, W., Koon, R. and Dickey, T. O. (1986) 'Frontal lobe disinhibition in Attention Deficit Disorder.' *Child Psychiatry and Human Development 16*, 221–234.

Comings, D. E. and Comings, B. G. (1987) 'A controlled study of Tourette syndrome: attention deficit disorders, learning disorders, and school problems.' *American Journal of Human Genetics 41*, 701–741.

Cornblatt, B. A. and Keilp, J. G. (1994) 'Impaired attention, genetics, and the pathophysiology of schizophrenia.' *Schizophrenia Bulletin 20*, 31–46.

Courchesne, E., Akshoomoff, N. A. and Ciesielski, K. (1990) 'Shifting attention abnormalities in autism: ERP and performance evidence.' *Journal of Clinical and Experimental Neuropsychology 12*, 77.

Courchesne, E., Townsend, J. P., Akshoomoff, N. A., Yeung-Courchesne, R., Press, G. A., Murakami, J. W. *et al.* (1994) 'A new finding in autism: impairment in shifting attention.' In S. H. Broman and J. Grafman (eds) *Atypical Cognitive Deficits in Developmental Disorders: Implications for Brain Function*, pp. 101–137. Hillsdale, NJ: Erlbaum.

Dawson, G., Meltzoff, A. N., Osterling, J. and Rinaldi, J. (1998) 'Neuropsychological correlates of early symptoms in autism.' *Child Development 69*, 1276–1285.

Dawson, G., Munson, J., Estes, A., Osterling, J., McPartland, J., Toth, K. *et al.* (2002) 'Neurocognitive function and joint attention ability in young children with autism spectrum disorder versus developmental delay.' *Child Development 73*, 345–358.

Dehaene, S. and Changeux, J. P. (1991) 'The Wisconsin Card Sorting Test: theoretical analysis and modeling in a neuronal network.' *Cerebral Cortex 1*, 62–79.

Dennis, M. (1991) 'Frontal lobe function in childhood and adolescence: a heuristic for assessing attention regulation, executive control, and the intentional states important for social discourse.' *Developmental Neuropsychology 7*, 327–358.

Diamond, A. and Goldman-Rakic, P. S. (1986) 'Comparative development in human infants and infant rhesus monkeys on cognitive functions that depend on prefrontal cortex.' *Society of Neuroscience Abstract 12*, 742.

Diamond, A., Prevor, M. B., Callender, G. and Druin, D. P. (1997) 'Prefrontal cortex cognitive deficits in children treated early and continuously for PKU.' *Monographs of the Society for Research in Child Development 62*, 1–205.

Dias, R., Robbins, T. W. and Roberts, A. C. (1996) 'Dissociation in prefrontal cortex of attentional and affective shifts.' *Nature 380*, 69–72.

Douglas, V. I. and Peters, K. G. (1979) 'Toward a clearer definition of the attentional deficit of hyperactive children.' In G. A. Hale and M. Lewis (eds) *Attention and Cognitive Development*, pp.173–247. New York: Plenum.

Duncan, J. (1986) 'Disorganization of behaviour after frontal lobe damage.' *Cognitive Neuropsychology 3*, 271–290.

Duncan, J. (2001) 'Frontal lobe function and the control of visual attention.' In J. Braun and C. Koch (eds) *Visual Attention and Cortical Circuits*, pp. 69–88. Cambridge, MA: MIT Press.

Farah, M. J. (1984) 'The neurological basis of mental imagery: a componential analysis.' *Cognition 18*, 245–272.

Fletcher, P., Happé, F., Frith, U., Baker, S. C., Dolan, R. J. and Frackowiak, R. (1995) 'Other minds in the brain: a functional imaging study of theory of mind in story comprehension.' *Cognition 57*, 2, 109–128.

Friedrich, F. and Rader, S. (1996) 'Component process analysis in experimental and clinical neuropsychology.' In M. Marirish and J. Moses (eds) *Theoretical Foundations of Clinical Neuropsychology for Clinical Practitioners*, pp. 59–79. Hillsdale, NJ: Erlbaum.

Frye, D., Zelazo, P. D. and Palfai, T. (1995) 'Theory of mind and rule-based reasoning.' *Cognitive Development 10*, 483–527.

Garretson, H. B., Fein, D. and Waterhouse, L. (1990) 'Sustained attention in children with autism.' *Journal of Autism and Developmental Disorders 20*, 101–114.

Gianutsos, R. (1991) 'Cognitive rehabilitation: a neuropsychological specialty comes of age.' *Brain Injury 5*, 353–368.

Gilotty, L., Kenworthy, L., Sirian, L., Black, D. O., and Wagner, A. E. (2002) 'Adaptive skills and executive function in autism spectrum disorders.' *Child Neuropsychology 8*, 241–248.

Goel, V. and Grafman, J. (1995) 'Are the frontal lobes implicated in planning functions? Interpreting data from the Tower of Hanoi.' *Neuropsychologia 33*, 623–642.

Goldman-Rakic, P. S. (1987) 'Circuitry of primate prefrontal cortex and regulation of behavior by representational memory.' In V. B. Mountcastle, F. Plum and S. R. Geiger (eds) *Handbook of Physiology: The Nervous System*, pp. 373–417. Bethesda, MD: American Physiological Society.

Grattan, L. M., Bloomer, R., Archambault, F. X. and Eslinger, P. J. (1990) 'Cognitive and neural underpinnings of empathy.' *The Clinical Neuropsychologist 4*, 279.

Griffith, E. M. (2002) 'Manipulating feedback normalizes perseveration in individuals with autism.' Unpublished doctoral dissertation, University of Denver.

Griffith, E. M., Pennington, B. F., Wehner, E. A. and Rogers, S. J. (1999) 'Executive functions in young children with autism.' *Child Development 70*, 817–832.

Happe, F., Ehlers, S., Fletcher, P., Frith, U., Johansson, M., Gillberg, C. *et al.* (1996) '"Theory of mind" in the brain: evidence from a PET scan study of Asperger syndrome.' *NeuroReport 8*, 197–201.

Happe, F., Briskman, J. and Frith, U. (2001) 'Exploring the cognitive phenotype of autism: weak "central coherence" in parents and siblings of children with autism: I. Experimental tests.' *Journal of Child Psychology and Psychiatry 42*, 299–307.

Harris, P. (1993) 'Pretending and planning.' In S. Baron-Cohen, H. Tager-Flusberg and D. J. Cohen (eds) *Understanding Other Minds: Perspectives from Autism*, pp. 228–246. New York: Oxford University Press.

Head, D., Bolton, D. and Hymas, N. (1989) 'Deficit in cognitive shifting ability in patients with obsessive-compulsive disorder.' *Biological Psychiatry 25*, 929–937.

Hill, E. L. and Russell, J. (2002) 'Action memory and self-monitoring in children with autism: self versus other.' *Infant and Child Development 11*, 159–170.

Hughes, C. (1996) 'Planning problems in autism at the level of motor control.' *Journal of Autism and Developmental Disorders 26*, 99–107.

Hughes, C. (1998) 'Executive function in preschoolers: links with theory of mind and verbal ability.' *British Journal of Developmental Psychology 16*, 233–253.

Hughes, C. (2001) 'Executive dysfunction in autism: its nature and implications for the everyday problems experienced by individuals with autism.' In J. A. Burack, T. Charman, N. Yirmiya and P. R. Zelazo (eds) *The Development of Autism: Perspectives from Theory and Research*, pp. 255–275. Mahwah, NJ: Erlbaum.

Hughes, C. (2002) 'Executive functions and development: emerging themes.' *Infant and Child Development 11*, 201–209.

Hughes, C. and Graham, A. (2002) 'Measuring executive functions in childhood: problems and solutions?' *Child and Adolescent Mental Health 7*, 131–142.

Hughes, C. and Russell, J. (1993) 'Autistic children's difficulty with mental disengagement from an object: its implications for theories of autism.' *Developmental Psychology 29*, 498–510.

Hughes, C., Russell, J. and Robbins, T. W. (1994) 'Evidence for executive dysfunction in autism.' *Neuropsychologia 32*, 477–492.

Hughes, C., Leboyer, M. and Bouvard, M. (1997) 'Executive function in parents of children with autism.' *Psychological Medicine 27*, 209–220.

Hughes, C., Plumet, M.-H. and Leboyer, M. (1999) 'Towards a cognitive phenotype for autism: increased prevalence of executive dysfunction and superior spatial span amongst siblings of children with autism.' *Journal of Child Psychology and Psychiatry 40*, 705–718.

Ingram, R. E. (1989) 'Information processing as a theoretical framework for child and adolescent psychiatry.' In M. H. Schmidt and H. Remschmidt (eds) *Needs and Prospects of Child and Adolescent Psychiatry*, pp. 25–36. Lewiston, NY: Hogrefe and Huber.

Jepsen, R. H. and von Thaden, K. (2002) 'The effect of cognitive education on the performance of students with neurological developmental disabilities.' *NeuroRehabilitation 17*, 201–209.

Kempton, S., Vance, A., Luk, E., Costin, J. and Pantelis, C. (1999) 'Executive function and attention deficit hyperactivity disorder: stimulant medication and better executive function performance in children.' *Psychological Medicine 29*, 527–538.

Kerns, K. A., Eso, K. and Thomson, J. (1999) 'Investigation of a direct intervention for improving attention in young children with ADHD.' *Developmental Neuropsychology 16*, 273–295.

Koczat, D. L., Rogers, S. J., Pennington, B. F. and Ross, R. G. (2002) 'Eye movement abnormality suggestive of a spatial working memory deficit is present in parents of autistic probands.' *Journal of Autism and Developmental Disorders 32*, 513–518.

Kurtz, M. M., Moberg, P. J., Gur, R. C. and Gur, R. E. (2001) 'Approaches to cognitive remediation of neuropsychological deficits in schizophrenia: a review and meta-analysis.' *Neuropsychology Review 11*, 197–210.

Levine, B., Robertson, I. H., Claire, L., Carter, G., Hong, J., Wilson, B. A. *et al.* (2000) 'Rehabilitation of executive functioning: an experimental-clinical validation of goal management training.' *Journal of the International Neuropsychological Society 6*, 299–312.

Liss, M., Fein, D., Allen, D., Dunn, M., Feinstein, C., Morris, R. *et al.* 2001) 'Executive functioning in high-functioning children with autism.' *Journal of Child Psychology and Psychiatry 42*, 261–270.

Logan, G. (1994) 'On the ability to inhibit thought and action: a user's guide to the stop-signal paradigm.' In D. Dagenbach and T. H. Carr (eds) *Inhibitory Processes in Attention, Memory and Language*, pp. 189–239. San Diego: Academic Press.

Logan, G. D., Cowan, W. B. and Davis, K. A. (1984) 'On the ability to inhibit simple and choice reaction time responses: a model and a method.' *Journal of Experimental Psychology Human Perception and Performance 10*, 276–291.

Lopez, B. R., Lincoln, A. J., Ozonoff, S. and Lai, Z. (2005) 'Examining the relationship between executive functions and restricted, repetitive symptoms of autistic disorder.' *Journal of Autism and Developmental Disorders 35*, 445–460.

Lueger, R. J. and Gill, K. J. (1990) 'Frontal-lobe cognitive dysfunction in conduct disorder adolescents.' *Journal of Clinical Psychology 46*, 696–706.

Luria, A. R. (1966) *The Higher Cortical Functions in Man.* New York: Basic Books.

Mateer, C. A. (1992) 'Systems of care for post-concussive syndrome.' In L. J. Horn and N. D. Zasler (eds) *Rehabilitation of Post-concussive Disorders*, pp. 143–160. Philadelphia: Henley and Belius.

Mateer, C. A., Sohlberg, M. M. and Youngman, P. (1990) 'The management of acquired attention and memory disorders following mild closed head injury.' In R. Wood (ed.) *Cognitive Rehabilitation in Perspective*, pp. 68–96. London: Taylor and Francis.

McEvoy, R. E., Rogers, S. J. and Pennington, B. F. (1993) 'Executive function and social communication deficits in young autistic children.' *Journal of Child Psychology and Psychiatry 34*, 563–578.

Miller, J. N. and Ozonoff, S. (2000) 'The external validity of Asperger disorder: lack of evidence from the domain of neuropsychology.' *Journal of Abnormal Psychology 109*, 227–238.

Moses, L. J. (2001) 'Executive accounts of theory-of-mind development.' *Child Development 72*, 688–690.

Mottron, L., Peretz, I., Belleville, S. and Rouleau, N. (1999) 'Absolute pitch in autism: a case study.' *Neurocase 5*, 485–501.

Mundy, P., Card, J. and Fox, N. (2000) 'EEG correlates of the development of infant joint attention skills.' *Developmental Psychobiology 36*, 325–338.

Neill, W. T., Lissner, L. S. and Beck, J. L. (1990) 'Negative priming in same-different matching: further evidence for a central locus of inhibition.' *Perception and Psychophysics 48*, 398–400.

Ozonoff, S. (1995) 'Executive functions in autism.' In E. Schopler and G. B. Mesibov (eds) *Learning and Cognition in Autism*, pp. 199–219. New York: Plenum.

Ozonoff, S. (1997) 'Components of executive function in autism and other disorders.' In J. Russell (ed.) *Autism as an Executive Disorder*, pp. 179–211. New York: Oxford University Press.

Ozonoff, S. (1998) 'Assessment and remediation of executive dysfunction in autism and Asperger syndrome.' In E. Schopler, G. B. Mesibov and L. Kunce (eds) *Asperger Syndrome and High-functioning Autism*, pp. 263–289. New York: Plenum.

Ozonoff, S. and Jensen, J. (1999) 'Specific executive function profiles in three neurodevelopmental disorders.' *Journal of Autism and Developmental Disorders 29*, 171–177.

Ozonoff, S. and McEvoy, R. E. (1994) 'A longitudinal study of executive function and theory of mind development in autism.' *Development and Psychopathology 6*, 415–431.

Ozonoff, S. and Strayer, D. L. (1997) 'Inhibitory function in nonretarded children with autism.' *Journal of Autism and Developmental Disorders 27*, 59–77.

Ozonoff, S. and Strayer, D. L. (2001) 'Further evidence of intact working memory in autism.' *Journal of Autism and Developmental Disorders 31*, 257–263.

Ozonoff, S., Pennington, B. F. and Rogers, S. J. (1991) 'Executive function deficits in high-functioning autistic individuals: relationship to theory of mind.' *Journal of Child Psychology and Psychiatry 32*, 1081–1105.

Ozonoff, S., Rogers, S. J., Farnham, J. M. and Pennington, B. F. (1993) 'Can standard measures identify subclinical markers of autism?' *Journal of Autism and Developmental Disorders 23*, 429–441.

Ozonoff, S., McMahon, W. M., Coon, H. and Lainhart, J. (2002) 'Neuropsychological profiles of autism and dyslexia families.' Paper presented at the Annual Meeting of the American Academy of Child and Adolescent Psychiatry, San Francisco, CA.

Ozonoff, S., Coon, H., Dawson, G., Joseph, R., Klin, A., McMahon, W. M. *et al.* (2004) 'Performance on CANTAB subtests sensitive to frontal lobe function in people with autistic disorder: evidence from the CPEA network.' *Journal of Autism and Developmental Disorders 34*, 139–150.

Pascualvaca, D. M., Fantie, B. D., Papageorgiou, M. and Mirsky, A. F. (1998) 'Attentional capacities in children with autism: is there a general deficit in shifting focus?' *Journal of Autism and Developmental Disorders 28*, 467–478.

Pennington, B. F. (1994) 'The working memory function of the prefrontal cortices: implications for developmental and individual differences in cognition.' In M. M. Haith, J. Benson, R. Roberts and B. F. Pennington (eds) *Future-oriented Processes in Development*, pp.243–289. Chicago: University of Chicago Press.

Pennington, B. F. and Ozonoff, S. (1991) 'A neuroscientific perspective on continuity and discontinuity in developmental psychopathology.' In D. Cicchetti and S. L. Toth (eds) *Rochester Symposium on Developmental Psychopathology, Volume III: Models and Integrations*, pp. 117–159. Rochester, NY: University of Rochester Press.

Pennington, B. F. and Ozonoff, S. (1996) 'Executive functions and developmental psychopathologies.' *Journal of Child Psychology and Psychiatry 37*, 51–87.

Pennington, B. F., Bennetto, L., McAleer, O. and Roberts, R. J. (1996) 'Executive functions and working memory: theoretical and measurement issues.' In G. R. Lyon and N. A. Krasnegor (eds) *Attention, Memory, and Executive Function*, pp. 327–348. Baltimore, MD: Paul H. Brookes.

Perner, J. and Lang, B. (1999) 'Development of theory of mind and executive control.' *Trends in Cognitive Science 3*, 337–334.

Perner, J. and Lang, B. (2002) 'What causes 3-year-olds' difficulty on the dimensional change card sorting task?' *Infant and Child Development 11*, 93–105.

Perner, J., Frith, U., Leslie, A. M. and Leekam, S. R. (1989) 'Exploration of the autistic child's theory of mind: knowledge, belief, and communication.' *Child Development 60*, 689–700.

Perner, J., Kain, W. and Barchfeld, P. (2002) 'Executive control and higher-order theory of mind in children at risk of ADHD.' *Infant and Child Development 11*, 141–158.

Perrine, K. (1993) 'Differential aspects of conceptual processing in the Category Test and Wisconsin Card Sorting Test.' *Journal of Clinical and Experimental Neuropsychology 15*, 461–473.

Pickles, A., Bolton, P. F., MacDonald, H., Bailey, A., LeCouteur, A., Sim, C. H. and Rutter, M. (1995) 'Latent-class analysis of recurrence risks for complex phenotypes with selection and measurement error: a twin and family history study of autism.' *American Journal of Human Genetics 57*, 717–726.

Pilling, S., Bebbington, P., Kuipers, E., Garety, P., Geddes, J., Martindale, B. *et al.* (2002) 'Psychological treatments in schizophrenia: II. Meta-analyses of randomized controlled trials of social skills training and cognitive remediation.' *Psychological Medicine 32*, 783–791.

Piven, J. (2001) 'The broad autism phenotype: a complementary strategy for molecular genetic studies of autism.' *American Journal of Medical Genetics 8*, 34–35.

Piven, J. and Palmer, P. (1997) 'Cognitive deficits in parents from multiple-incidence autism families.' *Journal of Child Psychology and Psychiatry 38*, 1011–1021.

Posner, M. I. (1980) 'Orienting of attention.' *Quarterly Journal of Experimental Psychology 32*, 3–25.

Price, B. H., Daffner, K. R., Stowe, R. M. and Mesulam, M. M. (1990) 'The comportmental learning disabilities of early frontal lobe damage.' *Brain 113*, 1383–1393.

Prior, M. R. and Hoffmann, W. (1990) 'Neuropsychological testing of autistic children through an exploration with frontal lobe tests.' *Journal of Autism and Developmental Disorders 20*, 581–590.

Purcell, R., Maruff, P., Kyrios, M. and Pantelis, C. (1998) 'Neuropsychological deficits in obsessive-compulsive disorder: a comparison with unipolar depression, panic disorder, and normal controls.' *Archives of General Psychiatry 55*, 415–423.

Rinehart, N. J., Bradshaw, J. L., Moss, S. A., Brereton, A. V. and Tonge, B. J. (2001) 'A deficit in shifting attention present in high-functioning autism but not Asperger's disorder.' *Autism 5*, 67–80.

Risch, N., Spiker, D., Lotspeich, L., Nouri, N., Hinds, D., Hallmayer, J. *et al.* (1999) 'A genomic screen of autism: evidence for a multilocus etiology.' *American Journal of Human Genetics 65*, 493–507.

Robbins, T. W., James, M., Owen, A. M., Sahakian, B. J., Lawrence, A. D., McInnes, L. and Rabbitt, P. M. A. (1998) 'A study of performance on tests from the CANTAB battery sensitive to frontal lobe dysfunction in a large sample of normal volunteers: implications for theories of executive functioning and cognitive aging.' *Journal of the International Neuropsychological Society 4*, 474–490.

Rumsey, J. M. (1985) 'Conceptual problem-solving in highly verbal, nonretarded autistic men.' *Journal of Autism and Developmental Disorders 15*, 23–36.

Rumsey, J. M. and Hamburger, S. D. (1990) 'Neuropsychological divergence of high-level autism and severe dyslexia.' *Journal of Autism and Developmental Disorders 20*, 155–168.

Russell, J., Mauthner, N., Sharpe, S. and Tidswell, T. (1991) 'The "windows task" as a measure of strategic deception in preschoolers and autistic subjects.' *British Journal of Developmental Psychology 9*, 331–349.

Russell, J., Jarrold, C. and Henry, L. (1996) 'Working memory in children with autism and with moderate learning difficulties.' *Journal of Child Psychology and Psychiatry 37*, 673–686.

Russell, J., Jarrold, C. and Hood, B. (1999a) 'Two intact executive capacities in children with autism: implications for the core executive dysfunctions in the disorder.' *Journal of Autism and Developmental Disorders 29*, 103–112.

Russell, J., Saltmarsh, R. and Hill, E. (1999b) 'What do executive factors contribute to the failure on false belief tasks by children with autism?' *Journal of Child Psychology and Psychiatry 40*, 859–868.

Rutter, M. and Bailey, A. (1993) 'Thinking and relationships: mind and brain (some reflections on theory of mind and autism).' In S. Baron-Cohen, H. Tager-Flusberg and D. J. Cohen (eds) *Understanding Other Minds: Perspectives from Autism*, pp. 481–504. New York: Oxford University Press.

Sandson, J. and Albert, M. L. (1984) 'Varieties of perseveration.' *Neuropsychologia 22*, 715–732.

Schachar, R. and Logan, G. D. (1990) 'Impulsivity and inhibitory control in normal development and childhood psychopathology.' *Developmental Psychology 26*, 710–720.

Semrud-Clikeman, M., Teeter, P. A., Parle, N. and Conner, R. T. (1995) 'Innovative approaches for working with children with ADHD.' Paper presented at the annual conference of the American Educational Research Association, San Francisco, CA.

Shu, B. C., Lung, F. W., Tien, A. Y. and Chen, B. C. (2001) 'Executive function deficits in non-retarded autistic children.' *Autism 5*, 165–174.

Sohlberg, M. M. and Mateer, C. A. (1986) *Attention Process Training (APT)*. Puyallup, WA: Washington Association for Neuropsychological Research and Development.

Sohlberg, M. M. and Mateer, C. A. (1987) 'Effectiveness of an attention training program.' *Journal of Clinical and Experimental Neuropsychology 9*, 117–130.

South, M., Ozonoff, S. and McMahon, W. M. (in press) 'Repetitive behaviour, executive function and central coherence in autism and Asperger syndrome.' *Autism: The International Journal of Research and Practice.*

Stevenson, C. S., Whitmont, S., Bornholt, L., Livesey, D. and Stevenson, R. J. (2002) 'A cognitive remediation programme for adults with attention deficit hyperactivity disorder.' *Australian and New Zealand Journal of Psychiatry 36*, 610–616.

Stone, V. E., Baron-Cohen, S. and Knight, R. T. (1998) 'Frontal lobe contributions to theory of mind.' *Journal of Cognitive Neuroscience 10*, 640–656.

Stuss, D. T. (1992) 'Biological and psychological development of executive functions.' *Brain and Cognition 20*, 8–23.

Swanson, J. M., Posner, M., Potkin, S. G., Bonforte, S., Youpa, D., Fiore, C. *et al.* (1991) 'Activating tasks for the study of visual-spatial attention in ADHD children: a cognitive anatomic approach.' *Journal of Child Neurology 6*, ss119–127.

Swettenham, J., Baron-Cohen, S., Charman, T., Cox, A., Baird, G., Drew, A. *et al.* (1998) 'The frequency and distribution of spontaneous attention shifts between social and nonsocial stimuli in autistic, typically developing, and nonautistic developmentally delayed infants.' *Journal of Child Psychology and Psychiatry 39*, 747–753.

Szatmari, P., Tuff, L., Finlayson, A. J. and Bartolucci, G. (1990) 'Asperger's Syndrome and autism: neurocognitive aspects.' *Journal of the American Academy of Child and Adolescent Psychiatry 29*, 130–136.

Task Force on Head Injury (1984) *Standards for Cognitive Rehabilitation.* Erie, PA: American Congress of Rehabilitation Medicine.

Thomson, J. (1994) 'Rehabilitation of high school-aged individuals with traumatic brain injury through utilization of an attention training program.' *Journal of the International Neuropsychological Society 1*, 149.

Tipper, S. P. (1985) 'The negative priming effect: inhibitory priming by ignored objects.' *Quarterly Journal of Experimental Psychology 37*, 571–590.

Turner, M. (1997) 'Towards an executive dysfunction account of repetitive behavior in autism.' In J. Russell (ed.) *Autism as an Executive Disorder*, pp. 57–100. New York: Oxford University Press.

Turner, M. (1999) 'Repetitive behavior in autism: a review of psychological research.' *Journal of Child Psychology and Psychiatry 40*, 839–849.

Van der Does, A. W. and Van den Bosch, R. J. (1992) 'What determines Wisconsin Card Sorting performance in schizophrenia?' *Clinical Psychology Review 12*, 567–583.

Wainwright-Sharp, J. A. and Bryson, S. E. (1993) 'Visual orienting deficits in high-functioning people with autism.' *Journal of Autism and Developmental Disorders 23*, 1–13.

Welsh, M. C., Pennington, B. F., Ozonoff, S., Rouse, B. and McCabe, E. R. B. (1990) 'Neuropsychology of early-treated phenylketonuria: specific executive function deficits.' *Child Development 61*, 1697–1713.

Williams, D. J. (1989) 'A process-specific training program in the treatment of attention deficits in children.' Unpublished doctoral dissertation, University of Washington.

Chapter 9

Language and Its development in the Autistic Spectrum Disorders

Isabelle Rapin

INTRODUCTION

The autistic spectrum disorders (pervasive developmental disorders in DSM-IV and ICD-10 (American Psychiatric Association 2000; World Health Organization 1992), referred to as autism for short in this chapter) are developmental disorders of the immature brain characterized by: (1) impaired social skills, empathy, and insight into others' thinking, (2) inadequate development of non-verbal and verbal communication, especially conversational skills and impoverished imagination, and (3) cognitive and behavioral rigidity and repetitive behaviors. Neither the level of cognitive competence, nor the presence of any other handicap, nor the biologic cause (etiology) of the brain dysfunction responsible for the disorder is a defining feature or rules it out. It is well established that the complex phenotype of autism can result, in a minority of cases, from a purely environmental relatively non-selective insult to the immature brain, for example an early infection like intrauterine rubella (Chess, Korn and Fernandez 1971), or from a single Mendelian gene defect like fragile-X or tuberous sclerosis with a widespread impact on brain development. In the majority of affected individuals autism reflects the cumulative consequences of a number of mutations or polymorphisms affecting some of the many genes that orchestrate the sequential unfolding of brain development (Muhle, Trentacoste and Rapin 2004). This multigenic etiology, in concert with the unique environmental impacts which each individual experiences, accounts for the wide variation in severity and symptomatology of the autistic phenotype (autistic spectrum), and for a recurrence risk of less than 10 percent within sibships.

Language is a rule-governed set of arbitrary signals every society develops as a means for communicating with others; it is also an important modality for thought. The auditory-vocal channel (speech) dominates communication, but there are many others, for example the visual-manual (sign languages, reading/writing) and tactile-vocal (Braille). All languages are arbitrarily multicoded systems created and shared by any communicating group. Some non-vocal coded language systems, like alphabets, map more or less directly onto the speech code; others such as music and mathematical notations or blue prints do not.

LANGUAGE ACQUISITION AND LEVELS OF LANGUAGE ENCODING

A schematic view of the multiple levels of language encoding is shown in Box 9.1. All normal children learn the oral language(s) of their speaking community rapidly and effortlessly as infants and preschoolers, although the age at which mastery of the various levels of language is achieved differs. The ear is mature at the end of the second trimester of pregnancy so that the infant hears *in utero*, mostly the sounds emanating from the mother, including her voice. Acquisition of the *phonologic (speech sound) code of speech* starts at birth. Infants hone their ability to perceive and segment phonologic contrasts relevant to the language(s) they hear and within months start practicing producing them, whereas contrasts they do not hear wither (Kuhl *et al.* 1997). Phonology encompasses not only the several dozen distinct phonemes (phonetics or individual speech sounds of languages) but also suprasegmental sound codes (prosody) that signal boundaries between longer utterances and the type of communication intended, for example a question, a declarative sentence, an angry outburst, or an endearment.

Box 9.1 Levels of language encoding

Phonology (speech sounds)

Phonetics	segmental
Prosody	suprasegmental

Grammar (connected utterances)

Syntax	word order, use of closed or small class words (articles, prepositions, etc.)
Morphology	word endings, etc.

Semantics (meaning of language)

Lexicon	dictionary of words in the brain
Meaning	of connected utterances

Pragmatics (intent of communication – conversational use of language)

Verbal	word choices, referencing, etc.
Non-verbal	direction of gaze, facial expression, turn-taking, gestures, body posture, prosody, etc.

Also starting at birth is the acquisition of *pragmatics* which convey the intent of the communication. *Non-verbal pragmatics* includes direction of gaze, gestures, facial expression, and body posture, nods, and other indicators of comprehension or reaction to the content of the received message; *verbal pragmatics* encompasses turn-taking, choice of intonation, topic, and words appropriate to the particular communicative interchange. Acquisition of non-verbal pragmatics comes first: it takes only a few weeks for infants to become aware that communication involves turning toward and fixating on the face of the person speaking to them, especially the eyes, and turn-taking with alternating periods of silence and vocal production. Infants' first expressive communication ('word') is generally pointing toward a desired target or to draw attention to it. Pointing usually emerges by about one year and is the clear indication that the infant understands that communication is power over another person's behavior.

Semantics encompasses the acquisition of a 'dictionary' of words (of signs in the deaf infant with signing parents) or lexicon stored in the brain and of the meaning of longer utterances. The lexicon also emerges around one year and grows throughout life. *Grammar*, the rules for creating multiword utterances that conform to the rules of the language of a speaking community, does not start to emerge until the child's lexicon has reached a critical size, usually between 50 and 100 words at around age two years. It takes a number of years for infants to master all the complicated rules for word order (syntax) or word inflections (morphology) that clarify the meaning of complex utterances by indicating the role of each word in multiword utterances and in longer strings like paragraphs.

INADEQUATE LANGUAGE ACQUISITION – DEVELOPMENTAL LANGUAGE DISORDERS (DLDs)

Given the complexities of the language code it is not surprising that the pace and ease of acquisition depend on and are influenced by many neuropsychologic abilities. Deficits like *inadequate hearing* and impaired conduction and processing of auditory signals in the brain will preclude the acquisition of language if severe, or jeopardize it to a greater or lesser degree if milder, because decoding phonology is the necessary first step toward language comprehension and acquisition. Memory and attention are also requisites for language learning. Infants must have an innate drive to communicate and seek social contact in order to orient toward other speakers and to work to make themselves intelligible to others. Although language generally develops in the face of less than severe cognitive disability, mental retardation does slow its emergence and decreases the richness of the lexicon and the ability to comprehend complex communications.

Because language is an input–processing–output function with parallel top-down loops to assist bottom-up operations, input disorders will preclude all subsequent operations at the language-learning age. Consequently *receptive deficits* in young children are necessarily mixed receptive-expressive disorders. In contrast *expressive disorders* may be 'pure' in the sense that reception and processing develop normally when impairment is at the level of output operations. Because the four levels of language (phonology, grammar, semantics, and pragmatics) take place in part hierarchically or sequentially and in part in parallel, phonologic and syntactic disorders are requisite for semantic processing, whereas *higher order processing (semantic) disorders* may exist in the absence of phonologic deficits and with deficits limited to complex grammatical and semantic comprehension, processing, and formulation. Disordered *verbal pragmatics* may be associated with any type of language deficit that impairs the comprehension of language, be it at the level of phonology, grammar, or semantics. Pragmatics is almost always adequate in children with isolated expressive disorders that spare phonologic, syntactic, and semantic comprehension and processing as the children are aware of the intent and power of communication. Inadequate *non-verbal pragmatics* sharply differentiates autism from DLD.

Thus one can simplify the DLDs by dividing them clinically into two broad groups with subtypes (Box 9.2). In the first group (A), production of well articulated, well formed sentences is impaired because phonology and basic grammatic rules are inadequate. This group encompasses two disorders, each with subtypes, differentiated on the basis of comprehension: mixed receptive/expressive disorders and expressive disorders. The second broad group (B) is characterized by adequate acquisition of the phonologic and grammatical codes and vocabulary, therefore the children produce intelligible well formed utterances, but with impaired semantics and acquisition of the more abstract grammatical rules of language. A salient deficit is often comprehension of such open-ended questions as 'who', 'what,' and 'where' in the absence of a proximate referent, 'either/or,' and especially 'why,' 'when,' and 'how' which normally-developing children learn to understand and use gradually, usually between ages three and five. Because children with language disorders at the level of semantics speak clearly and understand simple multiword utterances such as one or two level commands and 'what's that' and concrete 'what,' 'who,' and 'where' questions in context, their comprehension deficits often pass unnoticed early on. Their failure to respond to more complex questions or their propensity to respond to a word rather than the gist of questions is regularly misinterpreted as failure to cooperate or as a thought disorder.

As stated earlier, the most salient language differences between children on the autistic spectrum and those with isolated DLDs are that (1) pragmatics, especially non-verbal pragmatics, is universally deficient in autism, (2) the language of verbal children with autism has abnormal features that are infrequent in children with DLD, and (3) the relative frequency of various types of language disorders differs in autism compared to DLDs, with 'pure' expressive disorders rare in autism and frequent in DLD and the so-called semantic-pragmatic disorder considerably more frequent in autism than in DLD (Table 9.1).

Box 9.2 Clinically defined subtypes of developmental language disorders (DLDs) in young children

A LOWER LEVEL PROCESSING DISORDERS

phonology (and syntax) affected, therefore the production of well-articulated speech is impaired

1 Input disorders

mixed receptive/expressive disorders affecting phonology, grammar, and semantics

Verbal auditory agnosia (VAA) inability to decode phonology:

precludes all subsequent language operations. Language development extremely delayed or absent via the acoustic channel, though it may develop via the visual or tactile channel *if* pragmatics is spared:

- Comprehension: little or none
- Expression: child non-verbal or minimally verbal with very poor phonologic production, generally very few poorly articulated and labored single words. May be associated with (not caused by!) oromotor deficit or *dysarthria* which is an oromotor deficit that affects swallowing and production of non-speech sounds and mouth movements as well as speech

Mixed phonologic-syntactic disorder language development delayed and impoverished at all levels

- Comprehension: limited, equal to, or somewhat better than expression
- Expression: dysfluent, often labored. May be associated with (not caused by!) dysarthria
  - Phonology: impaired
  - Grammar: simplified, short utterances
  - Lexicon: impoverished

2 Expressive disorders

speech development delayed, comprehension and higher level language processing not affected

Dysfluent (verbal dyspraxia) often associated with, but not caused by, dysarthria

- Comprehension: unimpaired
- Expression: extremely impaired, especially if associated with a severe dysarthria (which is not causative but contributory!). Verbal output may be limited to vowel sounds or to a few

consonant sounds in the face of intact or approximately intact comprehension at all levels of language

Fluent (or more fluent)   speech programing deficit

- Comprehension: unimpaired
- Expression
  - Phonology: may produce a ± unintelligible jargon
  - Grammar: unimpaired or impaired by difficulty programming coherent discourse
  - Semantics: unimpaired or may have word retrieval difficulty

B   HIGHER ORDER PROCESSING DISORDERS
phonology and syntax at most mildly impaired

Lexical-syntactic disorder   language development delayed

- Comprehension: adequate at the word level, impaired for connected speech
- Expression: fluency variable
  - Phonology: early – frequent jargon, later OK
  - Grammar: early – immature, later OK
  - Semantics: early – severe word finding problems: pseudo-stuttering, lexicon impoverished. Impaired programming of discourse

Semantic-pragmatic disorder   expressive language development usually not delayed

- Comprehension: unimpaired at the word or simple sentence level, impaired for discourse, especially open-ended question forms. Typically comprehension is paradoxically worse than expression
- Expression: fluency unimpaired, chatty, may be verbose
  - Phonology: unimpaired
  - Grammar: unimpaired
  - Semantics: average or (extremely) large often atypical lexicon, perseverative or poorly constrained discourse
  - Pragmatics: impaired conversational skill.

NOTE 1   PRAGMATICS
- *Non-verbal pragmatics*   universally impaired in the autistic spectrum disorders (ASDs); preserved or at most mildly impaired in 'specific' (uncomplicated) developmental language disorders (DLDs; also known as specific language impairment or SLI)

- *Verbal pragmatics* depends largely on the severity of the language disorder, notably comprehension, in both DLDs and ASDs

NOTE 2 ABNORMAL FEATURES SUGGESTING AN ASD RATHER THAN A DLD

- *Striking pragmatic impairment* non-verbal and verbal, lack of awareness of the power of language and of a drive to communicate, speaking to speak rather than to communicate
- *Atypical prosody*
- *Echolalia* immediate or delayed (formulaic language, scripted speech), perseveration
- *Esoteric word choice*
- *Comprehension of discourse paradoxically more impaired than expression*
- *Purely expressive disorders* not characteristic of children with an ASD!

Table 9.1 Most salient differences between the language disorders of children with autism and those with developmental language disorders

Differentiating deficits	Autistic spectrum disorders (ASDs)	Developmental language disorders (DLDs)
Non-verbal pragmatics	Very impaired	Mildly impaired
Verbal pragmatics	Very impaired	Mildly impaired
Prosody	Very impaired	Mildly impaired
Abnormal features (e.g. echolalia, scripts, and pronoun reversal)	Striking	Almost never
Verbal auditory agnosia	More common than in DLD	Uncommon (but frequent in acquired epileptic aphasia)
Mixed receptive/expressive disorders	Common	Common
Expressive disorders	Almost never	Common
Semantic/pragmatic disorder	Common	Uncommon
Lexical/syntactic disorder	Common	Common

EARLY STUDIES OF LANGUAGE DISORDERS IN CHILDREN WITH AUTISM

There are a variety of plausible reasons for children on the autistic spectrum to have inadequate and, in most cases, delayed development of language. Early formal studies focused on pragmatic deficits because lack of the drive to communicate non-verbally is so salient in these children. Even verbal children and adults on the spectrum have prominent pragmatic deficits such as inadequate conversational skills, sparse and unpredictable speech or inability to switch topics with their conversational partner, gaze avoidance, failure to respond when addressed, and other obviously deviant characteristics. It was assumed for a long time that non-verbal or minimally verbal children with autism chose not to speak rather than were unable to speak. The fact that the rare utterances of some children were spoken clearly and were often sparse multiword exclamations was viewed as corroborating the interpretation that the children's problem was not language itself but a manifestation of their social deficit. Persistent failure for the emergence of any speech was attributed to their mental retardation; the possibility that lack of language might play a major contributing role to the retardation was not considered, perhaps because early investigators did not view autism as an organic brain disorder.

Many studies focused on the peculiarities of speech in children on the autistic spectrum who did speak and spoke clearly (Tager-Flusberg 2003). Their vocabularies are often remarkably large but atypical, and their speech is marked by such obviously deviant features as immediate echolalia, delayed echolalia or formulaic language (the reciting of overlearned scripts in more or less appropriate context), incessant repetitive questioning, and atypical prosody such as a singsong or uninflected (robotic) voice or a rising tone in utterances that make assertions sound like questions. Immediate and delayed echolalia and compulsive questioning may mask incomprehension as they obviate the need to formulate an apt response or initiate communication (Prizant and Rydell 1984). Lack of insight into another person's agenda (theory of mind) (Leslie and Frith 1988) and inattention to facial expression and body language (Schultz *et al.* 2003), (Klin *et al.* 2002), which are contributory features to or consequences of autistic individuals' social inadequacies, may play a role in lack of sensitivity to prosody (suprasegmental phonologic code) and non-verbal pragmatics and, therefore, to their inadequate acquisition. Young verbal children's pragmatic deficits are salient in that they do not take the point of view of their conversational partner into account, often speak ad nauseam of their topic, and have a great deal of difficulty switching topics or listening to what their partner has to say.

It was not until my late colleague, the developmental psycholinguist Dr. Doris Allen, and I studied the language skills of children who were non-verbal or minimally verbal as well as those of verbal children that it became clear that language disorders involving phonology and grammar occur in children with autism as well as in those with DLD (Rapin 1997; Rapin and Dunn 2003). Recent genetic studies have provided a biologic basis for our behavioral observations (Bradford *et al.* 2001; Wassink *et al.* 2001) by disclosing linkage to chromosome 7q31–33 and the *WNT2* gene, but only in late talking individuals with autism who had first order relatives who were either late talkers or late readers. As it is clear that the most prevalent cause of both developmental language disorders and of dyslexia is phonologic processing deficiency (Shaywitz 2003), the implication is that impairment of phonologic decoding akin to that in these families is largely responsible for severely compromised comprehension and impoverished poorly articulated expressive language in some non-verbal or poorly-verbal children with autism. Dr. Allen and I proposed that taking into consideration both the input–processing–output operations of language in the brain and the four encoded levels of language indicates that young children with autism have several subtypes of language disorders, and that these are similar in many ways to those we had identified clinically in young children with DLD (Box 9.2). What follows is a description of these subtypes as a function of age.

AGE-DEFINED CLINICAL SUBTYPES OF LANGUAGE DEFICITS IN INDIVIDUALS ON THE AUTISTIC SPECTRUM
Infants

Autism is rarely diagnosed in infancy despite the fact that many parents are aware before the age of one year that there is something wrong with their infant, and despite the fact that recent research has shown that it is often possible to spot an affected child by analyzing home videos of infants on their first birthday parties (Osterling, Dawson and Munson 2002). What parents are sensitive to are early social/pragmatic deficits: infants who do not sustain gaze, infants who do not like the parent–child interaction of cuddling and who may arch their backs and scream at attempts to hug them, infants who do not put up their arms and greet a parent who comes to pick them up after a nap and are content to stay in their crib making no demands for attention for unusually long periods, and quiet infants who do not babble a great deal. Whether lack of babbling (repetitive consonant–vowel utterances which appear in the second half of the first year) is the first sign of a phonologic processing deficit has not been determined formally, but is plausible.

Toddlers/preschoolers

There are three main ways in which autism presents in this age group: (1) delayed or failure to develop expressive language; (2) language that develops at the expected age but that has aberrant features; and (3) regression of language skills.

(1) POTENTIAL DEFICITS IN CHILDREN WITH ABSENT OR DELAYED EXPRESSIVE LANGUAGE

Parents' first awareness that something is amiss with their child is likely to be *delay or failure of first words to emerge*. Parents will often bring this concern to their physician, only to be reassured that there is a great deal of variability among children in the unfolding of early language abilities (Thal and Bates 1990). Many physicians cite the tendency for boys, who are of course those most likely to be on the autistic spectrum (and to have

DLDs), to speak later than girls as a reason for the delay. The parents may be told not to compare one of their children with the others and to come back in several months. Instead, the following possibilities need to be considered.

Hearing impairment

In toddlers/preschoolers who do not speak or in whom language develops very late, the first order of business is to determine whether hearing is normal. This mandates a competent pure tone audiogram, but as behavioral testing requires the infant to tolerate earphones and to respond reliably by orienting toward the stimulated ear in order to see a visual reinforcer that appears on that side of the booth, the child must be able to tolerate earphones and to be at least somewhat cooperative. Unless the test provides unequivocal results, physiologic tests, that is otoacoustic emissions or auditory brainstem evoked responses to tonal stimuli, must be obtained without delay. It is never enough to accept the parents' report that the child hears as there are unfortunate children who are both hearing impaired and autistic (Jure, Rapin and Tuchman 1991), and overlooking a hearing loss, in particular a high tone loss that may pass unnoticed clinically, is an egregious error.

Inadequate comprehension of speech

Once hearing has been shown to be normal, the question is how well the child comprehends speech. This is often difficult to determine because of uncertainty about whether lack of response to a question or of compliance to a verbal command denotes failure to understand speech, inattention, lack of motivation, or negativism. Lack of comprehension is therefore necessarily inferential and is based on verbal and non-verbal responses to a verbal input. It is imperative not to base this inference on a single instance or a parents' report as they are likely to provide inadvertent visual cues. Evaluating comprehension is crucial because it is requisite to the emergence of speech.

Non-fluent phonologic decoding deficits

Children whose hearing is demonstrably normal yet are non-verbal or minimally verbal and who appear to comprehend very few or essentially no verbal commands without visual cues may be suffering from the most severe input disorder, *verbal auditory agnosia*, in which lack of ability to decode phonology precludes all further language operations (Box 9.2). Some of these children have epileptiform activity in their perisylvian cortex which is presumed to interfere with the function of the primary or secondary auditory cortex (Klein, Tuchman and Rapin 2000). This language disorder is infrequent. If the decoding disorder for phonology is less severe and speech comprehension impaired rather than absent, children's utterances are likely to be sparse, imperfectly articulated, effortful, their vocabulary to be limited and their grammar simplified, in some cases to the point of speech consisting mostly of single words or uninflected two word utterances. Verbal auditory agnosia and the less severe and considerably more prevalent *mixed receptive/expressive dysfluent language deficit* are likely to be variants on a continuum, as both are characterized by impaired receptive and expressive phonology, deficient grammar, and a meager lexicon. What differentiates children with autism from those with the same developmental language disorder without autism is their profoundly impaired pragmatics.

Pragmatic deficits

These need to be looked for specifically. Caretakers must be asked whether the child attempts to communicate by gesture, whether the infant points to desired objects or to draw parents' attention to a salient event or object of interest. Does the infant have a means for expressing wants besides attempting to reach the desired object without help, pulling the parent by the hand toward it, or screaming? Does the infant shake the head to communicate 'no,' or just push away an undesirable object, or sink to the floor to indicate refusal to comply? Does the infant look up when called by name? Deaf toddlers and those with specific language deficits without autism attempt to communicate by any mean available to them and in fact will invent their own gesture language to do so, in contrast to toddlers on the autistic spectrum who appear to have little or no need to communicate and, when they do, it is in the very primitive ways just described.

Non-fluent higher order language processing deficits

Rather than having difficulty with the phonologic code, with its resultant mixed receptive/expressive deficit and curtailed and inadequate phonologic and grammatic production, there are toddlers/preschoolers on the autistic spectrum whose deficit is at the semantic and, of course, at the pragmatic level as well. If expressive language is delayed, it may start with a fluent jargon, often produced without clear communicative intent, namely speaking with the back turned and without expecting a response or the need for a communicative partner. When intelligible speech develops, the semantic deficit is characterized by an impoverished lexicon and, in some children, with such severe word retrieval deficits that the children sound like stutterers. When words appear, phonology improves rapidly to the point where speech is intelligible. Grammar may be simplified early on but also tends to catch up. Some of them have prominent echolalia, repeating what was just said rather than responding with a self-generated utterance. Prominent and persistent echolalia (echolalia is a normal but transient stage in learning to speak) should bring up the possibility of either inadequate comprehension or difficulty with sentence generation. These are the children who understand simple commands but whose deficit can be brought out by asking them questions, especially open ended 'wh–' questions like 'why,' 'when,' and 'how.' Allen and Rapin's name for this quite frequent type of language deficit is the *lexical-syntactic deficit*, which is also quite prevalent in non-autistic children, but without the salient pragmatic deficits and characteristic features of autistic speech.

(2) HIGHER ORDER LANGUAGE PROCESSING DEFICITS IN FLUENT CHILDREN WITHOUT DELAYED SPEECH

Not all toddlers/preschoolers fail to speak at the expected age, but when early language develops it is likely to have aberrant features (e.g. Tager-Flusberg 2003). They have another subtype of higher order language processing deficit, the fluent so-called *semantic-pragmatic subtype*. Because they speak at the expected age, this earns such children the label of Asperger syndrome provided they are not mentally retarded; that is, provided their IQ is at least 70. Although they share many of the features with the less fluent children just described, they differ from them in their chattiness and large, often esoteric vocabularies. Their speech is characterized less by immediate echoes than by the production of overlearned scripts and perseveration on favorite topics, and by incessant questioning. These children are the 'little professors' with prodigious rote memories who may endear themselves to admiring adults by the depth of their knowledge of some obscure topic but whose peers shun them because they would rather talk than play. Whether the semantic-pragmatic subtype exists in non-autistic children as well was disputed (Boucher 1998). It is seen in some hydrocephalic children (Fletcher, Barnes and Dennis 2002) and children with Williams syndrome (Laws and Bishop 2004), most of whom do not qualify for an autistic spectrum deficit because social skill may be one of their strengths.

A great deal of linguistic research has been devoted to the study of the semantic-pragmatic language disorder and its associated deficits. Good resources are the series of papers devoted to this topic (Boucher 1998), the studies by Bishop and colleagues reviewed in her book on receptive language disorders (Bishop 1997), Tager-Flusberg's review of language in autism (Tager-Flusberg 2003), and a study of electrophysiologic correlates of semantic deficits in intelligent children with autism (Dunn, Gomes and Sebastian 1996).

(3) LANGUAGE STAGNATION OR REGRESSION, RELATION TO ACQUIRED EPILEPTIC APHASIA

The third way in which autism presents in toddlers/preschoolers is *loss of language skills, together with a regression in sociability and play*. At least one in three parents reports that, at a mean age of 18–24 months, but in some cases as early as one year, whatever communication skill the infant had developed fades insidiously or, occasionally, abruptly or, in some cases, fails to develop further for many months. Some of the toddlers seemed entirely normal prior to the regression although, in retrospect, other parents had overlooked evidence for delay in the use of gestures or the appearance of single words. In some very young toddlers what goes away is imitation of meaningful gestures such as waving goodbye or of the gestures called for in a nursery song. When regression occurs very early it is difficult to be certain of the antecedent normality of the child, although availability of home videos (Osterling *et al.* 2002) has vindicated clinicians who elicited a history of language regression by direct questioning of parents (Kurita 1996; Kurita, Kita and Miyake 1992).

Our group has performed a number of studies of the relation of language regression and autism to epilepsy (defined in all of these studies as a history of at least two unprovoked seizures). In a cohort of 585 children on the autistic spectrum evaluated by Tuchman (Tuchman and Rapin 1997), parents reported that language had regressed at a mean age of 21 months in 30 percent of cases, and that 11 percent had epilepsy as just defined. Among 392 children (two-thirds of the cohort) with an available sleep EEG, the EEG was epileptiform in 21 (19%) of the 113 non-epileptic children who had undergone a regression and in 22 (10%) of 222 with neither regression nor epilepsy (EEGs were of course much more likely (approximately 60 percent) to be epileptiform in children who had epilepsy, whether or not they had regressed). In another study of 176 preschoolers with autism, 27 percent of parents reported regression of single words (Rapin 1996, p.84). A brief questionnaire to 177 parents in a third cohort disclosed that age at language regression was an important variable: regression before age three years was associated with autistic features in 91 percent of children and with epilepsy in 14 percent, whereas the trend was reversed after age three years: epilepsy in 58 percent and autism in 53 percent of children (Shinnar *et al.* 2001). This effect of age was duplicated in a fourth cohort of 196 children with histories of language regression, 98 percent of whom had autistic features (Sy *et al.* 2003). Asked whether there were antecedent events that might have triggered the regression, parents invoked a variety of non-specific intercurrent illnesses, reactions to immunizations, and traumatic life events, although the relevance of these memories is unproven as some parents reported several potential triggers, but the time between alleged trigger and regression varied a great deal casting doubt on the reliability of their answers (Shinnar *et al.* 2001). Extensive epidemiologic evidence has not persuaded parents, who understandably seek an explanation for untoward events, that vaccines and environmental intoxications are contemporary with, but not responsible for, the emergence of autism. As stated earlier, the principal etiology of the autism spectrum disorders is complex multigenic effects on prenatal brain development that vary among affected individuals, even, occasionally, within the same family (Muhle *et al.* 2004). This is not to deny that the vagaries of each individual's environmental circumstances influences the behavioral expression of these genetic traits.

There has been a great deal of speculation about the potential role of clinical or subclinical epilepsy in language/autistic regression of toddlers (Deonna 1991; Holmes, McKeever and Saunders 1981; Lewine *et al.* 1999). The reason is that the very much rarer unexplained loss of language in later childhood is invariably associated with epilepsy or an epileptiform EEG that is exacerbated by slow wave sleep (acquired epileptic aphasia or Landau Kleffner syndrome) (Ballaban-Gil and Tuchman 2000; Klein *et al.* 2000). A study of 149 children with histories of language regression who underwent all-night EEG monitoring (McVicar *et al.* 2005) indicates that 69 percent of them were on the autistic spectrum. Once again regression occurred earlier, at 26 months on average, in those on the autistic spectrum than in those who were not whose mean age at regression was 39 months. Eight per cent of children with autistic features had had at least two unprovoked seizures but only 2 per cent of them had an epileptiform overnight EEG; in contrast, 33 percent of children who were not on the autistic spectrum had epilepsy and 57 percent had an epileptiform EEG and thus fulfilled criteria for acquired epileptiform aphasia.

In summary, this series of studies on the relation of epilepsy to language loss in autism shows unequivocally that a history of very early language regression must be taken very seriously because it is the harbinger of an autistic spectrum disorder in the great majority of toddlers. It also shows that epilepsy or an epileptiform EEG is unlikely to be the major culprit in early language/autistic regression even though it may play a role in a minority of the children and that the opposite is true of children whose language regresses at school-age, with a considerable overlap between the two ages.

If epilepsy plays a subsidiary role in language/autistic regression, other possibilities need to be considered. Some cases might plausibly arise because of enhanced genetic predisposition to the deleterious effects of unidentified environmental influences. Linkage to genes relevant to immunity (Torres *et al.* 2002), together with an increased prevalence of autoimmune disorders in the families of children with autism (Comi *et al.* 1999), suggested that immunology might increase susceptibility to autism or autistic regression upon exposure to generally benign non-specific infections or well tolerated immunizations (Korvatska *et al.* 2002). Live measles vaccine (Miller 2003) and toxic effects of the ethyl mercury (thimerosal) used as a preservative in many vaccines have recently received a great deal of publicity (Kimmel 2002). Reports of an increase in the prevalence of the autistic spectrum disorders (a so-called autistic epidemic) (Croen *et al.* 2002), together with an escalating number of vaccines administered to infants and toddlers at the peak age of language regression and of the diagnosis of autism, fueled the hypothesis of a causal relation. This remains a hypothesis to be investigated further, although extensive epidemiological studies have failed to corroborate these hypotheses (e.g. Andrews *et al.* 2004; Heron and Golding 2004; Madsen *et al.* 2002 in Pichichero *et al.* 2002). The evidence for an autism epidemic seems to reflect mostly an increase in the identification of mild cases by both professionals and the public, fueled by awareness that a diagnosis of autism buys more intensive intervention for toddlers/preschoolers than a non-specific label like developmental delay (Fombonne 2003).

School-age children

The good news is that in most children with autism, like in those with uncomplicated developmental language disorders, language generally improves with maturation, provided the child is not profoundly autistic or cognitively impaired. The most informative study of outcome as a function of the clinically-defined language deficits subtypes of toddlers and preschoolers would be a longitudinal study of children whose language was evaluated several times between its emergence and later ages. Most of the studies to date are cross-sectional studies, the majority of them of verbal children. As part of a larger study, a group of specifically trained neurologists had the opportunity to score 83 children on the autistic spectrum at preschool, seven or nine years. Preliminary analysis indicates that the neurologists had scored the expressive language of two-thirds of lower-functioning children versus one-third of the higher-functioning group (whose expressive skills started out higher of course) as improved and as had the receptive skills of slightly more than half of both groups.

The classic descriptions of the language of children on the autistic spectrum have focused on school-age and adolescence, with particular emphasis on bright individuals labeled Asperger syndrome even though some of them had delayed onset of language, and therefore rigorous application of the DSM-IV/ICD-10 criteria would classify them as having either high-functioning autism (autistic disorder without mental retardation and with adequate verbal ability) or PDD-NOS. (Whether there is a biologic difference between Asperger syndrome, high functioning autism, and PDD-NOS is questionable (Myhr 1998).) It is well established that emergence by age five years of functional speech (that is, speech used for communication, not just echolalia, scripts, or elicited utterances) is a more reliable predictor of a favorable outcome than the severity of the dysfunction at preschool (Eisenmajer *et al.* 1998; Lord and Paul 1997), this despite the infrequent later emergence of speech in a heretofore non-verbal or minimally verbal older child. Provision of a visual mode of communication such as pictures (Bondy and Frost 1998) or sign language (Bonvillian, Nelson and Rhyne 1981) for those who remain non-verbal greatly enhances their quality of life. An occasional non-verbal child with an ASD will learn to read prior to the emergence of speech as reading may serve as scaffolding for speech.

I know of no study which used the clinical classification described in this chapter to determine whether the language subtypes in children on the spectrum were stable or predictive of school-age language. Clinical experience suggests that as children receive language training and mature, those who were classified in the lexical subtype at preschool, and probably some of the less severely affected children in the mixed phonologic-syntactic subtype, develop the characteristics of those with the classic semantic-pragmatic subtype, but longitudinal research based on the analysis of spontaneous language samples is needed.

Many of the children who underwent a language regression as toddlers regain speech and it seems to me (but again without formal data to support this supposition) that they do not fall exclusively into any one of the clinically defined language subtypes. The majority recover language, some completely or virtually completely except for residual pragmatic, prosodic, and semantic deficits. The vast majority of those who 'recover' retain enough autistic features to remain at the mild end of the autistic spectrum. A few remain non-verbal or minimally verbal with impaired phonologic production and limited comprehension; as expected, such children are generally moderately to severely mentally retarded and more severely autistic than those able to speak.

It is important to mention here that there are children who undergo a catastrophic autistic regression (*disintegrative disorder*) as preschoolers or at school-age (Fombonne

2002). Almost all become and remain mute life-long, severely autistic, and retarded. Although disintegrative disorder is generally stated to have a worse outcome than autism (Volkmar and Cohen 1989), a recent study (Kurita, Osada and Miyake 2004) disputes this, albeit in a small number of children because the disorder is mercifully rare. Whether disintegrative disorder and the infinitely more prevalent autistic regression are distinct or related disorders is not known, but both appear to have heterogeneous etiologies.

Adolescents and adults

Despite many descriptions of language in adolescence and adulthood, long term longitudinal studies are sparse. Ballaban-Gil and colleagues (Ballaban-Gil *et al.* 1996), on the basis of structured phone interviews to a parent, reevaluated 48 individuals without severe mental retardation, 26 with documented or estimated normal or near normal intelligence and 22 with mild to moderate cognitive impairment; one neurologist had diagnosed all of them in childhood as being on the autistic spectrum. Expressive language had improved in 54 percent and was stable in 19 percent of the 26 with normal or near normal intelligence, compared to improvement in 36 percent and stability in 59 percent of the 22 with mild or moderate cognitive impairment. Parents reported that expressive ability had worsened in 15 percent and 5 percent of the children in these two groups, but numbers are so small as to make this difference unreliable. The language of children seen for the first time below age six years was twice as likely to have improved as that of children seen between ages 6 and 12 years. Mawhood and colleagues (Mawhood, Howlin and Rutter 2000) reassessed at age 23–24 18 men who had been given a diagnosis of autism in childhood and whose mean non-verbal IQ (PIQ) at the time was 70 or better (mean PIQ 94, verbal IQ (VIQ) 66). They found that VIQ had increased substantially to 82 in the nine individuals retested but that their PIQ had dropped by ten points. Only 8 of the 18 were speaking in full sentences and four were still essentially non-verbal. Language comprehension in childhood was the strongest predictor not only of language in adulthood but also of social skills and overall function. As was true in their early twenties, all the men's social skills remained deficient in mid-adult life and only one had obtained independent employment (Howlin, Mawhood and Rutter 2000).

NEUROLOGIC CORRELATES OF LANGUAGE IMPAIRMENT IN THE AUTISTIC SPECTRUM DISORDERS
Imaging

There is now a growing literature on morphometric imaging in autism, but very few of them address language specifically. In a series of studies, Herbert and colleagues compared 16 school-age boys identified at preschool as having autistic disorder and a non-verbal IQ of at least 80 to two groups of age and handedness-matched controls:

normally-developing boys and boys with DLD. The many similarities between the brains of boys with DLD and autism brains were salient and included increased white matter volume in both due to selective enlargement of superficial white matter which contains late myelinating intrahemispheric cortico-cortical fibers (Herbert *et al.* 2004). Even though, at the whole brain level, there was no asymmetry between the hemispheres in any of the three groups, there were cortical differences between regions, a notable one being that language-related frontal cortex was larger on the right in autism, larger on the left in normal controls (Herbert *et al.* 2002). Parcellation into smaller cortical areas revealed that this rightward shift was more marked in autism than DLD, that more parcellation units in other association cortices were asymmetrical in autism than DLD, and that the asymmetry reflected enlargement on the right rather than loss of volume on the left, consonant with brain enlargement in both disorders (Herbert *et al.* 2005). A single functional MRI study disclosed failure of voice-selective activation of the left superior temporal sulcus despite normal activation to non-vocal sounds in autism (Gervais *et al.* 2004).

Electrophysiology

In hearing children with autism, refined behavioral and physiologic studies have failed to demonstrate any impairment of peripheral or subcortical auditory function (Gravel *et al.* in press). There are a small number of children with both peripheral hearing losses and an autistic spectrum disorder (Jure *et al.* 1991), many of them with either syndromic deafness or a hearing loss due to a definable condition like an infection that damaged both the ear and the brain. No doubt these presumably unrelated deficits interact, but I know of no convincing evidence for an increase in the prevalence of autism in early non-syndromic deafness unassociated with brain dysfunction, in contrast with blindness which does seem to be a risk factor for autism (Hobson, Lee and Brown 1999), although both are still controversial statements in need of further research based on modern diagnostic criteria.

Severely impaired four- to eight-year-old children with autism, compared to children with mental deficiency and normal controls, were found to have a significant delay and lower amplitude in the early obligatory cortical event-related response (ERP) component N1c to tones (Bruneau *et al.* 1999), pointing to deficient processing of auditory stimuli in very young severely impaired children with autism. This component, which has a latency of 130–170 msec, appears to be generated in lateral temporal auditory association cortex, as opposed to the earlier N1b component with a latency of 100–110 msec generated in primary auditory cortex in the supratemporal plane which is not delayed following either tones or speech sounds in autism. In eight- to ten-year-old children with autism, N1c latency to tones was similar to normally developing controls but delayed over the left hemisphere in response to words. This N1c finding was replicated in another sample of eight- to nine-year-olds but not found in 11–12-year-old children with autism (Dunn *et al.* 1996). Another study of high-functioning children provided physiologic evidence for a deficit in language presented to the auditory modality: there was no deviance in the early automatic response (mismatch negativity) to occasional deviance in simple or complex tones or vowels, whereas the P3a component, an index of attentional orienting, was absent but only for vowel changes, which points to the 'speechiness' of the auditory stimulus as determinant of deviance (Ceponiene *et al.* 2003).

Differences in semantic processing at both the word (lexical) and sentence levels have been identified comparing normal children to those with autism. Children with autism have difficulty automatically organizing words presented to the visual or auditory modality into superordinate categories for efficient storage. For example, when asked to generate categorical words, such as 'animals,' young children with autism offered atypical exemplars (Dunn *et al.* 1996); this suggested that they had stored each exemplar individually so that rare exemplars were just as likely to be retrieved from the lexicon as prototypic exemplars of the abstract superordinate category 'animal' which summarizes features shared by many familiar members of the group. Even high-functioning adults have deficits integrating new meaning into a context, which jeopardizes the creating of networks in memory to categorize words and ideas efficiently (Frith and Happe 1994). A physiologic abnormality of the N4 wave which occurs some 400 msec post stimulus presentation and indexes processing of the semantic relatedness between a word and its context was found only in eight- to nine-year-old but not 11–12-year-old children with autism; it consisted of failure of the infrequent presentation of an out-of-category word to produce the expected increase in the amplitude of the N4 wave (Dunn *et al.* 1996). That the abnormality was limited to the younger children confirms improvement of lexical semantic function with longer exposure to language.

IMPLICATIONS FOR LANGUAGE INTERVENTION IN AUTISM

As detailed in this chapter, research to date indicates that children with autism suffer from a variety of language deficits. As effective intervention requires that remediation address each child's particular deficits, this mandates a searching evaluation of the child's receptive and expressive deficits at each level of language. The first step is always to make sure that there is no peripheral hearing loss. In hearing children with severe comprehension deficits for speech it is mandatory to supplement the auditory modality by the visual. The most immediate measure is to limit the complexity and length of utterances and to speak mostly of the here-and-now, that is, to speak of what is happening as it is happening, for example of shoes as they are going onto the feet and of cookies as they are being offered. What this strategy does is provide a visual referent to the words being spoken. Presenting communications using sign language (Bonvillian 1991), pictures (Frost and Bondy 1994), a communication book, written language, a computer, or other augmentative communication devices (National Research Council 2001), far from retarding the emergence of speech, may help it and, in any case, may reduce frustration significantly by enhancing comprehension and providing the child with an alternate channel for expression. In fluent children, it is important to keep in mind that comprehension of discourse and of question forms may be deficient in the face of an extensive vocabulary so that strategies to improve comprehension and conversational skills need to be provided (Minshew, Meyer and Dunn 2003).

As all children on the autism spectrum have pragmatic deficits, these must be addressed in all of them. Children must be taught and given the opportunity to practice pragmatic skills such as glancing up when addressed, looking a conversational partner in the eye, responding verbally or non-verbally when spoken to, and curtailing perseveration on favorite topics and repeated questioning. The techniques to assist non-fluent children to develop better articulation and grammatical skills are similar to those used with non-autistic children who have a mixed receptive/expressive DLD, but they can only be introduced effectively to children on the spectrum who have improved their joint attentional and pragmatic skills sufficiently to be reasonably motivated to interact and comply with demands (Allen and Mendelson 2000; Allen, Mendelson and Rapin 1989; Koegel 2000). This is where systematic conditioning approaches like Applied Behavior Analysis (ABA) come into play because they are often rather rapidly effective for eliciting imitative speech in young non-verbal preschoolers, provided, that is, that their cognitive deficits are not severe or profound (Dunn *et al.* 1996; Lovaas 1981). But children with autism need to progress beyond echolalia and speech on demand. This is the focus of the many other language interventions in current use which share the common goal of fostering in more naturalistic functional contexts the communicative use of speech, or a visual language in non-verbal or poorly intelligible children (Ozonoff *et al.* 2003).

REFERENCES

Allen, D. A. and Mendelson, L. (2000) 'Parent, child, and professional: meeting the needs of young autistic children and their families in a multidisciplinary therapeutic nursery model.' In S. Epstein (ed.) *Autistic Spectrum Disorders and Psychoanalytic Ideas: Reassessing the Fit*, pp. 704–731. Hillsdale, NJ: The Analytic Press.

Allen, D. A., Mendelson, L. and Rapin, I. (1989) 'Syndrome specific remediation in preschool developmental dysphasia.' In J. H. French, S. Harel, P. Casaer, M. I. Gottlieb, I. Rapin and D. C. De Vivo (eds) *Child Neurology and Developmental Disabilities*, pp. 233–243. Baltimore, MD: Paul Brookes.

American Psychiatric Association (2000) *Diagnostic and Statistical Manual of Mental Disorders. Fourth edition, text revision: DSM-IV-TR* (4th edn). Washington, DC: American Psychiatric Association.

Andrews, N., Miller, E., Grant, A., Stowe, J., Osborne, V. and Taylor, B. (2004) 'Thimerosal exposure in infants and developmental disorders: a retrospective cohort study in the United Kingdom does not support a causal association.' *Pediatrics 114*, 584–591.

Ballaban-Gil, K. and Tuchman, R. (2000) 'Epilepsy and epileptiform EEG: association with autism and language disorders.' *Mental Retardation and Developmental Disabilities Research Reviews 6*, 300–308.

Ballaban-Gil, K., Rapin, I., Tuchman, R. F. and Shinnar, S. (1996) 'Longitudinal examination of the behavioral, language, and social changes in a population of adolescents and young adults with autistic disorder.' *Pediatric Neurology 15*, 217–223.

Bishop, D. V. M. (1997) *Uncommon Understanding: Development and Disorders of Comprehension in Children.* Hove, East Sussex, UK: Psychology Press.

Bondy, A. S. and Frost, L. A. (1998) 'The picture exchange communication system.' *Seminars in Speech and Language 19*, 373–388.

Bonvillian, J. D. (1991) 'Manual communication and autism: factors relating to sign language acquisition.' In P. Siple and S. D. Fisher (eds) *Theoretical Issues in Sign Language and Research. Vol 2, Psychology.* Chicago, IL: University of Chicago Press.

Bonvillian, J. D., Nelson, K. E. and Rhyne, J. M. (1981) 'Sign language and autism.' *Journal of Autism and Developmental Disorders 11*, 125–137.

Boucher, J. (1998) 'Clinical Forum. SPD as a distinct diagnostic entity: logical considerations and directions for future research.' *International Journal of Language and Communication Disorders 33*, 71–81.

Bradford, Y., Haines, J., Hutcheson, H., Gardiner, M., Braun, T., Sheffield, V. *et al.* (2001) 'Incorporating language phenotypes strengthens evidence of linkage to autism.' *American Journal of Medical Genetics 105*, 539–547.

Bruneau, N., Roux, S., Adrien, J. L. and Barthelemy, C. (1999) 'Auditory associative cortex dysfunction in children with autism: evidence from late auditory evoked potentials (N1 wave-T complex).' *Clinical Neurophysiology 110*, 1927–1934.

Ceponiene, R., Lepisto, T., Shestakova, A., Vanhala, R., Alku, P., Naatanen, R. *et al.* (2003) 'Speech-sound-selective auditory impairment in children with autism: they can perceive but do not attend.' *Proceedings of the National Academy of Sciences of the U.S.A. 100*, 5567–5572.

Chess, S., Korn, S. J. and Fernandez, P. B. (1971) *Psychiatric Disorders of Children with Congenital Rubella.* New York: Brunner/Mazel.

Comi, A. M., Zimmerman, A. W., Frye, V. H., Law, P. A. and Peeden, J. N. (1999) 'Familial clustering of autoimmune disorders and evaluation of medical risk factors in autism.' *Journal of Child Neurology 14*, 388–394.

Croen, L. A., Grether, J. K., Hoogstrate, J. and Selvin, S. (2002) 'The changing prevalence of autism in California.' *Journal of Autism and Developmental Disorders 32*, 207–215.

Deonna, T. W. (1991) 'Acquired epileptiform aphasia in children (Landau-Kleffner syndrome).' *Journal of Clinical Neurophysiology 3*, 288–298.

Dunn, M., Gomes, H. and Sebastian, M. (1996) 'Prototypicality of responses in autistic language disordered and normal children in a verbal fluency task.' *Child Neuropsychology 2*, 99–108.

Eisenmajer, R., Prior, M., Leekam, S., Wing, L., Ong, B., Gould, J. *et al.* (1998) 'Delayed language onset as a predictor of clinical symptoms in pervasive developmental disorders.' *Journal of Autism and Developmental Disorders 28*, 527–533.

Fletcher, J. M., Barnes, M. and Dennis, M. (2002) 'Language development in children with spina bifida.' *Seminars in Pediatric Neurology 9*, 201–208.

Fombonne, E. (2002) 'Prevalence of childhood disintegrative disorder.' *Autism 6*, 149–157.

Fombonne, E. (2003) 'Epidemiological surveys of autism and other pervasive developmental disorders: an update.' *Journal of Autism and Developmental Disorders 33*, 365–382.

Frith, U. and Happe, F. (1994) 'Autism: beyond "theory of mind".' *Cognition 50*, 115–132.

Frost, L. and Bondy, A. (1994) *PECS: The Picture Exchange Communication System Training Manual.* Cherry Hill, NJ: Pyramid Educational Consultants.

Gervais, H., Belin, P., Boddaert, N., Leboyer, M., Coez, A., Sfaello, I. *et al.* (2004) 'Abnormal cortical voice processing in autism.' *Nature Neuroscience 7*, 801–802.

Gravel, J. S., Dunn, M., Lee, W. and Ellis, M. A. (in press) 'Peripheral audition of children on the autistic spectrum.' *Journal of Speech, Language, and Hearing Research.*

Herbert, M. R., Harris, G. J., Adrien, K. T., Ziegler, D. A., Makris, N., Kennedy, D. N. *et al.* (2002) 'Abnormal asymmetry in language association cortex in autism.' *Annals of Neurology 52,* 588–596.

Herbert, M. R., Ziegler, D. A., Makris, N., Filipek, P. A., Kemper, T. L., Normandin, J. J. *et al.* (2004) 'Localization of white matter volume increase in autism and developmental language disorder.' *Annals of Neurology 55,* 530–540.

Herbert, M. R., Ziegler, D. A., Deutsch, C. K., O'Brien, L. M., Kennedy, D. N., Filipek, P. A. *et al.* (2005) 'Brain asymmetries in autism and developmental language disorders: a nested whole-brain analysis.' *Brain 128,* 213–226.

Heron, J. and Golding, J. (2004) 'Thimerosal exposure in infants and developmental disorders: a prospective cohort study in the United Kingdom does not support a causal association.' *Pediatrics 114,* 577–583.

Hobson, R. P., Lee, A. and Brown, R. (1999) 'Autism and congenital blindness.' *Journal of Autism and Developmental Disorders 29,* 45–56.

Holmes, G. L., McKeever, M. and Saunders, Z. (1981) 'Epileptiform activity in aphasia of childhood: an epiphenomenon?' *Epilepsia 22,* 631–639.

Howlin, P., Mawhood, L. and Rutter, M. (2000) 'Autism and developmental receptive language disorder – a follow-up comparison in early adult life. II: Social, behavioural, and psychiatric outcomes.' *Journal of Child Psychology and Psychiatry and Allied Disciplines 41,* 561–578.

Jure, R., Rapin, I. and Tuchman, R. F. (1991) 'Hearing-impaired autistic children.' *Developmental Medicine and Child Neurology 33,* 1062–1072.

Kimmel, S. R. (2002) 'Vaccine adverse events: separating myth from reality.' *American Family Physician 66,* 2113–2120.

Klein, S. K., Tuchman, R. F. and Rapin, I. (2000) 'The influence of premorbid language skills and behavior on language recovery in children with verbal auditory agnosia.' *Journal of Child Neurology 15,* 36–43.

Klin, A., Jones, W., Schultz, R., Volkmar, F. and Cohen, D. (2002) 'Visual fixation patterns during viewing of naturalistic social situations as predictors of social competence in individuals with autism.' *AMA Archives of General Psychiatry 59,* 809–816.

Koegel, L. K. (2000) 'Interventions to facilitate communication in autism.' *Journal of Autism and Developmental Disorders 30,* 383–391.

Korvatska, E., Van de Water, J., Anders, T. F. and Gershwin, M. E. (2002) 'Genetic and immunologic considerations in autism.' *Neurobiology of Disease 9,* 107–125.

Kuhl, P. K., Andruski, J. E., Chistovich, I. A., Chistovich, L. A., Kozhevnikova, E. V., Ryskina, V. L. *et al.* (1997) 'Cross-language analysis of phonetic units in language addressed to infants.' *Science 277,* 684–686.

Kurita, H. (1996) 'Specificity and developmental consequences of speech loss in children with pervasive developmental disorders.' *Psychiatry and Clinical Neurosciences 50,* 181–184.

Kurita, H., Kita, M. and Miyake, Y. (1992) 'A comparative study of development and symptoms among disintegrative psychosis and infantile autism with and without speech loss.' *Journal of Autism and Developmental Disorders 22,* 175–188.

Kurita, H., Osada, H. and Miyake, Y. (2004) 'External validity of childhood disintegrative disorder in comparison with autistic disorder.' *Journal of Autism and Developmental Disorders 34,* 355–362.

Laws, G. and Bishop, D. (2004) 'Pragmatic language impairment and social deficits in Williams syndrome: a comparison with Down's syndrome and specific language impairment.' *International Journal of Language and Communication Disorders 39,* 45–64.

Leslie, A. M. and Frith, U. (1988) 'Autistic children's understanding of seeing, knowing and believing.' *British Journal of Clinical Psychology 6,* 315–324.

Lewine, J. D., Andrews, R., Chez, M., Patil, A. A., Devinsky, O., Smith, M. *et al.* (1999) 'Magnetoencephalographic patterns of epileptiform activity in children with regressive autism spectrum disorders.' *Pediatrics 104*, 405–418.

Lord, C. and Paul, R. (1997) 'Language and communication in autism.' In D. J. Cohen and F. R. Volkmar (eds) *Handbook of Autism and Pervasive Developmental Disorders* (2nd edn), pp.195–225. New York: John Wiley and Sons.

Lovaas, O. I. (1981) *Teaching Developmentally Disabled Children: The Me Book.* Autism, TX: Pro-Ed.

Madsen, K. M., Hviid, A., Vestergaard, M., Schendel, D., Wohlfahrt, J., Thorsen, P. *et al.* (2002) 'A population-based study of measles, mumps, and rubella vaccination and autism.' *New England Journal of Medicine 347*, 1477–1482.

Mawhood, L., Howlin, P. and Rutter, M. (2000) 'Autism and developmental receptive language disorder – a comparative follow-up in early adult life. I: Cognitive and language outcomes.' *Journal of Child Psychology and Psychiatry and Allied Disciplines 41*, 547–559.

McVicar, K. A., Ballabin-Gil, K., Rapin, I., Moshé, S. L. and Shinnar, S. (2005) 'Epileptiform EEG abnormalities in children with language regression.' *Neurology 65*, 129–131.

Miller, E. (2003) 'Measles-mumps-rubella vaccine and the development of autism.' *Seminars in Pediatric Infectious Diseases 14*, 199–206.

Minshew, N. J., Meyer, J. A. and Dunn, M. (2003) 'Autism spectrum disorders.' In S. Segalowitz and I. Rapin (eds) *Child Neuropsychology* (2nd edn) pp.863–896. Amsterdam: Elsevier Science.

Muhle, R., Trentacoste, S. V. and Rapin, I. (2004) 'The genetics of autism.' *Pediatrics 113*, e472–e486.

Myhr, G. (1998) 'Autism and other pervasive developmental disorders: exploring the dimensional view.' *Canadian Journal of Psychiatry 43*, 589–595.

National Research Council (2001) *Educating Children with Autism.* Washington, DC: National Academy Press.

Osterling, J. A., Dawson, G. and Munson, J. A. (2002) 'Early recognition of 1-year-old infants with autism spectrum disorder versus mental retardation.' *Development and Psychopathology 14*, 239–251.

Ozonoff, S., Rogers, S. J. and Hendren, R. L. (eds) (2003) *Autism Spectrum Disorders: A Research Review for Practitioners.* Washington, DC: American Psychiatric Publishing.

Pichichero, M. E., Cernichiari, E., Lopreiato, J. and Treanor, J. (2002) 'Mercury concentrations and metabolism in infants receiving vaccines containing thimerosal: a descriptive study.' *Lancet 360*, 1737–1741.

Prizant, B. M. and Rydell, P. (1984) 'An analysis of the functions of immediate echolalia in autistic children.' *Journal of Speech and Hearing Research 27*, 183–192.

Rapin, I. (ed.) (1996) *Preschool Children with Inadequate Communication: Developmental Language Disorders, Autism, Low IQ.* London: MacKeith Press.

Rapin, I. (1997) 'Trastornos de la communicación en el autismo infantil.' In J. Narbona and C. Chevrie-Muller (eds) *El languaje del niño.* Barcelona: Masson.

Rapin, I. and Dunn, M. (2003) 'Update on the language disorders of individuals on the autistic spectrum.' *Brain and Development 25*, 166–172.

Schultz, R. T., Grelotti, D. J., Klin, A., Kleinman, J., Van der, G. C., Marois, R. *et al.* (2003) 'The role of the fusiform face area in social cognition: implications for the pathobiology of autism.' *Philosophical Transactions of the Royal Society of London, B: Biological Sciences 358*, 415–427.

Shaywitz, S. E. (2003) *Overcoming Dyslexia: A New and Complete Science-based Program for Overcoming Reading Problems at Any Level.* New York, NY: Alfred A. Knopf.

Shinnar, S., Rapin, I., Arnold, S., Tuchman, R. F., Shulman, L., Ballaban-Gil, K. *et al.* (2001) 'Language regression in childhood.' *Pediatric Neurology 24*, 185–191.

Sy, W., Djukic, A., Shinnar, S., Dharmani, C. and Rapin, I. (2003) 'Clinical characteristics of language regression in children.' *Developmental Medicine and Child Neurology 45*, 508–514.

Tager-Flusberg, H. (2003) 'Language impairments in children with complex neurodevelopmental disorders: the case of autism.' In Y. Levy and J. Schaeffer (eds) *Language Competence Across Populations: Toward a Definition of Specific Language Impairment*, pp. 297–321. Mahwah, NJ: Lawrence Erlbaum Associates.

Thal, D. and Bates, E. (1990) 'Continuity and variation in early language development.' In J. Colombo and J. Sagan (eds) *Individual Differences in Infancy: Reliability, Stability, and Prediction*. Hillsdale, NJ: Erlbaum.

Torres, A. R., Maciulis, A., Stubbs, E. G., Cutler, A. and Odell, D. (2002) 'The transmission disequilibrium test suggests that HLA-DR4 and DR13 are linked to autism spectrum disorder.' *Human Immunology 63*, 311–316.

Tuchman, R. F. and Rapin, I. (1997) 'Regression in pervasive developmental disorders: seizures and epileptiform EEG correlates.' *Pediatrics 99*, 560–566.

Volkmar, F. R. and Cohen, D. J. (1989) 'Disintegrative disorder or "late onset" autism.' *Journal of Child Psychology and Psychiatry and Allied Disciplines 5*, 717–724.

Wassink, T. H., Piven, J., Vieland, V. J., Huang, J., Swiderski, R. E., Pietila, J. *et al.* (2001) 'Evidence supporting WNT2 as an autism susceptibility gene.' *American Journal of Medical Genetics (Neuropsychiatric Genetics) 105*, 406–413.

World Health Organization (1992) *The ICD-10 Classification of Mental and Behavioural Disorders: Clinical Descriptions and Diagnostic Guidelines (10th edn)*. Geneva: World Health Organization.

Chapter 10

Development and Behavioural Profiles of Children with Autism and Asperger Syndrome

Susan Leekam

INTRODUCTION

I first heard the term 'Asperger syndrome' 20 years ago when I accompanied my sister-in-law Elizabeth and her son Ivan on a visit to a child psychiatrist. Ivan was 19 years old and had an odd pattern of behaviours since childhood. As none of the experts he had seen had been able to clearly diagnose his problem, we hoped that this new consultation would give a better insight into his difficulties. That day, Ivan received a diagnosis of Asperger syndrome, a condition that was virtually unknown at the time. The psychiatrist was Lorna Wing and the date was 1984, only a few years after she had written her paper on Asperger syndrome (Wing 1981).

It is a long time since that day when I first met Lorna Wing and she diagnosed Ivan, but the impact of that day still remains. Although Ivan was too old by then to benefit from specialized education, he was still able to gain access to adult services and residential accommodation that was more tailored to his needs. All this, and the fact that his diagnosis brought increased understanding of his condition by the people who work with him, has helped him and his family enormously. There is no doubt that Ivan's life was changed immeasureably by being able to gain an understandable diagnosis.

Since Lorna Wing's landmark paper on Asperger syndrome, there has been an extraordinary increase in the clinical, research and media attention given to this condition. The term Asperger syndrome has come far from the unknown status it had when she first wrote her landmark paper. It is now virtually a household term. In a recent article, Wing (2005) describes how public and professional conceptions about Asperger syndrome have changed since her original writings. There is now greater recognition of

Wing's original idea that autism is a broad spectrum of disorders, forming a continuum with normal functioning (Wing 1988). In reflecting on the changes in thinking about Asperger syndrome and its impacts, both Frith (2004) and Wing (2005) argue for the benefit of this increased understanding by the public and professionals.

Alongside the benefits of an expanded understanding of Asperger syndrome there has also been great controversy about its status as a separate subgroup. In 1993 and 1994, the international classification systems were revised leading to the description of a separate subgroup category for Asperger syndrome. This gave it a separate status in both behavioural and developmental terms. The new appearance of separate diagnostic criteria for Asperger syndrome caused considerable debate.

Asperger himself had not delineated any specific criteria for Asperger syndrome. Wing (1991) also described Asperger syndrome as part of the autistic spectrum. While the new official subgroupings were seen as an advantage in terms of giving recognition to a milder form of autism, there were many unanswered questions about what actually distinguished Asperger syndrome and autism as two separate subgroups.

In the 1990s I had the opportunity to explore some of these questions with Margot Prior and Richard Eisenmajer in Australia and Lorna Wing and Judith Gould in England. Our work together allowed us to investigate in detail the behavioural patterns of children with autistic spectrum disorders. We were interested in carrying out research that would address the debate about the utility versus the futility of defining distinct subgroupings. However, we also wanted to understand better the types of behavioural patterns that made up the spectrum of autism and how these connected to various cognitive and developmental variables.

In this chapter I discuss our collaborative work on subgroupings and the conclusions that we drew from this work. One thing that has emerged from this research and from the work of others in the field has been an increased interest in questions about development. Recent findings about the relationship between Asperger syndrome and autism have made us wonder about the way that the behavioural profiles we see in autism emerge from early childhood to later life and how the behaviours themselves constrain the potential for development. So in this chapter I also explore some new ideas about the way that early behavioural and developmental profiles might help to identify developmental pathways for children with autistic spectrum disorders.

ARE THERE SUBGROUPS IN THE AUTISTIC SPECTRUM?

Shortly after Ivan's diagnosis I trained as a researcher in autism. In my initial research I was investigating potential cognitive markers for autism. A compelling new idea at that time was the view that it was possible to identify a specific cognitive impairment that could explain the social and communicative difficulties in autism. The idea was that this cognitive impairment could also be linked to a brain system or genetic locus providing a causal account that connected underlying impairment to the overt behavioural pattern or phenotype. This idea was enormously influential in providing a key turning point in research in autism (Leslie 1987; Frith 1989; Baron-Cohen 1995).

The central hypothesis was that children with autism have a mentalizing deficit – that they are unable to detect and take account of other people's inner mental states. This lack of awareness of what other people were thinking or feeling by even high-functioning children constrasts with the awareness of typically developing children who are able to make inferences about others' mental states from the first few years of life. The marked failure to mentalize or show a 'theory of mind' was first demonstrated in a research study carried out by Baron-Cohen, Leslie and Frith (1985). These authors used a simple story-based task in which the child makes an inference about another person's mistaken belief. Evidence for this deficit was striking (see Baron-Cohen, Tager-Flusberg and Cohen 2000 for review) and was widely replicated using this and similar tasks.

Initially the mentalizing hypothesis was tested out with high-functioning children who had 'core' or classic autism. As broader definitions of autism become the norm, however, children with milder features and/or high mental age came to be included in the research studies. Increasingly, when a broader view of autism was used, the results looked different. The specific cognitive impairment for children with autism compared with those who did not have autism was no longer found. These results raised questions for researchers, and clinicians needed to think about the association between particular sets of symptoms within the autistic spectrum and particular cognitive or neuro-cognitive impairments. Was it the case that specific subgroups of children with particular behavioural or developmental characteristics would be more likely to have this particular mentalizing deficit? If children with a cognitive disability in mentalizing were found to belong to a different subtype of autistic disorder then perhaps this could be used as a diagnostic marker to distinguish subgroups within the autistic spectrum of disorders. Our study therefore aimed to investigate whether this cognitive ability might provide a measure of external validity for the existence of subgroups.

As part of this enterprise, we first needed to understand more about the behavioural patterns themselves. What are the different behavioural patterns found in children with diagnoses of autistic spectrum disorder? Do particular kinds of symptoms naturally cluster into subgroupings? Could these subgroupings be looked at in a 'bottom-up' way, by seeing what types of features are statistically most likely to connect together? In our first collaborative study we aimed to elicit subgroupings in exactly this way by using a statistical technique called cluster analysis.

In this project we collected detailed information about the range of behavioural features of a large group of high-functioning children, all with autistic spectrum disorders, in both South-East Australia and in England (Prior et al. 1998). This project had several components to it. The first was to identify what kinds of behavioural items cluster together in children with autism. The second was to investigate whether a specific cognitive ability might account for these groupings. There was a third component however. Since we also took measures of the child's developmental history and other measures of their current language, it was possible to examine the extent to which both language delay and current verbal ability might be accounting for subtypes of autistic features.

We started the study by recruiting a large sample of 135 individuals aged from 3 to 21 years that had been assessed and diagnosed by different clinicians at assessment centres in both England and Australia. Children were recruited who had a range of subgroup diagnoses of pervasive developmental disorders such as high-functioning autism (HFA), Asperger syndrome (AS), pervasive developmental disorder not otherwise specified (PDD-NOS) or simply 'autistic features'. All these children were highfunctioning with a minimum verbal mental age of approximately three to four years.

Parents of all the children in both countries were then interviewed using the Autism Spectrum Disorders Checklist (Rapin 1996). The interview collected two kinds of information – information about diagnostic behaviours specifically seen in autism and information about background history. Behavioural information included information about Wing and Gould's (1979) three domains of the 'triad of impairments'. These are impairments in social interaction, communication/imagination and restrictions/repetitions in self-chosen behaviour. There were 110 items in the checklist covering social interaction (body language, greeting, comfort seeking/giving, awareness of others' feelings, awareness of social rules, imitation and play, joint referencing), communication/imagination (comprehension and use of language, speech characteristics, non-verbal communication, imagination and pretence) and restrictions and repetition in self-chosen behaviour (stereotyped movements, preoccupations with objects, sensory responses, patterns of interest, maintenance of sameness). We also collected background history variables, including information on pregnancy and birth, developmental milestones, health problems, family history, age of onset. In addition we took a measure of current vocabulary comprehension. We then carried out a cluster analysis that would empirically separate the data into the groupings that best classified the behavioural, verbal ability and background history variables.

As mentioned earlier, we aimed to discover what the subgroupings emerging from these cluster analyses would look like. For example, would the clusters that emerged from the analysis resemble the children's original clinical subgroupings? Three clusters emerged that best fitted the data. We called these Cluster A, Cluster B and Cluster C. Interestingly these empirically directed clusters did not map perfectly onto the clinical groupings that the children had when they came into the study. Fifty per cent of children who had clinical diagnoses of high-functioning autism were in Cluster A but the rest were evenly distributed across the two clusters. More than half of the children who had clinical diagnoses of Asperger syndrome fitted a second cluster but 30 per cent of them were in Cluster A which fitted the more autistic-like picture. This result itself supported the intuition that clinicians are diagnosing children in ways that resemble a continuous spectrum of disorders rather than in separate groupings.

Leaving aside the original clinical diagnoses, what kinds of current behaviours were distinguished by each of the empirically derived clusters and how did they differ from each other? To answer this, we looked at the diagnostic symptoms within the categories of social interaction, communication and restricted/repetitive behaviours. Three groupings of children emerged from the analysis. Their behaviours differed from each other in terms of the severity. Cluster C children had fewer problems across all domains, Cluster B children were most like the children we would recognize as having Asperger syndrome while Cluster A children were most autism-like. Cluster B and Cluster C children were more aware of friendships and social relations than Cluster A children and were keen to communicate their interests. Half of Cluster B children and most of Cluster C children had joint attention skills, compared with only very few of Cluster A children. In contrast Cluster A children were more socially isolated and socially impaired. While Cluster A and Cluster B children were similar in some respects, they were differentiated by their social and communicative development. Yet in other areas of behaviour, for example unusual sensory responses (smelling or scratching surfaces, fascination with sounds or lights), Cluster A and Cluster B were alike and together these two clusters differed from Cluster C.

Given that the Cluster A (autism-like) and Cluster B (Asperger-like) groupings could be differentiated on the basis of their social and communication development, does this mean that their social and communication behaviours were quite different from each other? When we looked in more detail at the social and communication features that were different between the cluster groupings, the critical distinction was not a qualitative difference in the actual presence or absence of particular features. Instead there seemed to be a difference in the degree or severity of symptoms. Severity of impairment in this respect refers to the nature of differentiating symptoms. For example in the social domain, children in Cluster A tended to ignore others and isolate themselves whereas those in Cluster B made approaches and sought friendship, although this was unsuccessful. Yet there were behaviours that did not differ at all between Cluster B and Cluster A (e.g. problems with greeting, discrimination of persons to whom to show affection, peer friendships) and there were also behaviours that did not differ between any of the three subgroups (e.g. impaired eye contact, recognizing another's personal space, relationships with peers, response to others' emotions, imaginative ability, tone of voice, non-verbal communication, idiosyncratic speech).

Next we looked at the extent to which the background variables such as language delay and current language level discriminated the cluster groups. We found that language delay did not separate the groups. This was a surprising result as language delay had previously been considered to be a candidate feature for differentiating Asperger syndrome from autism. What about current language ability? Here the result was quite different. There was a strong difference between the clusters in terms of current verbal ability (vocabulary comprehension) factors. Children in the A group had a lower verbal ability/mental age than children in B or C. Again this was an interesting finding given that the cluster groups were not selected on the basis of their mental age but groups were empirically driven on basis of a range of behaviours. Given that Cluster A children had a lower level of current language, this might account for some of the social-communication differences between this group and Cluster B.

To summarize, the cluster analysis produced three cluster groups that differed in their patterns of behaviour. These clusters did not map perfectly onto the original clinical diagnosis. The critical difference between them relied on the severity of diagnostic behaviours rather than absolute differences and the groupings were differentiated by current verbal mental age but not by language delay.

As mentioned earlier, our study aimed to investigate whether particular behavioural symptom profiles in autism might link to the mentalizing deficit identified in earlier studies. If so, and this cognitive ability could meaningfully differentiate certain groups of children, then this might be an important marker for clinical subtypes and account for why some children in the autistic spectrum pass while others fail tests of 'mentalizing'. All the children in the sample were given a standard experimental task of 'mentalizing' (also known as 'theory of mind' tests). These tests assessed children's ability to infer another person's mental state.

The results showed that children in Cluster A were significantly less likely to pass tests of theory of mind than those in Clusters B or C. Does this then mean that theory of mind provides a reliable marker for subtypes of pervasive developmental disorder (PDD)? Before drawing this conclusion it is important to remember that the groups could be differentiated not only on their theory of mind skills but also on the basis of their current verbal mental age. So one possibility is that there are not one but two markers for subgrouping – theory of mind ability and verbal ability. Each would provide independent markers for the subgrouping. However, our own research, and the research of others in the field, shows that theory of mind (mentalizing) and verbal ability are themselves strongly related to each other. So if there should be just one marker of the subgroupings, which one should it be? This question has been widely debated in the literature (see Garfield, Peterson and Perry 2001 for discussion). Many now make the case that language experience is critical for theory of mind ability although the direction of the causal relationship is not fully understood. On the basis of the data from this study, we argue that theory of mind is not a specific marker for subtypes of pervasive developmental disorder. Instead, given the overall picture of functioning found in these children we suggest that language competence has a general influence on all domains of functioning of which mentalizing ability is one.

What then should we conclude from this study of subgroupings of the autistic spectrum and the connection between mentalizing and behavioural profiles? Our results showed that it *is* possible to empirically subdivide the autistic spectrum into separate subgroups. However, it seems that these subgroupings do not represent distinct, all or none categories but can be distinguished on the basis of severity of social and cognitive impairment and verbal ability and theory of mind and it is suggested that these abilities are linked. So we would argue that the best way to see the subgroupings is as within a spectrum of autistic disorders with severity of social and cognitive impairment being the primary basis for group differences. This is not to say that meaningful groupings cannot be identified where it is helpful to do so. As Prior (2003) points out, 'the label so often depends on the mental lens through which the labeler looks' (p.296). We simply conclude that, given the graded nature of severity and the number of exceptions appearing when subcategorizations are applied, it is usually more sensible to see the subgroups as part of a wider autistic spectrum.

THE BEHAVIOURAL AND DEVELOPMENTAL PROFILES OF INDIVIDUALS WITH ASPERGER SYNDROME

In the study of high-functioning children described above, we found three empirically derived subgroupings. These subgroupings did not map directly onto the clinical groupings identified by clinicians. Furthermore, when we applied the behavioural and developmental criteria for Asperger syndrome defined by the official international classification systems of DSM-IV (American Psychiatric Association 1994) and ICD-10 (World Health Organization 1993), we found that some official behavioural and developmental criteria did not fit our subgroupings at all. For example, ICD-10 research criteria for Asperger syndrome specifies that children with Asperger syndrome have 'no clinically significant delay in spoken or receptive language or cognitive development'. Yet language delay did not differentiate any of the cluster groupings in our study.

Could the DSM-IV and ICD-10 criteria for Asperger syndrome be wrong? The clinical experience of members of our team together with the findings from the research study gave us good reason to question the validity of these criteria. There were two aspects of the criteria in particular that did not seem to fit the clinical picture. The first was the requirement for normal cognitive development and lack of developmental delay. This means that the child is required to have normal cognitive functioning currently and should not have had any delays in the acquisition of single words or phrases nor any delays in their self-help and adaptive skills. The second was the absence of any criteria requiring impairment in current speech and language suggesting that the child might have no abnormalities in their use of communication or language. Neither of these requirements seems to fit Asperger's original descriptions.

Asperger ([1944] 1991) himself did not lay down diagnostic criteria but amongst his descriptions he did describe a range of abnormalities of language including odd intonation, inappropriate use of speech and pronoun reversal. Also in two case histories he described children who were delayed in starting to speak. Although he described their high intelligence, he noted that this clinical picture could be found in those with poor ability, even in children with severe mental retardation. The official DSM/ICD criteria therefore seemed to be describing a different sub-group than the group that Asperger originally described.

We wondered, as did other researchers at the time, what would happen if the official criteria for DSM-IV and ICD-10 were to be literally applied? How many cases of Asperger syndrome would we expect to see amongst children referred to clinicians with suspected autistic spectrum disorders if these official criteria were used? We attempted to answer this question in our next study (Leekam *et al.* 2000a). We started out on this study in the mid-1990s when the specific ICD-10 and DSM-IV criteria for Asperger syndrome were still new and just beginning to be adopted by clinicians. We wanted to know how useful these precise criteria would actually be if applied in the way that was intended by these international classification systems. As ICD-10 and DSM-IV criteria are similar, the criteria we worked with for this study were the ICD-10 diagnostic criteria for research (World Health Organization 1993).

The study had another aim. This was to compare the diagnostic criteria of ICD-10 with a different set of criteria proposed by Gillberg (1991) that more closely resembled Asperger's own descriptions. Although other criteria for Asperger syndrome also existed at this time (Tantam 1988; Szatmari, Brenner and Nagy 1989), we chose the Gillberg criteria because these criteria included all the behavioural features covered by two other systems and because the only prevalence study at the time had used Gillberg's criteria (Ehlers and Gillberg 1993). A few adaptations were made to the Gillberg criteria in order to fit them more closely with Aperger's own original descriptions.

The adapted Gillberg criteria differed from the ICD-10 criteria in two important ways. The first concerned the ICD-10 requirement for lack of developmental delay. The adapted Gillberg criteria did not include this requirement. This meant that unlike ICD-10, Gillberg's Asperger syndrome could be diagnosed even in cases where an individual had early language delay or had language levels below their chronological age or had a low IQ.

The second difference between the ICD-10 criteria and Gillberg's criteria relates to the current speech and language behaviour. For ICD-10, the diagnostic criteria for Asperger syndrome includes no criterion for language and communication deficits. In contrast, Gillberg's criteria for Asperger syndrome includes a category specifically devoted to abnormalities of speech and language. This category includes the following items – lack of appreciation of humour, interprets language literally, non-reciprocal communication, long-winded speech, odd tone of voice and uses different voices for no reason. To obtain a diagnosis of Asperger syndrome according to the Gillberg criteria you must have at least three of these impairments in speech and language.

Gillberg's criteria, then, rely on current behaviours rather than on developmental or ability variables. The criteria consist of six categories of impairment. These include speech and language peculiarities (described above), social interaction (odd quality of social interaction, lack of empathy, poor peer interaction, inappropriate behaviour in public), narrow interests (limited pattern of activities, repetitive routines, collects facts), repetitive routines (rituals, talks repetitively), non-verbal communication problems (body language, facial expression, staring) and motor clumsiness (gross gait, games, hand–eye, head bowed, fine motor). The Gillberg criteria therefore include more numerous criteria for current behaviour overall as well as more specific criteria that can identify problems such as motor clumsiness.

For this study, the clinicians L. Wing and J. Gould obtained detailed information from parents or other carers over a four-year period as part of their assessment process at the National Autistic Society's Centre for Social and Communication Disorders. Almost all of the referrals to this Centre have disorders in the autistic spectrum. Information was collected using the Diagnostic Interview for Social and Communication Disorders (the DISCO), a semi-structured interview schedule that elicits information on more than 300 aspects of development and behaviour. The DISCO has been designed to include a set of algorithms or rules that correspond with specific diagnostic categories. These include the diagnostic criteria for pervasive developmental disorders and their sub-groupings according to DSM-III-R, DSM-IV (American Psychiatric Association 1994) and ICD-10 (World Health Organization 1993) as well as Gillberg's criteria for Asperger syndrome (Ehlers and Gillberg 1993), in addition to the criteria for other diagnostic systems such as Kanner's (Kanner and Eisenberg 1956) and Wing and Gould's (1979) criteria. The reliability of the DISCO has been established (Wing *et al.* 2002) and its algorithms have been reported (Leekam *et al.* 2002).

The sample for this study consisted of 200 children and adults aged 32 months to 38 years. The complete DISCO interview was carried out, enabling information to be extracted that fitted the criteria for ICD-10 subgroups of both childhood autism and Asperger syndrome as well as Gillberg's Asperger syndrome. Information about lack of developmental delay, a requirement for the ICD-10 diagnosis, was obtained from the DISCO items relating to toileting, self-feeding, dressing, washing, independence and response to instructions. In addition, formal psychological assessments were carried out to collect information about current IQ level and language ability.

The first question we were interested in was how many individuals would qualify for a diagnosis of Asperger's syndrome when the ICD-10 criteria for Asperger syndrome were applied to each case. We found only three individuals who fitted the ICD-10 criteria exactly. However, not only did these individuals meet ICD-10 criteria for Asperger syndrome, they also met the criteria for either childhood autism or atypical autism. This finding appeared to justify our concerns about the official ICD-10 criteria for Asperger syndrome. This finding also supported our earlier finding that language delay does not predict different subgroups of current clinical behaviours. These findings support Szatmari's conclusion that obtaining an Asperger syndrome diagnosis as defined by the official international classifications systems is 'virtually impossible' (Szatmari *et al.* 1995, p.1669).

Our second aim was to compare ICD-10 and Gillberg's criteria for Asperger syndrome. We found that in contrast to the strict criteria for ICD, Gillberg's criteria identified 45.5 per cent of our population of 200 participants with Asperger syndrome. This is a comparable percentage to that found by other research studies (Ehlers *et al.*

1997). Although ability level was not itself included with the criteria, Gillberg's criteria selected a group that tended to have better language and more intellectual interests. Nearly two-thirds of individuals with the Gillberg diagnosis had current cognitive and language levels in the age-appropriate range. However, high ability and normal development was by no means the only profile to be found. Half of the individuals had language delays in childhood, one-third had language levels below their chronological age and a quarter had low IQ.

Examination of the current behavioural items used in the Gillberg diagnosis revealed that four of the categories – repetitive behaviour, speech and language, non-verbal communication and motor clumsiness – discriminated the Asperger group from the rest of the sample, while two, social impairment and narrow interests, did not. The reason for this was that the incidence of these criteria was already very high in the non-Asperger group (92 per cent and 94 per cent respectively). It should be noted that all the other Gillberg criteria were also commonly found in many of the individuals who were not diagnosed with Gillberg's Asperger syndrome. As many as 80 per cent of the group who did not qualify for a Gillberg Asperger diagnosis also had motor clumsiness and 83 per cent had odd or absent non-verbal communication.

To summarize, we found only three individuals in our large group of 200 individuals with autistic spectrum disorders who could be diagnosed with Asperger syndrome using ICD-10 criteria. So ICD-10 may create a subgroup but it is not a very helpful one. Indeed Eisenmajer *et al.* (1996) suggest that clinicians are not even using ICD criteria but instead are diagnosing Asperger syndrome on the basis of research and case studies. Given the inadequacy of the current diagnostic criteria to meaningfully identify Asperger syndrome and the growing view that high-functioning autism and Asperger syndrome are the same thing, Mayes and Calhoun (2003) recommend that the current version of DSM-IV criteria for Asperger syndrome should be deleted. Our results suggest that the same should apply for ICD-10.

How then should we describe the behavioural and developmental profiles of individuals with Asperger syndrome? If we apply Gillberg's criteria in contrast with the ICD-10 criteria a clearer pattern of behaviours is identified that more closely fit Asperger's original description. The most common picture is of an intellectually able individual with repetitive routines, peculiarities in speech and language, odd, one-sided non-verbal communication and motor clumsiness. Again, this pattern indicates a mildness of degree of impairment rather than any distinct behavioural profile. Furthermore, this pattern may belong to the majority but it by no means fits all.

What does seem clear from the results of both of our studies is that early developmental history in terms of language delay and early adaptive skills cannot differentiate children with Asperger syndrome from other children with autistic spectrum disorders. While this discredits the ICD-10 criteria it is also an interesting finding in its own right. In our large sample, we found that between 80 and 90 per cent of all individuals with ASD had delays in adaptive functioning skills such as self-help, curiosity, fetching and carrying and 60 per cent had delays in language. What is remarkable is that delays in self-help and adaptive skills and in language acquisition are so prevalent even in children with fluent language and high ability. This lack of motivation to carry out self-care skills that other people will do for you and the lack of curiosity in a wider sense may be an important part of the developmental picture for children with autistic spectrum disorders. These kinds of problem may also be some of the most difficult to change as Howlin (2000) notes in her follow-up study on the outcomes of older individuals with autism.

SUBGROUPINGS BASED ON CURRENT LANGUAGE, COGNITIVE AND BEHAVIOURAL PROFILES

Both of the studies described above suggest that when you find differences between subgroups within the autistic spectrum that these are best characterized by differences in degree of current behaviour. Our two studies as well as other research studies (see Mayes and Calhoun 2003 for review) also suggest that it is not a successful strategy to subdivide groupings on the basis of early developmental variables such as language delay or early adaptive function. Groupings are not clearly distinguished on that basis. Instead, both of the studies described above and in other research have shown that behavioural groupings are best distinguished on the basis of current verbal and cognitive profiles.

Although the picture emerging from recent research is that degree of severity in terms of current behavioural features and ability level (current language and cognitive function) provides the best discriminators of subgroupings, nevertheless, even this criterion does not always apply. In our study using Gillberg's criteria for Asperger syndrome, for example, we found that 20 per cent of individuals fitting the description for Asperger syndrome had IQs below 70 and 36 per cent had language below the level of their chronological age. Frith (2004) in tackling the question of what criterion should be used to separate Asperger syndrome from autism confirms the view that mildness of symptoms and ability level are not *sufficient* factors on which to separate Asperger syndrome from autism. This point is confirmed by some of the cases that Asperger himself described and by the findings of our studies reported above. In these studies we see that some individuals have learning disabilities combined with milder symptoms, while there are others who have high ability and more extreme symptoms. Therefore, although the subtyping of children with autism according to mildness of their symptoms and ability level might provide a guide for the clinician, the application of hard and fast categorization rules based on these factors will always be imprecise.

Given the difficulty that has plagued previous research attempts to identify distinct subgroupings and the conclusion that a spectrum concept best characterizes these disorders, is there any point in continuing to look for more precise criteria on which to subcategorize children within autistic spectrum? Surprisingly, despite the concerns surrounding previous research, many still argue strongly for the need to identify subtypes. What distinguishes these more recent research studies, however, is the attempt to break out of the circularity of attempting to describe existing subgroupings on the basis of the symptoms or ability factors that are already part of the diagnosis. These new approaches to subtyping involve research with children who have diagnoses across the autistic spectrum. The research investigations then look at patterns of behaviour and/or neuropsychological tests that are not part of the standard diagnostic picture and attempt to link them to specific patterns of neuropathology and/or to clinical characterististics of other disorders.

The case for subtyping is summarized by Szatmari (1999) and Rutter (2000). These authors argue that identifying subtypes is important in order for progress to be made in our understanding of the genetics of autism and underlying patterns of neuropathology. Tager-Flusberg and Joseph's (2003) work for example aims to focus on aspects such as language difficulties that are not identifying features for the disorders. They then connect these aspects to patterns of brain structure or genetic markers that are found not only in autism but also in other language disorders.

In one study, Kjelgaard and Tager-Flusberg (2001) took children who had a range of autistic spectrum disorders (ASDs). They looked at their language profiles using a battery of language tests that measure a range of different skills and then used MRI scanning to detect brain activation differences that might be related to these profiles. To conduct this study they first tested the children across a range of language functions. This resulted in three subgroups that had different levels of overall language ability – normal, borderline and impaired. They then tested these groups on a marker test for specific language impairment (SLI), a phonological skills task that involved assessing their ability to process language sounds. This task has not previously been linked to problems in autism. However, the authors found that this test distinguished between children with ASD who had normal language from those with impaired or borderline language. They also found that children with impaired language were poor on past tense markers (grammatical errors). This detailed examination of the language profiles therefore provided evidence to support the case that autism and SLI are overlapping disorders.

To complete their study of these subgroups, Kjelgaard and Tager-Flusberg (2001) then asked whether children with ASD and language impairment showed the same atypical brain structure as seen in children with SLI. In fact as predicted, they did find reversed asymmetry in the frontal language area, a similar finding to that found in SLI. Tager-Flusberg and Joseph (2003) suggest that dividing groups on the basis of language may also be useful for identifying genes associated with autism in cases where autism is either associated or not associated with SLI.

The usefulness of dividing groups on the basis of current language ability has also been proposed by Reitzel and Szatmari (2003). Szatmari makes the interesting claim that the traditional distinction between autism and Asperger syndrome could be turned on its head if we consider language impairment to be separately associated with each group. He argues that, instead of Asperger syndrome being thought of as a variant of autism, on the contrary, autism should be thought of as a variant of Asperger syndrome in which children have autistic spectrum disorder together with an additional handicap of SLI. These children frequently also have mental retardation in addition to the pragmatic language problems found in Asperger syndrome. This simple distinction may not provide a precise conceptualization but it offers an important new way of thinking about the problems experienced by children with autism. It is also in line with recent changes of thinking about the similarities in language impairment across different clinical groups (Bates 2004).

So far, I have outlined a proposal for subtyping on the basis of language impairment. Is there also a case for subtyping on the basis of non-verbal ability also? Recently, Joseph, Tager-Flusberg and Lord (2002) have subgrouped children in terms of their relative rather than absolute differences in both verbal and non-verbal ability. Traditionally it has long been claimed that people with autism have a standard psychological profile in autism in which non-verbal ability is higher than verbal ability. Subsequent researchers including Tager-Flusberg and Joseph have refuted this standard picture. Instead they have shown that when children are tested on standard psychological tests, some have a profile in which non-verbal ability is better than verbal ability, others have a profile of verbal ability greater than non-verbal ability and some show equal ability on verbal and non-verbal tests. Tager-Flusberg and Joseph have then explored the link between these three profiles in the light of both behavioural symptoms and neural pathology. In terms of the link between cognitive profile and symptoms, they found that individuals with discrepantly high non-verbal IQ (NVIQ), relative to verbal IQ scores, have more impairments in reciprocal social interaction than would be expected on the basis of their absolute level of ability and their level of language skills.

Following this finding, the authors considered the possible neuropathology that might be related to this unbalanced pattern of high NVIQ, low language and poor reciprocal interaction. One proposal they make follows the developmental explanation that this pattern of functioning could be the outcome of a different pattern of neurocognitive development early in life. The suggestion is that isolated visuo-perceptual strengths may be related to increased neuronal growth or reduced connectivity in the brain. One way of testing this would be to look at head and brain size. Tager-Flusberg and Joseph examined head circumference and brain volume and found that the group with discrepantly high NVIQ relative to verbal IQ had enlarged brain volume in addition to enlarged head circumference.

Non-verbal IQ is a very general basis on which to subtype children. Should the basis for subtyping go beyond general cognitive factors such as non-verbal IQ and include more specific cognitive variables? Frith (2004) agued for two specific cognitive candidates, mentalizing difficulties and weak central coherence indicated by lack of top-down cognitive control. The case of mentalizing ability, discussed earlier, has been used to trace impairments in brain functioning. For example, a recent study by Castelli *et al.* 2002) used tests of theory of mind to demonstrate reduced activation in parts of the brain considered to be the 'social brain' in ten individuals with autism.

While links between neural pathology and specific cognitive function are certainly suggested by these studies, whether they will provide good candidates for subtyping remains to be tested. What is not clear is whether any subtyping relating to mentalizing ability would be independent or tied to subtyping based on language ability. One of the most exciting challenges that lies ahead is the task of disentangling the nature of the causal relation between theory of mind, language and social communicative symptoms of autism. We know that language is an important mediator for symptoms of autism including social interaction. We also know that mentalizing ability is related to verbal ability (de Villiers 2000). Further developmental research following the transactional approach of Mundy and Neal (2001) is needed to trace the links between symptoms, theory of mind and language and their neuropathological origins.

Finally, could subtyping of the autistic spectrum rely on specific behavioural rather than cognitive or neural markers? Recently our own research has focused on specific behavioural symptoms that are not part of required criteria for autism but like the impairments in language are showing themselves to be strongly associated with a pro-portion of high-functioning individuals on the autistic spectrum. It is expected that these aspects of impairment will also show neuropathological markers, although research on this is yet to be conducted.

One pervasive problem is the difficulty with sensory responsiveness. Several studies show that this might form a potential marker for the social and communication problems in autism warranting further investigation along the lines taken by Tager-Flusberg and Joseph by looking at the patterns of dysfunction associated with this problem. In the first study of high-functioning children, described earlier in this paper (Prior *et al.* 1998), we found three different empirically derived subgroupings when we put children's diagnostic features into a cluster analysis. Clusters A and B differed from Cluster C by being more likely to have unusual sensory responses. Clusters A and B, however, differed from each other to some extent by their degree and awareness of social interactional problems. This finding suggests that meaningful subgroups might be based on the combination of sensory and social interactional features.

In a new study with colleague Carmen Nieto from Spain (Leekam *et al.* in press), we have been able to make a more detailed description of both the behavioural and the developmental characteristics that are associated with these sensory impairments. First, we collected details from parents using the Diagnostic Interview of Social and Commu-nication Disorders (Wing *et al.* 2002; Leekam *et al.* 2002). Details were collected of abnormalities in three domains of sensory abnormalities: proximal abnormalities (including a range of different tactile and olfactory behaviours), auditory abnormalities (including unusual responses to or fascination with particular sounds) and visual abnor-malities (including unusual attention to specific aspects of visual stimuli such as their brightness or movement). To test the degree to which sensory abnormalities might be related to language problems and ability levels we included comparison groups that had typical development, a group that had mental retardation and a group that had language impairments but no mental retardation.

The results showed that children with autism had significantly more sensory abnormalities than all these comparison groups. A particularly marked contrast was found between the high-functioning children with ASD on the one hand and children with only language impairment (SLI) or the typical development group. Approximately 85 per cent of children with autism had sensory abnormalities regardless of whether their IQ was above or below 70. Another finding was that these ASD children were more likely to have multi-modal abnormalities. That is, they were likely to have abnormalities in more than one sensory domain while comparison groups of learning disability or language impairment did not. Amongst the autism group, by far the most common abnormality was the proximal class.

Having established that a large proportion of autistic individuals have sensory abnormalities and that these abnormalities differ from comparison children and are found across several different modalities, we carried out another study with a larger sample of 200 individuals with a range of impairments across the autistic spectrum. We found that sensory abnormalities persist across age and IQ. Of the three main categories outlined above (proximal, auditory and visual) only the visual category showed significant reduction in symptoms with age and IQ. Unusual visual responses were more frequent in younger children with lower IQ than in older and more able individuals. In future research we plan to study the behavioural, cognitive and physiological profiles of children with and without sensory abnormalities in different modalities. These profiles may, like Tager-Flusberg's and Joseph (2003) research, provide an interesting comparison with the profiles of children from other atypical groups such as children with visual or hearing impairment.

Another problem that provides a potential behavioural subgroup within the spectrum of autistic disorders is the occurrence of disorders of posture and movement in the autistic spectrum (Wing and Shah 2000). As Wing (2005) reports, these catatonic features affect approximately 10 per cent of adolescents and adults with autistic spectrum disorders. Like the sensory difficulties, this problem is not only found in people with low ability. 'Autistic catatonia' (Hare and Malone 2004) may therefore provide a meaningful subgroup within the autistic spectrum.

To summarize, research to date has shown that there is no consistent profile in which individuals with Asperger syndrome have either higher verbal ability, poorer non-verbal ability or more motor problems than individuals with autism. As Frith (2004) points out in her review of the literature, genetic studies point to the same aetiology for both groups and neuroanatomical studies also show certain features of brain pathology that are present regardless of IQ. Given the common basis at both the biological and behavioural level for an autistic spectrum, the notion of differentiating subgroups of Asperger syndrome and autism according to the international classifica-tion systems is unjustified. However, many researchers consider that other distinctions are helpful. For example, recent attempts to subdivide the autistic spectrum according to neurocognitive profiles help to narrow down the definition of the phenotype, providing implications for future genetic and neurobiological research. These studies are provid-ing insights into overlaps between clinical groups outside of autism and challenging previous assumptions about the separateness of different disorders. Finally, new work on symptoms that co-occur with diagnostic symptoms points to the possibility of behavioural subgrouping that may be more valuable than previous distinctions between Asperger syndrome and autism in helping us to understand patterns of association and risk factors for autism.

DEVELOPMENTAL QUESTIONS ABOUT AUTISTIC SPECTRUM DISORDERS

As discussed above, although research findings over the last ten years have undermined the idea of distinct diagnostic subgroups based on ICD-10 and DSM-IV criteria, new attempts are being made to identify subgroupings using language, cognitive and behav-ioural factors that are not part of the essential diagnostic picture. These studies may help us to understand better the conditions under which certain behavioural profiles might overlap with other disorders and/or be associated with biological markers. However, many of the distinctions used for subgrouping are based on the child's *current* profile of functioning. What about early development factors? Surely if we are interested in understanding how autism emerges and what the potential is for improvement, we need to understand better how these behavioural profiles change over time.

Given that developmental considerations have been strongly highlighted in the clinical literature (Wing 1996), it is surprising that little research attention has been paid to this dimension, especially as there seem to be so many important developmental questions to answer. For example, why is it that two individuals may start off with very impaired early development, for example with delays in language and adaptive skills, but then one child will improve and show few related difficulties later in childhood while the other will not? Or why is it that, for some children, problems do not appear to be apparent early in development but then appear later leading to a late diagnosis? Could there have been some subtle problems in early development that were missed by parents?

The focus on these kinds of developmental questions is now gaining momentum (e.g. Charman *et al.* 2001; Mundy and Neal 2001) but theoretical and methodological approaches still tend to be rooted within non-developmental traditions. These tradi-tions tend to focus on trying to uncover common underlying factors that may explain the cause of autism. Attention to developmental issues is still underrepresented compared to the study of other developmental disorders such as SLI or Williams syndrome (Bishop 1997; Karmiloff-Smith 1998). There may be many reasons for this.

One reason may be that some of the research investigating developmental outcomes in autism tends to focus on stability in outcome rather than change, although there are exceptions to this (Piven *et al.* 1996). In addition, a good proportion of previous research on outcomes has focused on 'core' autism rather than the broader autistic spectrum. Once the focus on the discrimination between autism and Asperger syndrome was no longer important, the concern has been with the broader autistic spectrum, and perhaps there should be renewed interest in the conditions under which change does or does not occur.

One of the puzzling findings that emerges from this research is that about early developmental delay. Our research findings and those of others show that when you compare the groups who do have language delay and those who do not, you do not see any differences in these two groups in terms of their autistic behaviours when they are older. These findings are supported by longitudinal research by Szatmari *et al.* (2000). Szatmari *et al.* found that delayed language onset did not predict later language outcomes but a language score a few years later did predict subsequent language outcome. Reitzel and Szatmari (2003) propose an important developmental explanation for these findings. They argue that, until the age of three years, children with autistic spectrum disorders are not easily differentiated from each other. Once some children start to develop speech in two to three word phrases after the age of three, however, they are able to use this as an opportunity to acquire better social and communication skills and academic skills. Even children who develop this ability after three years can still take advantage of what these newly acquired language skills have to offer later on.

Could this also help to account for an unusual finding by Eisenmajer *et al.* (1998)? Richard Eisenmajer followed up the cluster analysis study described earlier and divided the children into two groups, according to whether they had language delay or did not. He then compared these two groups in terms of whether the language delay group would have a different pattern of autistic symptoms than the normal language onset group. He also looked at other developmental history variables such as delay in reaching motor milestones. There were two main findings. The first was that children who had language delays also had other general developmental delay in achieving their motor milestones and lower receptive language abilities. The second was that language delayed children did not differ in their autistic behaviours from the non-language delayed children except if you took into account the age at which they were diagnosed. The children who had language delay and who were diagnosed earlier (before six years) had more autistic symptoms than the non-language delay group. However, those who had language delay and were also diagnosed at an older age (after six years) showed no difference in behavioural profile to the non-language delay group.

What does this result mean? First, it is important to remember that many children in this large sample (about half of them) had language delay. Second, if we assume that children in the early diagnosis group had more autistic features early in life as well as later, it is likely that problems related to these features combined with their language delay and led them getting their early diagnosis. What kinds of early associated difficulties might put this particular language delay group at greater risk for a poor outcome than the language delay group who were picked up for diagnosis later? From the data we have analysed so far, it is not clear. One would expect that delays in language would be related to other basic delays in developmental milestones such as delayed toileting or self-help skills. However, this is not the case. Our Asperger syndrome study revealed that as many as 80–90 per cent have these kinds of problems. This means that even children without language delay have these kinds of developmental delays.

Another contender for the difference in developmental trajectory for the two language delay groups may be the difference in early non-verbal communication skills, especially in joint attention. Joint attention refers to the ability to coordinate attention between people and objects and is strongly related to language ability in typically developing children. Joint attention ability is also believed to be related to the development of theory of mind. If children do not show these early signs of non-verbal interaction and also have language delay they might be more likely to be referred for an early diagnosis.

Sigman and Ruskin (1999) carried out one of the few longitudinal studies of autism to follow up children's joint attention and other problems. Sigman and Ruskin followed up 51 of 70 children who had been diagnosed at age three to five years. The children were seen eight to nine years after their original diagnosis. Sigman and Ruskin predicted that children who showed more joint attention and symbolic play would make greater gains in language. This is what they found. Long term gains in language were predicted by responsiveness of others' bid for joint attention and by play. Joint attention ability was also related to changes in IQ amongst a subset who moved across the borderline from mental retardation to non-mental retardation. The authors found that individual differences in joint attention and play and emotional responsiveness have consequences for later development. If more non-verbal communication is shown early in development then more language is also shown later in development. Even more specifically, if the child is able to follow gaze early then they will make more long-term gains in language. Interestingly the impact of joint attention on later development is independent of early intelligence though this clearly helps. Early joint attention also predicts greater social engagement with peers.

We have also been carrying out a series of studies on joint attention in children with autism. Our early work took children of different ages and verbal abilities and we tested gaze-following experimentally and observationally. We found very strong developmental effects that were related to verbal mental age (Leekam, Hunnisett and Moore 1998). Subsequently we worked with preschool children and again found that the problem was largely confined to the children with greatest cognitive and language delay – when compared with non-autistic developmentally delayed children their problems were extremely marked (Leekam *et al.* 2000b). Our most recent research shows that even when you take an extremely basic element of social interaction – social orienting in response to name call – this is highly associated with language ability (Leekam and Ramsden 2006). Furthermore, this association is more strongly associated in the autism group than in the non-autism group.

It is difficult to explain in a simple way the different developmental trajectories that might appear as a consequence of early delays and difficulties. One idea we are working on relates to the bi-directionality of language and joint attention development (Leekam 2005). This proposal is that as language improves, children can use it to build their non-verbal skills. Another idea is that there is a dynamic relationship between sensory experience and social interaction. We suggest that early sensory difficulties may restrict opportunities for the infant to develop both social and sensory responsiveness. For example a restricted response when hearing a voice does not facilitate the infant to come into visual contact with that person which further restricts the opportunity for further engagement and thereby does not provide further sensation that is socially modulated (Leekam and Wyver 2004). This explanation might help to account for common patterns of associated impairments in sensory responsiveness, social impairments and adaptive self-directed behaviour.

To summarize, the answers to many developmental questions only become possible when we start to move away from the focus on prescribed subgroups and think about development. One question that still requires an answer is why one child with developmental delay goes on to develop more severe autistic impairments while another does not. Future longitudinal studies that trace developmental changes in infants with language and other developmental delays may help to identify the risk factors and critical points of timing that lead children towards different outcomes.

CONCLUSION

My research story started with a visit to a child psychiatrist 20 years ago. Progress in understanding Asperger syndrome has come a long way since then. Public recognition of Asperger syndrome has promoted awareness of the broader concept of a spectrum of disorders, with milder edges forming a continuum with normal functioning. This concept of an autistic spectrum (Wing 1996) has helped to change our thinking because it challenges the idea about rigid categories that separate distinct psychological conditions, influencing the way that other conditions are thought about, for example forms of specific language impairment and attention deficit disorder. In terms of education and management, this awareness of milder forms of autism has also led to greater understanding and support for people like Ivan that would not have been possible years ago.

Looking back over the years, Ivan had so many unmistakeable behavioural features of autism that, despite his good language, it is inconceivable that his diagnosis would have been missed if he were a young child today. Yet even now, many children who come to receive a diagnosis of Asperger syndrome still do not have their condition recognized until later in childhood or even adulthood. This is ironic because these are the children who may have the greatest prospects for learning and improvement. It is to be hoped that acceptance of the broader concept of the autistic spectrum, together with an increased focus on developmental issues, may enable us not only to identify these children better but also to assist more effectively in their potential for development.

REFERENCES

American Psychiatric Association (1994) *Diagnostic and Statistical Manual of Mental Disorders* (4th edn) (DSM-IV). Washington, DC: APA.

Asperger, H. [1944] (1991) 'Autistic psychopathy in childhood.' Translated and annotated by U. Frith (ed.). *Autism and Asperger Syndrome*. New York: Cambridge University Press.

Baron-Cohen, S. (1995) *Mindblindness: An Essay on Autism and Theory of Mind*. Cambridge, MA: MIT Press.

Baron-Cohen, S., Leslie, A. and Frith, U. (1985) 'Does the autistic child have a "theory of mind"?' *Cognition 21*, 37–46.

Baron-Cohen, S., Tager-Flusberg, H. and Cohen, D. (eds) (2000) *Understanding Other Minds: Perspectives from Developmental Cognitive Neuroscience*. Oxford: Oxford University Press.

Bates, E. (2004) 'Explaining and interpreting deficits in language development across clinical groups: where do we go from here?' *Brain and Language 88*, 248–253.

Bishop, D. V. M. (1997) *Uncommon Understanding: Development and Disorders of Language Comprehension*. Hove, UK: Psychology Press.

Castelli, F., Frith, C. D., Happé, F. and Frith, U. (2002) 'Autism, Asperger syndrome and brain mechanisms for the attribution of animated shapes.' *Brain 125*, 1839–1849.

Charman, T., Burack, J., Yirimaya, N. and Zelazo, P. R. (eds) (2001) *Development and Autism: Perspectives from Theory and Research*. Mahwah, NJ: Lawrence Erlbaum Associates.

de Villiers, J. (2000) 'Language and theory of mind: what are the developmental relationships?' In S. Baron-Cohen, H. Tager-Flusberg and D. Cohen (eds) *Understanding Other Minds: Perspectives from Developmental Cognitive Neuroscience*. Oxford: Oxford University Press.

Ehlers, S. and Gillberg, C. (1993) 'The epidemiology of Asperger syndrome.' *Journal of Child Psychology and Psychiatry 34*, 1327–1350.

Ehlers, S., Nyden, A., Gillberg, C., Dahlgren-Sandberg, A., Dahlgren, S. O., Hjelmquist, E. and Oden, A. (1997) 'Asperger syndrome, autism and attention disorder: a comparative study of the cognitive profiles of 120 children.' *Journal of Child Psychology and Psychiatry 38*, 207–217.

Eisenmajer, R., Prior, M., Leekam, S., Wing, L., Gould, J., Welham, M. and Ong, B. (1996) 'Comparison of clinical symptoms in autism and Asperger's Disorder.' *Journal of American Academy of Child and Adolescent Psychiatry 35*, 11, 1523–1531.

Eisenmajer, R., Prior, M., Leekam, S., Wing, L., Ong, B., Gould, J. and Welham, D. (1998) 'Delayed language onset as a predictor of clinical symptoms in pervasive developmental disorders.' *Journal of Autism and Developmental Disorders 28*, 6, 527–534.

Frith, U. (1989) *Autism: Explaining the Enigma*. Oxford: Blackwell.

Frith, U. (2004) 'Emanuel Miller lecture: confusions and controversies about Asperger syndrome.' *Journal of Child Psychology and Psychiatry 45*, 4, 627–686.

Garfield, J. L., Peterson, C. C. and Perry, T. (2001) 'Social cognition, language acquisition and the development of theory of mind.' *Mind and Language 16*, 5, 494–541.

Gillberg, C. (1991) 'Clinical and neurobiological aspects of Asperger syndrome in six family studies.' In U. Frith (ed.) *Autism and Asperger Syndrome*. New York: Cambridge University Press.

Hare, J. D. and Malone, C. (2004) 'Catatonia and autistic spectrum disorders.' *Autism 8*, 183–196.

Howlin, P. (2000) 'Outcome in adult life for more able individuals with autism or Asperger syndrome.' *Autism 4*, 1, 63–68.

Joseph, R. M., Tager-Flusberg, H. and Lord, C. (2002) 'Cognitive profiles and social-communicative functioning in language and learning impaired children.' *Journal of Child Psychology and Psychiatry 6*, 807–881.

Kanner, L. and Eisenberg, L. (1956) 'Early infantile autism.' *American Journal of Orthopsychiatry 26*, 55–65.

Karmiloff-Smith, A. (1998) 'Development itself is the key to understanding developmental disorders.' *Trends in Cognitive Science 2*, 389–398.

Kjelgaard, M. and Tager-Flusberg, H. (2001) 'An investigation of language impairment in autism: implications for genetic subgroups.' *Language and Cognitive Processes 16*, 287–308.

Leekam, S. R. (2005) 'Why do children with autism have a joint attention impairment?' In N. Eilan, C. Hoerl, T. McCormack and J. Roessler (eds) *Joint Attention: Communication and Other Minds.* Oxford: Oxford University Press.

Leekam, S. R. and Ramsden, C. A. H. (2006) 'Dyadic orienting and joint attention in preschool children with autism'. *Journal of Autism and Developmental Disorders.* http://springerlink.metapress.com

Leekam, S. R. and Wyver, S. (2004) 'Beyond "modularity" and innateness: sensory experience, social interaction and symbolic development in children with autism and blindness.' In L. Pring (ed.) *Autism and Blindness.* London: Whurr Publishers.

Leekam, S. R., Hunnisett, E. and Moore, C. (1998) 'Targets and cues: gaze following in children with autism.' *Journal of Child Psychology and Psychiatry 39*, 7, 951–962.

Leekam, S. R., Libby, S., Wing, L., Gould, J. and Gillberg, C. (2000a) 'Comparison of ICD-10 and Gillberg criteria for Asperger syndrome.' *Autism 4*, 1, 11–28.

Leekam, S. R., Lopez, B. and Moore, C. (2000b) 'Attention and joint attention in preschool children with autism.' *Developmental Psychology 36*, 2, 261–273.

Leekam, S. R., Nieto, C., Wing, L., Gould, J. and Libby, S. (in press) 'Describing the sensory abnormalities of children and adults with autism.' *Journal of Autism and Developmental Disorders.*

Leslie, A. (1987) 'Pretense and representation: the origins of "theory of mind".' *Psychological Review 94*, 412–426.

Mayes, S. D. and Calhoun, S. L. (2003) 'Relationship between Asperger syndrome and high functioning autism.' In M. Prior (ed.) *Learning and Behavior Problems in Asperger Syndrome.* New York: Guilford Press.

Mundy, P. and Neal, R. (2001) 'Neural plasticity, joint attention and a transactional social-orienting model of autism.' *International Review of Research in Mental Retardation 23*, 139–168.

Piven, J., Harper, J., Palmer, P. and Arndt, S. (1996) 'Course of behavioural change in autism: a retrospective study of high-IQ adolescents and adults.' *Journal of the American Academy of Child Adolescent Psychiatry 35*, 4, 523–529.

Prior, M. (2003) 'What do we know and where should we go?' In M. Prior (ed.) *Learning and Behavior Problems in Asperger Syndrome.* New York: Guilford Press.

Prior, M., Eisenmajer, R., Leekam, S., Wing, L., Gould, J. and Ong, B. (1998) 'Are there subgroups within the autistic spectrum? A cluster analysis of a group of children with autistic spectrum disorders.' *Journal of Child Psychology and Psychiatry 39*, 6, 893–902.

Rapin, I. (1996) 'Preschool children with inadequate communication: developmental language disorders, autism or low IQ.' *Clinics in Developmental Medicine*, No. 139. London: MacKeith Press.

Reitzel, J-A. and Szatmari, P. (2003) 'Cognitive and academic problems.' In M. Prior (ed.) *Learning and Behavior Problems in Asperger Syndrome.* New York: Guilford Press.

Rutter, M. (2000) 'Genetic studies of autism: from the 1970s into the millennium.' *Journal of Abnormal Child Psychology 28*, 3–14.

Sigman, M. and Ruskin, E. (1999) 'Continuity and change in the social competence of children with autism, Down syndrome, and developmental delay.' *Monographs of the Society for Research in Child Development 64*, 1, 256.

Szatmari, P. (1999) 'Heterogeneity and the genetics of autism.' *Journal of Psychiatric Neuroscience 24*, 159–165.

Szatmari, P., Brenner, R. and Nagy, J. (1989) 'Asperger syndrome: a review of clinical features.' *Canadian Journal of Psychiatry 34*, 554–560.

Szatmari, P., Archer, L., Fisman, S., Streiner, D. L. and Wilson, F. (1995) 'Asperger's syndrome and autism: differences in behaviour, cognition and adaptive functioning.' *Journal of American Academy of Child and Adolescent Psychiatry 34*, 1662–1671.

Szatmari, P., Bryson, S., Streiner, D., Wilson, L. and Ryerse, C. (2000) 'Two-year outcome of preschool children with autism and Asperger's syndrome.' *Americal Journal of Psychiatry 157*, 1980–1987.

Tager-Flusberg, H. and Joseph, R. M. (2003) 'Identifying neurocognitive phenotypes in autism.' *Transactions of the Royal Philosophical Society. London B*, 303–314.

Tantam, D. (1988) 'Asperger's syndrome.' *Journal of Child Psychology and Psychiatry 29*, 245–255.

Wing, L. (1981) 'Asperger's syndrome: a clinical account.' *Psychological Medicine 11*, 115–129.

Wing, L. (1988) 'The continuum of autistic characteristics.' In E. Schopler and G. Mesibov (eds) *Diagnosis and Assessment in Autism*. New York: Plenum Press.

Wing, L. (1991) 'The relationship between Asperger's syndrome and Kanner's autism.' In U. Frith (ed.) *Autism and Asperger Syndrome*. Cambridge: Cambridge University Press.

Wing, L. (1996) *The Autistic Spectrum*. London: Constable.

Wing, L. (2005) 'Reflections on opening Pandora's box.' *Journal of Autism and Developmental Disorders 35*, 2, 197–203.

Wing, L. and Gould, J. (1979) 'Severe impairments of social interaction and associated abnormalities in children: epidemiology and classification.' *Journal of Autism and Developmental Disorders 9*, 11–29.

Wing, L. and Shah, A. (2000) 'Catatonia in autistic spectrum disorders.' *British Journal of Psychiatry 176*, 357–362.

Wing, L., Leekam, S. R., Libby, S. J., Gould, J. and Larcombe, M. (2002) 'The Diagnostic Interview for Social and Communication Disorders: background, inter-rate reliability and clinical use.' *Journal of Child Psychology and Psychiatry 43*, 307–325.

World Health Organization (1993) *The ICD-10 Classification of Mental and Behavioral Disorders: Diagnostic Criteria for Research*. Geneva: WHO.

Chapter 11

The Neuroanatomy of the Brain in Autism

Current Thoughts and Future Directions

Margaret L. Bauman and Thomas L. Kemper

Infantile autism is a behaviorally defined disorder, first described by Kanner in 1943. Symptoms classically become apparent prior to three years of age and include impaired social skills, delayed and disordered language, and isolated areas of interest. Poor eye contact, abnormal responses to sensory stimuli, event, and objects, an insistence on sameness, and strong rote memory skills are also characteristic. Physical appearance is usually unremarkable and motor findings, when present, are frequently subtle. Motor milestones are generally achieved on time.

For a period of time, bad parenting and environmental factors were believed to be responsible for having caused the disorder. Gradually, however, with the observation that many of those affected had abnormalities on their electroencephalograms (Small 1975), and a higher than expected incidence of seizures (Deykin and MacMahon 1979), evidence for a neurological cause began to mount. Some of the earliest efforts to address this question utilized neurophysiologic technology, with resulting studies reporting abnormalities of auditory-nerve and brainstem-evoked responses (Student and Schmer 1978; Tanguay *et al.* 1982) and rapid eye movement sleep patterns (Tanguay *et al.* 1976). Although more recent investigations have failed to confirm these original observations (Rumsey *et al.* 1984; Courchesne *et al.* 1985), they nonetheless played an important role in initiating the path toward further neurobiologic research in autism.

Among biological abnormalities so far described in autism, neuroanatomic observations provide some of the strongest evidence. Results from postmortem and imaging studies have implicated the involvement of many major structures of the brain including the limbic system, cerebellum, corpus callosum, basal ganglia, and brainstem. However, many of these findings have been inconsistently reported. Moreover, there is little direct information regarding the neurobiology of the autistic brain during early development since most of the postmortem studies have been limited to investigations involving older children and adults. Nevertheless, available data provides evidence for a prenatal onset of at least some of the neuroanatomic abnormalities so far observed in these brains.

Our understanding of the neuroanatomical substrate of the autistic brain has been compromised largely by the limited availability of suitable autopsy material, technical factors, and the lack of an animal model. One of the first neuropathologic studies of an autistic brain was published by Aarkrog (1968) who described 'slight thickening of the arterioles, slight connective tissue increase in the leptomeninges, and cell increase' in a right frontal lobe biopsy. Some years later, in 1976, Darby published a review of 33 cases of childhood psychosis in which he suggested a relationship between limbic system lesions and the affective features of autism, but no specific pathology was described. Subsequently, in 1980, Williams *et al.* examined autopsy material obtained from four individuals with autistic features, looking primarily for cell loss and gliosis. No consistent abnormalities were observed.

In 1985, observations of the brain of a 29-year-old well-documented man with autism was reported, studied in comparison with an identically processed age and sex-matched control, using the technique of whole brain serial section (Bauman and Kemper 1985). Both brains were examined by means of a comparison microscope, multiple sections being studied side by side in the same field of view. The most significant findings were confined to regions of the limbic system and cerebellar circuits. No abnormalities were found in any regions of the cortex, an observation further supported by a detailed analysis of cortical neuronal and glial cell counts in another autistic brain by Coleman *et al.* (1985) and by repeated surveys of the original and an additional six autistic brains processed in whole brain serial section (Kemper 2004, personal communication). However, in 1998, Bailey *et al.* found neocortical malformations to be a prominent feature in their autopsy material. In four out of their six cases, they found evidence of thickened cortices, areas of increased neuronal density, irregular laminar patterns, increased numbers of neurons in layer I, and abnormally oriented pyramidal cells. More recently, Casanova *et al.* (2002) have reported that, in comparison to controls, the cerebral cortex in the autistic brain demonstrates more numerous minicolumns, and that these minicolumns, as seen in the autistic brains, appear to be smaller and more compact in configuration in the three cortical areas studied. Given these interesting but as yet unreplicated findings, the presence, consistency, and significance of cerebral cortical abnormalities in the autistic brain remains uncertain. How these observational differences relate to the clinical heterogeneity of the subjects studied and to the disorder in general will be an important focus of future research.

Since their initial case report, Bauman and Kemper have studied eight additional clinically well-documented autistic brains using the same methodology of whole brain serial section (1996). None of these cases showed any gross abnormalities and patterns of myelination appeared to be comparable to that of controls. A careful survey through multiple serial cortical sections was likewise unremarkable when compared with controls with the exception of small neuronal cell size and increased cell packing density in the anterior cingulate gyrus in all eight brains, an observation not appreciated in the original case. In addition, a small heterotopic lesion was observed on the infra-orbital region in one hemisphere in one autistic child with a history of a severe seizure disorder, and multiple heterotopic cells were observed in the cerebellar molecular layer in a second autistic child with significant developmental delay (Kemper and Bauman 1998). For the most part, however, no consistent cortical abnormalities were evident in any of these cases.

Areas of the forebrain that have been found to be abnormal have included the hippocampus, subiculum, entorhinal cortex, amygdala, mammillary body, anterior cingulate gyrus, and septum. All of these regions are known to be related to each other by interconnecting circuits and comprise a major portion of the limbic system of the brain. In comparison with controls, these areas showed reduced neuronal cell size and increased cell packing density (increased numbers of neurons per unit volume) bilaterally (Bauman and Kemper 1994). Golgi analysis of CA1 and CA4 pyramidal neurons has shown decreased complexity and extent of dendritic arbors in these cells (Raymond et al. 1996). In the amygdala, the most significant increase in cell packing density was noted in the most medially placed nuclei. With the exception of a single child of normal intelligence but with significant behavioral dysfunction, the lateral nucleus has appeared to be uninvolved.

Small neuronal size and increased cell packing density was also observed in the medial septal nucleus (MSN). However, in the nucleus of the diagonal band of Broca (NDB) of the septum, a different pattern of abnormality was noted. In this nucleus, the neurons were adequate in number but were unusually large in the brains of all of the autistic children less than 13 years of age when compared to controls. In contrast, the cells of the NDB in all of the autistic brains older than 21 years of age were small and pale and markedly decreased in number (Kemper and Bauman 1998). At this time, there is no autopsy material available from autistic adolescents that have been processed in whole brain serial section and, thus, it is unknown when and how rapidly these changes might occur during this period of time.

Outside of the limbic system, the most apparent and consistent abnormalities have been confined to the cerebellum and related inferior olive. All of the autistic brains reported to date, regardless of age, sex, or cognitive abilities, have shown a significant decrease in the number of Purkinje cells, primarily effecting the posterolateral neocerebellar cortex and adjacent archicerebellar cortex of the cerebellar hemispheres (Arin, Bauman and Kemper 1991). Similar anatomic findings have been reported by Ritvo et al. (1986) and more recently by Bailey et al. (1998), thus making the presence of reduced numbers of Purkinje cells the most reproducible pathological observation in the autopsied autistic brain. However, since then, immunocytochemical studies, using calcium-binding proteins, have been conducted in the cerebella of six autistic brains in comparison with four age and sex-matched controls. Although eight of the ten brains studied showed no difference in the numbers of Purkinje cells between Nissl and calcium-binding protein sections, two brains showed significantly lower numbers of Purkinje cells on the Nissl stained sections when compared with calcium-binding sections. This observation raises questions with regard to the quality of previously reported Nissl stained material, and the possible effect of agonal changes and/or post-mortem handling of the brain tissue, at least in some cases (Whitney *et al.*, in preparation). Despite reports of hypo- and hyperplasia of the vermis with magnetic resonance imaging (MRI) (Courchesne, Townsend and Saitoh 1994), we have found no change in Purkinje size or cell number in this cerebellar region (Bauman and Kemper 1996). Reduced numbers of Purkinje cells in the cerebellar hemispheres have been observed in both childhood and adult cases, in individuals with and without a history of seizures or medication usage, and appear to be unrelated to cognitive function. With few exceptions, there has been an absence of glial hyperplasia (Bauman and Kemper 1996; Bailey *et al.* 1998) suggesting that the cerebellar lesions have been acquired early in development. Animal studies have shown a progressively decreasing glial response after cerebellar lesions occurring at increasingly earlier ages (Brodal 1940).

In addition to the presence of reduced numbers of Purkinje cells, abnormalities have also been observed in the fastigeal, globose, and emboliform nuclei in the roof of the cerebellum, which like the NDB appear to alter with age. In these three nuclear groups, all of the adult brains have shown small pale neurons that are significantly decreased in number. In contrast, in all of the childhood brains (ages 5–13 years), the neurons in these same nuclear groups, in addition to those of the dentate nucleus, have been found to be enlarged and plentiful in number (Bauman and Kemper 1994).

A similar pattern of change in cell size has also been observed in the inferior olive of the brainstem but the number of neurons has been found to be preserved. Given the known close relationship of the olivary climbing fiber axons to the Purkinje cell dendrites (Holmes and Stewart 1908), the preservation of the olivary neurons in the face of a significant reduction in Purkinje cell number strongly supports a prenatal origin for the cerebellar abnormalities. Studies in the fetal monkey indicate that the olivary climbing fiber axons synapse with the Purkinje cell dendrites in a transitory zone beneath the Purkinje cells called the laminas dessicans, thus forming a single unit (Rakic 1971). In the human fetus, this zone is no longer present after 28–30 weeks' gestation (Rakic and Sidman 1970). Thus, given the resulting tight bond between the olivary neurons and the Purkinje cells after this time, loss or damage to the cerebellar Purkinje cells results in an obligatory retrograde loss of olivary neurons (Holmes and Stewart 1908; Norman 1940; Greenfield 1954). Since, in the autistic brain, the number of the olivary neurons is preserved, it is likely that whatever event resulted in the reduction of the Purkinje cells in these cases it has to have occurred before this tight bond has been established, and thus before 28–30 weeks' gestation.

Abnormalities in the brainstem have also been observed in a small number of cases. Rodier *et al.* (1996) has described dysgenesis of the facial motor nucleus and agenesis of the superior olivary nuclei in a single case with autism and Moebius syndrome. The nature and location of these findings would suggest an onset during the first four weeks post-conception, during the time of neural tube closure. Bailey *et al.* (1998) have described the presence of ectopic neurons lateral to the olives bilaterally in one case and malformation of the olive in three cases, thus providing further pathological evidence for a prenatal onset of this disorder. A review of our own material has yielded olivary nuclear malformations, similar to those reported by Bailey *et al.* (1998) in some cases. A more systematic analysis of serially sectioned brainstem material from autistic subjects and age and sex-matched controls is currently underway.

Based on the findings in the cerebellum, combined with brainstem and cerebral cortical abnormalities in some cases (Rodier *et al.* 1996; Bailey *et al.* 1998), there appears to be reasonable evidence to suggest that at least some of the brain abnormalities observed in the autistic brain are of prenatal origin. However, there is a growing appreciation that the underlying neurobiological mechanisms involved in autism may reflect an on-going process. Further, there is the possibility that postnatal factors may also be important. It has been observed, for example, that overall brain weight in children with autism is statistically heavier than that of age- and sex-matched controls, while the weight of the autistic adult brain tends to be lighter than that of controls (Bauman and Kemper 1997, 2005). This observation is consistent with reports that, although autistic children tend to be born with normal head circumferences, the trajectory of head growth in these children tends to significantly accelerate, beyond that seen in typically developing children, during the preschool years (Lainhart *et al.* 1997; Courchesne, Carper and Akshoomoff 2003). Imaging studies have indicated increased brain volume in autism, most prominent between the ages of two and four-and-a-half years of age, a feature which later appears to plateau during adolescence (Courchesne *et al.* 2001). Although both gray and white matter volumes have been reported to be increased, the major changes appear to involve the cerebral and cerebellar white matter. Subsequently, Carper *et al.* (2002) observed that, although several brain regions have shown increased gray and white matter enlargement in two- to three-year-old autistic children, the greatest volumetric increase was found to be in the frontal lobe, with the occipital lobe being unaffected. More recently, Herbert *et al.* (2004) have reported that the white matter increase in both autistic and language disordered children appears to primarily involve the radiate white matter which myelinates later than the deep white matter, a concept that seems to be consistent with the unusual postnatal head growth reported in autism.

In addition, microscopic observations of enlarged cells in some brain regions in autistic children, and small pale cells that are reduced in number in these same areas in adults, strongly indicate changes with age. Clinically and pathologically, this process does not appear to be a degenerative one and may reflect the brain's attempt to compensate for its atypical circuitry over time. Future research will need to address the timing and pathogenesis of these changes and to consider how the resulting findings may impact on the clinical features of the disorder.

The observation of postnatal brain enlargement is intriguing and a number of hypotheses have been posed to explain its origins. A number of possible neurobiological mechanisms have been proposed to explain this apparent early brain 'overgrowth' including increased neurogenesis, decreased neuronal cell death, increased production of non-neuronal brain tissues (i.e. glial cells), decreased synaptic pruning, and abnormalities of myelin. At this time, there is no firm pathological evidence to support any of these suggested hypotheses. Finding the answer to these questions may go a long way toward advancing our understanding of the underlying pathogenic mechanisms which lie at the basis of this disorder.

While it will be imperative to continue to further define and refine neuroanatomic observations in the autistic brain, it will be equally important to expand our knowledge of the underlying neurochemical profile of these brains, most especially in the regions already determined to be anatomically abnormal. To date, Chugani et al. (1997) has reported decreased serotonin synthesis in the dentatothalamocortical pathway in seven autistic boys using positron emission tomography (PET). Fatemi et al. (2001) has described reduced amounts of reelin and Bcl-2 proteins in 44 percent of the autistic cerebella studied. Reelin is important for brain development and appears to play a role in the process of synapse elimination and Bcl-2 is important for programmed cell death. Blatt et al. (2001) have noted reduced binding of GABAa receptors in the hippocampus in the brains of four autistic adults studied in comparison to controls, but found no significant changes in kainate, cholinergic, or serotonergic receptors. Perry et al. (2001) have reported a decrease in nicotinic receptors in tissue obtained from autistic frontal and parietal cortex, with a decrease in M1 receptors only in the parietal cortex. Although the basal forebrain failed to show similar findings, this region showed a marked increase in brain-derived neurotrophic factor (BDNF). Since then, this same research group has noted a decrease in three of four nicotinic receptors in the cerebellum but no abnormalities of either M1 or M2 receptors or in choline acetyltransferase activity in this same area (Lee et al. 2002). Thus, studies such as these began the expansion of our knowledge base about the neurobiology of autism and future investigations should continue to explore the underlying neurochemistry of the autistic brain.

In conclusion, our understanding of the neurobiology of autism has advanced substantially over the past twenty years but there is still much to be learned. There is an urgent need for an animal model to address numerous questions, which, because of the limited availability of suitable human autopsy material and the technical limitations involved in the study of the human brain, cannot be adequately addressed at this time. Analysis of other body tissues such as blood, urine, and spinal fluid have resulted in inconsistent findings and related neuropharmacological research has been discouraging in many cases. Neurochemical evaluation of brain tissue obtained from autistic subjects is beginning to emerge but has been hampered by small sample size and the quality of the tissue available for study. It is hoped that, with advancements in technology coupled with a better definition of the genetic, neurochemical, and neuroanatomic profiles in autism and its broader phenotype, our understanding of the pathogenesis and neurobiology of the disorder will be expanded substantially, and ultimately this information will lead to earlier identification and more effective interventions and treatment.

REFERENCES

Aarkrog, T. (1968) 'Organic factors in infantile psychoses and borderline psychoses: retrospective study of 45 cases subjected to pneumoencephalography.' *Danish Medical Bulletin 15*, 283–288.

Arin, D. M., Bauman, M. L. and Kemper, T. L. (1991) 'The distribution of Purkinje cell loss in the cerebellum in autism.' *Neurology 41* (Suppl), 307.

Bailey, A., Luthert, P., Dean, A., Harding, B., Janota, I., Montgomery, M. *et al.* (1998) 'A clinicopathological study of autism.' *Brain 121*, 889–905.

Bauman, M. L. and Kemper, T. L. (1985) 'Histoanatomic observations of the brain in early infantile autism.' *Neurology 35*, 866–874.

Bauman, M. L. and Kemper, T. L. (1994) 'Neuroanatomic observations of the brain in autism.' In M. L. Bauman and T. L. Kemper (eds) *The Neurobiology of Autism*, pp.119–145. Baltimore, MD: Johns Hopkins University Press.

Bauman, M. L. and Kemper, T. L. (1996) 'Observations on the Purkinje cells in the cerebellar vermis in autism.' *Journal of Neuropathology and Experimental Neurology 55*, 613.

Bauman, M. L. and Kemper, T. L. (1997) 'Is autism a progressive process?' *Neurology 48* (Suppl), 285.

Bauman, M. L. and Kemper, T. L. (2005) 'Structural brain anatomy in autism: what is the evidence?' In M. L. Bauman and T. L. Kemper (eds) *The Neurobiology of Autism* (2nd edn), pp.121–135. Baltimore, MD: Johns Hopkins University Press.

Blatt, G. J., Fitzgerald, C. M., Guptill, J. T., Booker, A. B., Kemper, T. L. and Bauman, M. L. (2001) 'Density and distribution of hippocampal neurotransmitter receptors in autism.' *Journal of Autism and Developmental Disorders 31*, 537–543.

Brodal, A. (1940) 'Modification of Gudden method for study of cerebral localization.' *Archives of Neurology and Psychiatry 43*, 46–58.

Carper, R. A., Moses, P., Tigue, Z. D. and Courchesne, E. (2002) 'Cerebral lobes in autism: early hyperplasia and abnormal age effects.' *Neuroimage 16*, 1038–1051.

Casanova, M. F., Buxhoeveden, D. P., Switala, A. E. and Roy, E. (2002) 'Minicolumnar pathology in autism.' *Neurology 58*, 428–432.

Chugani, D. C., Musik, O., Rothermel, R., Behen, M., Chakraborty, P., Mangner. T. *et al.* (1997) 'Altered serotonin synthesis in the dentatothalamocortical pathway in autistic boys.' *Annals of Neurology 42*, 666–669.

Coleman, P. D., Romano, J., Lapham, L. and Simon, W. (1985) 'Cell counts in cerebral cortex in an autistic patient.' *Journal of Autism and Developmental Disorders 15*, 245–255.

Courchesne, E., Courchesne, R. Y., Hicks, G. and Lincoln, A. J. (1985) 'Functioning of the brain stem auditory pathway in non-retarded autistic individuals.' *Electroencephalography and Clinical Neurophysiology 51*, 491–501.

Courchesne, E., Townsend, J. and Saitoh, O. (1994) 'The brain in infantile autism.' *Neurology 44*, 214–228.

Courchesne, E., Karns, C. M., Davids, H. R., Ziccardi, R., Carper, R. A., Tigue, Z. D. *et al.* (2001) 'Unusual brain growth patterns in early life in patients with autistic disorder.' *Neurology 57*, 245–254.

Courchesne, E., Carper, R. and Akshoomoff, N. (2003) 'Evidence of brain overgrowth in the first year of life in autism.' *Journal of the American Medical Association 290*, 337–344.

Darby, J. H. (1976) 'Neuropathologic aspects of psychosis in childhood.' *Journal of Autism and Childhood Schizophrenia 6*, 339–352.

Deykin, E. Y. and MacMahon, B. (1979) 'The incidence of seizures among children with autistic symptoms.' *American Journal of Psychiatry 136*, 1312–1313.

Fatemi, S. H., Stary, J. M., Halt, A. R. and Realmuto, G. R. (2001) 'Dysregulation of reelin and Bcl-2 proteins in autistic cerebellum.' *Journal of Autism and Developmental Disorders 31*, 529–535.

Greenfield, J. G. (1954) *The Spino-cerebellar Degenerations.* Springfield, IL: C. C. Thomas.

Herbert, M. R., Ziegler, D. A., Makris, N., Filipek, P. A., Kemper, T. L., Normandin, J. J. *et al.* (2004) 'Localization of white matter volume increase in autism and developmental language disorder.' *Annals of Neurology 31*, 530–540.

Holmes, G. and Stewart, T. G. (1908) 'On the connection of the inferior olives with the cerebellum.' *Brain 31*, 125–137.

Kanner, L. (1943) 'Autistic disturbances of affective contact.' *Nervous Child 2*, 217–250.

Kemper, T. L. (2004) Personal communication.

Kemper, T. L. and Bauman, M. L. (1998) 'Neuropathology of infantile autism.' *Journal of Neuropathology and Experimental Neurology 57*, 645–652.

Lainhart, J. E., Piven, J., Wzorek, M., Landa, R., Santangelo, S. L., Coon, H. *et al.* (1997) 'Macrocephaly in children and adults with autism.' *Journal of the American Academy of Child and Adolescent Psychiatry 36*, 282.

Lee, M., Martin-Ruiz, C., Graham, A., Court, J., Jaros, E., Perry, E. *et al.* (2002) 'Nicotinic receptor abnormalities in the cerebellar cortex in autism.' *Brain 125*, 1483–1495.

Norman, R. M. (1940) 'Cerebellar atrophy associated with etat marbre of the basal ganglia.' *Journal of Neurology and Psychiatry 3*, 311–318.

Perry, E. K., Lee, M. L. W., Martin-Ruiz, C. M., Court, J., Volsen, S., Merritt, J. B. *et al.* (2001) 'Cholinergic activity in autism: abnormalities in the cerebral cortex and basal forebrain.' *American Journal of Psychiatry 158*, 1058–1066.

Rakic, P. (1971) 'Neuron–glia relationship during granule cell migration in developing cerebellar cortex. A Golgi and electron microscopic study in macacus rhesus.' *Journal of Comparative Neurology 141*, 282–312.

Rakic, P. and Sidman, R. L. (1970) 'Histogenesis of the cortical layers in human cerebellum, particularly the lamina dessicans.' *Journal of Comparative Neurology 139*, 7473–7500.

Raymond, G. V., Bauman, M. L. and Kemper, T. L. (1996) 'The hippocampus in autism: a Golgi analysis.' *Acta Neuropathologica 91*, 117–119.

Ritvo, E. R., Freeman, B. J., Scheibel, A. B., Duong, T., Robinson, H., Guthrie, D. and Ritvo, A. (1986) 'Lower Purkinje cell counts in the cerebella of four autistic subjects: initial findings of the UCLA-NSAC autopsy research report.' *American Journal of Psychiatry 146*, 862–866.

Rodier, P. M., Ingram, J. L., Tisdale, B., Nelson, S. and Roman, J. (1996) 'Embryological origins for autism: developmental anomalies of the cranial nerve nuclei.' *Journal of Comparative Neurology 370*, 247–261.

Rumsey, J. M., Grimes, A. M., Pikus, A. M., Duara, R. and Ismond, D. R. (1984) 'Auditory brainstem responses in pervasive developmental disorders.' *Biological Psychiatry 19*, 1403–1417.

Small, J. G. (1975) 'EEG and neurophysiologic studies of early infantile autism.' *Biological Psychiatry 10*, 4, 385–397.

Student, M. and Schmer, H. (1978) 'Evidence from auditory nerve and brainstem evoked responses for an organic lesion in children with autistic traits.' *Journal of Autism and Childhood Schizophrenia 8*, 13–20.

Tanguay, P. E., Ornitz, E. M., Forsythe, A. B. and Ritvo, E. R. (1976) 'Rapid eye movement (REM) activity in normal and autistic children during REM sleep.' *Journal of Autism and Childhood Schizophrenia 6*, 275–288.

Tanguay, P. E., Edwards, R. M., Buchwald, J., Schwofel, J. and Allen, V. (1982) 'Auditory brainstem evoked responses in autistic children.' *Archives of General Psychiatry 38*, 174–180.

Whitney, E. R., Kemper, T. L., Bauman, M. L. and Blatt, G. J. (in preparation) 'Calcium-binding proteins in the Purkinje cells of the Autistic cerebellum.'

Williams, R. S., Hauser, S. L., Purpura, D. P., Delong, G. R. and Swisher, C. W. (1980) 'Autism and mental retardation.' *Archives of Neurology 37*, 749–753.

Chapter 12

Cortical Circuit Abnormalities (Minicolumns) in the Brains of Autistic Patients

Manuel F. Casanova

INTRODUCTION

Autism is classified as a pervasive developmental disorder of childhood. It is called pervasive because it affects a wide portion of abilities (domains) usually attained during childhood. In autism affected domains include language, socialization, and motor behavior (APA, DSM-IV, 1994). Not all abilities are affected equally or globally and various combinations of individual symptoms may markedly improve or worsen with time. In some patients basic difficulties are reduced by development of compensatory strategies. Contrariwise, other autistics may not develop their skills. Thus, language impairment may continue in some patients as life-long muteness. Paradoxically, a mute autistic patient may exhibit a reduction (improvement) in stereotype movements and/or an increase in circumscribed interests. This variability in symptomatology, expressed over time, makes it difficult to identify and treat core deficits, to operationalize criteria (e.g. age of symptom onset) in clinical trials or epidemiological studies, and to interpret comorbid symptoms.

Diagnosis of autism requires that symptoms be present before three years of age. Affected children have problems looking at faces, turning when their names are called, performing symbolic play, and pointing at interesting objects. Autism may present in infancy as impaired attachment or more typically, in toddlers, with delayed speech and lack of interest in others (Rapin 1997). Related symptoms include sleep and eating disturbances and excessive anxiety. Mental retardation is regarded as a comorbid condition which may be severe or profound in almost half of all examined patients (coded separately under Axis II of DSM-IV). Paradoxically, some 10 percent of affected individuals exhibit savant-like skills that cluster around some narrow domain, e.g. numerical and calendar calculation, artistic (drawing) and musical proficiency.

Autism exemplifies a series of incongruous abilities. An underlying organic condition is suspect by disparities in IQ performance: higher performance IQ than verbal IQ scores. Patients may thus outperform normal controls in tasks related to block design and visual illusions. In addition, although some patients seem insensitive to pain, others exhibit a hypersensitivity to the texture of clothing or touching of their skin. Ornitz (1989) has proposed that these disturbances may reflect an inability to modulate the sensory system. Other investigators believe that autism results from low-level perceptual processing of incoming stimuli or what has been called a bottom-up approach (O'Riordan 2000). This theory supports a cortical abnormality in dampening of filtered information.

Although once considered rare, the prevalence of autism is estimated as 1 per 1,000, making it the most common among the severe neurodevelopmental disorders of childhood (Gillberg and Wing 1999). Autistic traits usually persist into adulthood, making it a 'life-long static developmental disorder' (Rapin and Katzman 1998). Although some pharmacological interventions can be attempted, there is no known cure for the disorder (Gordon *et al.* 1993).

BIOLOGICAL UNDERPINNINGS
Genetics

Ever since the disorder was first described by Kanner (1943), the etiology of autism has remained unknown. Postnatal environmental factors may play a minor role, and stand in contrast to prominent genetic and neurodevelopmental contributions to the disorders (Bailey, Phillips and Rutter 1996; Lotspeich and Ciaranello 1993). Genetic determinants have been strongly suggested by the large male predilection (males are affected more than females in a ratio of 3.5:1 to 5:1) and by the concordance rates for autism in monozygotic twins. Thus, the rate for concordance of monozygotic twins varies between 40 percent and 70 percent and reports for dizygotic twins range between 0 and 9 percent (Bailey *et al.* 1995; Smalley 1991).

A recurrence rate, estimated as 3 percent to 8 percent for affected families, is about 100 times higher than the rate in the general population. Other studies have shown an excess of cognitive delays in the biological relatives of autistic children, and the increased incidence of social impairments in their parents and other biological relatives. The calculated heritability of autism exceeds 90 percent, leading researchers to claim that 'autism is one of the most strongly genetic psychiatric disorders' (Turner, Barnby and Bailey 2000).

Both twins and family studies suggest that autism is a multi-locus disorder with one model suggesting two to ten genes as underlying the susceptibility to autism (Turner *et al.* 2000). However, the mode of inheritance remains unknown and segregation analyses have been inconclusive (Jorde *et al.* 1991). The identification of a genetic marker has been hampered by sample heterogeneity, lack of specific phenotype, and presumed polygenetic origin of autism.

Developmental onset

A number of associated medical conditions and physical anomalies suggest that the neuropathology of autism occurs early during gestation. Approximately one-third of patients with Moebius syndrome have comorbid autistic syndrome (Strömland *et al.* 2002). This rare disorder is characterized by a congenital palsy (i.e. paralysis) of the sixth and seventh cranial nerves. At physical examination autistic patients exhibit other malformations generally attributed to a developmental process. The most common among these malformations is the posterior rotation of the external ears. Small feet and normal to large hands and a reduction in the interpupillary distance have also been noted (Rodier, Bryson and Welch 1997).

A recent report that 5 percent of thalidomide victims have autism further supports the developmental nature of the autistic lesion with timing near to the closure of the neural tube during fetal gestation (Rodier *et al.* 2002; Rodier 1996). The fact that 'autistic' thalidomide patients have ear abnormalities and normal limbs indicates that the drug may have triggered the disorder some 20 to 24 days after conception (Rodier 2000). This timing coincides with recent report that the brains of autistic individuals exhibit supernumerary minicolumns. Minicolumns (*vide infra*) are basic units of cortical circuitry whose numbers are defined during the first 40 days of gestation (Casanova *et al.* 2002a). The developmental nature of the insult would exclude participation of some postnatal events currently incriminated in the pathophysiology of autism (e.g. immunizations) (Casanova *et al.* 2002a).

Neuropathology

Neuropathological studies in autism have provided for varied findings affecting many regions of the central nervous system. Most studies have focused on the limbic system; a composite of anatomical structures relating moods to bonding and social connectedness. The limbic system is arranged as a ring encircling the thalamus. Within this circuit, physiologically complementary structures oppose each other, e.g. amygdala and hippocampus. The organizational plan seems reasonable as the amygdala is involved in deciding whether memories are important and the hippocampus is involved in saving information. Ultimately, saved information should be important and what is not important should not be saved (Gordon 1995).

The importance we attach to information is thus heavily weighed by affective processing. Recognizing a face as belonging to one's mother may soothe an infant, but not one with an amygdala lesion. This is because even from an early age, both amygdala and hippocampus have worked in concert to identify the face of the mother with food, water, and other comforts. Autistic patients show abnormal judgment about trustworthiness of faces, but no impairment when the same information is lexical in nature (Adolphs, Sears and Piven 2001). The results suggest that both hippocampus and amygdala may be affected in patients with autism.

It is of importance that neuropathological studies have provided a possible correlate to socioemotional symptoms in autism, e.g. emotional connotative value of faces. These studies show a reduction in neuronal size and increased cell packing density for both amygdala and hippocampus (Kemper and Bauman 1993). However, the studies did not employ stereological techniques, making the interpretation of the subjective findings somewhat obscure. Although a developmental lesion has been postulated, the findings could also represent simple cell atrophy, hypoxia, or an appraisal bias. Other reported findings (Raymond, Bauman and Kemper 1996) such as limited dendritic arbors and illustrations of sharply angulated discontinuities in somatic projections (silver-impregnation studies) are common indicators of postmortem artifacts.

Many of the examined patients in neuropathological studies suffered from co-morbid conditions, i.e. mental retardation and epilepsy. It is therefore difficult to discern whether the reported findings represent a core feature of the condition or whether they are secondary to a concurrent illness. The controversy revolves primarily around patho-logical findings in the cerebellum, an area of pathoclisis for epilepsy and hypoxia. Although the existence of the reported reductions in the number of Purkinje cells (Kemper and Bauman 1993) is not questioned, the nature of the loss is the basis of con-tention. Aplastic or dysplastic phenomena of the cerebellum, particularly of the vermis, are associated with malformations of the medulla (Friede 1989) and corresponding folia (Harding and Copp 1997). Thus far, reported abnormalities of the inferior olives or pyramidal tracts, both of them structures within the medulla, have not played a promi-nent role in the pathology of autism. Reports of enlarged neurons in the inferior olive of younger autistic patients and shrunken, pale-staining ones, in older patients, have been based on qualitative, non-stereological, appraisals (Bauman and Kemper 1985; Kemper and Bauman 1993).

In autism, reported reductions in Purkinje cell counts occur in the midst of little, if any, granular cell loss or gliosis. Since the glial reaction is immature during early stages of gestation, the inference is that Purkinje cell loss is a developmental defect and not the result of hypoxia. However, these observations may have equated glial proliferation with glial hypertrophy, a phenomenon that is lost in the chronic stages of a lesion. Acute astrocytic reactions are seen in the first few days after insults such as trauma, infarcts, and infections. However, the reaction tapers off after several weeks or months (Hirano 1985). Chronic fibrillary gliosis may be better visualized with the Holzer or phosphotungstic acid-hematoxylin stain (PTAH) than with glial fibrillary acid protein (GFAP) immunohistochemistry. In autism, a hypertrophic-type gliosis would not be expected if the original insult (e.g. hypoxia from seizures) occurred years before the patient's demise.

The interpretation of cerebellar findings as secondary to hypoxia (seizures) may also help explain the presence of 'atrophic' areas in the orbitofrontal cortex and anterior temporal region of autistic patients as contusions secondary to falls during seizures or self-injurious behavior (Williams *et al.* 1980). A similar explanation may hold for the sporadic presence of neurofibrillary tangles in fairly young autistic patients: in analogy to the neurofibrillary tangles found in dementia pugilistica, these degenerative changes may be secondary to trauma (Hof *et al.* 1991). Unsurprisingly, head trauma with loss of consciousness raises the risk of developing Alzheimer's disease by about 1.7 times (Gordon 1995).

Studies by Fatemi and colleagues (2001) have endeavored to investigate the putative developmental nature of the reported cerebellar findings in autism. In these studies the levels of reelin have been measured in the cerebellar cortex of five autistic (seizure status unknown) and eight control subjects. Reelin is a glycoprotein that has been associated with neuronal migration and lamination disturbances (Fatemi *et al.* 1999). Results of the studies have shown a 40 percent reduction in reelin. This glycoprotein has also been reported as diminished following postnatal hypoxia (Curristin *et al.* 2002). In autism the preagonal condition of the patients as well as the possibility of seizures offer confounds to significant alterations in reelin levels. Furthermore, no one, during the last few decades of neuropathological studies in autism, has described the characteristic reversal in the normal pattern of lamination observed in the Reeler mouse cortex.

More difficult to dismiss have been neuropathological findings intrinsic to the neocortex. Evidence for abnormalities of the cerebral cortex began to appear as different studies (structural imaging, autopsy studies, and physical examination) all supported the fact that the brain of autistic individuals is, on average, larger than normal. This finding remains significant after controlling for height, gender, the presence of epilepsy, and other medical disorders (Fombonnne *et al.* 1999; Piven *et al.* 1996). The relationship of brain size and performance IQ is less clear. Arguably, changes in brain size result from enlargement of some areas and reductions in others (Koenig, Tsatsamis and Volkmar 2001; Piven *et al.* 1996). Brain growth may be noticeable during the first few postnatal years and then plateaus. The gray/white matter ratio is altered favoring an expansion by the white matter, particularly the short corticocortical projections (Herbert *et al.* 2004).

Reported cortical abnormalities (structural imaging) include polymicrogyria, macrogyria, and schizencephaly (Piven *et al.* 1990). These changes suggest a disturbance in cell migration during the early stages of brain development. More recently, Bailey and colleagues (1998) have described postmortem evidence of neocortical abnormalities in the brains of four out of six examined autistic patients, i.e. laminar disturbances, heterotopias. The four cases were megalencephalic (larger head size) but selection was not unbiased. This was the first study to report abnormalities of the cerebral cortex and to advocate a central role for the cortex in providing an explanation for the seizures and deficits in higher order cognitive abilities in autism. They further proposed that autism involved widespread areas of the brain, rather than isolated anatomical structures (Bailey *et al.* 1998).

Neocortical abnormalities in autism are also evident by clinical symptomatology, the localization of saccadic and pursuit eye movements, and functional MRI studies showing a reduction in regional connections and localized specialization of circuitry (Just *et al.* 2004; Luna *et al.* 2002; Sweeney *et al.* 2004). Thus, approximately one-third of autistic patients develop seizures before three years of age or during puberty (11 years to 14 years) (Volkmar and Nelson 1990). Furthermore, epileptiform (EEG) abnormalities are common in autism, i.e. being reported in 21 percent of children receiving sleep recordings (Tuchman and Rapin 1997). This is of interest because, by adulthood, a third of autistic individuals will have experienced at least two unprovoked seizures (Volkmar and Nelson 1990; Olsson, Steffenburg and Gillberg 1988). Researchers have commented that 'The unusual pattern and onset (adolescence) and the frequency of seizures in persons with autism are strong indications of a neuropathological process' (Dykens and Volkmar 1997). The presence of seizures and deficits in complex behaviors has been classically associated to dysfunction of cerebral association cortex. Furthermore the absence of blindness, deafness, paralysis, or sensory deficits suggests that the primary sensory and motor cortices are spared.

A review of the medical literature suggests the presence of cortical pathology in autism. Furthermore, abnormalities of brain growth, gray/white matter ratios, and disturbances in cell migration may all be related to a core deficit within neocortical minicolumns. A recent review of minicolumnopathies (Casanova 2005) enunciates many characteristics of importance to autism, among them: (1) impairment of higher cortical functions, (2) changes in symptomatology (profile and/or severity) accrued to aging, (3) the presence of comorbid symptoms, (4) multiple neurotransmitter systems affected, (5) gender differences in symptom expression, (6) complex genetic and epigenetic influences, (7) language impairment and alterations of cerebral dominance, (8) change in prevalence through different generations, (9) frontal lobe syndrome, (10) abnormalities in EEG, especially in higher (gamma) frequencies, (11) abnormalities in brain size, gyrification, and gray/white matter ratios, and (12) the presence of heterotopias.

MINICOLUMNS

All subcortical arrangements are primarily nucleoid in type. The cortex has been the first structure during mammalian evolution to develop both a radial and laminar arrangement. Subcortical lesions cause specific deficits manifested, for example, as movement abnormalities of the appendages. In contrast, some cortical lesions provide for graded symptoms that can't be related to individual cellular components. Clinical observations therefore suggest the existence of a cortical 'system' where the properties of the whole far exceed the sum of its parts. These cortical systems are called either modules or hierarchical levels. At present there is sufficient information to designate as modules four different, but intertwined, anatomical structures: (1) minicolumns, (2) multiple minicolumns, (3) macrocolumns, and (4) large scale networks of macrocolumns (Casanova *et al* .2003a). Within these arrangements connectivity is more prominent within than between modules. An additional characteristic of modules is that their components (e.g. neurons) tend to share similar stimulus/response properties.

The minicolumn occupies the lowest level within the hierarchical arrangements of the neocortex (Mountcastle 1998). In the human primate brain, minicolumns are the composite of pyramidal cell arrays, myelinated bundles and apical dendritic bundles. Double-bouquet cells arrange themselves in reproducible patterns that define the periphery of the minicolumn (DeFelipe *et al.* 1990). It is less clear whether some astrocytes with interlaminar processes occur in a pattern similar to those of double-bouquet cells. Such a disposition, if present, would help provide for the spatial definition of minicolumns (Colombo 2001; Colombo *et al.* 2000).

The developmental process affords many opportunities for minicolumns to acquire individual specificity. They vary in regards to their cellular composition (number and type of neuron), afferent connectivity, efferent outflow, local and horizontal connectivity, and synaptic patterns. Unsurprisingly, numerous researchers have reported on this lack of 'clone-like' uniformity of cell minicolumns: variability in the thickness of dendritic and axonal bundles, the number of fibers within bundles, column width, amount of neuropil space, and the cell density within a column based on the gray level index (GLI) (Buxhoeveden and Casanova 2002; Ichinohe *et al.* 2003; Lohmann and Koppen 1995; Peters and Sethares 1996; Schmolke and Kunzle 1997). Peters and Payne (1993) found highly specific differences in apical dendrite bundle connectivity patterns between areas 17 and 18. Csillik *et al.* (1998) and Barone and Kennedy (2000) found evidence for distinctive patterns of NADPH in columns. It is apparent that a high degree of variation exists in both the cellular and fiber bundle components of columns.

There is no single technique that allows for the simultaneous visualization of all minicolumnar components, i.e. pyramidal cell arrays, myelinated bundles, and apical dendritic bundles (Buxhoeveden and Casanova 2005). When making reference to minicolumns we are generalizing conclusions based on evidence derived from only one of its components. In this chapter the term minicolumn has been used primarily to denote pyramidal cell arrays. Critics of morphological classification systems suggest that such attempts may be misguided, that no two neurons are exactly the same, and that each cell has unique characteristics. Using shape and size criteria are reasonable, albeit not ideal, ways of attempting cell classification and studying minicolumns as pyramidal cell arrays. For these and other reasons researchers have used alternate methods to study apical dendritic bundles and double-bouquet cells, i.e. silver impregnation stains and/or immunocytochemistry. These techniques provide for subjective appraisal of cells and their components but otherwise provide biased quantitative measurements. It is well known that silver impregnation techniques like Golgi are not quantitative. Similarly, incubation conditions for immunocytochemical reactions seldom allow the intensity of staining to vary directly with the amount of antigen nor do they prevent excess diffusion of antibody. Even when optimized, lack of immunocytochemical staining does not exclude the presence of antigen (Casanova and Kleinman 1990). The failure of immunocytochemical staining to reveal quantitative features of the object of biological interest is known in stereology as a recognition bias. This bias cannot be quantitated, corrected, or removed when reporting results based on pseudo-optical imaging. These reasons have made many 'minicolumnar researchers' concentrate their efforts on pyramidal cell arrays as visualized with Nissl stains.

Pyramidal cells have a longitudinal access that allows researchers to examine how they register with each other through different cortical lamina. When visualized with Nissl stains the cellular skeleton of minicolumns reminds us of pearls in a string (Figure 12.1).

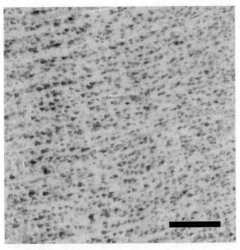

Figure 12.1 Minicolumns in lamina III, Brodmann area 22, from a 71-year-old male. Scalebar: 200 μm. Minicolumns are oriented perpendicularly to the pial surface, which lies to the right of the image

This linear configuration is broken by tangential lamina of predominantly granular/ stellate cells the soma of which lack a longitudinal axis. This cellular bias explains why minicolumns are not easily discernible in granular cortex, e.g. striate cortex (Figure 12.2).

Similarly, despite the orderly arrangements of apical dendrites, pyramidal cell arrays are not evident in allocortex, i.e. archicortex (hippocampal complex) and paleocortex (pyriform cortex). Contrariwise, a systematic increase in pyramidal cell size when going from caudal to rostral portions of the brain makes minicolumns easily visualized within the frontal lobe, e.g. motor strip (Figure 12.3).

Minicolumns maintain their linearity and cellular constituency despite the presence of tissue contortions (Figure 12.4).

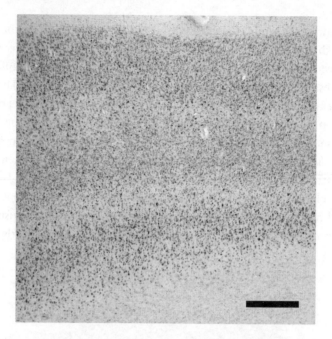

Figure 12.2 Primary visual cortex (also called striate cortex) corresponds to area 17 of Brodmann's map. The predominance of granule cell makes difficult the visualization of any vertical bias in the cortex. The tissue came from the brain of a 67-year-old female. Scalebar: 400 μm

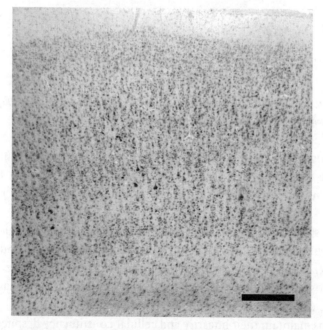

Figure 12.3 Motor cortex (Brodmann area 4) from the same brain as Figure 12.2 (q.v.). Several giant pyramidal cells (Betz) are clearly visible. Scalebar: 400 μm

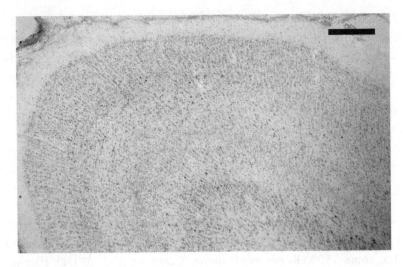

Figure 12.4 Minicolumnar orientation varies continuously across the folding of the cortex, maintaining their orientation perpendicular to the surface. Scalebar: 400 μm

The basic one-cell thick arrangement of minicolumns is preserved and only splayed apart by gyrification. For this reason minicolumns may be considered a basic unit of anatomy. The origin of pyramidal cell arrays stems from the ontogenetic minicolumn of Pasko Rakic (Figure 12.5).

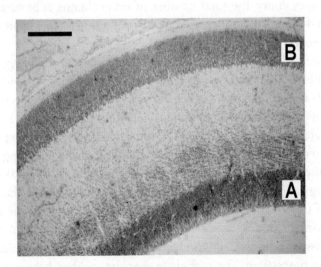

Figure 12.5 Developing cerebral cortex at 12 weeks of gestation. Young cells migrating from the germinal zone (A) form ontogenetic columns (B), thought to be the precursor to the minicolumn. Scalebar: 200 μm

The genesis of minicolumns stems from symmetrical divisions of germinal periventricular cells that establish the total number of minicolumns. A later series of asymmetric divisions provides for the total number of (pyramidal) cells within the minicolumn. Inhibitory cells follow a different (tangential) migratory pathway to the neocortex. Minicolumns span layers II through VI of the neocortex. All cellular elements are represented in the minicolumn. The sole exception is the Cajal-Retzius cells which are derived from the primordial plexiform layer.

Rockel, Hiorns and Powell's (1980) early study purporting to find cell number homogeneity in arbitrary 30 μm vertical slabs has been revised. Later findings show no uniformity in the number of neurons in different cortical areas (Beaulieu 1993; Skoglund, Pascher and Berthold 1996).

Thus, the total number of neurons within a minicolumn varies greatly depending on the region of interest and species. The greatest number of cells can be found within the striate cortex, some 250 cells per minicolumn (Casanova *et al.* 2003a). Paradoxically minicolumns within the striate cortex tend to be the narrowest, thus sustaining the great increase in cellular density in this brain region.

Putative factors affecting the total number of minicolumns include: (1) the number of founder cells, (2) the duration of the cell-division cycle, (3) the number of successive cell cycles during the period of neurogenesis,(4) modes of cell division, and (5) selective cell death (Rakic and Kornack 2001). Contrary to other specimens in which neurogenesis lasts until the postnatal period, human neurogenesis is defined before the last trimester of pregnancy. Since the total number of minicolumns appears to be defined during gestation, findings of an increased number of minicolumns in autism suggest a developmental process during embryogenesis.

Thick Nissl stained sections (e.g. celloidin) allow visualization of large fragments of pyramidal cell arrays. Thinner sections (e.g. paraffin embedded) provide for column fragmentation (Z-axis artifact) into smaller chains of pyramidal cells. It is not coincidental that the original descriptions of pyramidal cell arrays employed thick sections. This was first appreciated early in the twentieth century, when von Economo (1929) identified cell cords encompassing all the known neuronal types and spanning the width of the cortex. Lorente de Nó (1949) was the first to posit a central role for these structures in brain physiology and equated them to a canonical circuit 'in which, theoretically, the whole process of transmission of impulses from the afferent fibre to the efferent axon may be accomplished'. Modern researchers have used celloidin as an embedding media to obtain thick tissue sections. Celloidin has the added advantage of reducing artifacts accrued to tissue processing. The technique employs neither heat nor dehydration through graded alcohols. It has the disadvantage of long processing times and the use of ether, which is considered an explosive material. Also, a sledge microtome may be needed to cut the sections through the hardened tissue blocks. Alternatives to celloidin include the use of a vibratome and cutting cryoprotected tissue with a cryostat. Still, even in thicker sections a significant percentage of cellular projections are not visible in Nissl stained tissue sections.

Modern computerized image analysis methods are capable of quantitating different parameters of minicolumnar morphometry (pyramidal cell arrays) (Casanova and Switala 2005). These parameters include, among others, minicolumnar width, cellular core and peripheral neuropil space, relative dispersion of cells, and mean cell distance (Figure 12.6) (Casanova and Switala 2005). All computerized image analysis measurements are made under the assumption that pyramidal cell arrays exist within a column of tissue and that samples through its cross section will be representative of the structure as a whole. This assumption does not appear to be correct. The space configured by dendritic bundles acquires polygonal shapes of variable size with aging (Skoglund *et al.* 2004). Nevertheless, the ability of computerized image analysis to compartmentalize the minicolumn is of importance as communication pathways are topographically segregated within this structure. Thus, the neuropil space at the periphery of the minicolumn contains mostly synapses, dendrites, and unmyelinated axons (Figure 12.7).

The central core compartment has the cell somas for neurons and both the thalamocortical and corticocortical projections (Buxhoeveden *et al.* 2000).

Figure 12.6 Computerized image analysis of the microscopic field shown in Figure 12.1 (q.v.). Clusters of cells (points) are indicated by their minimum distance spanning trees (heavy lines). The mean length of edges, i.e. line segments, of the tree provides the mean interneuronal distance within a minicolumn. Regions of low cell density (light lines) delimit the minicolumnar fragments. The distance from these boundaries to the cells in the fragment provides a measurement of peripheral neuropil, while the distance from cluster to cluster, measured perpendicular to their orientation, estimates the minicolumn's full width

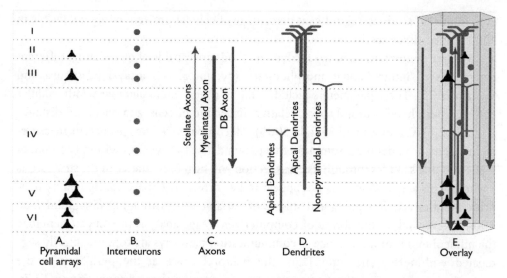

Figure 12.7 Cell somas, myelinated axons, and the stems of pyramidal cells' apical dendrites define the minicolumn core. Unmyelinated axons and dendritic arbors tend to occupy the neuropil on the periphery of the minicolumn. Reprinted by permission of Sage Publications, from Casanova et al. (2003a) 'Disruption in the inhibitory architecture of the cell minicolumn: implications for autism.' The Neuroscientist 9, 6 , 496–507. Copyright © Sage Publications 2003

Minicolumnar findings in autism and other conditions

In later work our group has reported smaller minicolumns in the brains of autistic patients. More specifically, we used a computerized image analysis system to examine pyramidal cell arrays in three different brain regions (Brodmann areas 2, 21, and 22). There were nine autistic patients and an equal number of controls in the study. The results indicated significant differences in the total number of minicolumns, in the horizontal spacing that separated the minicolumns, and in their internal structure (relative dispersion of cells) (Casanova *et al.* 2002b). A subsequent study using a different method (gray level index) corroborated the initial findings (Casanova *et al.* 2002a). It thus appears that in autism an increased number of minicolumns combined with fewer cells per column (or their greater dispersal) results in no global difference in neuronal density.

Studies in the cortex of autistic patients have not demonstrated differences in cell density (Bailey *et al.* 1998; Coleman *et al.* 1985), nor have we. This is of great interest as an increased number of radial units (minicolumns) in the presence of normal neuronal density argue against the possibility of a shrinkage artifact. In order for the number of minicolumns to increase while preserving the same cellular density per unit of tissue, the average individual minicolumn must contain fewer cells. The configuration of minicolumns is closely linked to cell density, so that changes in one should be detectable in the other. By contrast, cell density does not necessarily translate to absolute cell numbers. A reduction in the spacing between neurons can result in increased cell density. For example, Selemon and Godlman-Rakic (1999) postulated that a reported 17 percent elevation in cell density in prefrontal cortex (Brodmann area 9) was caused by a reduction in the spacing between cells (interneuronal or neuropil space). To this effect Buxhoeveden *et al.* (2000) examined minicolumns of Brodmann area 9 in the brains of schizophrenic patients, and found a 14 percent reduction in the spacing between cell somas within minicolumns compared to normal controls. Furthermore, the latter investigators found the greatest reduction of interneuronal spacing in the core region of the minicolumn with a smaller decrease in the peripheral neuropil space. This demonstrates that relationships between cell number, density, and minicolumns can be detected and quantified.

Our morphometric studies now include patients with Asperger disorder, considered by many to be a higher-functioning autism (Casanova *et al.* 2002c). We examined two cases with Asperger syndrome and 18 controls. We anticipated that the findings in our patients would be qualitatively the same but less severe than those observed in autism. Minicolumns in one patient differed significantly from those found in normal patients. Only one brain region appeared to be affected, Brodmann area 22 (part of Wernicke's language region) ($p = 0.032$, after applying the Bonferroni correction). Specifically minicolumns were smaller and their component cells more dispersed than normal. Other Brodmann areas examined, i.e. 9 and 22, did not provide for significant results. Nor did the brain of a second Asperger patient show significant findings. However, changes accrued to aging in this second patient (age 79) may have obscured minicolumnar abnormalities. It has been reported that minicolumns become wider and less vertical with aging (Casanova *et al.* 2002c). The minicolumnar abnormalities observed in Asperger syndrome are similar in morphometry but less severe in magnitude and distribution than those previously reported in autism. Further studies are needed using larger series of patients before reaching a final conclusion.

To further investigate the specificity of the reported minicolumnopathies, we studied other cases in which various etiologies cause a behavioral syndrome that closely resembles autism, e.g. congenital rubella, Kluver-Bucy syndrome, tuberous sclerosis, and Rett syndrome. The first such etiology we identified was Rett syndrome: a progressive neurological disorder affecting primarily females (Casanova *et al.* 2003b). It is characterized by the early regression of acquired language, cognitive functions, social skills, and purposeful hand function. Patients with Rett syndrome are often misdiagnosed as autistic and, unsurprisingly, they are both classified as pervasive developmental disturbances of childhood. Otherwise, Rett syndrome is a completely different neurological disorder than autism. Besides having described midline midbrain and nuclear brainstem abnormalities, its severe cognitive impairments implicate equally severe cerebral cortical dysfunction.

For the purpose of our studies we obtained digitized images of cortex from five Rett syndrome patients and one patient each with congenital rubella, Kluver-Bucy, and tuberous sclerosis. The series also included 40 subjects as controls. The tissue was celloidin embedded, sectioned at 35 μm and Nissl stained. The images (at 100 ×

magnification) were taken from Brodmann areas 9, 21, and 22 in layer III of the left hemisphere. Columnar width measurements for these images were obtained with computerized image analysis (Casanova and Switala 2005). Each area was analyzed separately with univariate ANOVA, with diagnosis included as a fixed factor and age (linear and quadratic terms) and sex included as covariates. The resultant confidence limits on the mean columnar width represented averages for men and women at 36 years of age. Diagnosis dependent effects were statistically significant only in one Brodmann area 21 (p = 0.012). Results for the two other Brodmann areas (BA) examined were as follows: BA 9, p = 0.085 and BA 22, p = 0.137. The significance was accrued by Rett syndrome patients who exhibited minicolumnar widths 12 μm smaller than those of controls. Computer modeling has shown that similar abnormalities may disturb information processing, biasing the signal to noise ratio in favor of the signal (Gustafsson 1997). A plot of the first two Fisher discriminant functions (Figure 12.8) revealed differences between the minicolumnopathy observed in Rett syndrome patients and that previously described in autism and Asperger syndrome.

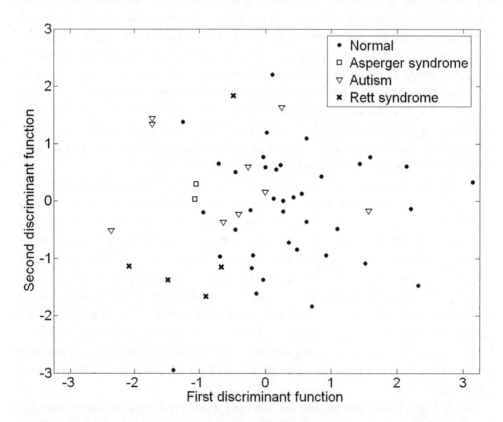

Figure 12.8 Data on minicolumnar width, interneuronal distance, peripheral neuropil, and the compactness of the cellular arrangement within minicolumns is reduced to two dimensions by computing the first two Fisher discriminant functions. These linear combinations of the original four-dimensional data best preserve the distinction between the groups (normal control, autism, etc.)

In our research we have used brains of Down syndrome (DS) patients as a control sample. The aim has been to study both mental retardation and brain size as possible confounds in the assessment of minicolumnar morphometry. Materials came from the Yakovlev-Haleem collection at the Armed Forces Institute of Pathology (Washington, DC). Normal controls consisted of seven samples, ages 4, 6, 16, 47, 53, 57, and 60 years. The seven Down syndrome subjects were aged 4, 6, 26, 29, 47, 56, and 56 years. Samples were obtained from the left and the right hemisphere. Sections were processed and examined in the same way as in our previously described studies (*vide supra*). In all, we measured some 600 cell minicolumns per brain for a total of approximately 8000 minicolumns in the series. To account for the effects of shrinkage, we compared the fresh and dehydrated volumes of both the normal and DS brains where possible. Data existed for all the children, but only three out of five normal adults and two out of five DS adults contained the pre- and post-fixation volumes. Based on the data available, both populations incurred similar amounts of shrinkage. Results from the study showed that minicolumns in the brains of DS patients were as large as normal controls even though their brains were much smaller. Moreover, minicolumns attained adult size much earlier than in controls (Buxhoeveden and Casanova 2004). The results are striking given the numerous histological studies showing a reduction of dendrites and synapses in these brains. In sharp contrast to DS, the brains of autistic patients are on average larger than the normative average but with narrower cell columns. Brain size is therefore not a confound to the reported minicolumnopathy of autistic patients.

Significance of minicolumnar findings

For a given brain size, the dimension (width) of minicolumns will determine their total number. Compared to the normal brain, the larger autistic brain contains smaller minicolumns and therefore many more information processing units. We may find an analogy to our findings in comparative anatomical studies. Across species, variations in size and number of minicolumns are common. Minicolumns in the visual cortex of the monkey (~30 μm) are much smaller than those of the cat (~56 μm) (Peters and Sethares 1991; Peters and Yilmaz 1993). Furthermore, the monkey brain is both bigger and has a larger span of visual cortex than cats. Thus, monkeys have more minicolumns both by virtue of the dimensions of their minicolumns and the size of their brain. Smaller minicolumns may have afforded monkeys (as contrasted with cats) a greater complexity of information processing and superior visual capabilities (Orban 1984). Similarly, smaller and more numerous minicolumns provide a putative explanation to the high degree of sensory discrimination and highly focused skills observed in patients with autism. It is however an insufficient explanation to other prominent symptomatology, e.g. seizures. In this regard two possible effects of the reported minicolumnopathy in autism should be considered, those related to thalamic innervation and the loss of peripheral neuropil space (an inhibitory deficit).

Without evidence to the contrary, the afferent thalamic terminal input is the same in both the brains of autistic patients and normal controls. Since minicolumns are smaller in the brains of autistic patients, the afferent input will contact more minicolumns. In addition, if the brains of normal and autistic patients contain identical dendritic arborization, by comparison each dendrite in the autistic patient will contact more minicolumns. The resultant greater spread of signal and columnar circuitry pattern differs from that found in the normal brain. One result is that the cortex of autistic patients acts as an amplifier system, biasing information processing towards enhancing incoming signals (Casanova, *et al.* 2002d, 2003a). This bias may explain some of the more publicized features of the autistic condition: hypersensitivity of all sensory modalities (e.g. flickering of fluorescent lights) and some eccentricities (e.g. eating the same foods, wearing the same clothes).

It has also been proposed that certain behavioral traits exhibited by autistic patients may be rooted in an imbalance between excitation and inhibition at the columnar level. Casanova *et al.* (2003a) argue for a decrease of inhibitory modulation in the brains of at least some autistic patients, especially those susceptible to seizure disorder and extreme hypersensitivity. To the degree that a loss of inhibition is present in autism, it may exist as a continuum. Only a third of these patients display a propensity for seizure disorders, and behavior is varied throughout the autistic spectrum disorder. We have further suggested that the decrease in minicolumn size may reflect a loss of GABAergic interneurons. The potential changes in minicolumnar configuration significantly involve interneuronal elements. These phenomena may result from a decrease in the peripheral neuropil space of minicolumns where most of the unmyelinated (inhibitory) projections are located.

An argument can be made that the specificity of GABAergic inhibition in the neo-cortex is focused around its mini- and macrocolumnar organization. GABAergic interneurons are vital to minicolumnar differentiation, which in turn affects signal processing. It is therefore of interest that computer models that alter excitation and inhibition levels provide for representations of core autistic symptoms. Some of these models have critically tied the fundamental shaping of the macrocolumn during development to the correct balance of excitation and inhibition of individual minicolumns (Favorov and Kelly 1994a, b). Gustafsson (1997) proposes that in autism there is a mismatch between excitation and lateral inhibition. He concludes there is too much inhibition, while Casanova *et al.* (2003a) propose the opposite, that there is too little inhibition. Finally, a neural network model for learning that removed GABA-receptor mediated inhibition of intrinsic fibers resulted in a decline in learning and recall (Wallenstein and Hasselmo 1997). This was thought to occur because sensory information was obscured by competing activity from intrinsic and afferent fibers (Wallenstein and Hasselmo 1997).

Hussman (2001) suggests that while autism may be caused by an array of defects in relatively independent systems, some arguments suggest reducing to a single dysfunction, i.e., cortical inhibition defect. The theory for a generalized GABA deficit in autism is known as 'suppressed GABAergic inhibition hypothesis' (Hussman 2001). One reason supporting this hypothesis is that pathology relating to GABA receptors is a common feature in several suspected etiologies of autism (Hussman 2001). Both disinhibition of GABAergic influence, or excessive stimulation of non-NMDA glutamate receptors, generate pathology similar to autism (Hussman 2001). Evidence from genetics is derived from the suspected gene sites for autism on chromosome 15 in which there are three GABA receptor subunit genes (GABRBe, GABRA5, GABRG3). Another suspected gene, chromosome 3, the GAT1 gene, makes protein that works with GABA.

In summary, the reported minicolumnar findings in autism explain many and varied aspects of the expressed symptomatology. The presence of supernumerary minicolumns provides for increased brain size and the possibility of altered gyrification (Hardan *et al.* 2004). Added minicolumns have a 1000-fold ratio of interconnectivity which results in altered gray:white matter ratios. Within this scheme, u-shaped corticocortical projections predominate leaving long commisural connections (e.g. corpus callosum) unaltered. This connectivity scheme enhances further processing of incoming signals (discrimination) at the expense of generalization (connections between topological different regions of interest). Smaller minicolumns also mean that a given span of thalamic afferents may innervate more of them. It is postulated that the larger number of minicolumnar units acting in unison within a macrocolumnar arrangement provides for an amplifier system. The fact that in the smaller minicolumns of autistic patients the outer neuropil compartment is affected more than their core underlies an inhibitory deficit. These characteristics of smaller minicolumns help explain the hypersensitivities, eccentricities, and seizure related phenomena observed in patients with autism.

ACKNOWLEDGEMENT

This chapter is based upon work supported by the Stanley Medical Research Foundation, the National Alliance for Autism Research, and NIMH grants MH61606, MH62654, and MH69991.

REFERENCES

Adolphs, R., Sears, L. and Piven, J. (2001) 'Abnormal processing of social information from faces in autism.' *Journal of Cognitive Neuroscience 13*, 2, 232–240.

APA (American Psychiatric Association) (1994) *Diagnostic and Statistical Manual of Mental Disorders* (4th edn). Washington, DC: APA.

Bailey, A., Le Couteur, A., Gottesman, I., Bolton, P., Simonoff, E., Yuzda, E. and Rutter, M. (1995) 'Autism as a strongly genetic disorder: evidence from a British twin study.' *Psychological Medicine 25*, 63–77.

Bailey, A., Phillips, W. and Rutter, M. (1996) 'Autism: toward an integration of clinical, genetic, neuropsychological, and neurobiological perspectives.' *Journal of Child Psychology and Psychiatry and Allied Disciplines 37*, 1, 39–126.

Bailey, A., Luthert, P., Dean, A., Harding, B., Janota, I., Montogomery *et al.* (1998) 'A clinicopathological study of autism.' *Brain 121*, 889–905.

Barone, P. and Kennedy, H. (2000) 'Non-uniformity of neocortex: areal heterogeneity of NADPH-diaphorase reactive neurons in adult Macaque monkeys.' *Cerebral Cortex 10*, 160–174.

Bauman, M. L. and Kemper, T. L. (1985) 'Histoanatomic observations of the brain in early infantile autism.' *Neurology 35*, 866–874.

Beaulieu, C. (1993) 'Numerical data on neocortical neurons in adult rat, with special references to the GABA population.' *Brain Research 609*, 284–292.

Buxhoeveden, D. and Casanova, M. F. (2002) 'The minicolumn hypothesis in neuroscience.' *Brain 5*, 125, 935–951.

Buxhoeveden, D. and Casanova, M. F. (2004) 'Accelerated maturation in brains of patients with Down syndrome.' *Journal of Intellectual Disability Research 7*, 48, 704–705.

Buxhoeveden, D. and Casanova, M. F. (2005) 'The cell column in comparative anatomy.' In M. F. Casanova (ed.) *Neocortical Modularity and the Cell Minicolumn*, pp.93–116. New York: Nova Science Publishers.

Buxhoeveden, D., Roy, E., Switala, A. and Casanova, M. F. (2000) 'Reduced interneuronal space in schizophrenia.' *Biological Psychiatry 47*, 7, 681–682.

Casanova, M. F. (2005) 'An apologia for a paradigm shift in the neurosciences.' In M. F. Casanova (ed.) *Neocortical Modularity and the Cell Minicolumn*. New York: Nova Science Publishers.

Casanova, M. F. and Kleinman, J. E. (1990) 'The neuropathology of schizophrenia.' *Biological Psychiatry 27*, 353–362.

Casanova, M. F. and Switala, A. (2005) 'Minicolumnar morphometry: computerized image analysis.' In M. F. Casanova (ed.) *Neocortical Modularity and the Cell Minicolumn*. New York: Nova Science Publishers.

Casanova, M. F., Buxhoeveden, D., Switala, A. and Roy, E. (2002a) 'Neuronal density and architecture (gray level index) in the brains of autistic patients.' *Journal of Child Neurology 17*, 7, 515–521.

Casanova, M. F., Buxhoeveden, D., Switala, A. and Roy, E. (2002b) 'Minicolumnar pathology in autism.' *Neurology 58*, 428–432.

Casanova, M. F., Buxhoeveden, D., Switala, A. and Roy, E. (2002c) 'Asperger syndrome and cortical neuropathology.' *Journal of Child Neurology 17*, 2, 142–145.

Casanova, M. F., Buxhoeveden, D. P. and Brown, C. (2002d) 'Clinical and macroscopic correlates of minicolumnar pathology in autism.' *Journal of Child Neurology 17*, 692–695.

Casanova, M. F., Buxhoeveden, D. and Gomez, J. (2003a) 'Disruption in the inhibitory architecture of the cell minicolumn: implications for autism.' *The Neuroscientist 9*, 6, 496–507.

Casanova, M. F., Buxhoeveden, D., Switala, A. and Roy, E. (2003b) 'Rett syndrome as a minicolumnopathy.' *Clinical Neuropathology 22*, 163–168.

Coleman, P. D., Romano, J., Lapham, L. and Simon, W. (1985) 'Cell counts in cerebral cortex of an autistic patient.' *Journal of Autism and Developmental Disorders 15*, 3, 245–255.

Colombo, J. A. (2001) 'A columnar-supporting mode of astroglial architecture in the cerebral cortex of adult primates?' *Neurobiology 9*, 1, 1–16.

Colombo, J. A., Fuchs, E., Hartig, W., Marotte, L. R. and Puissant, V. (2000) '"Rodent-like" and "primate-like" types of astroglial architecture in the adult cerebral cortex of mammals: a comparative study.' *Anatomy and Embriology 201*, 111–120.

Csillik, B., Nemcsok, J., Boncz, I. and Knyihar-Csillik, E. (1998) 'Nitric oxide synthase and the acetylcholine receptor in the prefrontal cortex: metasynaptic organization of the brain.' *Neurobiology 6*, 4, 383–404.

Curristin, S. M., Cao, A., Stewart, W. B., Zhang, H., Madri, J. A., Morrow J. S. and Ment, L. R. (2002) 'Disrupted synaptic development in the hypoxic newborn brain.' *Proceedings of the National Academy of Sciences of the United States of America 99*, 16729–16734.

DeFelipe, J., Hendry, S., Hashikawa, T., Molinari, M. and Jones, E. G. (1990) 'A microcolumnar structure of monkey cerebral cortex revealed by immunocytochemical studies of double bouquet cell axons.' *Neuroscience 37*, 3, 655–673.

Dykens, E. M. and Volkmar, F. R. (1997) 'Medical conditions associated with autism.' In D. J. Cohen and F. R. Volkmar (eds) *Handbook of Autism and Pervasive Developmental Disorders* (2nd edn), pp.388–407. New York: John Wiley and Sons.

Fatemi, S. H., Emamian, E. S., Kist, D., Sidwell, R. W., Nakajima, K., Akhter, P. *et al.* (1999) 'Defective corticogenesis and reduction in Reelin immunoreactivity in cortex and hippocampus of prenatally infected neonatal mice.' *Molecular Psychiatry 4*, 2, 145–154.

Fatemi, S. H., Stary, J. M., Halt, A. R. and Realmuto, G. R. (2001) 'Dysregulation of Reelin and Bcl-2 proteins in autistic cerebellum.' *Journal of Autism and Developmental Disorders 31*, 6, 529–535.

Favorov, O. V. and Kelly, G. (1994a) 'Minicolumnar organization within somatosensory cortical segregates, I: development of afferent connections.' *Cerebral Cortex 4*, 408–427.

Favorov, O. V. and Kelly, G. (1994b) 'Minicolumnar organization within somatosensory cortical segregates, II: emergent functional properties.' *Cerebral Cortex 4*, 428–442.

Fombonne, E., Roge, B., Claverie, J., Courty, S. and Fremolle, J. (1999) 'Microcephaly and macrocephaly in autism.' *Journal of Autism and Developmental Disorders 29*, 2, 113–119.

Friede, R. L. (1989) *Developmental Neuropathology* (2nd edn), p.347. Berlin: Springer-Verlag.

Gillberg, C. and Wing, L. (1999) 'Autism: not an extremely rare disorder.' *Acta Psychiatrica Scandinavica 99*, 6, 399–406.

Gordon, B. (1995) *Memory: Remembering and Forgetting in Everyday Life.* Baltimore, MD: Intelligence Amplification, Inc.

Gordon, C. T., State, R. T., Nelson, J. E., Hamburger, S. D. and Rapoport, J. L. (1993) 'A double blind comparison of clomipramine, desipramine and placebo in the treatment of autistic disorder.' *Archives of General Psychiatry 50*, 441–447.

Gustafsson, L. (1997) 'Inadequate cortical feature maps: a neural theory of autism.' *Biological Psychiatry 42*, 1138–1147.

Hardan, A. Y., Jou, R. J., Keshavan, M. S., Varma, R. and Minshew, N. J. (2004) 'Increased frontal cortical folding in autism: a preliminary MRI study.' *Psychiatry Research 131*, 3, 263–268.

Harding, B. and Copp, A. J. (1997) 'Malformations.' In D. I. Graham and P. L. Lantos (eds). *Greenfield's Neuropathology*, pp. 397–533. London: Arnold.

Herbert, M. R., Ziegler, D. A., Makris, N., Filipek, P. A., Kemper, T. L., Normandin, J. J. *et al.* (2004) 'Localization of white matter volume increase in autism and developmental language disorder.' *Annals of Neurology 55*, 4, 530–540.

Hirano, A. (1985) 'Neurons, astrocytes, and ependyma.' In R. L. Davis and D. M. Robertson (eds) *Textbook of Neuropathology*, pp.1–91. Baltimore MD: Williams and Wilkins.

Hof, P. R., Krabe, R., Bovier, P. and Bouras, C. (1991) 'Neuropathological observations in a case of autism presenting with self-injury behavior.' *Acta Neuropathologica 82*, 321–326.

Hussman, J. P. (2001) 'Suppressed GABAergic inhibition as a common factor in suspected etiologies of autism.' *Journal of Autism and Developmental Disorders 31*, 2, 247–248.

Ichinohe, N., Fujiyama, F., Kaneko, T. and Rockland, K. S. (2003) 'Honeycomb-like mosaic at the border of layers 1 and 2 in the cerebral cortex.' *Journal of the Neurological Sciences 23*, 4, 1372–1382.

Jorde, L. B., Hasstedt, S. J., Ritvo, E. R., Mason-Brothers, A., Freeman, B. J., Pingree, C. *et al.* (1991) 'Complex segregation analysis of autism.' *American Journal of Human Genetics 49*, 932–938.

Just, M. A., Cherkassky, V. L., Keller, T. A. and Minshew, N. J. (2004) 'Cortical activation and synchronization during sentence comprehension in high-functioning autism: evidence of underconnectivity.' *Brain 127*, 8, 1811–1821.

Kanner, L. (1943) 'Autistic disturbances of affective contact.' *Nervous Child 2*, 217–250. Reprinted in L. Kanner (ed.) (1973) *Childhood Psychosis: Initial Studies and New Insights.* Washington, DC: V. H. Winston.

Kemper, T. and Bauman, M. (1993) 'The contribution of neuropathologic studies to the understanding of autism.' *Neurologic Clinics 11*, 1, 175–187.

Koenig, K., Tsatsamis, K. D. and Volkmar, F. R. (2001) 'Neurobiology and genetics of autism: a developmental perspective.' In J. A. Burack, T. Charman, N. Yirmiya and P. R. Zelazo (eds) *The Development of Autism: Perspectives from Theory and Research*, pp. 81–101. Mahwah, NJ: Erlbaum.

Lohmann, H. and Koppen, H. J. (1995) 'Postnatal development of pyramidal dendritic and axonal bundles in the visual cortex of the rat.' *Journal für Hirnforschung 36*, 1, 101–111.

Lorente de Nó, R. (1949) 'Cerebral cortex architecture, intracortical connections, motor projections.' In J. F. Fulton (ed) *Physiology of the Nervous System* (3rd edn), Chapter 15, pp.288–330. Oxford: Oxford University Press.

Lotspeich, L. J. and Ciaranello, R. D. (1993) 'The neurobiology and genetics of infantile autism.' *International Review of Neurobiology 35*, 87–129.

Luna, B., Minshew, N. J., Garver, K. E., Lazar, N. A., Thulborn, K. R., Eddy, W. F. and Sweeney, J. A. (2002) 'Neocortical system abnormalities in autism: an fMRI study of spatial working memory.' *Neurology 59*, 6, 834–840.

Mountcastle, V. B. (1998) *Perceptual Neuroscience: The Cerebral Cortex.* Cambridge, MA: Harvard University Press.

Olsson, I., Steffenburg, S. and Gillberg, C. (1988) 'Epilepsy in autism and autistic like conditions: a population-based study.' *Archives of Neurology 45*, 666–668.

Orban, G. A. (1984) *Studies in Brain Function, Vol. II: Neuronal Operation in the Visual Cortex.* Berlin: Springer.

O'Riordan, M. (2000) 'Superior modulation of activation levels of stimulus representations does not underlie superior discrimination in autism.' *Cognition 77*, 2, 81–96.

Ornitz, E. M. (1989) 'Autism at the interface between sensory and information processing.' In G. Dawson (ed.) *Autism: Nature, Diagnosis and Treatment*, pp.174–207. New York: Guilford Press.

Peters, A. and Payne, B. R. (1993) 'Numerical relationship between geniculocortical afferents and pyramidal cell modules in cat primary visual cortex.' *Cerebral Cortex 3*, 69–78.

Peters, A. and Sethares, C. (1991) 'Layer IVA of rhesus monkey primary visual cortex.' *Cerebral Cortex 1*, 6, 445–462.

Peters, A. and Sethares, C. (1996) 'Myelinated axons and the pyramidal cell modules in monkey primary visual cortex.' *Journal of Comparative Neurology 365*, 2, 232–255.

Peters, A. and Yilmaz, E. (1993) 'Neuronal organization in area 17 of cat visual cortex.' *Cerebral Cortex 3*, 49–68.

Piven, J., Berthier, M. L., Starkstein, S. E., Nehme, E., Pearlson, G. and Folstein, S. (1990) 'Magnetic resonance imaging evidence for a defect of cerebral cortical development in autism.' *American Journal of Psychiatry 147*, 734–739.

Piven, J., Arndt, S., Bailey, J. and Andreasen, N. (1996) 'Regional brain enlargement in autism: a magnetic resonance imaging study.' *Journal of the American Academy of Child and Adolescent Psychiatry 35*, 530–536.

Rakic, P. and Kornack, D. R. (2001) 'Neocortical expansion and elaboration during primate evolution: a view from neuroembryology.' In D. Falk and K. R. Gibson (eds) *Evolutionary Anatomy of the Primate Cerebral Cortex*, pp. 30–56. Cambridge, England: Cambridge University Press.

Rapin, I. (1997) 'Autism.' *New England Journal of Medicine 337*, 2, 97–104.

Rapin, I. and Katzman, R. (1998) 'Neurobiology of autism.' *Annals of Neurology 43*, 1, 7–14.

Raymond, G. V., Bauman, M. L. and Kemper, T. L. (1996) 'Hippocampus in autism: a Golgi analysis.' *Acta Neuropathologica 91*, 117–119.

Rockel, A. J., Hiorns, R. W. and Powell, T. P. (1980) 'The basic uniformity of structure of the neocortex.' *Brain 103*, 221–224.

Rodier, P. M. (2000) 'The early origins of autism.' *Scientific American 282*, 2, 56–63.

Rodier, P. M. (2002) 'Converging evidence for brain stem injury in autism.' *Development and Psychopathology 14*, 3, 537–557.

Rodier, P. M., Ingram, J. L., Tisdale, B., Nelson, S. and Romano, J. (1996) 'Embryological origin for autism: developmental anomalies of the cranial nerve motor nuclei.' *Journal of Comparative Neurology 370*, 2, 247–261.

Rodier, P. M., Bryson, S. E. and Welch, J. P. (1997) 'Minor malformations and physical measurements in autism: data from Nova Scotia.' *Teratology 55*, 5, 319–325.

Schmolke, C. and Kunzle, H. (1997) 'On the presence of dendrite bundles in the cerebral cortex of the Madagascan lesser hedgehog tenrec and the red-eared pond turtle.' *Anatomy and Embryology 196*, 3, 195–213.

Selemon, L. D. and Goldman-Rakic, P. S. (1999) 'The reduced neuropil hypothesis: a circuit based model of schizophrenia.' *Biological Psychiatry 45*, 17–25.

Skoglund, T. S., Pascher, R. and Berthold, C. H. (1996) 'Aspects of the quantitative analysis of neurons in the cerebral cortex.' *Journal of Neuroscience Methods 28*, 70(2), 201–210.

Skoglund, T. S., Pascher, R. and Berthold, C. H. (2004) 'Aspects of the organization of neurons and dendritic bundles in primary somatosensory cortex of the rat.' *Neuroscience Research 50*, 2, 189–198.

Smalley, S. L. (1991) 'Genetic influences in autism.' *Psychiatric Clinics of North America 14*, 1, 125–139.

Strömland, K., Sjögreen, L., Miller, M., Gillberg, C., Wentz, E., Johansson, M. *et al.* (2002) 'Mobius sequence: a Swedish multidiscipline study.' *European Journal of Paediatric Neurology 6*, 1, 35–45.

Sweeney, J. A., Takarae, Y., Macmillan, C., Luna, B. and Minshew, N. J. (2004) 'Eye movements in neurodevelopmental disorders.' *Current Opinion in Neurology 17*, 1, 37–42.

Tuchman, R. F. and Rapin, I. (1997) 'Regression in pervasive developmental disorders: seizures and epileptiform electroencephalogram correlates.' *Pediatrics 88*, 1211–1218.

Turner, M., Barnby, G. and Bailey, A. (2000) 'Genetic clues to the biological basis of autism.' *Molecular Medicine Today 6*, 238–244.

Volkmar, F. R. and Nelson, D. S. (1990) 'Seizure disorders in autism.' *Journal of the American Academy of Child and Adolescent Psychiatry 29*, 127–129.

von Economo, C. F. (1929) *The Cytoarchitectonics of the Human Cerebral Cortex*. Oxford, UK: Oxford University Press.

Wallenstein, G. V. and Hasselmo, M. E. (1997) 'GABAergic modulation of hippocampal population activity: sequence learning, place field development, and the phase precession effect.' *Journal of Neurophysiology 78*, 1, 393–408.

Williams, R. S., Hauser, S. L., Purpura, D. P., DeLong, G. R. and Swisher, C. N. (1980) 'Autism and mental retardation: neuropathologic studies performed in four retarded persons with autistic behavior.' *Archvies of Neurology 37*, 749–753.

Chapter 13

Genetic Research into the Autistic Disorder

Ángel Díez-Cuervo

INTRODUCTION

The autistic disorder or infantile autism is a disorder of neurological development caused by a dysfunction of the central nervous system of variable aetiology, and which is diagnosed as a behavioural syndrome. The onset of symptoms occurs within the first three years of life and its principal manifestations are a qualitative impairment of reciprocal social interaction and communication (verbal and non-verbal) and the development of restrictive, repetitive and stereotypic patterns of behaviour, interests and activity in general. About 70 per cent of the individuals suffering from this disorder present mental retardation of variable severity.

At present, it is accepted that the mental disorders and complex behaviours, and hence autism, are polygenic disorders, meaning that they are the consequence of a group of interdependent genes, located at different points in the genome and which require a minimum but necessary number of genes to develop, though this number is not always the same. The proposed hypothesis is that each one of the genes which is involved gives rise to a small quantity of risk for the disorder and that only when this quantity exceeds a certain threshold does the individual present the complete phenotype (Jones and Szatmari 2002). The initial genetic studies in families with multiple incidences (with more than one affected child) would suggest the existence of two to ten interacting autism susceptibility genes (Pickles *et al.* 1995). However, subsequent genome research suggests that the individual must inherit at least 15 to 20 genes (genetic heterogeneity) (Risch *et al.* 1999), which interact synergically to express the autism phenotype. Of these genes, some will act in all cases and others in various combinations, influencing the severity or expression of the phenotype, and it has been stated that the autistic disorder is the most genetic of the neuropsychiatric syndromes.

GENETIC STUDIES IN TWINS

Studies performed in twins (Bailey *et al.* 1995; Folstein and Rutter 1977; Smalley, Asarnow and Spence 1988; Steffenburg *et al.* 1989) conclude that monozygotic twins (MZ, coming from a single fertilized ovum) have a concordance rate (the probability that both twins are autistic) of over 60 per cent for the complete syndrome, whereas no concordance is found between dizygotic twins (DZ, from two different ova). This high rate of concordance in MZ twins provides solid proof of a genetic cause for autism. Furthermore, it has been shown that up to 76 per cent of MZ twins who are not concordant for autism present cognitive disorders, disturbances of language and/or social deficits in comparison with 0 per cent in DZ twins. Also, when the twins were re-evaluated for broader autistic phenotypes, including communication and social abilities, the percentage concordance rose from 60 per cent to 92 per cent in MZ twins and did not reach 10 per cent in DZ twins (Bailey *et al.* 1995; Le Couteur *et al.* 1996). A follow-up study (Bolton and Rutter 1990) showed that almost all MZ twins with cognitive disorders who were not diagnosed as autistic in the first study subsequently presented significant difficulties in reciprocal social interaction. In another study (Steffenburg *et al.* 1989), the concordance in MZ twins did not vary after inclusion of the cognitive disorder, whereas the concordance rose from the initial 0 per cent to 30 per cent in the DZ twin group.

These results suggest that, as MZ twins shared 100 per cent and DZ twins 50 per cent of their genes, other factors must be involved in the concordance rates, factors which may have acted on only one of the twins and, possibly, that one of the discrepant MZ twins may have sustained a random epigenetic mutation in early embryonic life which altered the expression of the genetic trait (Muhle, Trentacoste and Rapin 2004). There is also discussion about the possible influence of MZ twins sharing one or having two placentas as, if the zygote divides between the fourth and seventh day, the twins will be monochorionic (found in two-thirds of MZ twins) whereas if this occurs within the 72 hours after fertilization, the MZ twins will be dichorionic; in this latter case, just as these twins differ in birthweight, blood cholesterol levels, cognitive function, etc. (Kaufman 1999), could an epigenetic mutation favouring autism occur in just one of the pair of dichorionic twins in early embryonic life?

Research into adopted MZ twins has also been considered, comparing twins brought up together with those who were brought up separately, in order to evaluate whether the influence of the genetic factor continues to be the same or if, in contrast, it differs, with environmental factors playing a more important role. This approach would be very strict and practically impossible to carry through, in view of the rarity with which the two situations will occur together; there are thus no studies of this type. It has also been suggested that discordance between MZ twins could be due to alterations suffered during labour, though this proposal has been rejected as the majority of obstetric complications are a consequence of abnormalities specific to the foetus, acquired in the initial stages of embryonic development, and are not the cause of autism, as may be observed from the high percentage of dystocic deliveries with non-autistic children (MRC 2001).

Some studies (Greenberg *et al.* 2001; Vukicevic and Siegel 1990) have suggested that the specific nature of twins (monozygosis, foetal hypoalimentation, placental insufficiency, etc.) is an important risk factor in the aetiology of autism. The results of another study (Hallmayer *et al.* 2002), with larger, well-defined samples, have rejected this suggestion, demonstrating that the high proportion found in affected twins is due to the high ratio of concordance rates in MZ twins. The conclusion is that twin studies support the hypothesis that the high prevalence of the autistic phenotype in affected families is principally due to genetic rather than environmental factors (Folstein and Rosen-Shidley 2001; Lauritsen and Ewald 2001).

FAMILIES: RECURRENCE IN SIBLINGS

Family studies have indicated a recurrence factor of 2.2–8 per cent among the siblings of affected probands, depending on the autism spectrum disorder (ASD) subgroups being studied (Chakrabarti and Fombonne 2001; Folstein and Rosen-Shidley 2001; Rutter *et al.* 1999). This would imply a 50 to 100-fold risk increase over the general population (Bailey *et al.* 1998b; Szatmari *et al.* 1998), much higher than for bipolar disorder, schizophrenia or alcoholism, although the recurrence rate in the siblings of autistic children cannot be determined accurately due to so-called 'genetic interruption' (Cook 2001; Slager *et al.* 2001), as families often decide not to have more children when they already have one or more affected offspring.

More discrete and variable phenotypic expressions of autism are more frequent in first-degree relatives of individuals with autism than in the general population. This is due to the so-called anticipation, which suggests the possibility of an increase in the severity of the phenotype over successive generations due to the involvement of multiple autism genes, though not sufficient to develop the complete syndrome (Pickles *et al.* 1995; Piven *et al.* 1997). For the same reason, the preponderance of other related developmental disorders, in particular language and communication disorders, repetitive and stereotypic behaviours, impaired social abilities, as well as other disturbances such as social phobia and the obsessive-compulsive disorder in non-autistic relatives of individuals with autism, suggests the existence of an underlying genetic susceptibility (Hollander *et al.* 2003; Murphy *et al.* 2000; Piven and Palmer 1999; Piven *et al.* 1991, 1994, 1997; Smalley, McCracken and Tanguay 1995). From these observations it may be concluded that autism is a polygenic disorder in which the interactions between several genes can give rise to the autistic phenotype in varying degrees of intensity (Bailey *et al.* 1998a; Bolton *et al.* 1994).

The current recommendation is to perform studies based on endophenotypes, which are quantifiable traits (neurobiological, psychological and others) of a syndrome (Gottesman and Gould 2003), and which offer potential advantages over the diagnostic category itself, as the inheritance of a trait usually corresponds to a few genes and their localization may therefore be easier. In autism, a principal endophenotype could be the cranial circumference, as a significant percentage of individuals with autism are born with a normal cranial circumference and present an increase in the growth of this parameter during early infancy (Lainhart *et al.* 1997). This is due, in part, to insufficient apoptosis (synaptic pruning and cell death), although only 20 per cent of children with autism satisfy criteria of macrocrania (Fombonne *et al.* 1999). Other phenotypes of interest include platelet hyperserotonaemia, the level of cognitive function, an impairment of language, communication or social abilities, the presence or absence of epileptic seizures, repetitive and restrictive behaviours, dysmorphologies and even the response to certain drugs.

CHROMOSOMAL ABNORMALITIES

Although a chromosomal abnormality has only been identified in 5–9 per cent of individuals with autism (Cook 2001; Folstein and Rosen-Shidley 2001; Fombonne *et al.* 1997; Wassink *et al.* 2001a), a number of manifestations (deletions, duplications or triplications, translocations, inversions, etc.) have been reported (Cook 1998; Gillberg 1998; Herzing *et al.* 2002; Lauritsen *et al.* 1999). These percentages vary depending on the characteristics of the study population, and are generally higher when individuals with autism and severe mental retardation and/or dysmorphias are included in the samples (Konstantareas and Homatidis 1999; Miles and Hillman 2000; Rutter *et al.* 1994). Current research is therefore studying more homogeneous samples with the autistic phenotype but without other concurrent abnormalities. Since large deletions or duplications contain hundreds or thousands of genes, finding the causative gene can be very difficult. It is therefore preferable to focus research on translocations or inversions in which only two breakpoints are found, giving a maximum of two candidate loci. Currently, special attention is being paid to the 2q37, 7q31 and 15q11–q13 regions, which have often been implicated in individuals with autism. Of these, the most frequently observed, in 1–4 per cent of individuals with autism, are duplications (Bolton *et al.* 2001; Boyar *et al.* 2001; Cook *et al.* 1997b; Flejter *et al.* 1996; Thomas *et al.* 2003), deletions (Nurmi *et al.* 2001; Schroer *et al.* 1998) and inversions (Borgatti *et al.* 2001; Cook 1998) in chromosome region 15q11–q13. The duplications usually present as interstitial repetitions of the proximal portion of the long arm of chromosome 15 and, occasionally, as an inverted duplication of the short arm and the proximal portion of the long arm of chromosome 15 (inv dup 15) (Cook 1998). All the duplications of the proximal part of chromosome 15q which give rise to autism have had a maternal route of inheritance (Boyar *et al.* 2001; Schroer *et al.* 1998). Although many duplications were *de novo* duplications, affected children had an unaffected mother with the same duplication (Browne *et al.* 1997; Cook 1998). Several studies have reported a 'chromosome 15 phenotype' which includes mental retardation, ataxia, language delay, epileptic seizures particularly developing during adolescence, and facial dysmorphia, which presents in some individuals with the ASD phenotype (Bolton *et al.* 2001; Boyar *et al.* 2001; Thomas *et al.* 2003).

Deletions in this region can give rise to very different monogenic disorders, such as the Angelman and Prader-Willi syndromes, which are associated with behavioural symptoms and which can resemble traits of the autistic phenotype, although they present very different somatic phenotypes. The cause of the Angelman syndrome may be a *de novo* deletion on the maternal chromosome 15q11–q13 (about 70% of cases) (Steffenburg *et al.* 1996), a mutation in gene *UBE3A* (20%), the absence of the maternal chromosome 15 with paternal uniparental disomy for chromosome 15 (3–7%), and impaired imprinting (3%), an epigenetic process which causes a different expression of the two alleles of a gene on the chromosomes of distinct parental origin, i.e. the gene is only expressed on one chromosome and is silent on the other, and the difference in the manifestations of the genetic disorders will depend on the sex of the progenitor transferring the genes. In the Prader-Willi syndrome, the causes are a deletion on the 15q11–q13 chromosome of paternal origin, mutations of the *SNRPN* gene, maternal uniparental trisomy with absence of the paternal chromosome 15, and impaired imprinting. In general, techniques more complex than karyotyping (molecular analysis, fluorescence in-situ hybridization (FISH), subtelomere tests, etc.) are required to detect the abnormalities described.

LINKAGE ANALYSIS OF THE COMPLETE GENOMIC IN MULTIPLEX FAMILIES

The findings in families with autistic children, and, in particular, in multiplex families (with more than one affected child), encourage us to perform linkage analysis studies in large samples of this type of family. This technique is based on the interchange of chromosomal material between homologous chromosomes which occurs during meiosis, leading to the crossing over of genetic material, such that two genes become closely related (linked) on the same chromosome of a homologous pair. The linkage technique enables us to search for markers (specific alleles) in families, identifying specific chromosomal regions of the genomes which the affected individuals inherit more frequently than would occur by chance, leading to a high probability of them containing genes possibly linked to a given disease, in this case implicated in the autistic disorder.

Since 1998, many studies and investigations of the complete genome have been performed in groups of multiplex families (Auranen *et al.* 2002, 2003; Bakker *et al.* 2003; Buxbaum *et al.* 2002; CLSA 1999, 2001; Hutcheson *et al.* 2003; Liu *et al.* 2001; Philippe *et al.* 1999; Risch *et al.* 1999; Shao *et al.* 2002a, 2002b, 2003; Yonan *et al.* 2003). These have suggested different chromosomal regions in which autism susceptibility loci may be found. According to these studies, a number of regions and different positional candidate genes may be implicated, on practically all chromosomes, although the results still do not allow us to conclude that the genes found make a decisive contribution to the susceptibility to autism. In some cases they may be related to other developmental disorders (language deficits, stereotypies, social interaction disorders and anomalous behaviours which are similar to autism), or they show a low power of replication in the different studies. It has been suggested that samples of at least 1,000 sibling pairs would be necessary to detect linkage to more specific regions with greater certainty.

After the first complete genome studies in the ASD, research has focused its attention on a region of chromosome 7q (Ashley-Koch *et al.* 1999; Badner and Gershon 2002; CLSA 1999; Gillberg 1998; IMGSAC 1998, 2001; Liu *et al.* 2001; Scherer *et al.* 2003). This is a long region with two distinct peaks at 7q21–Q22 and 7q32–Q36, and in which translocations and inversions have been located (Ashley-Koch *et al.* 1999; Tentler *et al.* 2001; Vincent *et al.* 2000; Warburton *et al.* 2000). Three distinct regions have been identified in the mapping of the breakpoints of the translocation, affecting genes *FOXP2*, *NPTX2* and *TCAG* (Scherer *et al.* 2003), and a mutation in gene *RAY1/ST7* (Vincent *et al.* 2002) which it has been possible to relate to the autism phenotype, although this has not been replicated in other studies.

Both gene *FOXP2* and gene *TCAG* are found to be mutated in individuals with language and speech disorders. Mutations of gene *WNT2* on 7q31, causing changes in amino acid metabolism, were found in two families with autism in which one of the affected parents transmitted the mutation to two affected offspring (Wassink *et al.* 2001b). Chromosomal region 7q22 was found to contain gene *RELN*, first identified in reeler mutant mice and subsequently in human autosomal recessive lysencephaly, caused by impaired neuronal migration, a cerebral abnormality reported in subjects with autism (Bailey *et al.* 1998a). Subsequent studies have not been able to find an association with the ASD (Bonora *et al.* 2003; Li *et al.* 2004) and research is currently being performed in post mortem brains of autistic individuals into abnormalities of expression of reelin, the protein product of this gene (Fatemi *et al.* 2001).

The conclusion of the various studies is that, in the large region of chromosome 7q21–Q36, variant genes exist which cause susceptibility to the ASD. Research must continue into these genes using fluorescent in-situ hybridization (FISH) techniques, as these are able to locate the exact position of the breakpoint, permitting visualization of the candidate susceptibility genes and the DNA fragments on the chromosomes at any stage of the cell cycle. Thanks to this technique, the human *neurobeachin* gene (*hNbea*) has been identified as a candidate for autism (Castermans *et al.* 2003) in a *de novo* translocation onto chromosome 13q [46,XY t (5;13) (q12.1; q13.2)]. In a linkage analysis (CLSA 1999), this gene was also identified on chromosome 13q as a candidate for autism. Mutations of gene *NLGNA*, located on chromosome Xp22.23, identified in two siblings with ASD, in their unaffected mother (Li *et al.* 2004) and in other individuals with autism (Thomas *et al.* 1999), are also apparently worthy of mention. This gene, together with the other members of the neuroligin family, is implicated in neuronal synapse formation and function (Rao *et al.* 2000; Scheiffele *et al.* 2000).

As a summary of the most important finding of the various studies, the following loci and genes may be indicated on chromosome 2q24–Q33: *cAMP-GEFII, Cd28/ctla 4, DLX1/DLX2, TBR1, CHN1, GAD1, CREB2/ATF2, NEUROD1, SLC25A12, SCRT, HOXD1*; on chromosome 3p25–p26: OXTR; on chromosome 6p21: *GRIK2/GLUR6*; on chromosome 7p15: *HOXA1*; on chromosome 7q21–q22: *DLX6, GRM3, NPTX2, RELN*; on chromosome 7q31–q34: *DBH, GRM8, RAY1/ST7, WNT2, IMMPL2, NRCAM, CORTBP2, LAMB1, UBE2H, CADPS2, HOXB1, PERG/MEST, SPCH1/FOXP2*; on chromosome 7q36.3: *VIPR2, EN-2*; on chromosome 11p15: *HRAS*; on chromosome 12q: *AVPR1a*; on chromosome 15q11–q13: *GABRB3, UBE3A/E6-AP, ATP10C*; on chromosome 16p13: *NMDA, TSC2*; on chromosome 17q11: *5HTT, SERT*; and on chromosome Xq13.1: *NLGN3, NLGN4* (Auranen *et al.* 2003; Jamain *et al.* 2003; Liu *et al.* 2001). Of all these findings, concordant results in a number of different studies have only been achieved with chromosome 7q.

The discordant and, sometimes, contradictory results of the studies and their lack of replication draw attention to the intrinsic complexity of the genetic heterogeneity of the disorder. It appears that the participation of multiple genes, with different degrees of penetrance, at several different susceptibility loci, is necessary to cause the condition; these genes are not always the same in all families (genetic, allelic and phenotypic heterogeneity). There is also an influence of other epigenetic factors (different sizes and characteristics of the samples, different technologies used, insufficient mapping, the influence of environmental factors, variations in the behavioural characteristics and cognitive function, etc.). The lack of replication found in the studies suggests that reality is more complex than the models used in its investigation and that, for the moment, variability in the results is inevitable (Bartlett *et al.* 2005). The largest and most encouraging study to date on the genetics of autism is currently under way. This is a study designed by the *NAAR Autism Genome Project*, with the collaboration of four *National Institutes of Health* in the US, to map the human genome in order to search for the autism susceptibility genes. About 170 experts in genetics in some 50 academic and research institutions in the US, Canada, United Kingdom, France, Sweden, Denmark and Germany are participating in this study. In an initial phase, the research will involve two studies of the human genome analysing 6,000 DNA samples from 1,500 families with multiple incidences (parents and two affected children), with the aim of identifying the genetic patterns which are common to these families. For this first phase of the research, the Affymetrix GeneChip® DNA Array technology, which enables a rapid and accurate examination of the human genome using markers of about 10,000 single nucleotide polymorphisms (SNPs), is being used in all the subjects examined. The SNPs are changes of a single base which occur in the human DNA and which are shared by individuals suffering a given disease. In the second phase, detailed mapping of the identified changes will be performed in order to create a map of the genes causing the phenotypes associated with autism. The results of this research will provide fundamental knowledge of the syndrome which will serve to improve its diagnosis, treatment and, most encouragingly, prevention.

STUDIES OF MONOGENIC DISORDERS

The current investigation of behavioural phenotypes provides evidence of the existence of a group of syndromes and diseases with specific genotypic and physical phenotypic (dysmorphological) characteristics, as well as motor, cognitive, linguistic and social abnormalities which is consistently associated with a biological disorder which permits their individualization (Flint and Yule 1994; O'Brien, Yule and Nyhan 1995). Sometimes, certain behavioural characteristics of these phenotypes coincide with manifestations characteristic of the autistic disorder. Genetic research has therefore also focused its attention on discovering what percentage of cases of autism is associated with specific monogenic behavioural phenotypes in order to be able to deduce its presence from clinical markers. Currently, these syndromes are diagnosed in approximately 10 per cent of individuals with autism (Gillberg and Coleman 1996; Rutter *et al.* 1994), although the autistic phenotype may be being applied with excessively broad criteria, the so-called *autistic traits*, which may give rise to a falsely high number of specific syndromes associated with the autistic disorder. The most important neurogenetic disorders include: Aarskog syndrome (translocation Xp11.21-*FGD1*), Angelman syndrome (described above), Cornelia de Lange syndrome (duplication in 3q26.3–q27 and mutations of *CHRD, THPO* and *GSC)* (unconfirmed), Down syndrome (non-disjuntion/trisomy 21, mosaicism and translocation), Duchenne's muscular dystrophy (Xp21-dystrophin), tuberous sclerosis complex (9q34-*TSC1* in 50 per cent of cases and 16p13-*TSC2* in the other 50 per cent), phenylketonuria (PKU) (12q22–q24-*PAH*), hypomelanosis of Ito (translocation of Xp21.1-*COL5A1*) (unconfirmed), Joubert syndrome (6q23.2–q23.3-*AHI1*), Lesch-Nyhan syndrome (Xq26–27-*HPRT*), Moebius syndrome (deletion 13q12.2 and/or translocation of 13q12.2–13) (unconfirmed), Neurofibromatosis type 1 (17q11.2-*NF1*), Noonan syndrome (12q.22-qter-*SHP2*, of maternal inheritance in the majority of cases), Prader-Willi syndrome (described above), Smith-Lemli-Opitz syndrome (11q12–q13-*DHCR7*), Smith Magenis syndrome (17p11.2-*NSMH1A*), Sotos syndrome (5q35-*NSD1*), Williams syndrome (7q11.23-*elastin*), and fragile-X syndrome (Xq27.3-*FMR1*). Although many of these disorders cannot be considered to be cases of idiopathic autism, their study continues with the aim of finding autism susceptibility genes (Baieli *et al.* 2003; Diez-Cuervo 2000; Dixon-Salazar *et al.* 2004; Fan and Farrell 1994; Gillberg and Steffenburg 1989; Golfin *et al.* 2001; Kent *et al.* 1999; Komoto *et al.* 1984; Morrow, Whitman and Accardo 1990; O'Brien *et al.* 1995; Ozonoff *et al.* 1999; Reiss *et al.* 1985; Rougeulle, Glatt and Lalande 1997; Stevenson *et al.* 1994; Tierney *et al.* 2001; Williams and Hersh 1998; Zappella 1993; Zwaigenbaum and Tarnopolsky 2003).

CANDIDATE GENES

Since the Human Genome Project has allowed the susceptibility loci of complex disorders to be identified (Spence 2001), research has used various methodologies to search for the association between the so-called candidate genes and autism. A candidate gene is one which the investigators suspect may be related to a specific illness or disorder. Differentiation is made between positional and functional genes. In the case of autism, the positional candidate genes are those which are located in a specific chromosomal region with a higher frequency in individuals suffering the disorder than in the general population, whereas the functional candidate genes are those which produce certain substances which are involved in the development, cytoarchitecture and function of different areas of the brain related to autism. The most solid candidate genes are those which satisfy both positional and functional conditions.

In order to attempt to find the association between specific genes and autism, research uses studies of the complete genome (genetic markers frequent in populations of multiplex autism families), cytogenetic studies (hereditary or spontaneous genetic abnormalities in a specific individual) and the linkage disequilibrium test, reducing the area of the previously identified search or examining the linkage to a specific gene. The ultimate objective of all these techniques is to identify the heritable genetic mutations on the candidate genes which play a role in cerebral development and alterations of which predispose an individual to developing autism or associated traits (Muhle *et al.* 2004).

To date, only a few studies of candidate genes in autism have provided solid evidence of an association, although these have not always been replicated in independent samples. The principal candidate genes include *HOXD1* on chromosome 2; *GAT1* and *OXTR* on chromosome 3; *FOXP2, HOXA1, HOXB1, RELN* and *WNT2* on chromosome 7; *GABRA5, GABRB3, GABRG3, UBE3A* and *ATP10C* on chromosome 15; and *NLGN3* and *NLGN4* on the X chromosome.

During development, the gene *HOXD1* acts on the cytoarchitecture of the prosencephalon (diencephalic structures: thalamus and hippocampus), and its relationship with autism was found in a subgroup of individuals with autism and language delay (Buxbaum *et al.* 2002).

The gene *GAT1* codes for a protein which acts in association with the neurotransmitter GABA (gamma-aminobutyric acid), an important inhibitory neurotransmitter in the mammalian central nervous system. The investigators suggest that an excess or dysfunction of GABA may overstimulate the brain, leading to hypervigilance behaviours, as are presented by a high percentage of individuals with autism. The gene *OXTR* produces the protein of the oxytocin receptor. In studies in animals, it has been reported that this gene is involved in early cerebral development. It is also found in the brain of human beings, but its involvement in cerebral development is unknown. Some studies performed in rats have confirmed that when higher quantities than normal of oxytocin are present, non-functional repetitive behaviours develop, such as reiterative cleaning of the face with the paws and stretching movements.

The gene *FOXP2* appears to be related to a disorder of speech and language, specifically with developmental verbal dyspraxia (difficulty to perform the facial movements necessary for verbal articulation) and problems of language processing. It is a candidate gene for autism in view of the language disorders which autistic individuals present, although replication has still not been achieved. The genes *HOXA1* and *HOXB1* are involved in development of the posterior encephalon (cerebellum and part of the brain stem), and they are considered to be candidate genes for autism because some individuals with this disorder have evidence of abnormalities in these areas of the encephalon on neuroimaging. However, variations in these genes have been found in individuals with and without autism, and their involvement is therefore unclear. The gene *RELN* is involved in neuronal proliferation and migration during foetal development. This gene has a polymorphic repetition of ten or more trinucleotides which varies between individuals (Persico *et al.* 2001). Investigators at Duke University examined the repetitions in the gene *RELN* in families participating in the Collaborative Autistic Disorder Team (CADT) study and in families in the Autism Genetics Resource Exchange (AGRE). They found no significant evidence of an association between the number of repetitions in the gene and the autistic disorder in the families in the CADT study, but they did find a possible association between the gene *RELN* with eight to ten repetitions and autism in the families in the AGRE. This line of investigation is therefore being continued. The gene *WNT2* is involved in neuronal migration and function during development of the foetal nervous system. Wassink *et al.* (2001b) found a variant in individuals with autism in the subgroup presenting severe language delay. Mutations in the mouse give rise to a behavioural phenotype characterized by a reduction in social interaction. The genes *GABRB3*, *GABRA5* and *GABRG3* have also been the subject of research and, of these, gene *GABRB3* is the one which appears to be most closely related to autism. It is expressed very early throughout the brain and an allelic association has been found in autism. Its absence in the mouse leads to the development of learning deficits, EEG abnormalities, seizures and motor restlessness (Buxbaum *et al.* 2002; Martin *et al.* 2000; Menold *et al.* 2001). The gene *UBE3A* is a candidate gene due to its position in the region 15q11–q13 and its known association with Angelman syndrome, with mutation and/or deletion of the copy inherited from the mother (Herzing *et al.* 2002; Nurmi *et al.* 2001; Veenstra-Vander Weele *et al.* 1999). This gene participates in the formation of the hippocampus and the Purkinje cells, areas frequently affected in individuals with autism. The gene *ATP10C* codes for a transporter ATPase which is involved in ion transport (Meguro *et al.* 2001). The region of chromosome 15 on which this gene is located was studied in a group of ten unrelated subjects presenting autism, finding variations which were not found in a second group of 115 subjects with autism, suggesting that this gene does not always appear to be related to autism. The authors concluded that the groups studied were too small to be able to draw significant conclusions and that further studies with larger samples of subjects with and without autism were required (Kim *et al.* 2002).

The genes *NLGN3* and *NLGN4* have been investigated in a study (Jamain *et al.* 2003). These genes produce the neuroligin proteins which are involved in message transmission between neurones. The investigators looked for changes in these two genes in 158 subjects with autism or Asperger syndrome, finding mutations of gene *NLGN3* in one family and of gene *NLGN4* in another, concluding that the mutations found could be implicated in some but not all families with autism and that further research with more numerous groups of families with autism was necessary.

The results of some studies have suggested that certain individuals with autism present disturbances of the cerebral neurotransmitters (serotonin, dopamine, GABA, etc.). These are closely related to early dysgenetic processes occurring in the cerebral cortex, the cerebellum and the brain stem as a consequence of impaired neuronal migration, an increase in neuronal proliferation and a reduction or absence of apoptosis. These disturbances of the neurotransmitters, documented in neurochemical, neuroimaging and autopsy studies, etc., may be a consequence of changes in the functional candidate genes which regulate their metabolism, for which reason they have been and continue to be a subject of research.

In one of these studies (Hérault *et al.* 1993), studying the *c-Harvey Ras* (*Hras*) oncogene, located on the short arm of chromosome 11 (11p15), a possible association was reported between the allele frequency of the *Hras RFLP* allele and the autistic disorder. In a subsequent study, the same authors (Hérault *et al.* 1994) studied 72 autistic individuals, without finding any significant difference in the frequency of the allele for the three loci studied on chromosome 11 between the autistic population and controls. Later, in another study (Hérault *et al.* 1995) with 55 autistic individuals, it was concluded that, apart from a possible association between autism and a marker located at the 3'-terminus of the coding sequences of gene *HRAS*, a second marker confirmed a possible association of the *HRAS* gene markers with the autistic syndrome, indicating autism-susceptibility for the DNA region of chromosome 11. Another study, which investigated autism as well as other psychiatric disorders, included 48 autistic individuals (Comings *et al.* 1996). This study suggested that the *HRAS* gene may participate in obsessive-compulsive behaviours and phobias observed in autism rather than in the syndrome itself.

Despite the fact that the results of the research on gene *HRAS* are not uniform, this type of study continues to be of obvious interest, since more than 25 per cent of individuals with autism present a state of hyperserotonaemia (Anderson *et al.* 1987; Cook 1990). This may have contributed to the formation of cerebral abnormalities at some stage of development, giving rise to certain behavioural characteristics of autism

(Anderson 2002; Chugani 2002), although it has still not been possible to confirm the mechanisms underlying this concept. Since 1961, when the first study of the blood levels of serotonin (5-HT) in children with autism and other children with mental retardation was started (Schain and Freedman 1961), there have been studies in which a high percentage of autistic individuals presented levels considered to be normal (Yuwiler *et al.* 1971) and others which indicate the contrary (Badcock, Spence and Stern 1987; Launay *et al.* 1988; Ritvo *et al.* 1970). It must also be taken into consideration that the reduction of the plasma levels of 5-HT does not always improve autistic behaviour, suggesting that hyperserotonaemia may correlate better with the degree of associated mental retardation or only with certain behavioural characteristics of autism.

Some studies suggest that the serotonin transporter gene (*5HTT, SERT*) may be implicated in the ASD after detecting an association in the 5' region of the gene both in studies of families with an affected child and in sibling pairs. Furthermore, the increase in platelet serotonin reuptake in hyperserotonergic first-degree relatives of individuals with ASD and the efficacy of the selective serotonin reuptake inhibitors on the stereotypic behaviours, anxiety and/or aggression sometimes associated with autism has meant that *SERT* may be considered a principal candidate gene (Bartlett *et al.* 2005; Cook *et al.* 1997a; Yonan *et al.* 2003), though other studies have not been able to confirm this.

In view of the therapeutic effects of the neuroleptics on the treatment of autism, certain results of neuroimaging studies, the knowledge of the existence of abnormal dopaminergic activity in the medial prefrontal cortex of children with autism (Ernst *et al.* 1997), and also the high blood, urinary and CSF catecholamine levels in some children with autism (Martineau *et al.* 1994), another line of research has focused its attention on the dopamine receptors, particularly receptor D2. However, similar conclusions to other studies have not yet been obtained.

Acetylcholine has also been suggested as a neurotransmitter associated with autism, based on the findings of autopsy studies of the parietal cortex and cerebellum of individuals with autism (Lee *et al.* 2002; Perry *et al.* 2001). Likewise, the glutaminergic system has been studied in the pathogenesis of autism, though definitive results have not yet been found.

The human homeobox genes *EN-1* and *EN-2*, located on chromosomes 2q13–q21 and 7q36.3, respectively (Köhler *et al.* 1993; Petit *et al.* 1995; Poole *et al.* 1988), have been evaluated in association studies and the authors concluded that several polymorphisms of gene *EN-2*, involved in cerebellar development, could be related to the physiopathology of autism. Other genes studied, such as *DLX1* and *DLX2* on chromosome 2q32, *GRIK2* on chromosome 6p21, *GRM8* on chromosome 7q31–q33 and *DBH* on chromosome 7q34, have still not been replicated and continue under investigation.

ANIMAL MODELS

The Brain Molecular Anatomy Project (BMAP) has been involved in cataloguing genes which are expressed in different parts of the brain during the different stages of development, building up a digital atlas of the brain of the mouse and other animals which will tell us how specific genes act and are expressed in certain regions of the brain in the different stages of development. This will facilitate the identification of genes in experimental animals and the possibility of their localization in the human being.

At present, animal models allow rapid breeding which facilitates the direct identification of patterns of hereditability and the number of loci involved. However, animal models, which have been shown to be useful for the study of certain diseases, cannot be used in autism, in the complete disorder, as it is very difficult to reproduce the variability and complexity of the behavioural phenotype and also because the anatomical phenotypes are due to a polygenic inheritance in the ASD and a monogenic inheritance in the mouse. Nevertheless, although animal models do not provide a perfect model of the disorder, they should be designed for the analysis of many biological variables and several behavioural variables (endophenotypes), as well as the relationship of these variables with the underlying cerebral neurobiological disturbances, without forgetting the importance of their use for the development of effective pharmacological treatment (Murcia, Gulden and Herrup 2005).

Current investigation is able to create animal models, usually using laboratory mice, by knocking out specific genes (knockout) or inserting new genes which modify their genomes (transgenic) during embryogenesis. Studies performed in transgenic mice indicate that the absence of the oxytocin gene (*Oxt*) causes a loss of social memory (Ferguson *et al.* 2000). Surgical and chemical techniques or infectious agents have also been used to induce lesions in the candidate regions of the brain, usually during development. The general conclusion is that it is necessary to improve the tools available to study these animal models and understand the results as these are still not well standardized (Andres 2002).

Genes have also been identified in the hippocampus, the amygdala and the cerebellum of the mouse associated with the regulation of neuronal cell growth, cell death and cell connectivity, as well as glial function (Grant *et al.* 1995; Tsirka *et al.* 1995), the structural abnormalities of which are very similar to those found in the brains of some individuals with autism. These homeobox (HOX) genes include *HOXA1* on chromosome 7p15, *HOXB1* on chromosome 7q31–q34 and *HOXD1* on chromosome 2q31–Q33 (Goodman and Scambler 2001; Ingram *et al.* 2000). Due to their scope of action, the nature of their effects and the regions of activity, it is considered that when these genes function in an anomalous manner, they may contribute to the genetic basis of some cases of idiopathic autism.

CONCLUSION

The current state of knowledge allows us to conclude that autism is a complex genetic syndrome involving many variants of different genes which, by interacting together, are able to cause susceptibility to the disorder. However, due to their complexity, it is still very difficult to identify the specific genes which contribute to this susceptibility in the majority of individuals with ASD. Despite this, the genetic studies performed in recent years must be considered very promising. Genetic study must be included in integrated neuroscientific research programmes, which also take into consideration environmental factors, neurobiology, neurophysiology, neuroimaging, neuropsychology, autopsy studies, cerebral tissue and DNA libraries, etc., in collaboration with the health care services. The aim of this research is to facilitate earlier diagnosis, provide more effective treatments, and even achieve cure and, above all, most encouragingly, to guarantee prevention of such a complex and devastating disorder.

REFERENCES

Anderson, G. M. (2002) 'Genetics of childhood disorders: XLV. Autism, part 4: serotonin in autism.' *Journal of American Academy of Child and Adolescent Psychiatry 41*, 1513–1516.

Anderson, G. M., Freedman, D. X., Cohen, D. J. *et al.* (1987) 'Whole blood serotonin in autistic and normal subjects.' *Journal of Child Psychology and Psychiatry 28*, 885–900.

Andres, C. (2002) 'Molecular genetics and animal models in autistic disorder.' *Brain Research Bulletin 57*, 109–119.

Ashley-Koch, A., Wolpert, C. M., Menold, M. M. *et al.* (1999) 'Genetic studies of autistic disorder and chromosome 7.' *Genomics 61*, 227–236.

Auranen, M., Vanhala, R., Varilo, T. *et al.* (2002) 'A genomewide screen for autism-spectrum disorders: evidence for a major susceptibility locus on chromosome 3q25–27.' *American Journal of Human Genetics 71*, 777–790.

Auranen, M., Varilo, T., Alen, R. *et al.* (2003) 'Evidence for allelic association on chromosome 3q25–27 in families with autism spectrum disorders originating from a subisolate of Finland.' *Molecular Psychiatry 8*, 879–884.

Badcock, N. R., Spence, G. J. and Stern, L. M. (1987) 'Blood serotonin levels in adults, autistic and non-autistic children, with a comparison of different methodologies.' *Annals of Clinical Biochemistry 24*, 625–634.

Badner, J. and Gershon, E. (2002) 'Regional meta-analysis of published data supports linkage of autism with markers on chromosome 7.' *Molecular Psychiatry 7*, 56–66.

Baieli, S., Pavone, L., Meli, C. *et al.* (2003) 'Autism and phenylketonuria.' *Journal of Autism and Developmental Disorders 33*, 201–204.

Bailey, A., Le Couteur, A., Gottesman, I. *et al.* (1995) 'Autism as a strongly genetic disorder: evidence from a British twin study.' *Psychological Medicine 25*, 63–77.

Bailey, A., Luthert, P., Dean, A. *et al.* (1998a) 'A clinicopathological study of autism.' *Brain 121* (Suppl), 889–905.

Bailey, A., Palferman, S., Heavey, L. *et al.* (1998b) 'A. Autism: the phenotype in relatives.' *Journal of Autism and Developmental Disorders 28*, 369–392.

Bakker, S. C., Van der Meulen, E. M., Buitelaar, J. K. *et al.* (2003) 'A whole-genome scan in 164 Dutch sib pairs with attention-deficit/hyperactivity disorder: suggestive evidence for linkage on chromosomes 7p and 15q.' *American Journal of Human Genetics 72*, 1251–1260.

Bartlett, C. W., Gharani, N., Millonig, J. H. *et al.* (2005) 'Three autism candidate genes: a synthesis of human genetic analysis with other disciplines.' *International Journal of Developmental Neuroscience 23*, 221–234.

Bolton, P. and Rutter, M. (1990) 'Genetic influences in autism.' *International Review of Psychiatry 2*, 67–80.

Bolton, P., Macdonald, H., Pickles, A. *et al.* (1994) 'A case-control family history study of autism.' *Journal of Child Psychology and Psychiatry 35*, 877–900.

Bolton, P., Dennis, N. R., Browne, C. E. *et al.* (2001) 'The phenotypic manifestations of interstitial duplications of proximal 15q with special reference to the autistic spectrum disorders.' *American Journal of Human Genetics 105*, 675–685.

Bonora, E., Beyer, K., Lamb, J. *et al.* (2003) 'Analysis of reelin as a candidate gene for autism.' *Molecular Psychiatry 8*, 885–892.

Borgatti, R., Piccinelli, P., Passoni, D. *et al.* (2001) 'Relationship between clinical and genetic features in "inverted duplicated chromosome 15" patients.' *Pediatric Neurology 24*, 111–116.

Boyar, F. Z., Whitney, M. M., Lossie, A. C. *et al.* (2001) 'A family with a grand-maternally derived interstitial duplication of proximal 15q.' *Clinical Genetics 60*, 421–430.

Browne, C. E., Dennis, N. R., Maher, E. *et al.* (1997) 'Inherited insterstitial duplications of proximal 15q: genotype–phenotype correlations.' *American Journal of Human Genetics 61*, 24–30.

Buxbaum, J. D., Silverman, J. M., Smith, C. J. *et al.* (2002) 'Evidence for a susceptibility gene for autism on chromosome 2 and for genetic heterogeneity.' *American Journal of Human Genetics 68*, 514–520.

Castermans, D., Wilquet, V., Parthoens, E. *et al.* (2003) 'The neurobeachin gene is disrupted by a translocation in a patient with idiopathic autism.' *Journal of Medical Genetics 40*, 352–356.

Chakrabarti, S. and Fombonne, E. (2001) 'Pervasive developmental disorders in preschool children.' *Journal of the American Medical Association 285*, 3093–3099.

Chugani, D. C. (2002) 'Role of altered brain serotonin mechanisms in autism.' *Molecular Psychiatry 7* (Suppl 2), S16–S17.

Collaborative Linkage Study of Autism (CLSA) (1999) 'An autosomal genomic screen for autism.' *American Journal of Medical Genetics 88*, 609–615.

Collaborative Linkage Study of Autism (CLSA) (2001) 'Incorporating language phenotypes strengthens evidence of linkage to autism.' *American Journal of Medical Genetics 105*, 539–547.

Comings, D. E., Wu, S., Chiu, C. *et al.* (1996) 'Studies of the c-Harvey-Ras gene in psychiatric disorders.' *Psychiatry Research 63*, 25–32.

Cook, E. H. (1990) 'Autism: review of neurochemical investigation.' *Synapse 6*, 292–308.

Cook, E. H. (1998) 'Genetics of autism.' *MRDD Research Reviews 4*, 113–120.

Cook, E. H. (2001) 'Genetics of autism.' *Child and Adolescent Psychiatric Clinics of North America 10*, 333–350.

Cook, E. H., Courchesne, R., Lord, C. *et al.* (1997a) 'Evidence of linkage between the serotonin transporter and autistic disorder.' *Molecular Psychiatry 2*, 247–250.

Cook, E. H., Lindgren, V., Leventhal, B. L. *et al.* (1997b) 'Autism or atypical autism in maternally but not paternally derived proximal 15q duplication.' *American Journal of Human Genetics 60*, 928–934.

Diez-Cuervo, A. (2000) 'Medical disorders and syndromes associated with autism.' In *Autismo. Una guía multimedia.* Madrid: PAUTA.

Dixon-Salazar, T., Silhavy, J. L., Marsh, S. E. *et al.* (2004) 'Mutations in the AHI1 gene, encoding jouberin, cause Joubert syndrome with cortical polymicrogyria.' *American Journal of Human Genetics 75*, 979–987.

Ernst, M., Zametkin, A. J., Matochik, J. A. *et al.* (1997) 'Low medial prefrontal dopaminergic activity in autistic children.' *Lancet 350*, 638.

Fan, Y. S. and Farrell, S. A. (1994) 'Prenatal diagnosis of interstitial deletion of 17(p11.2p11.2) (Smith-Magenis syndrome).' *American Journal of Human Genetics 49*, 253–254.

Fatemi, S. H., Stary, J. M., Halt, A. R. *et al.* (2001) 'Dysregulation of Reelin and Bcl-2 proteins in autistic cerebellum.' *Journal of Autism and Developmental Disorders 31*, 529–535.

Ferguson, J. N., Young, L. J., Hearn, E. F. *et al.* (2000) 'Social amnesia in mice lacking the oxytocin gene.' *Nature Genetics 25*, 284–288.

Flejter, W. L., Bennett-Baker, P. E., Ghaziuddin, M. *et al.* (1996) 'Cytogenetic and molecular analysis of inv dup (15) chromosomes observed in two patients with autistic disorder and mental retardation.' *American Journal of Medical Genetics 61*, 182–187.

Flint, J. and Yule, W. (1994) 'Behavioural phenotypes.' In M. Rutter, E. Taylor and L. Hersov (eds) *Child and Adolescent Psychiatry*, pp. 666–687. Oxford: Blackwell Scientific.

Folstein, S. E., Rosen-Shidley, B. (2001) 'Genetics of autism: complex aetiology for a heterogeneous disorder.' *Nature Reviews Genetics 2*, 943–955.

Folstein, S. and Rutter, M. (1977) 'Infantile autism: a genetic study of 21 twin pairs.' *Journal of Child Psychology and Psychiatry 18*, 297–321.

Fombonne, E., Du Mazaubrun, C., Cans, C. *et al.* (1997) 'Autism and associated medical disorders in a French epidemiological survey.' *Journal of American Academy of Child and Adolescent Psychiatry 36*, 1561–1569.

Fombonne, E., Roge, B., Claverie, J. *et al.* (1999) 'Microcephaly and macrocephaly in autism.' *Journal of Autism and Developmental Disorders 29*, 113–119.

Gillberg, C. (1998) 'Chromosomal disorders and autism.' *Journal of Autism and Developmental Disorders 28*, 415–425.

Gillberg, C. and Coleman, M. (1996) 'Autism and medical disorders: a review of the literature.' *Developmental Medicine and Child Neurology 38*, 191–202.

Gillberg, C. and Steffenburg, S. (1989) 'Autistic behaviour in Moebius syndrome.' *Acta Paediatrica Scandinavica 78*, 314–316.

Golfin, A., Hoefsloot, L. H., Bosgoed, E. *et al.* (2001) 'PTEN mutation in a family with Cowden syndrome and autism.' *American Journal of Medical Genetics 105*, 521–524.

Goodman, F. R. and Scambler, P. J. (2001) 'Human HOX gene mutations.' *Clinical Genetics 59*, 1–11.

Gottesman, I. and Gould, T. D. (2003) 'The endophenotype concept in psychiatry: etymology and strategic intentions.' *American Journal of Psychiatry 160*, 636–645.

Grant, S. D. N., Karl, K. A., Kieber, M. A. *et al.* (1995) 'Focal adhesion kinase in the brain: novel subcellular localization and specific regulation by Fyn tyrosin kinase in mutant mice.' *Genes and Development 9*, 190–192.

Greenberg, D. A., Hodge, S. E., Sowinski, J. *et al.* (2001) 'Excess of twins among affected sibling pairs with autism: implications for the etiology of autism.' *American Journal of Human Genetics 69*, 1062–1067.

Hallmayer, J., Glasson, E. J., Bower, C. *et al.* (2002) 'On the twin risk in autism.' *American Journal of Human Genetics 71*, 941–946.

Hérault, J., Perrot, A., Barthélémy, C. *et al.* (1993) 'Possible association of C-Harvey-ras-1 (HRAS-1) marker with autism.' *Psychiatry Research 46*, 261–267.

Hérault, J., Petit, E., Buchler, M. *et al.* (1994) 'Lack of association between three genetic markers of brain growth factors and infantile autism.' *Biological Psychiatry 35*, 281–283.

Hérault, J., Petit, E., Martineau, J. *et al.* (1995) 'Autism and genetics: clinical approach and association study with two markers of HRAS.' *American Journal of Medical Genetics 60*, 276–281.

Herzing, L. B., Kim, S. J., Cook, E. H. *et al.* (2001) 'The human aminophospholipid-transporting ATPase gene ATP10C maps adjacent to UBE3A and exhibits similar imprinted expression.' *American Journal of Human Genetics 68*, 1501–1505.

Herzing, L. B., Cook, E. H. Jr. and Ledbetter, D. H. (2002) 'Allele-specific expression analysis by RNA-FISH demonstrates preferential maternal expression of UBE3A and imprint maintenance within 15q11–q13 duplications.' *Human Molecular Genetics 11*, 1707–1718.

Hollander, E., King, A., Delaney, K. *et al.* (2003) 'Obsessive-compulsive behaviors in parents of multiplex autism families.' *Psychiatry Research 117*, 11–16.

Hutcheson, H. B., Bradford, Y., Folstein, S. E. *et al.* (2003) 'Defining the autism minimum candidate gene region on chromosome 7.' *American Journal of Medical Genetics 15*, 90–96.

IMGSAC (1998) 'A full genome screen for autism with evidence for linkage to a region on chromosome 7q.' *Human Molecular Genetics 7*, 571–578.

IMGSAC (2001) 'A genome wide screen for autism: strong evidence for linkage to chromosomes 2q, 7q and 16p.' *American Journal of Human Genetics 69*, 570–581.

Ingram, J. L., Stodgell, C. J., Hyman, S. L. *et al.* (2000) 'Discovery of allelic variants of HOXA1 and HOXB1: genetic susceptibility to autism spectrum disorders.' *Teratology 62*, 393–405.

Jamain, S., Quach, H., Betancur, C. *et al.* (2003) 'Mutations of the X-linked genes encoding neuroligins NLGN3 and NLGN4 are associated with autism.' *Nature Genetics 34*, 27–29.

Jones, M. B. and Szatmari, P. (2002) 'A risk-factor model of epistatic interaction, focusing on autism.' *American Journal of Medical Genetics 114*, 558–565.

Kaufman, A. S. (1999) 'Genetics of childhood disorders: II. Genetics and intelligence.' *Journal of the American Academy of Child and Adolescent Psychiatry 38*, 626–628.

Kent, L., Evans, J., Paul, M. *et al.* (1999) 'Comorbidity of autistic spectrum disorders in children with Down syndrome.' *Developmental Medicine and Child Neurology 41*, 153–158.

Kim, S., Herzing, L. B. K., Veenstra-Vander Weele, J. *et al.* (2002) 'Mutation screening and transmission disequilibrium study of ATP10C in autism.' *American Journal of Medical Genetics 114*, 137–143.

Köhler, A., Logan, C., Joyner, A. L. *et al.* (1993) 'Regional assignment of human homeobox-containing gene EN-1 to chromosome 2q13–q21.' *Genomics 15*, 233–235.

Komoto, J., Usui, S., Otsuki, S. *et al.* (1984) 'Infantile autism and Duchenne muscular dystrophy.' *Journal of Autism and Developmental Disorders 14*, 191–195.

Konstantareas, M. M. and Homatidis, S. (1999) 'Chromosomal abnormalities in a series of children with autistic disorder.' *Journal of Autism and Developmental Disorders 29*, 275–285.

Lainhart, J. E., Piven, J., Wzorek, M. *et al.* (1997) 'Macrocephaly in children and adults with autism.' *Journal of American Academy of Child and Adolescent Psychiatry 36*, 282–290.

Launay, J. M., Ferrari, P., Haimart, M. *et al.* (1988) 'Serotonin metabolism and other biochemical parameters in infantile autism.' *Neuropsychobiology 20*, 1–11.

Lauritsen, M. B. and Ewald, H. (2001) 'The genetics of autism.' *Acta Psychiatrica Scandinavica 103*, 411–427.

Lauritsen, M. B., Mors, O., Mortensen, P. B. *et al.* (1999) 'Infantile autism and associated autosomal chromosome abnormalities: a register-based study and a literature survey.' *Journal of Child Psychology and Psychiatry 40*, 335–345.

Le Couteur, A., Bailey, A., Goode, S. *et al.* (1996) 'A broader phenotype of autism: the clinical spectrum in twins.' *Journal of Child Psychology and Psychiatry 37*, 785–801.

Lee, M., Martin-Ruiz, C., Graham, A. *et al.* (2002) 'Nicotinic receptor abnormalities in the cerebellar cortex in autism.' *Brain 125*, 1483–1495.

Li, J., Nguyen, L., Gleason, C. *et al.* (2004) 'Lack of evidence for an association between WNT2 and RELN polymorphisms and autism.' *American Journal of Medical Genetics 126* (Suppl), 51–57.

Liu, J., Nyholt, D., Magnussen, P. *et al.* (2001) 'A genomewide screen for autism susceptibility loci.' *American Journal of Human Genetics 69*, 327–340.

Martin, E. R., Menold, M. M., Wolpert, C. M. *et al.* (2000) 'Analysis of linkage disequilibrium in gamma-aminobutyric acid receptor subunit genes in autistic disorder.' *American Journal of Medical Genetics 96*, 43–48.

Martineau, J., Herault, J., Petit, E. *et al.* (1994) 'Catecholaminergic metabolism and autism.' *Developmental Medicine and Child Neurology 36*, 688–697.

Meguro, M., Kashiwagi, A., Mitsuya, K. *et al.* (2001) 'A novel maternally expressed gene, ATP10C, encodes a putative aminophospholipid translocase associated with Angelman syndrome.' *Nature Genetics 28*, 19–20.

Menold, M. M., Shao, Y., Smith, C. *et al.* (2001) 'Association analysis of chromosome 15 GABA-A receptor subunit genes in autistic disorder.' *Journal of Neurogenetics 15*, 245–259.

Miles, J. H. and Hillman, R. E. (2000) 'Value of a clinical morphology examination in autism.' *American Journal of Medical Genetics 91*, 245–253.

Morrow, J. D., Whitman, B. Y. and Accardo, P. J. (1990) 'Autistic disorder in Sotos syndrome. A case report.' *European Journal of Pediatrics 149*, 567–569.

MRC (2001) *Review of Autism Research. Epidemiological and Causes.* London: MRC.

Muhle, R., Trentacoste, S. V. and Rapin, I. (2004) 'The genetics of autism.' *Pediatrics 113*, 472–486.

Murcia, C. L., Gulden, F. and Herrup, K. (2005) 'A question of balance: a proposal for new mouse models of autism.' *International Journal of Developmental Neuroscience 23*, 265–275.

Murphy, M., Bolton, P. F., Pickles, A. *et al.* (2000) 'Personality traits of the relatives of autistic probandos.' *Psychological Medicine 30*, 1411–1424.

Nurmi, E. L., Bradford, Y., Chen, Y. *et al.* (2001) 'Linkage disequilibrium at the Angelman syndrome gene UBE3A in autism families.' *Genomics 77*, 105–113.

O'Brien, G., Yule, W. and Nyhan, W. L. (eds) (1995) *Behavioural Phenotypes.* Cambridge: University Press.

Ozonoff, S., Williams, B. J., Gale, S. *et al.* (1999) 'Autism and autistic behavior in Joubert syndrome.' *Journal of Child Neurology 14*, 636–641.

Perry, E. K., Lee, M. L., Martin-Ruiz, C. M. *et al.* (2001) 'Cholihergic activity in autism: abnormalities in the cerebral cortex and basal forebrain.' *American Journal of Psychiatry 158*, 1058–1066.

Persico, A., D'Agruma, L., Maiorano, N. *et al.* (2001) 'Reelin gene alleles and haplotypes as a factor predisposing to autistic disorder.' *Molecular Psychiatry 6*, 150–159.

Petit, E., Herault, J., Martineau, J. *et al.* (1995) 'Association study with two markers of a human homeogene in infantile autism.' *Journal of Medical Genetics 32*, 269–274.

Philippe, A., Martinez, M., Guilloud-Bataille, M. *et al.* (PARISS) (1999) 'Genome-wide scan for autism susceptibility genes.' *Human Molecular Genetics 8*, 805–812.

Pickles, A., Bolton, P., Macdonald, H. *et al.* (1995) 'Latent-class analysis of recurrence risks for complex phenotypes with selection and measurement errors: a twin and family history study of autism.' *American Journal of Human Genetics 57*, 717–726.

Piven, J. and Palmer, P. (1999) 'Psychiatric disorder and the broad autism phenotype. Evidence from a family study of multiple-incidence autism families.' *American Journal of Psychiatry 156*, 557–563.

Piven, J., Chase, G. A., Landa, R. *et al.* (1991) 'Psychiatric disorders in the parents of autistic individuals.' *Journal of American Academy of Child and Adolescent Psychiatry 30*, 471–478.

Piven, J., Wzorek, M., Landa, R. *et al.* (1994) 'Personality characteristics of the parents of autistic individuals.' *Psychological Medicine 24*, 783–795.

Piven, J., Palmer, P., Jacobi, D. *et al.* (1997) 'Broader autism phenotype: evidence from a family history study of multiple-incidence autism families.' *American Journal of Psychiatry 154*, 185–190.

Poole, J. J., Law, M. L., Kao, F. T. *et al.* (1988) 'Isolation and chromosomal localization of the human En-2 gene.' *Genomics 4*, 225–231.

Rao, A., Harms, K. J. and Craig, A. M. (2000) 'Neuroligation: building synapses around the neurexin-neuroligin link.' *Nature Neuroscience 3*, 747–749.

Reiss, A. L., Feinstein, C., Rosenbaum, K. N. *et al.* (1985) 'Autism associated with Williams syndrome.' *Journal of Pediatrics 106,* 247–249.

Risch, N., Spiker, D., Lotspeich, L. *et al.* (1999) 'A genomic screen of autism: evidence for a multilocus etiology.' *American Journal of Human Genetics 65,* 493–507.

Ritvo, E. R., Yuwiler, A., Geller, E. *et al.* (1970) 'Increased blood serotonin and platelets in early infantile autism.' *Archives of General Psychiatry 23,* 566–572.

Rougeulle, C., Glatt, H. and Lalande, M. (1997) 'The Angelman syndrome candidate gene, UBE3A/E6-AP, is imprinted in brain.' *Nature Genetics 17,* 14–15.

Rutter, M., Bailey, A., Bolton, P. *et al.* (1994) 'Autism and known medical conditions: myth and substance.' *Journal of Child Psychology and Psychiatry 35,* 311–322.

Rutter, M., Silberg, J., O'Connor, T. *et al.* (1999) 'Genetics and child psychiatry, II: Empirical research findings.' *Journal of Child Psychology and Psychiatry 40,* 19–55.

Schain, R. J. and Freedman, D. X. (1961) 'Studies on 5 hydroxyindole metabolism in autistic and other mentally retarded children.' *Journal of Pediatrics 58,* 315–320.

Scheiffele, P., Fan, J., Choih, J. *et al.* (2000) 'Neuroligin expressed in nonneuronal cells triggers presynaptic development in contacting axons.' *Cell 101,* 657–669.

Scherer, S. W., Cheung, J., MacDonald, J. R. *et al.* (2003) 'Human chromosome 7: DNA sequence and biology.' *Science 300,* 767–772.

Schroer, R. J., Phelan, M. C., Michaelis, R. C. *et al.* (1998) 'Autism and maternally derived aberrations of chromosome 15q.' *American Journal of Medical Genetics 76,* 327–336.

Shao, Y., Wolpert, C. M., Raiford, K. L. *et al.* (2002a) 'Genomic screen and follow-up analysis for autistic disorder.' *American Journal of Medical Genetics 114,* 99–105.

Shao, Y., Raiford, K. L., Wolpert, C. M. *et al.* (2002b) 'Phenotypic homogeneity provides increased support for linkage on chromosome 2 in autistic disorder.' *American Journal of Human Genetics 70,* 1058–1061.

Shao, Y., Cuccaro, M. L., Hauser, E. R. *et al.* (2003) 'Fine mapping of autistic disorder to chromosome 15q11–q13 by use of phenotypic subtypes.' *American Journal of Human Genetics 72,* 539–548.

Slager, S. L., Foroud, T., Haghighi, F. *et al.* (2001) 'Stoppage an issue for segregation analysis.' *Genetic Epidemiology 20,* 328–339.

Smalley, S. L., Asarnow, R. F. and Spence, M. A. (1988) 'Autism and genetics.' *Archives of General Psychiatry 45,* 953–961.

Smalley, S. L., McCracken, J. and Tanguay, P. (1995) 'Autism, affective disorders, and social phobia.' *American Journal of Medical Genetics 60,* 19–26.

Spence, M. A. (2001) 'The genetics of autism.' *Current Opinion in Pediatrics 13,* 561–565.

Steffenburg, S., Gillberg, C., Hellgren, L. *et al.* (1989) 'A twin study of autism in Denmark, Finland, Iceland, Norway, and Sweden.' *Journal of Child Psychology and Psychiatry 30,* 405–416.

Steffenburg, S., Gillberg, C., Steffenburg, U. *et al.* (1996) 'Autism in Angelman syndrome: a population-based study.' *Pediatric Neurology 14,* 131–136.

Stevenson, R. E., May, M., Arena, J. F. *et al.* (1994) 'Aarskog-Scott syndrome: confirmation of linkage to the pericentromeric region of the X chromosome.' *American Journal of Medical Genetics 52,* 339–345.

Szatmari, P., Jones, M. B., Zwaigenbaum, L. *et al.* (1998) 'Genetics of autism: overview and new directions.' *Journal of Autism and Developmental Disorders 28,* 351–368.

Tentler, D., Brandberg, G., Betancur, C. *et al.* (2001) 'A balanced reciprocal translocation t(5;7)(q14;q32) associated with autistic disorder: molecular analysis of the chromosome 7 breakpoint.' *American Journal of Medical Genetics 105,* 729–736.

Thomas, N. S., Sharp, A. J., Browne, C. E. *et al.* (1999) 'Xp deletions associated with autism in three females.' *Human Genetics 104,* 43–48.

Thomas, J. A., Johnson, J., Peterson Kraai, T. L. *et al.* (2003) 'Genetic and clinical characterization of patients with an interstitial duplication 15q11–q13, emphasizing behavioral phenotype and response to treatment.' *American Journal of Medical Genetics 119*, 111–120.

Tierney, E., Nwokoro, N. A., Porter, F. D. *et al.* (2001) 'Behavior phenotype in the RSH/Smith-Lemli-Opitz syndrome.' *American Journal of Medical Genetics 98*, 191–200.

Tsirka, S. E., Gualandris, A., Amaral, D. G. and Strickland, S. (1995) 'Exitotoxin-induced neuronal degeneration and seizure are mediated by tissue plasminogen activator.' *Nature 377*, 340–344.

Veenstra-Vander Weele, J., Gonen, D., Leventhal, B. L. *et al.* (1999) 'Mutation screening of the UBE3A/E6-AP gene in autistic disorder.' *Molecular Psychiatry 4*, 64–67.

Vincent, J. B., Herbrick, J. A., Gurling, H. M. *et al.* (2000) 'Identification of a novel gene on chromosome 7q31 that is interrupted by a translocation breakpoint in an autistic individual.' *American Journal of Human Genetics 67*, 510–514.

Vincent, J. B., Petek, E., Thevarkunnel, S. *et al.* (2002) 'The RAY1ST7 tumor-suppressor locus on chromosome 7q31 represents a complex multi-transcript system.' *Genomics 80*, 283–288.

Vukicevic, J. and Siegel, B. (1990) 'Pervasive developmental disorder in monozygotic twins.' *Journal of American Academy of Child and Adolescent Psychiatry 29*, 897–900.

Warburton, P., Baird, G., Chen, W. *et al.* (2000) 'Support for linkage of autism and specific language impairment to 7q3 from two chromosome rearrangements involving band 7q31.' *American Journal of Medical Genetics 96*, 228–234.

Wassink, T., Piven, J. and Patil, S. R. (2001a) 'Chromosomal abnormalities in a clinic sample of individuals with autistic disorder.' *Psychiatric Genetics 11*, 57–63.

Wassink, T., Piven, J., Vieland, V. *et al.* (2001b) 'Evidence supporting WNT2 as an autism susceptibility gene.' *American Journal of Medical Genetics. Supplement 105*, 406–413.

Williams, P. G. and Hersh, J. H. (1998) 'Brief report: the association of neurofibromatosis type 1 and autism.' *Journal of Autism and Developmental Disorders 28*, 567–571.

Yonan, A. L., Alarcón, M., Cheng, R. *et al.* (2003) 'A genomewide screen of 345 families for autism-susceptibility loci.' *American Journal of Human Genetics 73*, 886–897.

Yuwiler, A., Ritvo, E., Bald, D. *et al.* (1971) 'Examination of circadian rhythmicity of blood serotonin and platelets in autistic and non-autistic children.' *Journal of Autism and Childhood Schizophrenia 1*, 421–435.

Zappella, M. (1993) 'Autism and hypomelanosis of Ito in twins.' *Developmental Medicine and Child Neurology 35*, 826–832.

Zwaigenbaum, L. and Tarnopolsky, M. (2003) 'Two children with muscular dystrophies ascertained due to referral for diagnosis of autism.' *Journal of Autism and Developmental Disorders 33*, 193–199.

Chapter 14

A Partnership between Parents and Professionals

Hilde de Clercq and Theo Peeters

It seemed logical to have a chapter on parent–professional collaboration written jointly by a parent and a professional. Because both of us work at a training centre, much of what we say has been inspired by a module we developed for our diploma courses in autism. A chapter covering the whole spectrum of autism disorders was too broad. So instead we focused on parents with children with low to border-line normal intelligence, although there may be some overlap with higher learners with autism and their parents. Most of our ideas are subjective – they come from personal experience rather than research data. We also decided to leave out as much professional jargon as possible.

The beginning of this chapter is about a crucial period in the collaboration between parents and professionals. It may be the most critical period of their lives, when they must decide whether they want to continue to collaborate with professionals or not. Therefore it is essential in this pre-diagnostic and diagnostic phase of their child's life that social services not only be excellent but also specifically adapted to the needs of autism.

Society should make enormous investments in 'empowering' parents with knowledge and practical help, because the quality of the future of citizens with autism will depend largely on the level of motivation and knowledge of parents. It is they who will push the professionals towards the extraordinary level of motivation that is necessary in autism.

We all know the expression 'the triad in autism'. In the past autism was often erroneously linked to just one symptom: 'being aloof'. In our contemporary understanding of autism, 'aloofness' is no longer seen as a necessary symptom for a diagnosis. Autism is considered as a syndrome (a combination) of groups of difficulties, especially those relating to: (1) a different social understanding, (2) different development of verbal and non-verbal communication, and (3) different imaginative and thinking styles.

We, however, have another 'triad' in mind, one that relates to the services that cater to the needs of parents with an autistic child in the earliest years and their relevance to future collaboration between parents and professionals. This triad consists of three of the services that should be linked:

1   *the diagnosis,* which works hand in hand with

2   *the assessment,* that then makes possible

3   *individualized educational guidelines,* preferably in the form of home-training.

The diagnosis provides the answer to the question: what is the matter with my child and what type of problems does he have? The diagnosis may be autism or atypical autism or something similar.

Then an assessment is needed since autism can be found in children with a wide range of intelligence levels. One needs to know whether this is a child with 'normal' intelligence, or with mild, moderate, severe or profound mental retardation.

And since people with autism develop unevenly, one also needs individual information about the most important developmental or functional areas (e.g. cognition, perception, eye–hand coordination, communication, self-help skills, social skills, leisure skills).

Educational guidelines, individual educational programmes (IEPs), and home training programmes are the individualized translations of assessment and observation results (taking into account the parents' priorities).

This, then, is our triad and it is what we will cover in this chapter. We will start by describing the three services so that we can understand why this cooperation is so necessary. We have developed it in the form of a little story.

DIAGNOSTIC AND ASSESSMENT DAY
The first home visit

The centre for developmental disorders receives a telephone call. The doctor at the other end of the line talks about family X and their four-year-old child who might have autism. Yes, they are very eager to receive more information and help as soon as possible.

Two people from the centre make a first appointment for a family visit. One is a child therapist, the other a family consultant. The child therapist, of course, focuses on the child's interests. But at the centre they have found that many services neglect the parents' priorities and possibilities. So a parent consultant is there too, to focus on the interests and survival tactics of the family. (Later on when the child therapist develops a home programme for the family it will be necessary to take into account things like the family's level of motivation, their degree of fatigue or energy and their need for immediate success.)

Child therapists have a tendency to develop programmes that may be ideal for the child (at least from a professional's point of view), but not for the parents. One of the important principles of the centre is that one reaches the child through the parents. If the parents are lost, so is the child. The two professionals have experienced both sides of the coin: the child therapist for this family has been a parent consultant for other families and vice versa.

For this first visit the child therapist has a few toys with him: form board puzzles, a ball, a hand puppet, etc. He will not diagnose the child, but only try to play with him and find out whether the child seems to belong to the family of children with a pervasive developmental disorder. The ability to play or not gives you immediate information relevant for the triad in autism. If you play together, you get an idea of their social under-standing with all its invisible rules, using verbal and non-verbal communication and imagination (especially with symbolic play one needs to go far 'beyond the information given').

Meanwhile, the parent consultant explains the services which the centre offers: what happens on a diagnostic day, the possibilities of having a home training programme afterwards. The parents will be asked if they will allow the centre to contact the other services that play a role in the child's life, such as his day centre. They will also be asked for permission to get all the written information that has been gathered about the child. They will be asked if the parents will permit the centre to invite a professional to the 'di-agnostic day'. This may be a teacher, a psychologist, a speech therapist, or whoever has had the best experience with the child up to that point.

Parents will also be invited to fill out forms or answer questions about the character-istics of autism and developmental milestones. These are very helpful questionnaires in placing the child in the context of the family and to clarify parents' expectations. The list contains questions such as:

- What is a typical day with your child?
- What do you find hardest to bear about your child's development?
- What gives you the most joy when you are with your child?
- What type of help do you need most urgently from us?
- What are your priorities? What does your child like most?
- What doesn't he like?

Simple as these questions may seem, they can make a lot of difference during the assess-ment of the child and may even determine whether the evaluation will be a success or whether the child will be 'untestable'. Here are some examples of how.

> Working with children, I like to lay my hands on their cheeks to show them I appreciate their efforts, but some children with autism cannot stand this. If I don't know this, I can end up spoiling the assessment from the onset.

I once asked a mother what I could do to help make the assessment go well. She said, 'Wear a grey sweater and everything will be all right.' I wore a grey sweater and the assessment went smoothly.

The diagnostic and assessment day

A good diagnosis and assessment are the starting points for an individualized educational programme and this is what this day is all about. (There are some necessary medical examinations, but they will not be described in this chapter.)

The clinical director will meet with his staff before the parents come in and everyone's role will be discussed. It will be a stressful day because the parents will have to digest so much difficult and challenging (though useful) information. The staff's schedule for the day should therefore be as predictable as possible. If procedures are not clear, the ensuing chaos and improvisation will certainly affect the parents, who already have enough on their plate.

First, there is a brief meeting with the parents and child. The clinical director summarizes the parents' priorities as he understands them and then asks the parents if they have understood them and whether any other priority or expectations should be added. He asks if there are any other questions that the parents would like to have answered in the afternoon, after the assessment. This is when the assessment results will be explained, especially with regard to the parents' priorities and questions.

The child therapist then invites the child to go with him to the assessment room. He will usually try to show a toy that is particularly attractive so that the child is motivated to follow him. If necessary, one of the parents will help him and the parent will stay or not, depending on the circumstances. (Personally I have had assessments when the child was 'untestable' with me, but became very 'testable' when his mother gave the instructions.)

The parent consultant, who has studied the parents' written and verbal information, will ask supplementary questions if necessary and then invite the parents to sit with him behind a one-way mirror. He will explain what skills are being examined and why and will ask if the parents are surprised at the reactions of their child. The consultant will be able to explain the difference in the child's skill level in structured versus unstructured situations, and the difference between his skill level in activities 'that speak for themselves' (like some of the hand–eye coordination tasks) and in activities that are more 'open' (like symbolic play). Usually he will also be able to show how 'problem behaviour' is linked to tasks that are too difficult and that the child usually is very cooperative if tasks are within his capacities.

It is very important that parents are present during the assessment and that they can watch everything so that there is common ground, a common experience, to discuss when professionals explain what the child's possibilities and difficulties were during the assessment.

The clinical director will also be present but his main responsibility is diagnosis. He will observe behaviours to supplement the information he already has from the parents' interview.

During the lunch break the child therapist will summarize the assessment results for the clinical director, the parent consultant and other professionals (e. g. from the child's day centre). The parents will not be present during this presentation for various reasons. First, the explanation of the results requires careful wording and the child therapist needs a rehearsal. During this meeting the clinical director and the parent consultant will provide any supplementary information which they received from the parents while they watched the assessment. Second, this is a chance to explain autism to the outside professionals who might not know as much about autism and therefore might be hesitant to ask questions or give information in front of the parents. Several beginning professionals, even though they now know that autism is biological in origin, fail to understand the pervasive nature of the condition and continue to question the parents' educational practices. They may think the parents' attitudes are incoherent, or too strict or too lenient. This is why it is so important to explain to them in a non-threatening atmosphere of mutual trust that such misunderstandings are normal, and these seemingly incoherent attitudes are more to do with having an especially difficult child than with bringing them up badly. You only need to look at the history of autism itself to see the incoherent attitudes professionals have had towards people with autism. No parent is born with an intuitive knowledge of autism, and even with the best information in the world, bringing up a child with autism is extremely demanding.

If no supplementary assessment or other information is needed, the diagnostic and assessment conversation starts. Tensions usually run high. The information they are going to receive is very difficult for parents to confront. And having to give the information is very difficult for professionals. Striking a good balance between presenting objective information and showing empathy with the parents' grief (usually) is not easy.

When parents learn that their child has autism and learning disability they often cry. Professionals may be so overwhelmed by these emotions that they cry with them. This is okay as long as it does not make them less efficient as professionals. Sometimes, however, they hurry to get beyond this troubling information and, in doing so, they may forget to explain relevant aspects of the child's development.

In a world of chaos, a child with autism needs structure and predictability. Professionals also need structure during those difficult interviews. They may find good structured information in the article 'Explaining mental retardation and autism to parents' (Shea 1984). It is beyond the scope of this chapter to reproduce the information in detail, but here is her step-by-step schedule that may be an interesting source of inspiration. Briefly:

1   Restate the parents' questions and concerns related to the child's development.

2   Explain that the child's development was assessed using standardized tests.

3   State that the assessment indicated that the child's development was delayed in some or all areas.

4   Follow this general information with specific test results.

5   Compare the child's chronological age and developmental level(s) and explain that the child's rate of development has been slower than average.

6   Reassure the parents that the child will continue to learn and develop, although his or her rate of development in the future will be slower than average.

7   Introduce the term *learning disability* as a synonym for slow development.

8   Explain that there are different degrees of *learning disability* that correspond to different rates of development.

9   State that the child is unlikely to catch up in development.

10   State that in addition to the *learning disability* the child has another developmental handicap called autism.

One way to explain autism is by looking at the general developmental age of the child and then point to the fact that his level of 'abstraction', in other words his talent to 'extract meaning' from his senses, seems to be less developed than his general developmental age suggests.

It is then possible to show other aspects of the triad, e.g. the child's developmental age is three, but his symbolic play skills are much less developed, his understanding of communication may basically still be at an object level, his talent to read emotions from the faces is very poor. Usually this explanation is linked to the parents' main concerns in the beginning, for example the child's bizarre communication, the bizarre relationship, his poor play skills.

Readers who are interested in Shea's guidelines should read her whole article which is full of useful comments. The first recommendation is particularly pertinent: start from the parents' priorities. What are their main concerns? What are the questions that have priority for them?

If the parents are especially concerned about the absence of speech, then begin the explanation with speech, e.g. during the assessment you observed that the child was very cooperative when solving the form board puzzle, but when we asked for a verbal response, such as imitating words, he was resistant, etc.

Some professionals have a tendency to explain an assessment in terms of their own interests and not in terms of the parents' priorities and then are surprised when parents don't have the 'appropriate' reactions. One may compare what happens in the context of an organ transplant – the body may reject the 'foreign' organ, just as parents may not accept 'foreign' information.

As mentioned before, when the professional explains the possibilities and difficulties in autism and mental retardation, especially in developmental areas like perception, imitation, eye–hand coordination and communication, it is easier and more meaningful if the parents were present during the assessment and have themselves seen what happened.

Some professionals prefer not to include parents in assessment sessions because they want to hide their ignorance and lack of expertise in autism. As always, if a professional who wants to help parents with autistic children is not specialized enough then his 'help' becomes a burden, not a help to parents. This is a pity, because, after all, who are these services for?

In her article, Shea also advises how to organize the session: no outside interruptions such as telephone calls, the afternoon session should be predictable (who explains what and in what order), there should be time for emotions (tissues available, since there might be tears, etc.).

One of the professionals should summarize the diagnostic sessions and put it into a written report so that parents do not have to take notes. It is also very important that the assessment and diagnostic report are written in an intelligible way, without professional jargon.

The period of extended diagnosis and the possibility of a home training programme

At the end of the diagnostic session parents are asked if they would like to have a programme they can carry out at home and, if so, how frequently (once a week, every fortnight, every month). Some parents may want this, others may not, but it is for the parents to decide. It is not up to us, professionals, to decide what parents should or should not do. If they do opt for a home programme the educational conclusions drawn from the diagnostic day will be shaped into an individualized programme by the child therapist and the parent consultant.

A home programme should not be seen as a sophisticated form of baby-sitting. During the limited period of a home programme (there may be other parents on the waiting list) the professionals will attempt to pass on to the parents what they know about autism and how to deal with various issues such as stress behaviour, communication development, etc., so that the parents will feel more competent and confident that they are 'special' parents for a special child.

Of course a home programme cannot work miracles but it can alleviate certain problems and restore a sense of dignity in the family. Autism is simply very difficult.

A home-trainer should be someone with lots of experience in autism and plenty of modesty, who will act as a guide more than as an expert.

Unfortunately some professionals think that problems in autism can be solved simply by daily schedules, spatial organization and visual help. It is important not to create false hopes. More experienced professionals know that they may be very helpful but that they are not going to work miracles. Autism is difficult for professionals as well and it is better to acknowledge this.

It is important to demonstrate a home training programme to the parents. They may seem ideal on paper, but do they work?

During my internship at TEACCH (Treatment and Education of Autistic and related Communications handicapped CHildren), in 1979 I had developed my first home training programme and was so proud of it. It was for a young boy who did not understand speech or pictures yet. It was all written out in great detail.

His parents were to ask him to come and sit at a table and show him a green box (green was his favourite colour).

1   Mother shows the green box and says 'Sit'.

2   He sits at the table.

3   His mother shows, etc.

The supervisor read the whole programme very carefully and then said, 'Yes, I think it is a clever programme, but now read it with me.'

1   Mama shows the green box and says 'Sit'.

2   He sits at the table.

He looked and said: 'What if he does not sit?'

This is a lesson I never forgot.

Autism is just not as simple as a young professional with his tendency towards cut and dried solutions may think, though it is normal to have 'echo-behaviour' and want to try out 'cookie cutter' approaches ('rigid thinking' confronted with situations that are too difficult...!). But this is why professionals who write out home programmes should demonstrate them themselves to the parents first. And if they fail? It wouldn't be such a bad thing. This way parents can see that autism is difficult for the so-called experts too. Next time when parents 'fail' they won't have to think any more that it is their fault.

Honesty obliges us to admit that autism can be very difficult, both for professionals and for parents alike. Autism is autism. Parents should not feel guilty when they 'fail'. It usually has nothing to do with lack of talent.

During this home training phase parents learn about autism and their child and about the educational cycle: how their child was assessed and the conclusions drawn from the assessment which were then shaped into an individualized educational programme (taking into account both the child's needs and the parents' priorities). This way parents learn that the home training programme in turn becomes another assessment which is regularly changed and adapted. This period is often called the 'extended diagnosis', since it is when parents learn what autism really means in their child.

Often, when the child is still very young, or when the diagnostic 'decision' is not so obvious, parents help gather information along with the home-trainers and often they come up with a diagnosis of autism by themselves. Then it only has to be confirmed later on by the professionals. This way parents learn that they are the experts on their own child, whereas the professionals are the experts on autism in general. In order to reach quality work both forms of expertise have to be put together.

(More formal and more complete information about this new 'triad' and other ethical aspects in autism may be found elsewhere (Schopler *et al.* 1984).)

INVOLVING PARENTS OF CHILDREN WITH AUTISM: WHY?

The description of the triad of services may have shown how vital it is to involve parents, but we want to develop this theme a little further.

In the dark psychogenic past of autism, the so-called experts thought that institutions were the best places for autistic children, because treating autism was seen as something best left to the experts. Now most people realize that for a child with autism (as for all children) the home is a better place, unless the parents cannot cope any more and the institution is exceptionally equipped to work with autistic children. Parents are in much closer contact with their children so they can use the periods when the child is open for discovering new aspects of life to best effect.

As parents, they have the advantage of being able to work with their child in a one on one situation which can only increase the possibility of acquiring new skills. And if they are involved, they may begin to regain hope, especially when they have gone through periods of feeling guilt and hopelessness.

On the other hand, if professionals make an assessment in an unfamiliar environment, the child will show atypical behaviours. What then? Does the so-called expert develop a programme for parents based on these atypical observations? We could go on, but the most obvious reason why professionals should collaborate with parents is logical, reasonable and clear: the child belongs to the parents and not to the professionals.

This means that parents have the right to be informed and a part of all evaluations, examinations and tests concerning the development of their child with autism. In fact they should not be treated any different from parents with 'ordinary' children. One wonders why parents with autistic children have to face so many difficulties just to get the most elementary information and rights for their own child. After all, the parents gave birth to the child and they are responsible for all the decisions that are going to be made in the future. How could they *not* be involved?!

Another urgent and necessary reason for engaging parents comes from the nature of autism itself. As we know, people with autism treat information they receive from the senses differently and have a tendency to associate new skills and new behaviours with certain details in the environment. Therefore, one needs to develop active generalization programmes. And parents should be the first ones to be involved.

Caregivers should consult parents about behaviour and skills at home so that they can be used in the professional environment as well. For example, a child with autism may have his own unique way of communicating and understanding and parents are the natural source of such information. After all, the parents have known the child from the start and have spent a lot of time with him. They know what the child understands, how the child understands, why the child cries, how the child expresses his needs and emotions. The parents may not use a 'professional' vocabulary, but they are the experts on their own children.

Think of Ricks's very old and nearly forgotten but always interesting study about early emotional vocalizations in ordinary and autistic children (Ricks and Wing 1976). He recorded different groups of children reacting in natural situations with their own parents in four situations evoking an emotion: joy (mother came into the room), desire to eat (one was preparing food), frustration (the food was presented and then was taken away) and surprise (a beautiful balloon was being blown up). In each of these situations the toddlers reacted and uttered their emotions by vocalizing. Ricks registered all these vocalizations and invited the parents to listen to them.

The parents were then asked two questions: the first one was 'Do you recognize your own child?' The parents of the normal children did not. Their children used 'universal vocalizations' to express their emotions and so there was little or no difference from one child to another. However, the parents of the children with autism were able to pick out the vocalizations of their children. Their children did not use these universal sounds. They had their own vocalizations that were only recognized and understood by their own parents.

The second question was: 'What is happening when the child makes the different types of vocalizations?' Parents of normal children could easily figure this out, as they could for the other 'normal' children and the children with Down syndrome or babies of parents who spoke another language, but they could not recognize the expressions of the children with autism. The parents of the children with autism could recognize the situation for their own child, but they, too, were unable to do it for the other children with autism. You are only able to understand this private babbling if you know the child very well.

This private, non-universal, idiosyncratic communication grows with the child. And even later in life parents and siblings are the best interpreters of the child's private verbal or non-verbal communications or actions. Professionals need to know this in order to really understand the person with autism.

Autism is very often described as a problem with 'meaning' and the parent is the key person to explain to the professionals 'how' and 'what' the child understands, and what private meaning he gives to cues in the environment. The parent has no need of a professional vocabulary – he intuitively 'understands' his child and knows him inside out. An example:

> Thomas puts his coat away and because of that he has a crick in his neck (stiff neck). He feels the pain and hears his teacher say: 'You made the wrong movement.'

During several days he felt the pain and from time to time he said: 'I made the wrong movement.' But when I checked his words he didn't seem to understand them fully.

He associated the pain with the words, linked them together and gave his own meaning.

Later on, when he had pain he would say: 'I made the wrong movement.'

Ever since that day, he hates to wear a coat… We know that he links it to the fact that all of a sudden he got this pain in his neck while hanging up his coat.

This is what 'autism thinking' is about: without using words such as 'concrete associations', 'echolalia', and 'idiosyncratic communication', the parents will be able to tell you where the expression comes from, what the child wants to express with it and why he doesn't like to wear a coat. Parents are excellent observers of their child and they can give you important additional information about the child's behaviour at home. Another example:

Laura has been taught to eat 'properly' at the day centre, but unfortunately the parents have never seen this progress at home. At home she eats with her fingers, never using a fork or a spoon.

This is important information, not because Laura's behaviour is worse at home than at the centre, but because she hasn't generalized the new skill.

This is important to know for the professionals who'll have to try (together with the parents) to teach the transfer of the skill to the home environment.

It is also very important for the parents: this way they learn that it is not their fault that Laura doesn't use a knife and fork at home. It is not 'poor education', nor is Laura disobedient. She is simply not generalizing spontaneously.

If parents understand this aspect of autism they'll also notice its opposite: that their child can do many things at home that she is not able to do at the day centre.

Both 'partners' will have to collaborate for the well-being of the child.

The caregivers from the centre will work with the parents to decide how they can help Laura to eat properly at home. At the same time the parents will help the professionals by giving them information about what strategies work at home, how Laura can be rewarded, what kind of things she detests, what strategies are ineffective and in what situations she'll probably get into a temper tantrum.

The parents can also give a lot of precious information about her sensory difficulties: her oversensitivity to certain noises, textures or smells.

Each child with autism seems to have his own 'user's guide', a kind of instructions manual. In the best situations this manual exists in a written form. It is kept at the school or the centre where the child is educated and is regularly reviewed and updated.

If caregivers are ill or leave the school or centre, those who replace them will then at least have the basic information. This prevents a lot of problems. And it is reassuring for the parents. Parents are the ones with the highest motivation to help their child, to give and to get the necessary and relevant information and to work on their child's development and emotional well-being. This way of collaborating sharpens that motivation.

This way of engaging the parents is the basis for help and at the same time the basis for any educational programme for the child – the child is helped through his parents. Involving the parents is also protection against over-specialisation. An 'expert' often has the tendency to interpret the behaviour or the test results of a child as a function of his own interests, which may be something the parents do not find particularly interesting. To counter-act this tendency, when a multi-disciplinary team develops a programme parents should (if they want) always be part of the team.

A good programme should reflect (in a reasonable way) the family needs and priorities. The home situation is the first setting where skills taught in the classroom are actually used. Priorities have to be discussed together. Example:

> A very motivated caregiver taught Johnny to ride a bicycle. The child was so motivated that he wanted to ride his bicycle on all his non-school days too. Unfortunately his parents lived on the eleventh floor in an apartment, with no garden and no space to cycle. Yet the same child was not even able to sit on a chair to do a jigsaw puzzle at home at the weekends. The parents begged for help.

Caregivers should try to take into account not only the interests of the child, but also the situation of the family. This may include questions like how much space do they have at home, how much time can the parents invest (do they have outside help? a professional life?) and how much money? Siblings also play a very important role in the whole issue of working together with families. Each individual member of the family has his or her own needs and the habits and values of the parents are as important as the habits and values of caregivers.

Parents know how to explain something to the child by using certain specific words, or intonation, gestures, movements, pictures or objects. Examples:

> Simon understands that he has to go to sleep if his mother switches off the television set.

> When David hears the weather forecast he thinks it's time for dinner.

Parents, however, are not born with the knowledge of autism. They do not always 'understand' the behaviour of their child within the framework of 'autism'. Example:

> Nadia's mother tells me that Nadia doesn't need visual help, because she understands a lot of verbal language.

'When we have to eat, I simply tell her that it's time to eat and Nadia comes to the kitchen.'

A few hours later it is time for lunch. Nadia's mother goes to the kitchen, takes a plate, shows it to Nadia and says 'eating time'. Nadia goes to the kitchen.

Here we see that the parent may know how to explain things to the child, but does not always realize whether this is full understanding of words or something else.

Here it was very clear that Nadia understood the instruction because she saw the plate. The visual information was stronger than the words.

It is up to the caregivers to explain these things to parents, beginning with very concrete examples, while emphasizing that although the parent intuitively did the right thing, the child may be reacting to objects, routine, intonation or space.

AN IDEAL PERSPECTIVE OF COLLABORATION

The ideal collaboration is when parents and professional have similar attitudes about the educational process. In the following pages a nearly ideal start for a successful collaboration (the 'triad of services') is described followed by the argument that parents should be included as much as possible because they, after all, are the ones who know their children best.

If there is a vertical and horizontal continuity of services (meaning that over the years at the clinical centre, at home and in the classroom there are the same coordinated efforts to help the children) then the basis for collaboration remains solid.

Here are some of the pre-conditions for a fruitful collaboration:

- parents and professionals must have a similar understanding of autism

- the person with autism must be able to grow up in an 'autism friendly' environment (that is, one adapted to autism where parents and professionals have been well-trained in autism)

- professionals must take the families' priorities into account

- there must be both a developmental perspective (where to start a programme with children) and a functional one (where to go to: for what type of adult life are we preparing our learners with autism?)

- the educational strategies must be specifically linked to autism (how do we teach them?).

FROM INSIGHTS INTO EACH OTHER'S DIFFICULTIES TOWARDS APPROPRIATE ATTITUDES TOWARDS ONE ANOTHER

Unfortunately, this ideal situation, in which parents and professionals have similar attitudes about autism, collaboration, the educational process and preparation for adulthood, is not common.

So a good place to start would be in developing such attitudes. One of the biggest problems is that many professionals do not have the faintest idea about how difficult it is for a family to survive with a child with autism. And parents often do not have any idea how limited professionals may be in their professional environment and how many frustrations they have of their own.

The following section is an overview of the different and difficult periods faced by the parents and the professionals. This is limited within the scope of this chapter to the (pre-)diagnostic years for the parents and to the school years for the professionals. More extended information is available at the Opleidingscentrum (email: info@ocautism.be; website: www.ocautisme.be). For further reading, see Harris and Powers 1984; Lord *et al.* 1993; Marcus 1984; Task Force on Autism 2001; Whitman 2004; Whitman and Lounds 2004.

SURVIVING WITH A CHILD WITH AUTISM
Getting a diagnosis for the child

This is a very stressful period for parents. In a normal world, having a child is a natural thing. Normal children develop in such a predictable way that one rarely thinks about abnormalities. So if you have a normal child you are unlikely to be familiar with terms like mental retardation, autism, developmental age, chronological age, psychological profile, evaluations, etc. For the parents of an autistic child, getting help is like taking their first steps into 'alien' territory. It means asking for and getting information and support in a strange new world.

So, it is not surprising that parents, unacquainted with this world, feel terribly frightened. Asking for help is not easy. Parents may feel guilty and their feelings of uncertainty and anxiety can turn this period of their life into a real nightmare.

Yet their needs and feelings must be taken seriously. Entering this world of 'disability, handicap, difficulties, abnormality' is not something they do lightly. They do it out of concern. This is why being able to trust the caregivers is so important. Everything is new and strange, and feelings can be overwhelming at times – good reasons, for example, to use a one-way screen in every evaluation situation. This way parents know and see exactly what the caregiver is trying to do with the child and afterwards the parents can give useful feedback. This makes it possible right from the beginning for the parents to see how their child behaves in different situations.

The stress and the feelings that parents of children with autism face in different periods of their life will also be described. Each child and parent is different. Situations can vary. So this is a subjective overview of what parents may experience as the most important issues.

The feelings cover more than just the period described. Some parents get the diagnosis for their child when the child is an adolescent and in a lot of cases the diagnosis is a real relief. Some people with autism are very proud of their 'autism', others want to be like other people. It is difficult to speak for each individual family.

Ambiguity – medical shopping

Autism is a very ambiguous disability. Many children with autism look 'normal', some of them are even beautiful and they may have splinter skills. All too often the splinter skills hide the delayed development and the real communication problems. This ambiguity is very puzzling for the parent. He is constantly torn between hope and despair. Example:

> Matthias is able to sing whole songs, he pronounces all the words correctly, and he sings them beautifully. On the other hand he has never asked for a biscuit or a piece of candy.
>
> He is able to find his way home even in places where he has been only once but if his parents change the furniture he seems to be lost in space.
>
> He never plays with his brother, but he is able to do a puzzle with 80 pieces.
>
> From time to time his parents think their child is deaf, but when a dog barks, he hears it before anyone else, and covers his ears.

Because of such ambiguities parents often get conflicting and unclear diagnoses. They are told that they worry too much, they are told to be patient, they are blamed for not being patient enough. And still the parents continue to hope.

Nevertheless, the parent knows that something is wrong with the child and often will blame himself for it. Maybe they did not bring him up properly, maybe the child is just acting up, maybe they weren't firm enough?

Unfortunately this is very often confirmed by the environment:

> 'a good smack on his bottom, that's all he needs'
>
> 'lock him up in the cellar for a short while, he'll soon toe the line'
>
> 'if he were mine…'

All the things that work with ordinary children seem to fail with the child with autism. The parent can see what is going wrong, but since he is the one bringing the child up, he thinks it is his fault. Feelings of guilt grow and grow.

This situation of 'doubt' certainly affects the atmosphere in the whole family.

Siblings no longer know how to react. Mummy cries all day long, she is exhausted. Daddy does nothing but read books on handicaps. Mum and Dad argue constantly;

they blame each other for having such a strange family. And Granny tells the children that their brother is a very naughty boy who is terribly spoiled.

> With undiagnosed autism, the parents must walk alone, with weights on both feet. (Akerley 1984)

Because of all the different and contradictory advice they are getting, parents end up going from professional to professional, from centre to centre, and from doctor to doctor, torn constantly between hope and despair. Mary Akerley (1998), herself a mother of a child with autism, uses the phrase 'medical shopping'.

Receiving the diagnosis

A distinction should be made between getting the diagnosis for your child in a psychoanalytical environment and in a biologically and educationally oriented environment.

In the first environment autism is still seen as a withdrawal into oneself due to a lack of love from the parents. The parent is not included in the programme but has to be cured himself. Feelings of guilt grow ever stronger. It goes without saying that all this affects the whole family. If it is the parents' fault, then what kind of mistakes did they make with their other children?

It can be worse. In countries where caregivers and parents still have not been given a good explanation of what autism actually is, this medical shopping may continue but in a different form and can be called 'therapy shopping'.

In some countries autism is still seen as something wonderful and mysterious and many so-called miraculous therapies promise a cure for the child. Feelings of guilt and despair continue to grow as the therapy fails to bring the promised cure.

And what about the parents who believe their child can be cured but don't have enough money to afford expensive therapies? How guilty must they feel? Believing their child can be cured but they cannot afford it?

If the caregivers have a realistic scientific view on autism, they will tell the parents that autism is not a result of poor education or a lack of love...but that *the child is special. Autism is a lifelong handicap and will never disappear.* Parents have the right to the truth. When parents hear this for the first time it may come as a terrible shock. The feelings of shock and mourning this brings do not necessarily pass in stages and they may never disappear.

They may fluctuate according to the different periods in the child's and the parents' lives. In many cases the parents have to fight to get the right diagnosis for their child. They may have read a lot about autism and may recognize the signs of autism in their child. They may fight for the diagnosis because, if the child gets the right label, he will have the right to get the appropriate education.

Other parents continue to compare their child with other children with autism, especially the ones who seem to have more problems. By doing this they try to convince themselves that their child cannot have autism.

It is important for caregivers to take into account all these feelings and emotions which parents may have in this difficult period. It often happens that the parents turn their anger on the person who tells them the truth about their child. This is very human and normal. Yet it is always better to tell them the truth in a gentle and sensitive way rather than to give them false hope. They will come back to the honest caregivers, because the only thing they want is to help their child.

If autism is a hard diagnosis for the parents, even harder is the diagnosis of 'mental retardation' that often goes together with 'autism'. The word 'autism' has been linked with 'mystery', 'splinter skills', 'Rainman', 'ambiguity', 'bright children', 'beauty', 'therapies' and this may cause a lot of confusion. The word 'autism' may also be associated with very special abilities. Example:

'Oh, your son is autistic? You can go to the casino with him!'

'Well, they are bright at mathematics…'

The terms 'mental retardation' and 'learning disability' are immediately associated with 'handicap'. And the word 'handicap' is a very loaded and heavy word. Some parents prefer the word 'autism' to 'mental handicap'. Only if one understands the real difficulties in autism does one realize that the word 'autism' is very limited. The word is too often used to refer to only one aspect of the syndrome: 'the withdrawal into oneself'. If the child shows interest in other people, then parents (and caregivers) may think that the diagnosis of autism is wrong.

Even if parents know something about autism and agree with the diagnosis, the label 'autism' is a heavy weight to carry. This is why it is important not to label the child, but the difficulties which he has. Example:

'Oh, you have four children. Which one is the autist?'

After 18 years, this is just as painful as it was when he was five. To add insult to injury, people may then hint that the parents have not 'accepted' his autism yet.

We talk about children 'with' autism. The child remains the same child, with his personality and all his features, but he is special and everything that is special and different in this case is called 'autism'. Even if parents are sure of the diagnosis life is not made easier by outsiders' insensitive questions and comments, like:

'Why do you complain? He is beautiful – have you never seen a child with Down syndrome?'

'Would you rather have a child in a wheelchair?'

It is hard for parents in this case to feel good about themselves and feelings of guilt again grow stronger and stronger.

SURVIVING IN A PROFESSIONAL ENVIRONMENT
Professional stress

When professionals talk openly to parents about the obstacles they have to face, parents are often surprised that many of their worries are shared by the professionals, that professionals' lives are not stress-proof either.

One shouldn't always emphasize the differences between parents and professionals; it is also important to see the similarities. Parents and caregivers are the 'advocates' of people with autism. Parents have a difficult life, but professionals have a difficult job. Both of them may be criticized and may be overtired.

Autism should also be seen as a political problem. The fight for a better life for people with autism, their families and caregivers is an important issue in which both play a very important role. Together they can educate politicians to provide better services, schools, group homes, employment, living centres, etc. for people with autism.

The following are some of the most frequent frustrations professionals feel.

- They feel isolated, especially when they work in regions where educational services for people with autism have just started up.

- Their director is not that interested in autism and does not provide enough support.

- They are less involved than their colleagues in the overall functioning of their institute. They are mostly with the children and have their breaks with them at separate times and so they are not able to eat with their colleagues and often have less free time than other members of staff.

- Because they have a better adult:child ratio (e.g. 2:7), their colleagues are jealous but do not (want to?) understand why this is necessary.

- Despite their hard work they are often criticized by outsiders who always seem to know better and have their own theories about education.

- There are few possibilities for comprehensive training in autism and so they often do not have the arguments to back themselves up when they are criticized. Explaining autism is not easy, especially not if the psychiatrist sees things differently.

- There is a lack of understanding around them of the specificity of autism and much confusion due to the ambiguity ('Looks normal, but behaves differently. Does he refuse or does he understand things differently?').

- Some parents seem to understand autism better than others. The ones who don't seem to understand autism do not realize that their child also has mental retardation and they have unrealistic expectations about their child's development.

- Some pupils are taught using one educational approach at one time of the day and then another one at other times (e.g. educational in the morning, psychoanalytical in the afternoon).

- Working in teams can be difficult.

- No extra time is given to develop new and adapted individualized programmes and activities.

- No extra time is provided for conversations and discussions with parents.

- Dealing with challenging behaviours is difficult with so little knowledge and so little support.

- Autism itself can prove too difficult for some professionals and some parents.

These frustrations are heard among even the most motivated professionals. A new type of frustration surfaces when directors appoint professionals who are not motivated to work with people with autism.

In the early 1990s in our country, Belgium, professionals 'chose' autism. But now that so many more people have been diagnosed with autism, new services have popped up everywhere. This may sound like progress, but not if autism is poorly understood and the professionals appointed to do the job have no special motivation. A professional should not accept a job 'in spite of the autism', but 'because of autism'. To work with 'special' children, professionals must be 'special' too (Gillberg and Peeters 1999).

We have described what a parent faces to survive with a child with autism. And we have seen what some of the greatest frustrations are that the professionals must deal with.

PARTNERSHIP BETWEEN PARENTS AND PROFESSIONALS: GUIDELINES FOR PROFESSIONALS

Here are some guidelines we think are important for professionals to keep in mind (inspired by Lee Marcus, at a TEACCH workshop during an internship in 1980).

The child's difficulties are not the result of being badly brought up

One needs to take into account and be very careful about interpreting the level of difficulties of the person with autism. For parents who have a child with autism with a very young developmental age the big issues are: speech, toilet training, feeding and sleeping problems.

For parents with a child with normal intelligence the problems are different: the child may talk all the time, he may be very repetitive, and in social situations be very naïve and/or be unaware of his differences.

Autism isn't easy. Although it is now accepted that autism is of biological origin, in some environments people continue to overemphasize the role of the parents in influencing the child's 'bad behaviour'. Parents then are criticized for being inconsistent in the way they are bringing up the child, either too permissive or too strict, as if the professional world had never been incoherent in its own interpretation of autism.

To be honest, if we looked at all the different 'methods' and 'therapies' in autism, we would not find much coherence in the professional world. Yet, professionals sometimes seem to suppose that parents have an intuitive knowledge of autism and put their behaviour under a microscope. This doesn't happen with parents of blind or deaf or ordinary children. Presumably the past, when one used to blame parents, continues to influence the present. It may also have to do with the incongruity of autism.

Parents have to deal with more than just having a child with autism

Having a child with autism doesn't mean that their other problems go away: there is still the stress of their other children, their marriage, their financial problems and difficulties at work.

Some parents are forced to quit their job because of their child with autism. This may lead to financial difficulties within the family. It is up to caregivers to try to find out what kind of financial support parents can get. It is important to inform parents about this spontaneously and reassure them that they should not feel 'guilty' or 'bad' because they will get some more money. Life with a person with autism can be expensive.

The contributions and worries of the other children in the family are often overlooked. They need to be informed about the handicap of their brother or sister. Parents have to try to give them ways and tools to explain autism to their friends, teachers and others.

It can be helpful for them to play a role in the education of their handicapped brother/sister. If this role is geared to their abilities, they'll be proud of being able to do something for him.

They may need contacts with other siblings of a child with autism: in the same way as their parents did in the beginning, they may think that they are the only one in the world with such a strange brother.

They need to see the strong points, the splinter skills of their brother/sister so they can tell other people about them. They also should have the opportunity to talk about their concerns with their parents. And they should have the chance to do things with the parent on their own.

The stress that comes with having a child with autism should not be underestimated

In 1975, at a time when the interpretation of the cause of autism was still largely psychogenic, a study was published, comparing maternal attitudes in Antwerp and London. In Belgium the approach was psychogenic. This study showed that the mental and physical health of mothers of children with autism was largely determined by the presence or absence of specific services for their children. Mothers in London scored much lower than the mothers in Flanders on the Malaise Inventory (a standardized list of psychosomatic complaints) and also much lower on the 'Feeling of social isolation' scale. Statistical analysis showed that the results on both questionnaires were correlated at a highly significant level.

One might argue that it was the mother's 'neurosis' that caused autism, but having a child with autism in a cultural climate where autism was poorly understood and little appropriate help was available could be a cause of that neurosis (Peeters 1978).

The study also suggested that having a child with autism caused more psychosomatic problems than having an otherwise handicapped child.

In the past one tended to focus on how the parents affected their child's behaviour, but once the problems of social reciprocity in autism were better documented, one could also take into account the effects of having a special child on the parents.

It should be clear that the availability of appropriate schools and services and how well autism is understood in these environments are the most important factors in reducing the level of stress in parents with autistic children. In a TEACCH survey the two most helpful coping strategies for parents were:

1   believing that my child's programme (TEACCH) has my family's best interest in mind

2   learning more about how I can help my child to improve (Bristol 1984).

Example:

> What's in a name? It is not because schools, centres or institutions give themselves the label of being 'autism-specialized' that they are... Being 'autism-specialized' covers much more than 'admitting pupils with autism'. It's a pity that during the most difficult period of Thomas's life as a teenager, the biggest part of our energy has to be invested in the lack of knowledge of many professionals. This does not only influence the level of anxiety and stress in Thomas, but unfortunately also has serious consequences for family life. I can only be grateful to those 'special' professionals who understood and still understand 'our special child' from within because a big part of his and our emotional well-being is dependent on it.

Seeing the family as part of society

For outsiders, the identity of parents of children with autism is often wrapped up with that one specific child with autism. In some cases that is okay. But sometimes it is not. Example:

> If I go to Thomas's school, people address me as 'the mother of Thomas'.
>
> Unfortunately, in other circumstances, I do not want to be only Thomas's mother, but also the mother of my three other children, somebody's wife, somebody's sister, somebody's friend, somebody's aunt... I also have a job, and although autism, because of its impact and pervasiveness, takes the biggest part of my life, I also want to be considered as a 'real person', 'a whole person', 'somebody with other characteristics than only being the mother of –'.

If we want to collaborate with parents it is very important to take into account these other aspects as well. It is not for professionals to 'judge' parents, but to try to understand them and their families in their social context.

Here is a nice example to illustrate this.

> She was a good teacher. She developed her own informal assessments and three times a year she assessed her children on work behaviour and work skills and checked to see if they had made any progress. She discussed the evolution with the parents and they seemed generally satisfied. One night at a parent–teacher conference, Anna's father repeated how glad he was that his daughter had such a good teacher.
>
> 'But,' he said, 'do you know what I really dream of? I'd so much like to take my daughter to the cafe and have her sit with me while I quietly drink my beer with my friends.'
>
> The teacher took this seriously and asked the bartender whether she could come with her pupil to the cafe, first at a time when there weren't any customers. Within six months Anna was sitting in the cafe with her father and all his friends, waiting while her father drank his beer.

Share not only the successes but also the worries and failures with the parents

Unfortunately sometimes professionals only turn to the parents when there is a serious crisis. And by then, it may be too late. One should start to collaborate with the parents right from the start in an atmosphere of honesty and trust. It is not much use to introduce yourself as an expert after you've been working with the child a year or two. It is also not very helpful to parents if everything you say and write about their child is only positive and full of joy and happiness.

The professional sees himself more as a guide than as 'the expert'

Professionals may have a better understanding (not always!) of autism in general, but parents are the experts on their own child. Professional knowledge may move educational decisions in certain directions, but parents have to help the professionals individualize their general knowledge. For some professionals it may be difficult to admit that they do not know everything. But pretending they do is worse! Parents must learn that a professional is not an Olympic god.

No professional secrets

It goes without saying that parents should be well informed about all medical and educational aspects concerning their children. If there are written reports, they should be given to parents and not simply circulated among professionals. Not having access to written information is not only humiliating for parents: it is a mortgage on a good collaboration.

Parents must have the final responsibility for their child

This guideline speaks for itself. If the professional wants to help those parents desperately seeking information and advice, he must share all the useful knowledge he has. One does not make assessments and keep them for one's own personal satisfaction.

Unfortunately the reality sometimes is very different. Here is an example of an incredible but true event. A certain psychologist administered an assessment, but did not want to communicate the results because she considered them 'medical secrets'.

Even though professionals share the responsibility for the child only for a short time they sometimes have trouble accepting that it is the parents who have the final say over their own child. This attitude is much less common with parents of deaf or blind children. Perhaps it is because of the lingering attitudes about autism in the past when parents were seen as the cause of their children's problems and therefore excluded from treatment ('parentectomy', on the contrary, was part of the treatment).

In a few countries mothers say that their children need education. Yet psychologists in some daycare centres insist on treating the children as if they were the mother, leaving the job of teaching communication and self-help skills to the real mothers. The world is turned upside down: the professional takes on the mother's role and the mother is forced to become the teacher.

There is something cruelly funny in autism. In some environments professionals think they are the 'authorities' and that they have the right to tell parents what they should do for their child: e.g. use visual help at home, be actively involved in the generalization of programmes and so on.

Important decisions unilaterally taken by professionals may be extremely humiliating to the parents. Even though it may be meant as helpful to the child, it is the parents ultimately who must decide. Sometimes, even with the best of intentions, parents may decide it is impossible to have their child at home. When the parents must face this decision, professionals should not be judgemental.

COLLABORATING

How can caregivers work with parents in a practical way? Here we will try to give a brief overview of the some of the best ways of collaborating, especially in terms of keeping both sides informed of the progress and the difficulties of the child. Naturally, each country will have to adapt these suggestions according to what is available in terms of schools, centres and families.

The parents' book or the communication booklet

This is a booklet that the child carries with him in his schoolbag and takes to and from school. Parents can write information in it about the child and so can the professionals. It may be about anything that is important to the education and well-being of the child: news about daily events, homework, communication, behaviour, siblings, or malaise, for example.

The most important function of the booklet is to keep parents and caregivers informed about anything that might affect the child so that all involved can react in an appropriate way. What it is not meant to be is more work for either party. If there is nothing to say, nothing needs to be written.

Nevertheless, this communication booklet is very often the only form of communication between school and home, whether there is anything special to mention or not. Children with autism (verbal as well as non-verbal ones) have a tendency to think in compartments, in contexts. We should not expect them to communicate spontaneously to their parents what they have done at school.

Even if they are verbal and have normal intelligence, they don't always spontaneously tell their parents what kind of homework they have, whether they are supposed to take their swimming bag the next day, etc.

Some children don't like to communicate about one context (e.g. school) when they are in another. To them this is logical: school is over for the day and now they are at home.

Some children don't have the communication skills, so it is irrelevant whether or not they are in the mood to communicate! (In this case learning to communicate about what happens at school can be one of the goals for the communication programme. Teachers could stick a photo of the swimming pool in the booklet, so that the child, using this type of visual help, gradually learns to communicate from one context to another.) Used this way, the communication booklet becomes an excellent means of getting basic information about their child's day to the parents.

The parents should be given honest information: not too negative, not over positive, but straightforward and sensitive. There is no point trying to protect the parents by writing that their child always behaves well, eats his food properly and never causes any problem in the centre or at school. This will only make the parents feel inadequate, thinking that it is only at home that their child is difficult.

On the other hand, if the information is too negative, parents may begin to doubt the quality of the service their child is being given, or they may be afraid that caregivers will give up. As we have already said, it is important to be informed about the difficulties each side is facing in order to maintain a good relationship of reciprocal trust.

For their part, the parents can provide the caregivers with important information about the child's behaviour at home: some children with autism have a tendency to link their stress behaviour to the home situation. They may behave perfectly at school, but explode when they get home.

Very often this happens when the day has been too stressful, or when there were sudden unannounced (or only verbally announced) changes in the programme or other unpredictable events, an overload of information that was too difficult, or sensory problems, etc.

If the caregivers read that the child has been exhibiting a lot of problem behaviour at home, they may try to find out what is causing the difficult behaviour. They can then keep notes on the behaviour: when and where it happens, is it always on Monday? Is it always after an excursion or a walk? or when the teacher was absent? or when the child has done activities with a new group of pupils?

For their part, parents can also provide useful information: e.g. that their child didn't want to eat, or has been ill during the night, or couldn't sleep.

The professional will then understand immediately why the child is upset or very tired in the classroom and so be prepared to make adaptations in the programme for the day.

Visits to the home

These informal visits are paid by teachers, psychologists, therapists, or the whole team. The idea is to observe the child in a different situation so that they can see for themselves the difference in the child's behaviour at home.

The best thing to do is to explain the reason for the visit ahead of time since it is not meant to make parents feel guilty, but to learn more about the child and thus be able to improve the quality of help. Sometimes these visits are used to teach the generalization of skills from the school environment to the home.

Parents should not expect professionals to make these visits in their spare time. Some schools and centres make provisions for these visits within the working hours of the professionals, others don't. If parents prefer not to have caregivers visiting their home, their wishes should be respected. Very often parents are ashamed of their home situation and they need time to learn to trust people. Or they simply don't like the idea. In this respect they are no different from parents of normal children and they have the right to their privacy.

Evenings for parents

These evenings are organized for many parents together and so they are not 'individualized' to the needs of each family. They can be seen as 'informal contacts' between school and home, but also between teachers and parents and even among parents themselves. The contacts parents have with each other can be positive. They may learn that other families face the same problems, and it can be reassuring to see how other parents cope with practical issues.

During these evenings of getting acquainted with the school, caregivers might explain to parents what the classroom looks like, how they work with the child, what their views are on autism, and what they hope to achieve in general with the children. Some caregivers show a video-document of the children in the classroom to the parents. They may organize this evening in the child's classroom at the beginning of the school year so that parents can see the world their child will inhabit during the day. Having such visual and concrete information is reassuring to parents.

Later in the school year the evening can be organized in a different way. Caregivers may invite a speaker (e.g. a home trainer), with lots of practical experience and a down-to-earth approach, to explain aspects of autism to parents. Parents may use a questionnaire to select the subjects that concern them most: e.g. toilet training, sleeping problems, sensory difficulties. After the speaker gives his presentation, the parents have time to ask questions. In this way, listening to other parents, they may realize that their own worries are not unique. And there is the added bonus that they can exchange advice with each other.

Meetings with the whole team

These meetings are more 'individualized'. The team along with the parents and possibly the home-trainer meet to discuss the child's individualized educational programme (IEP).

Usually the team is a multidisciplinary group of 'generalists', having the same or similar training and the same philosophy on autism. The team consists of all the caregivers who work with the child: his teachers, educators, psychologist, social assistant, director of the school, psychiatrist (depending upon the situation, e.g. in a moment of crisis, it may be very important that a medical doctor is present). Directors, though they cannot be present at every IEP meeting, should be available if necessary.

Home-trainers are very important at the IEP meetings, because they can act as a bridge between the family and the professional environment.

Some parents like to be included in the IEP discussion; others do not. The latter, when faced with a group of professionals, may fear that they will not be able to express their priorities, or even their sorrows.

The IEP meeting gives the parents an opportunity to see the 'coordinator' (very often a psychologist) together with the most important caregiver (e.g. teacher or educator) so that they can discuss their child privately in depth. Some parents are comfortable in such an atmosphere. But others may consider this way of working a waste of time.

The parent may have important information that they want to pass on to the team but they decide to wait for the next IEP, even though the information could have been usefully discussed earlier. But parents' feelings are important and, if parents feel overwhelmed at this meeting, it is better to talk to them privately at another time. A good coordinator needs to sense the secret worries and frustrations which the parents feel. Very often this meeting is the only chance these parents have to talk about their problems. It is not surprising that they may not like group situations.

A good coordinator will also be the motor behind a successful collaboration between parents and professionals. This is important because, if parents lose confidence, it can spoil a lot of hard work.

When starting an IEP conversation professionals can give parents an overview of the past, and discuss what failed and what is now emerging in terms of the priorities discussed in the earlier IEP. Also parents who want to work on certain skills will get the chance to talk about their successes and failures. Based upon the previous IEP, together they can formulate future goals: will they continue with what they did before and introduce the next step or do they have other urgent new goals? Example:

> Recently Johnnie made a lot of progress in self-help skills: in the day care centre he can take a shower all by himself. But he is not yet able to wash his hair. He needs help. It would be a logical priority to teach this. On the other hand, his father says that he has the impression that Johnnie gets demotivated having to learn new things all the time. And he is afraid that his son is not going to like the centre if they emphasize self-help skills too much. His suggestion of practising what Johnnie already knows will motivate his son and will make him feel successful.
>
> On the other hand, Johnnie is very motivated to learn a foreign language. It might be a good idea to set up new goals in this field. It would make Johnnie feel like a real teenager.

Again, the information exchanged must be honest. Sometimes it is helpful if caregivers talk about their own frustrations and the goals that have not been achieved in spite of their efforts. Sometimes parents have their own strategies that work with their child. Talking about the child's progress is not only rewarding for the caregivers but very motivating for the parents.

From time to time parents may have overly high expectations. Seeing and hearing the step-by-step methods that professionals use to teach the child with autism may give parents insight into the demanding and intensive work professionals do with their child.

Not only must autism be taken into consideration, but also the needs of the family and the child within the family setting. Emotional development is as important as the development of skills. Therefore again parents are able to provide information about the child's characteristics and personality.

Some of the most important issues that are discussed in the IEP are communication, social skills, play skills, free time skills, work behaviour and work skills, domestic skills and self-help skills, academic skills (e.g. reading, writing, mathematics, history, geography) and emotional well-being. This is a good moment to discuss the global evolution of the child as well and possible problems at home or at school along with the generalization of skills.

As a result of the conversation professionals have with parents, they will jointly formulate priorities and set up educational objectives. And of course, parents will get a written report about the IEP meeting.

Collaboration made to measure

'Collaboration made to measure: better together' is the name of a document where real forms of collaboration between parents and professionals are described in order to avoid misunderstanding about each other's expectations (Shiltmans and Vermeulen 1998). It is a guide packed with suggestions for a realistic form of collaboration and has been developed by the 'Vlaamse Vereniging Autisme' (The Parental Society in Flanders, Belgium). Parents and professionals can use the document to keep each other informed about their individual expectations and possibilities. This way both the quality of services and their collaboration can be improved.

Both parents and professionals fill out forms about the child and what they know about him in their own situations, along with their priorities, goals and ways of collaborating. The parents are invited to answer questions about what they want and what they can do, through a simple system of 'yeses' and 'nos'.

LEARNING FROM PARENTS

Let's start at the beginning. In 1943 Leo Kanner, after having observed 11 children over five years, invited the scientific world to study these special children who had 'infantile autism'. It is a pity that he came up with the name 'autism' because it caused a great deal of confusion for many decades (and it still does in several European countries), but it goes without saying that his role in autism has been enormous.

Today we are still impressed by his accurate observations, but where did he get most of his information? He got it from the parents. It is appropriate that everyone still knows the name 'Leo Kanner', but it is not right that nobody remembers the role the parents played by giving their detailed diaries to Leo Kanner (Akerley 1984).

When outsiders look at skilful professionals who adapt their communication styles to people with autism and use only the essential words, they are often being suspected of being 'cold' or 'rigid'. One might wonder whether Leo Kanner and other professionals in the 1940s came to that conclusion because they had not yet found out what parents know: that our overflow of words ('logorrhea') only confuses people with autism.

As we have already said, in the best of cases, professionals might be the experts on autism overall (though not always), but parents are the experts of their own child. Nothing can replace the combination of knowledge and 24/7 care and experience. It is as if they have autism in their blood. Professionals should use the wisdom of burned-out parents more often. Our governments should also put more money into *preventing* their burn-out!

As suggested in the beginning of the chapter: this investment should start very early on by developing the 'triad of early intervention'; that is, services where diagnosis is immediately linked to assessment and individualized educational help in the form of home training programmes.

One should accept and act accordingly so that the future of people with autism depends more on the knowledge of their parents than on the knowledge of professionals. Parents who understand autism will push professionals towards the level of motivation that is needed to understand and guide people with autism. Moreover a government that accepts this level of commitment will not only gain in humanitarian values but will also save itself a lot of money. Well-informed parents should understand that there is now a 'validated consensus' in the understanding and guidance of people with autism (not in every little detail, of course: a lot of creativity is required for an individualized application of general principles). Well-informed parents will also be better protected against 'miracle cures' that appear regularly on the 'market of despair' and they will know (as is not the case in many countries) that providing help to their child is not a question of shopping around for a 'method' or a 'therapy'.

Of course, not all parents understand autism, nor do all professionals. Autism may be as difficult for some parents as it is for some professionals, but well-informed parents can observe schools and institutions that claim to have expertise in autism and judge how little real practical understanding they actually have. It is amazing how parents continue to be so patient. It is true that they often do not have much choice for their children nor do they always have the same range of options available that parents of 'standard' children have. But still...

Several years ago a professional asked a doctor (who was herself a parent of a child with autism) where she learned such patience. The professional said: 'If I were the father of a child with autism and saw the sometimes criminal ignorance of people and the way some professionals make life for my child so difficult, I think I would kill someone.'

This parent–doctor smiled and said, very patiently, 'How many would you kill, one, five, fifty, hundred...?'

Linked to this patience, there is also a deep but often hidden vulnerability in parents. There was once a boy with autism who wrote that all day at school he kept his 'social mask' on. There was only one person in the world with whom he felt safe taking it off.

That was his mum. She got the whole tornado of frustrations vented on her. But what about the parents? When do they get to take off their 'social masks of tolerance'?

Paul Theroux has written about people's secret lives, their hidden agendas, the internal life that is often more valuable than the external one. Parents of children with autism often have this secret agenda, full of hidden feelings, which they don't reveal to professionals, but which contains oceans of truth about autism. Why don't they make it public?

Has it to do with the 'long toe terror' (Williams 1998) and their strategy of protection, which is sometimes the only form of self-defence they have left, the last means they have to protect their children? In some ways they are trying to protect themselves and their children but, in other ways, they are protecting the professionals.

One often has the impression that people who have suffered, who have overcome crises, often understand and appreciate life at its essence. Think of parents' risk of burn-out and their survival skills. The misunderstandings, the sleepless nights, the chronic fatigue. Most 'neurotypical' parents would reach their limits sooner or they would succumb, but parents with children with autism often go beyond the limit of their possibilities. The very special and deep love for their children leaves them no other choice.

In *Philip and the Others* (written in 1995 by the Dutch author Cees Nooteboom) there is the story of the strange uncle Alexander who gave young Philip a wise lesson about life. He said that you first have to realize that this world is the ugliest world imaginable and when you really understand this, then you will discover again a new love for the small things in life that others don't even see any more.

In an interview with Alvarez, author of *The Savage God* (1971), a book about suicide in literature, Alvarez explained to one of the authors how he had survived a suicide attempt. He said that it cured him of the sickness he called 'Americanism': the idea that there is a solution for every problem. He realized that there were problems with no solution and this acceptance made him a wiser person.

In a way the years spent dealing with autism seem to have 'purified' some parents. They no longer complain so much about the little things they miss or that other people have more than they do. Crises are the most creative periods in your life, but only if you survive them. Can parents really survive 'autism'? Their best chance is in a culture where the government has created a lifelong continuity of services specialized in autism.

Didn't Kundera write that the level of civilization can best be measured by the level of protection it offers to its most vulnerable citizens?

REFERENCES

Akerley, M. (1984) 'Developmental changes in families with autistic children: a parent's perspective.' In E. Schopler and G. Mesibov (eds) *The Effects of Autism on the Family*. New York: Plenum Press.

Akerley, M. (1988) 'What's in a name?' In E. Schopler and G. Mesibov (eds) *Diagnosis and Assessment in Autism*. New York: Plenum Press.

Alvarez, A. (1971) *The Savage God: A Study of Suicide.* Harmondsworth: Penguin.

Bristol, M. (1984) 'Family resources and successful adaptation to autistic children.' In E. Schopler and G. Mesibov (eds) *The Effects of Autism on the Family.* New York: Plenum Press.

Gillberg, C. and Peeters, T. (1999) *Autism: Medical and Educational Aspects.* London: Whurr Publishers.

Harris, S. and Powers, M. (1984) 'Behavior therapists look at the impact of an autistic child on the family system.' In E. Schopler and G. Mesibov (eds) *The Effects of Autism on the Family.* New York: Plenum Press.

Kanner, L. (1943) 'Autistic disturbances of affective contact.' *Nervous Child 2,* 217–250.

Lord, C., Bristol, M. and Schopler, E. (1993) 'Early intervention for children with autism and related developmental disorders.' In E. Schopler, M. Van Bourgondien and M. Bristol (eds) *Preschool Issues in Autism.* New York: Plenum Press.

Marcus, L. (1984) 'Coping with burnout.' In E. Schopler and G. Mesibov (eds) *The Effects of Autism on the Family.* New York: Plenum Press.

Nooteboom, C. (1995) *Philip en de anderen.* Amsterdam: Querido.

Peeters, T. (1978) 'Autism. Maternal attitudes and services: a cross-cultural study.' MSc in Communication, University of London.

Peeters, T. (2000) 'The role of training in developing services for persons with autism and their families.' *International Journal of Mental Health 29,* 2, 49–59.

Ricks, D. and Wing, L. (1976) 'Language, communication and the use of symbols.' In L. Wing (ed.) *Early Childhood Autism.* Oxford: Pergamon Press.

Schiltmans, C. and Vermeulen, P. (1998) *Beter samen. Samenwerking creëert kwaliteit.* Gent: Vlaamse Dienst Autisme.

Schopler, E., Mesibov, G., Shigley, R. Hal and Bashford, A. (1984) 'Helping autistic children through their parents: the TEACCH model.' In E. Schopler and G. Mesibov (eds) *The Effects of Autism on the Family.* New York: Plenum Press.

Shea, V. (1984) 'Explaining mental retardation and autism to parents.' In E. Schopler and G. Mesibov (eds) *The Effects of Autism on the Family.* New York: Plenum Press.

Task Force on Autism (2001) 'Chapter 3: Parents as partners.' In *The Report of the Task Force.* Dublin: Government Publications.

Whitman, T. (2004) 'Recommendations to parents, therapists/educators, researchers and policy-makers.' In T. Whitman (ed.) *The Development of Autism: A Regulatory Perspective.* London: Jessica Kingsley Publishers.

Whitman, T. and Lounds, J. (2004) 'Family stress and coping.' In T. Whitman (ed.) *The Development of Autism: A Regulatory Perspective.* London: Jessica Kingsley Publishers.

Williams, D. (1998) *Autism: An Inside-Out Approach.* London: Jessica Kingsley Publishers.

Contributors

Margaret L. Baumann, MD, is at the Departments of Pediatrics and Neurology, Massachusetts General Hospital, is Associate Clinical Professor at the Department of Neurology, Harvard Medical School, and is Adjunct Associate Clinical Professor at the Department of Pathology and Laboratory Medicine, Boston University School of Medicine, Boston, Massachusetts, US.

Manuel F. Casanova, MD, is Professor of Psychiatry and Behavioral Sciences, Professor of Anatomical Sciences and Neurobiology, Professor of Neurology, Senior Member of the Graduate Faculty, University of Louisville, US.

Hilde de Clercq is a trainer in autism at the Opleidingscentrum Autisme, Antwerp, Belgium (www.ocautisme.be).

Ángel Díez-Cuervo is a Consultant Neurologist and Psychiatrist, Scientific Advisor, Spanish Parents Association of People with Autism (APNA), Spain.

Eric Fombonne is Canada Research Chair in Child Psychiatry, Professor of Psychiatry, McGill University, Head of McGill University Division of Child Psychiatry and Director of the Department of Psychiatry at the Montreal Children's Hospital, Canada.

Pedro M. González is from the Association of Parents of People with Autism (Asociación de Padres de Personas con Autismo, APNA), Spain.

Peter Hobson is at the Developmental Psychopathology Research Unit, Tavistock Clinic and Institute of Child Health, University College London, UK.

Thomas L. Kemper, MD, is Professor at the Departments of Neurology, Anatomy and Neurobiology and Pathology, Boston University School of Medicine, Boston, Massachusetts, US.

Laura Grofer Klinger is at the University of Alabama, US.

Mark R. Klinger is at the University of Alabama, US.

Susan Leekam is at the Department of Psychology, University of Durham, UK.

María Llorente Comí, is from the Association of Parents of People with Autism (Asociación de Padres de Personas con Autismo, APNA), Spain).

Catherine Lord, PhD, is at the University of Michigan Autism and Communication Disorders Center, US.

Juan Martos Pérez is from the Association of Parents of People with Autism (Asociación de Padres de Personas con Autismo, APNA), Spain.

Peter Mundy, PhD, is Professor of Psychology and Director of the Marino Autism Research Institute, University of Miami, US.

Carmen Nieto is from the Association of Parents of People with Autism (Asociación de Padres de Personas con Autismo, APNA), Spain.

Sally Ozonoff is a Professor in the Department of Psychiatry and Behavioral Sciences M.I.N.D. Institute, University of California–Davis, US.

Theo Peeters is a trainer in autism at the Opleidingscentrum Autisme, Antwerp, Belgium (www.ocautisme.be).

Rebecca L. Pohlig is at the University of Alabama, US.

Sherri Provencal, PhD, is in the Department of Psychology, University of Utah, US.

Isabelle Rapin is at the Saul R. Korey Department of Neurology, the Department of Pediatrics, and the Rose. F. Kennedy Center for Research in Mental Retardation and Human Development, Albert Einstein College of Medicine, Bronx, New York, US.

Mikle South, PhD, is in the Department of Psychology, University of Utah, US.

Danielle Thorp, PhD, is Psychology Intern at the Louis de la Porte Florida Mental Health Institute, University of South Florida, US.

Sally Wheelwright is at the Autism Research Centre, Departments of Experimental Psychology and Psychiatry, University of Cambridge, UK.

Subject Index

Note: page numbers in *italics* refer to information contained in tables, page numbers in **bold** refer to diagrams.

Author Index